ORGANIZATION AND REPRESENTATION IN PERCEPTION

Edited by
JACOB BECK
University of Oregon

LEA LAWRENCE ERLBAUM ASSOCIATES, PUBLISHERS
1982   Hillsdale, New Jersey   London

Lawrence Erlbaum Associates, Inc., Publishers
365 Broadway
Hillsdale, New Jersey 07642

Library of Congress Cataloging in Publication Data
Main entry under title:

Organization and representation in perception.

   ''Based on a conference on 'Processes of perceptual
organization and representation' held in Abano, Italy,
in June 1979''—Introd.
   Includes bibliographical references and indexes.
   1. Perception—Congresses. 2. Gestalt psychology—
Congresses. 3. Human information processing—Congresses.
I. Beck, Jacob.
BF311.67   153.7   82-7463
ISBN 0-89859-175-9   AACR2

Printed in the United States of America
10 9 8 7 6 5 4 3 2 1

Contents

To the Memory of
James J. Gibson

Acknowledgments

The conference on Processes of Perceptual Organization and Representation was supported by grants from the National Science Foundation and the Consiglio Nazionale Ricerche of Italy. This book was edited while on sabbatical leave at the Computer Vision Laboratory of the Computer Science Center at the University of Maryland, supported by National Science Foundation Grant MCS-79-23422. I am indebted to Professor Azriel Rosenfeld, Director of the Computer Vision Laboratory, for providing the support and facilities that greatly aided the preparation of this book.

List of Contributors

Fred Attneave, Department of Psychology, University of Oregon, Eugene, Oregon 97403

Jacob Beck, Department of Psychology, University of Oregon, Eugene, Oregon 97403

Sten Sture Bergström, Department of Applied Psychology, Umeå University, S-901 87 Umeå, Sweden

David H. Foster, Department of Communication and Neuroscience, University of Keele, Staffordshire ST5 5BG, England

Walter Gerbino, Istituto Di Psicologia, Università Di Trieste, Trieste, Italy

Eleanor J. Gibson, Department of Psychology, Cornell University, Ithaca, New York 14853

James J. Gibson,* Department of Psychology, Cornell University, Ithaca, New York 14853

Julian Hochberg, Department of Psychology, Columbia University, New York, New York 10027

Gaetano Kanizsa, Istituto Di Psicologia, Università Di Trieste, Trieste, Italy

Emanuel Leeuwenberg, Department of Experimental Psychology, University of Nijmegen, Nijmegen, The Netherlands

Herschel W. Leibowitz, Department of Psychology, The Pennsylvania State University, University Park, Pennsylvania 16802

William Maguire, Department of Psychology, State University of New York at Buffalo, Buffalo, New York 14226

Fabio Metelli, Istituto Di Psicologia, Università Di Padova, Padova, Italy

Stephen E. Palmer, Department of Psychology, University of California, Berkeley, Berkeley, California 94720

D. N. Perkins, Graduate School of Education, Harvard University, Cambridge, Massachusetts 02138

Robert B. Post, Department of Psychology, The Pennsylvania State University, University Park, Pennsylvania 16802

Frank Restle,* Department of Psychology, Indiana University, Bloomington, Indiana 47405

Azriel Rosenfeld, Computer Science Center, University of Maryland, College Park, Maryland 20742

Giovanni B. Vicario, Istituto Di Psicologia, Università Di Padova, Padova, Italy

Naomi Weisstein, Department of Psychology, State University of New York at Buffalo, Buffalo, New York 14226

Mary C. Williams, Department of Psychology, State University of New York at Buffalo, Buffalo, New York, 14226

Mario Zanforlin, Istituto Di Psicologia, Università Di Padova, Padova, Italy

*Deceased

Introduction

This book is based on a conference on "Processes of Perceptual Organization and Representation" held in Abano, Italy, in June 1979. The alternative approaches of Gestalt theory and information processing theories provided an effective framework for clarifying many of the basic unresolved issues relating to perceptual organization and representation. Gestalt and information processing theories share the assumption that perception is mediated by an underlying representation that can be studied through modeling. The models of Gestalt psychology and of information processing theories differ in an important way. Gestalt theory proposed nonsymbolic self-regulating analog physical processes to model the operation of underlying perceptual processes. Köhler, for example, proposed a model in which perceptual organization reflected the action of electrochemical fields due to the spatial distribution of neural excitation resulting from visual stimulation. Information processing theories, in contrast, propose language-like symbolic representations to model underlying perceptual processes. Leeuwenberg (see Chapters 2 and 3) proposes a formal language to describe the encoding of patterns and objects by the visual system. Both direct experimental tests (Lashley, Chow, and Semmes, 1951; Sperry, Miner, & Meyers, 1955) and subsequent neurophysiological research have made Köhler's hypothesis of direct current flows highly unlikely. The idea of an analog representation in which the functional properties of the perceptual system do not depend on symbolic manipulation, however, remains appealing.

Attneave (Chapter 1) is concerned with the Gestalt "Law of Prägnanz," which holds that the psychological organization of a stimulus will be as "good" as the prevailing stimulus conditions allow. The concept of Prägnanz is interpreted

1

differently in analog and symbolic models. In analog models, Prägnanz corresponds to the tendency toward a goal state or state of equilibrium associated with an analog physical process. In symbolic models, within which a stimulus can be described, Prägnanz corresponds to the preference for a simple description. Attneave argues that an internal analog representation of stimulus properties and relations is necessary to solve the problem of how the visual system implements a Prägnanz principle. Descriptions in a coding language of all permissible interpretations of a stimulus would require an exhaustive search in order to find the most economical encoding. Because a proximal stimulus is often consistent with a large number of distal alternatives, Attneave rejects this as implausible. An alternative possibility is a hill-climbing model that directly seeks the most economically described interpretation. The difficulty with a hill-climbing model is to devise a feedback mechanism by which the complexity of a description could guide the system to its goal-state. What is needed, Attneave proposes, is a system that will seek the goal-state not through computational procedures but through a diffuse interplay of forces as in classical Gestalt models. Attneave uses neural dipoles to model perceived tridimensional space. Permissible three-dimensional interpretations of a proximal stimulus are represented by sets of dipoles which interact through complex causal and recursive sequences. The perception of a particular distal shape results from mutual facilitation of like values (e.g., dipoles representing equal distal lengths) and inhibition of unlike values (e.g., dipoles representing different distal lengths) on variables, such as length, on which uniformity is the goal-state.

The dipole system does not take advantage of all varieties of regularity in progressing to the end state. There are two types of limitations. First, there are limitations inherent to the representation itself. The dipole system will seek an interpretation that maximizes right angles but not an interpretation that maximizes equality of angles. The representation of angles would require tripoles. Second, Attneave proposes that the mutual facilitation and inhibition of dipoles representing like and unlike distal properties has evolved adaptively. Helmholtz pointed out that the contour of an occluding surface does not change direction when it meets the contour of an occluded surface. Good continuation of a contour at a juncture represents an ecologically important regularity that is embodied in the model by the mutual facilitation of collinear dipoles. Attneave, however, does not accept an overall principle of Prägnanz. An accepted characteristic of figural goodness in both Gestalt and information processing models is symmetry. It is not made a basis for mutual reinforcement between dipoles because the experimental evidence concerning its effectiveness is weak (see Perkins, Chapter 4). The view of Prägnanz as operating on individual stimulus properties that have evolved adaptively enables Attneave to answer a question originally posed by Mach: Why is it that "the visual system acts in conformity with a principle of economy and at the same time with a principle of probability." (Mach, 1959). The acceptance of a Prägnanz principle, even a qualified one, presumes that the visual system does not respond solely to specific visual cues but formulates general rules reflecting regularities in the environment. The reality of such rules is indicated when they lead to nonveridical perceptions. Perceptual rules, such as good continuation, appear to depend on the contour and shape characteristics of stimuli more than on their meaning. Kanizsa and Gerbino (Chapter 9) present drawings in which the principle of good continuation leads to perceptions that are counter to past experience with the represented objects.

Restle (Chapter 2) begins with a description of Leeuwenberg's coding theory. The coding system consists of (a) primitive elements; (b) compositional rules that describe relations and transformations among the primitives; and (c) a principle of Prägnanz or of minimum information. The principle of minimum information asserts that the preferred psychological organization of a stimulus is that which minimizes the complexity of the code specifying the stimulus, for example, the number of symbols required to describe a figure or object. Restle seeks to integrate Gestalt theory with information processing theories through the use of Leeuwenberg's coding theory. He shows how the Gestalt laws of grouping, the Gestalt concepts of figural goodness, and field forces, the theory of stimulus invariants, and the information processing substages of feature extraction, coding, and comparing are directly translatable into the language and concepts of coding theory. Restle also sees coding theory as providing a common framework for the contributions of many of the conference participants and shows how what they said may be interpreted within coding theory. There are a very large number of combinatorial ways of putting together parts of a visual pattern. As just indicated, a difficult problem for a theory like Leeuwenberg's is how the visual system is able in milliseconds to search through the possible interpretations to find the most economical interpretation. One possibility is that the number of permissible interpretations to which a principle of minimum information is applied to is reduced by preprocessing. Linking processes based on connectedness and proximity which occur early in visual processing (see Beck, Chapter 15) or geometric constraints that limit perception to veridical interpretations (see Perkins, Chapter 4) may greatly reduce the number of permissible interpretations that need to be compared. Restle, however, argues for an unrestricted principle of perceptual simplicity. He takes the view that Leeuwenberg's coding theory is a descriptive theory that provides algorithms for computing what will be seen given a stimulus. It is not a process theory and does not assume that the actions carried out in applying the algorithms are the same as the actions carried out by the perceptual system.

The theory of minimum information is still in its formative stages and is not complete. Leeuwenberg's coding theory measures only structural or syntactic complexity. Two patterns that differ only in the relative sizes of figural elements would have the same measure of complexity. The perception of a pattern, however, also depends on metric properties. Patterns A and B have the same structural information but are seen differently because of the quantitative differences

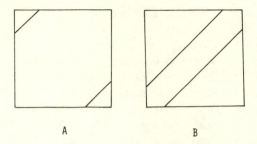

A   B

FIG. I.1.   Metric differences make A and B look different.

between them (see Fig. I.1). Leeuwenberg (Chapter 3) introduces a new measure of "impulse load" for measuring metric complexity. The measure is applied to the Müller-Lyer illusion. He also suggests that metric values may be encoded through constraints imposed on a pattern by alternative structural codes. A complete analysis of perceptual simplicity needs to take into account, however, not only structural and metric information but also semantic information. The perception of a caricature depends on the meanings conveyed by distinctive features. The semantic and syntactic properties of visual patterns appear to be interrelated (Green & Courtis, 1966). The theory of perceptual simplicity requires developing an understanding of how structural complexity, metric complexity, and semantic complexity combine.

Perkins (Chapter 4) is concerned with the perception of outline drawings. Outline drawings of geometric solids and surfaces tilted in space are projectively ambiguous because they can be the projection of many different three-dimensional objects. Nonetheless, such drawings are usually seen to represent specific shapes and slants. How is the perceptual system able to determine surface shape and slant? Perkins hypothesizes that the perceptual system is organized to arrive at a percept that is veridical, simple, and probable. The perception of outline drawings involves two distinct processes. First, an analog process that tends toward a state of minimum energy produces an interpretation of a local region of a figure. Second, a hypothesis-making process propagates the local interpretation over an entire figure. Both the analog and hypothesis-making process are veridical and respect the requirements of projective geometry. That is, perceptual interpretations that are clearly geometrically impossible do not occur. The experiments reviewed indicate that the perceptual system seeks to maximize many types of regularity such as rectangularity (equality of right angles), equal sidedness, symmetry, coplanarity, and so forth. The fact that not all types of regularity are of equal importance suggests that the visual system is also sensitive to the probability of a representation. Rectangularity, for example, is preferred by the visual system to equal sidedness and symmetry. An analog process can be postulated, as Attneave proposed, in which the system as a whole would progress to the desired interpretation with no separate hypothesis-making extension process. The problem, according to Perkins, with a single analog process is that it is not in accord with perceptual experience (see Hochberg, Chapter 10).

Palmer (Chapter 5) presents an information processing analysis of perceptual phenomena given prominence by Gestalt psychology. He is concerned with perceptual organization, figural structure, the emergent properties of a shape, spatial constancies, and the fact that often global properties seem to be processed before local properties. To account for these differing phenomena, Palmer brings together Garner's hypothesis of rotation and reflection subsets, an analysis of shape constancy in terms of transformational invariance, and a hypothesis of a multiplicity of spatial analyzers, which he calls reference frames. Gestalt qualities arise from analyzing stimuli in parallel by different reference frames. Phenomena such as emergent and global shape properties are the result of encoding stimuli at different levels of resolution. Good figures are those figures that produce the fewest different outputs for rotation and reflection subsets of reference frames. Spatial constancies are based on the application of internal compensatory transformations. Reference frames are related to each other by transformations of translation, rotation, reflection, and dilation. Two patterns are judged to be the same and independent of a spatial transformation if applying the information that the transformation has taken place brings the internal representation of one pattern into agreement with that of the other.

Although the focus of the book is directed at the human visual system, the approach to perceptual problems taken by computer scientists is not irrelevant. At the level of problem specification—the representation of stimulus information and of the computational requirements—the concepts and methods of processing pictorial information by computer becomes highly relevant. Computer vision deals with many of the same problems as perceptual psychology. Common problems are the extraction of features and relations, segmentation, organization, and hypothesis-testing. Rosenfeld (Chapter 6) describes an iterative local adjustment scheme, known as "relaxation," that has recently been developed for use in computer image analysis and recognition. As already mentioned, perceptual information is often ambiguous and disambiguation plays an important role in many stages of the perceptual process. Relaxation eliminates possible interpretations of a stimulus by applying constraints to the interpretations of neighboring local parts of a stimulus. Although there is no mathematical proof that relaxation yields optimal global interpretations, in practice, relaxation methods appear to yield low-ambiguity, high consistency results after only a few iterations. Information processing models of pattern perception assume, as the first stage in constructing a structural description of a stimulus, the abstraction of features such as lines, edges, angles, and other assumed perceptual elements. How these features are abstracted, however, is unclear. Neurophysiological units, such as simple and complex cells, will fire to a variety of stimulus features and cannot serve as direct detectors of perceptual elements. Relaxation methods can be used to extract information about pattern features. Rosenfeld gives examples of applying relaxation to several visual problems, including curve detection and graph matching. The relaxation methods described by Rosenfeld are digital processes. Because an analog process can be simulated digitally, the analog processes proposed by Attneave for dipoles and by Perkins for interpreting local segments of an image can be modelled within the type of system described by Rosenfeld.

Gibson's contribution to the conference is represented by two chapters. Gibson's ecological theory argues that perception is based on the direct pickup of information by the active perceptual systems of men and animals. The first Chapter (7) was a paper prepared for, but not read at, the conference and is a description of the properties of surfaces that animals and men have to cope with. Visual stimulation is structured by surfaces of the environment and information for the meaningful properties of a surface is directly available in the visual stimulus. Gibson's talk at the conference was based on notes in which he stated the points on which he agreed and disagreed with Gestalt theory. Professor Gibson did not write up his talk before his death, and his talk is summarized by Professor Eleanor Gibson, his wife, in Chapter 8. James Gibson accepted the Gestalt criticism of perceptual elements but rejected the distinction between a phenomenal and physical world (i.e., epistemological dualism). He reinterpreted Köhler's "physiche gestalten," Wertheimer's laws of organization, Rubin's distinction between figure and ground, and Koffka's distinction between proximal and distal stimuli. Perception also does not involve processes of synthesis that can be understood through modeling. There are no processes of sensory organization or of hypothesis testing. Gestalt theory and information processing theories have in common that their theories of perception were strongly influenced by the study of pattern perception. The laws of organization, for Gibson, are pictorial expressions of the information available in the ambient array of light specifying surfaces in the environment. Theories of perception based on the study of drawings and pictures mistakenly assume that the main problem is to resolve ambiguities that do not arise in nonpictorial perception. What there is to be perceived are substances, surfaces, planes, objects, and events as they occur in the environment. These are the perceptual realities and they are rarely ambiguous. Moreover, these realities of the perceptual environment need to be understood in terms of the actions they afford rather than in terms of the visual experiences they evoke.

A view common to both Gestalt and information processing theories is that no sharp distinction is to be drawn between perceptual and cognitive processes. Kanizsa and Gerbino (Chapter 9) argue forcefully against this view. A basic error, in their view, is that Gestalt psychology sought to explain thinking in terms of perceptual processes and information processing theories seek to explain perception in terms of cognitive processes. The function of perceptual processes is the segmentation and organization of the visual field into figural units. Perceptual processes involve field-like analog representations that model stimulus relations. The function of cognitive processes is to describe, categorize, and interpret what is seen. Cognitive processes involve symbolic representations that are manipulated to produce other symbolic descriptions. In amodal completion, perception and cognition involve different ways of going beyond the stimulus information. Amodal completion refers to the psychological completion of a figure that is not completely visible because it is covered by another object. Perceptual amodal completion involves a direct perceptual effect. Kanizsa and Gerbino present numerous examples showing that amodal completion may increase the perceived amount of a quality or may even create a new visual figure. Cognitive amodal completion involves a two-step process. Perceptually, there is a sensory representation of an incomplete figure followed by a cognitive interpretation that recognizes that the object is complete but not entirely visible. Kanizsa and Gerbino argue that cognitive processes do not produce a perceptual effect. Interpolation of missing parts that occurs readily through perceptual processes may, in fact, be quite difficult when carried out by cognitive processes.

Hochberg (Chapter 10) is critical of both Gestalt theory and Gibson's theory of direct perception. Though among the first to develop a quantitative model of figural organization based upon a minimum principle, he now believes such attempts to be misguided. A minimum principle assumes that the organization of the whole determines the perceived structure of a form or object. Hochberg presents demonstrations showing that a wholistic perceptual process does not always determine the appearance of the parts. Perception is also not a direct response to visual stimulation. There are limits to the pickup of stimulus information. When one considers carefully the structure of the eye, serious doubts arise about how accurately higher-order stimulus variables may be picked up. Hochberg adopts the theoretical position of Mill and Helmholtz. Percepts are mental constructions that use local as well as nonlocal cues to construct schematic maps of objects and events. Perceptions of objects are not physical objects; perceived space need not follow physical law or exhibit global consistency. Artists such as De Chirico and Escher have shown how visual cues that are inconsistent with each other can be combined to produce perceptual objects and spaces which are physically impossible.

Metelli, a founder of the Italian School of Gestalt psychology, presents an analysis of what characterizes Gestalt-oriented perceptual research (Chapter 11). Typical characteristics of Gestalt-oriented research are careful phenomenological description, a concern with structure and organization, the empirical testing of whether perception is the result of past experience, and a concern with formulating qualitative theoretical hypotheses to guide research. Metelli presents examples of how careful phenomenological observation has led to the discovery of new phenomena and of how the structure of a stimulus influences the appearance of parts of the stimulus. He acknowledges that the overall structure does not determine what will be seen in all instances. The challenge posed by Hochberg, however, remains to be met: What are the conditions when a wholistic perceptual process determines what will be seen?

Weisstein, Maguire, and Williams, Zanforlin, and Vicario (Chapters 12, 13, and 14) present further examples of how global relations affect perception. Weisstein et al. show that motion affereffects may depend on Gestalt-like processes. Motion aftereffects typically found from localized retinal stimulation can be obtained within areas of the visual field that have not been stimulated by moving contours. The illusion involves high-level motion and contour mechanisms and depends on perceived depth, a nonlocal aspect of the configuration. They suggest that the Gestalt-like character of perception is often masked because of the prepotence of peripheral processes dependent on local retinal stimulation.

Gestalt theory assumes that monocular form perception preceded and was necessary for stereoscopic perception. The introduction of random dot stereograms by Julesz has shown that monocular form recognition is not necessary for steropsis. Binocular depth can arise from either disparity between monocularly organized figures or from disparities between the dots composing the stereograms. The former depends on the preliminary processing of a form in terms of Gestalt laws whereas the latter does not. Zanforlin presents demonstrations showing that binocular depth perception is a function of the relative strengths of organizational forces and fusional forces. He argues that organizational forces and fusional forces need to be distinguished and considered separately. Zanforlin also considers the difficult question of how the visual system eliminates false localizations. He argues that elimination of false localizations depends on figural cues as well as on processes that search for a disparity shift that maximizes the number of stimulus points that are in registration. Vicario presents demonstrations designed to illustrate that various Gestalt organizing principles found in vision also occur in audition. Using a Moog synthesizer, he demonstrated to conference participants auditory dependence, alternative groupings, hidden figures, and amodal completion.

I write in Chapter 15 about textural segmentation. Textural segmentation is a function of stimulus differences that can be discriminated prior to a narrowing or focusing of attention. I hypothesize that the retinal intensity array is transformed into "textural elements" as a result of a small number of linking operations based on connectivity, proximity, and good continuation. Textural segmentation is based on differences of first-order statistics of nonrelational properties, such as the slopes, sizes, colors, and brightnesses of textural elements. Wertheimer proposed a number of principles or laws of organization to describe how the parts of a visual display or of a figure tend to be grouped. The laws of organization are conjectured to fall into three classes that serve different functions. One function is the transformation of the intensity array into elements that subserve texture and form perception. A second function is the aggregation of textural elements into groups of similar elements. Similarity grouping is hypothesized to be an instance of textural segmentation and depends on the discrimination in parallel of stimulus differences. A third function is the organization of elements in perceiving a visual form. Organizational principles such as closure, and similarity (as it relates to the transformations relating two figures) enable an economical encoding of a stimulus. These principles are corollaries of the Gestalt Law of Prägnanz or of figural goodness.

Foster (Chapter 16) is concerned with two specific problems of shape perception: the discrimination of collinearity from noncollinearity and the encoding of the angle between two connected lines. He presents evidence that these features are encoded categorically by the visual system. Categorical internal representations change discretely based on the response to critical pattern features. More generally, Foster proposes an information processing model of shape perception based on three assumptions: (a) the internal representation of a form consists of local features and spatial relations between these features; (b) the assignment of a form to an internal representation is probabilistic; and (c) the probability of discriminating between two forms is determined by the probability that they are assigned different internal representations. Leibowitz and Post (Chapter 17) review recent evidence from psychophysical studies in man and neurophysiological experiments with animals suggesting that visual information may be processed by two different systems specialized for either object recognition and identification (the focal system) or spatial orientation, locomotion, and localization in space (the ambient system). The focal system involves the visual cortex whereas the ambient system involves midbrain structure. Patients with lesions in the visual cortex which result in scotomas in their visual fields can sometimes avoid bumping into a visual target when moving about though they can not see stationary objects. In fact, some people can move about surprisingly well despite the fact that they are clinically diagnosed as blind. In these people, there has been damage to the cortical structures subserving focal vision but not to the midbrain structures subserving ambient vision. Liebowitz discusses the role of these two visual systems in perceiving size, shape, and motion. The ambient system, for example, appears to exhibit size constancy but not shape constancy. This reflects the important role played by the spatial localization of stimuli in size constancy. Shape constancy, in contrast, is solely a function of the focal system.

Johansson has proposed a vector extraction model for motion perception. Bergström (Chapter 18) applies a vector component analysis to the problem of perceiving the shape and color of a surface. The visual system is assumed to analyze the light reflected to the eyes into common and residual components. The common component corresponds to the perceived illumination. The residual components are analyzed into a variable component corresponding to the three dimensional shape of an object and a constant component corresponding to the color of the object. Bergström presents demonstrations showing the effect of superimposing different luminance gradients on the perception of two-dimensional pictures of colored rectangular areas. He also reports that a temporal modulation of luminance can evoke the perception of rigid objects moving in depth. Bergström argues that the interrelated perceptions of reflectance, illumination, and three-dimensional shape all emerge simultaneously from the direct analysis of the luminances in the retinal image into vector components.

Taken as a whole, the chapters reflect current theorizing concerning the problems of organization and representation. They make it apparent that no single, agreed on, overall theoretical approach to the problems of organization and representation exists. The chapters, however, succeed in clarifying fundamental problems, indicating new directions for research, and focusing attention on the advances in theoretical understanding necessary for developing a consistent theoretical foundation.

Jacob Beck
Eugene, Oregon

REFERENCES

Green, R. T., & Courtis, M. C. Information theory: the metaphor that failed. *Acta Psychologica,* 1966, *25,* 12–36.

Lashley, K. S., Chow, K. L., & Semmes, J. An examination of the electrical field theory of cerebral integration. *Psychological Review,* 1951, *58,* 123–136.

Mach, E. *The analysis of sensations.* New York: Dover, 1959 (5th ed., orig. 1906).

Sperry, R. W., Miner, N., & Meyers, R. E. Visual pattern perception following subpial splicing and tantalum wire implantations in the visual cortex. *Journal of Comparative and Physiological Psychology,* 1955, *48,* 50–58.

1 Prägnanz and Soap Bubble Systems: A Theoretical Exploration

Fred Attneave
University of Oregon

INTRODUCTION

The Gestalt "Law of Prägnanz" held (to paraphrase Koffka, 1935) that psychological organization will be as "good" as the prevailing stimulus-constraints allow. "Goodness" was an undefined concept which could entail either maxima or minima, but in recent years it has most often been considered equivalent to homogeneity, or regularity, or simplicity (Attneave, 1954, 1972; Attneave & Frost, 1969; Hochberg & Brooks, 1960; Hochberg & McAlister, 1953; Leeuwenberg, 1971; Musatti, 1931; and others). In this restricted interpretation, the Law of Prägnanz is identifiable with Mach's (1959, orig. 1906) earlier "principle of economy," which he discussed along with a coordinate "principle of probability" in perception.

A principle of economy or Prägnanz can be supposed to operate only within some region of indeterminacy, some range of permissible alternative perceptions, left open by the stimulus constraints: we do not see an irregular polygon as a circle, however much "better" the latter might be. Prägnanz has been evoked to explain the resolution of at least two types of indeterminacy. One of these involves segregation and grouping, the partitioning of a field into perceptual units. (See Leeuwenberg's chapter in this volume for some good examples, which his system handles quite successfully.) The other, which overlaps the first, involves the classical problem of monocular depth perception, the perception of a tridimensional world given a two-dimensional picture in which each element could, in principle, image any distance whatever. A considerable body of evidence is consistent with the view that the emergence of depth is at least partially controlled by a preference for simpler over more complex alternative arrangements (Attneave & Frost, 1969; Hochberg & Brooks, 1960; and others). This chapter is concerned with possible systems that might accomplish such a result.

The "minimum principle," as stated by Hochberg (1968) holds that "our nervous systems organize the perceived world in whatever way will keep changes and differences to a *minimum*." The essential next question is: changes and differences on what variables? We do not know a priori, but possibilities with at least superficial plausibility include such variables as length or spacing (of lines, contours, edges, etc.), slope, curvature, and value of angle. It is important to recognize that these are in every case *abstractions* from the sensory array; they are "higher order" variables (at least second order, as we shall see), even in their proximal form.

Two very general possibilities may be suggested for systems of perceptual organization that might minimize variability, or maximize uniformity, on the variables that are relevant. The first category I shall call "soap bubble systems," using a familiar and evocative metaphor that has become something like a trademark of the Gestalt school. More literally, I refer to systems that progress to equilibrium states by way of events in interconnected and recursive causal sequences so numerous that their effects must be considered in the aggregate rather than individually. (In such a fashion, a real soap bubble moves into an end-state characterized by minimum surface area enclosing a fixed volume.) How a psychoneural system for achieving spatial organization could work in this manner has never been very clear, however. About the only effort of the Gestalt psychologists in this direction was a somewhat feeble one: Köhler's (Köhler & Wallach, 1944, etc.) hypothesized field of electrical potentials and direct currents (depending essentially on luminance and luminance gradients) in the cortex. An experiment of Lashley, Chow, and Semmes (1951) showed that Köhler's proposal was simply wrong, but more to our present point is the fact that it was formally inadequate: the DC brain fields, if they did exist, would not operate to minimize variability at even the very modest levels of abstraction that have relevance to our problem.

Another possibility is that the perceptual system selects, from any given set of permissible alternatives, the one that can be described most simply. This is the view that I have taken in the past, having suggested some 25 years ago that perception is a process of "economical description" (Attneave, 1954). At that time, objective methods for describing visual shapes and patterns were fairly primitive, but subsequently Leeuwenberg (1971) has given us his ingenious and elegant system for composing descriptions that are essentially complete and more or less nonredundant. The information content of those descriptions can be quantified in units of structural information, "logons" in the terminology of MacKay (1950). It should be understood that any kind of uniformity or regularity in a form or pattern makes possible some corresponding economy in the description. For different ways of perceiving an ambiguous pattern, different descriptions can be written, and Leeuwenberg and his associates have found considerable evidence that the perception is typically that which corresponds to the most economical description (Leeuwenberg, 1971; van Tuijl, 1980). The design of a perceptual system capable of *discovering* the simplest description poses formidable problems, however. I have suggested (Attneave, 1972) that it would have to be a "hill-climbing" system; that this might consist of (a) an analog medium representing external 3-D space, the contents of which could take any form not violating the stimulus-constraints; feeding into (b) a digital or propositional mechanism which would generate continually updated descriptions of the model and feed back "hot-cold" signals in response to perturbations in the model, depending on whether the change simplified or complicated the description, thereby guiding the system into a stable state. These suggestions were never specific enough to have much value, however, and I have been so far unable to develop them in any way that is minimally satisfying; for example, by characterizing the terrain on which the hill-climber would operate, that is to say, the dimensions on which the suitably reinforced perturbations might occur in a system that worked in the desired manner.

In view of these difficulties, I have recurrently wondered whether some version of the soap bubble alternative might not, after all, be tenable. Like the hill-climbing system, a soap bubble system would presumably require a tridimensional field or manifold for spatial representation. Unlike the former, it would not be dependent on feedback from a propositional level; rather it would be moved toward an equilibrium state by some diffuse interplay of forces within the analog medium itself.

Considering the topic of the present conference, I set myself this exercise: to start from the general point of view of the classical Gestalt psychologists and try to design a psychoneural system of the soap bubble type that might at least partially account for monocular perception of tridimensional space, without being grossly incompatible with current knowledge in neurophysiology. It should be understood that what follows is a theoretical exploration: I shall try to suggest hypotheses that are worth consideration along with their alternatives, but my interest at present is rather in what is possible than in what is true.

A SOAP BUBBLE SYSTEM

The hypothesis with which we start is that like values are mutually facilitating, and unlike values mutually inhibitory, on variables on which uniformity is to be a goal-state. Whatever their nature or level of abstraction all such variables should be interdependent, and consistent with one another at equilibrium; therefore their effects must be integrated in a common medium. We shall suppose that this common ground is a neuronal manifold representing external space, in which the two dimensions of the visual field are complemented by a third dimension of depth or distance, different distances being represented by different "sheets" of neurons.

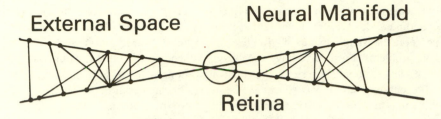

External Space   **Neural Manifold**

Retina

FIG. 1.1.   The stimulation of a given point on the retina may originate at any one of an infinite number of points, equal in direction but different in distance, in external space. Likewise, there are many *pairs* of external points, differing in separation and orientation, that might stimulate the same retinal pair. It is proposed that a pair of like-stimulated retinal points activates, in a neural manifold, a ''projective set'' of dipoles representing possible sources of external stimulation. The task of the system is to choose, from these many possibilities, one that corresponds closely to the external situation.

Suppose further that the representational 3-space contains numerous *dipoles*, each of which consists of a pair of end-points in the neural manifold linked by reciprocal or reverberatory excitation to a third unit unique to the dipole. Initially a dipole will be activated if its end-points correspond or project to a pair of retinal points that are in approximately the same state of stimulation. (For present purposes of exposition, ''same state'' may be taken to depend simply upon luminance. More plausibly, it might refer to the states of units that represent contours or other discontinuities abstracted by antecedent processes.) These dipoles can vary within the tridimensional manifold in 6 independent ways: (1) length, that is, separation of endpoints; (2) horizontal location; (3) vertical location; and (4) depth or distance (of, say, the midpoint); (5) tilt or orientation in the frontal or retinal plane; and (6) slant in depth, or deviation from the frontal plane. (Alternatively, the 6 degrees of freedom follow simply from variation of 2 points on 3 dimensions.) Thus if a pair of retinal points are stimulated alike, they will tend to excite a set of dipoles corresponding to those lines in external space whose end-points would project the same image, that is, to that retinal pair, as illustrated in Fig. 1.1. Note that the members of the set have two degrees of freedom for variation, which add to four degrees of freedom among retinal pairs to make up the six described above.

When all the dipoles in such a projective set are equally activated, the representation is maximally ambiguous. The system will employ two types of interaction to resolve the ambiguity. First, the dipoles within each projective set will mutually inhibit one another, so that an increase in activity of one will cause a decrease in activity of the others, and in the stable end-state one dipole will suppress all its competitors. Second, each active dipole will facilitate nearby dipoles (in other projective sets) that are akin to it in ways to be specified; in other words, mutual facilitation or reverberation will occur among the dipoles within certain kinship sets, decreasing as a function of the separation between the dipoles. Thus, roughly speaking, the dipole that wins out over its rivals in a projective set will be the one that has the most active kindred allies nearby, but the multifarious, recursive, "soap bubble" nature of the process leading to the end-state is fairly evident.

When one dipole becomes dominant in a projective set, this means that some *surface,* or element thereof, is perceived at the place and orientation represented by that dipole. If the system works properly (i.e., perceives correctly), it must do so by capitalizing on ecologically prevalent surface regularities of the sort involved in the invariances emphasized by J. J. Gibson (1950) in his work on "momentary stimulation," and I shall draw heavily on Gibson's illustrations in what follows.[1] Let us see what "kinship" relationships between dipoles might reflect such surface regularities.

The most obvious of these is (*1*) *Equality of length.* (This does not refer to the lengths of dipoles considered as neural entities, but to the extents in external 3-space that they represent; likewise "Parallelism," "Coplanarity," etc., are defined in terms of the real-world referents of the dipoles in question.) Whenever a Gibsonian "texture-gradient" arises from more or less uniform elements on a physical surface, mutual facilitation among equal-length dipoles will be greatest in a neural analog of that surface, and the dipoles therein will tend to "lock in" with one another and become dominant. With a modest amount of prior processing, mutual facilitation based on equality of length will further capitalize on regularities associated with boundaries of surfaces, thus providing a mechanism for the "relative size cue" to depth (differences in proximal size perceived as differences in distance), and possibly for the tendency to see an object in an orientation consistent with equality of its edges (Attneave & Frost, 1969; Attneave, 1972).

Because surfaces tend to be continuous, another plausible basis for mutual reinforcement is (2) *Coplanarity.* Bear in mind that curved surfaces may be considered locally coplanar, and that the postulated interfacilitation will be heavily weighted by proximity. A further reason for such weighting is that surfaces end, and we wish to prevent one surface from interfering unnecessarily with the locating of another with which it is not coplanar. (3) *Parallelism,* or equality of 3-D slope, is another important kinship relation, applying to cases in which "linear perspective" is effective (i.e., when proximally convergent lines are perceived as parallel on a receding surface). Interfacilitation based on (4) *Collinearity* will create a tendency for lines to be represented as tridimensionally

---

[1] When I saw Gibson outside the meeting room just after giving this talk I assured him, only half in fun, that it was really a Gibsonian system I had been presenting, that I was merely trying to make an honest man of him by suggesting mechanisms for effects he had pointed out years before. He responded with a pantomime of speechless horrification which anyone who knew him will find it easy to visualize.

collinear if they can be (i.e., if their proximal projections are collinear), over and beyond the like tendencies based on Coplanarity and Parallelism. (5) *Inclusion* will have a similar effect, but in its case an asymmetry of mutual facilitation may be desirable, with the influence of including on included dipole being greater than the reverse. To these may be added (6) *Connectedness,* in the sense of sharing an end point, although its effects require no new assumptions: it follows from the internal structure of the dipoles that any two with a common end-point in the manifold must facilitate each other. (Any two such dipoles will always be coplanar, but not necessarily collinear.) Thus proximal connectedness will tend to be perceived as distal connectedness.

Note that relationships 2 through 5 form a nested sequence, each being a special case of the one before it. For example, any two parallel dipoles are coplanar, but it is supposed that they facilitate each other more than do dipoles that are coplanar but not parallel, and so on. The relevance of the interactions that have been suggested to the Gestalt organizational principles of similarity, good continuation, and proximity is obvious enough, but I would remind the reader that we are restricting ourselves (so far, at least) to relations that may exist between dipoles; that is, points in space considered two at a time. (Of this, more later.) Before examining some further possible types of kinship which raise interesting questions of principle, let me illustrate how those already suggested might work.

Figure 1.2 depicts a proximal stimulus array, the familiar Gibsonian perspective of a tile floor or similar surface, in which a variety of factors combine to produce the perception of a receding ground-plane. The pairs of like-stimulated points a, b, c, d, and e, are all collinear, and pair a is moreover *included* in the span of b. Each of these pairs (and each of many other collinear and nested pairs not shown) excites a corresponding projective set of dipoles as in Fig. 1.1. There are innumerable possible selections of dipoles from these sets that would represent curved or angular lines or aggregates of unconnected segments at diverse distances and slants, but mutual facilitation based on collinearity and inclusion will result in the selection of a kinship-set of dipoles that are collinear tridimensionally as well as on the retina. (This result seems trivial only if one fails to appreciate the inherent ambiguity of a line in the retinal image, and hence the need for a disambiguating mechanism.) Collinearity and inclusion do not determine a unique tridimensional line, however; other factors must select from the alternatives that remain.

One of these is "linear perspective" among the radial lines that appear to extend from near to far. From the projective sets of pairs such as e, f, g, h, and i, mutual facilitation based on parallelism will result in the selection of dipoles that are tridimensionally parallel to one another and hence, concomitantly, determinate in tridimensional slant or or orientation; accordingly the lines to which they belong will appear to recede.

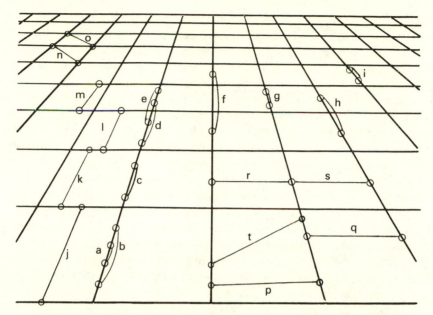

FIG. 1.2.   A visual array in which various factors converge to produce the perception of a slanting surface. Any pair of like-stimulated retinal elements (of which pairs *a* through *t* are examples) may activate a "projective set" of dipoles, as indicated in Fig. 1.1.

The Equal-Length kinship demands more discussion. We would like it to work in such a way that, in the present example, the surface will be perceived in an orientation consistent with equal distal spacing of the horizontal lines, which are of course unequally spaced proximally. Thus, if mutual facilitation between the projective sets of pairs *j, k, l,* and *m,* causes dipoles of equal length to become dominant, those dipoles will lie in the desired orientation. The same is true for interaction between particular pairs like *n* and *o.* It is not true, however, for interaction between, say *m* and *n.* These extents should not be represented as equal (or in an orientation consistent with equality) in the final outcome. A partial solution, it would appear, is to restrict mutual facilitation between equal-length dipoles to those that are also parallel to one another.

Note further that there is an alternate route, involving Equal Length, by which "linear perspective" may operate. In the case of pairs bridging radial lines, like *p, q,* and *r,* if interfacilitation causes dipoles of equal length to become dominant they will vary concomitantly in distance in a manner consistent with perception of the receding plane—but, again, only if they are parallel in that plane. In other situations mutual facilitation between nonparallel dipoles may be desirable, but in any case some nonlinear combination of Equality of Length and Parallelism, whereby facilitation based on the former is much greater when the dipoles are parallel than when they are not, is strongly indicated, This will not appreciably increase the complexity of the system. (In order to appraise the potentialities of a very simple system, I am deliberately avoiding some possible applications of Equal Length that are not implausible, but that would require substantial "preprocessing" for the definition of sameness of state in proximal pairs.)

One may object that even between dipoles that are at once equal in length and parallel, interfacilitation will have unwanted effects in many cases; for example, when the proximal pairs are collinear, or when (in an array like Fig. 1.2) they have one foot on a radial line and the other on a horizontal line. Similarly, interaction between the dipoles of pairs like t and r will favor one set of planes, interaction between the dipoles of t and p a different set, both inconsistent with the perceived or target plane. In all such cases, the distance between like-stimulated points varies randomly, and interfacilitation among dipoles of equal length will likewise have random effects. But being random, they will tend to cancel one another out, the more so if the number of dipoles involved is large; to the degree that they do not, they will constitute noise in the system. In the case of collinear pairs, mutual facilitation based on tridimensional collinearity and inclusion will operate to override the noise. The more general point, however, is that stabilizing effects will be *coherent* only in a particular plane (the one perceived), because the number of channels for recursive facilitation will be greater in this plane than in any other.

Most of the possible pairs of points in Fig. 1.2 will obviously be in the same state because they both fall on blank areas, between the lines. Interfacilitation between their various projective sets will yield almost purely random and therefore useless effects, but in such profusion that they may certainly be expected to cancel out. The *only* coherent effect operating on these sets in the present example will be that of coplanarity, whereby the blank areas will be brought into the plane determined by neighboring lines.

Now, it is well understood that such monocular stimulus factors as we have been considering, whatever their mode of operation, provide information about relative size and distance but not about absolute size and distance.[2] Nevertheless, I have postulated a neural manifold in which dipoles represent determinate separations between points each of which represents some absolute distance from the observer. How are these absolute values to be determined? Veridical determination will presumably require some source of information extraneous to the dipole system: the diverse possibilities include convergence, "familiar size" operating via higher cognitive centers, and contact with a hand or foot. But once the absolute distance of a single point is fixed in a coherent array, this constraint

---

[2]A trick that enjoyed some popularity during the eighteenth century employed a peephole in a door, through which a well-furnished room could be seen. Upon opening the door the viewer was astonished to find a completely different room inside. What he had seen through the peephole was a scale model, a room from a doll's house, in a box attached to the door.

will be propagated through the dipole system to determine the absolute distances of other points in a manner consistent with the regularities to which the system is responsive. In the absence of any information whatever about absolute distance (as is very nearly the case in Fig. 1.2, for example), the system must nonetheless settle upon *some* specific set of mutually dependent absolute values, determined either by chance or by weak internal biases comparable to Gogel's (1973) "spe-cific distance tendency," simply because it will be in an unstable state until it does so.

Let us now consider two further kinds of kinship between dipoles that might be introduced into the system. One of these is *Symmetry*. A Prägnanz or econ-omy principle suggests that a figure that is distally symmetrical but viewed obliquely (so that its proximal projection is asymmetrical) should be perceived in the plane of the symmetry. The Equal-Length kinship would tend to produce this result since for every pair of points in a (bilaterally) symmetrical figure there is a similar pair of points with the same separation, but the tendency might be a rather weak one because the interfacilitation would be only within separate pairs of dipoles, and the paired dipoles would not typically be parallel to each other. We could further postulate, however, a more specific mutual facilitation between "symmetrical" dipoles, defined as parallel dipoles with a common perpendicular bisector, which would have many more recursive channels through which to circulate facilitation. The question that arises here is one of psychological fact. Kanizsa (1975) has argued against the perceptual importance of symmetry, par-ticularly in the determination of figure-ground relationships. At one point in the present conference I asked Professor Kanizsa if he knew of any empirical evi-dence showing whether or not perceived slant tends to maximize symmetry; he replied that he knew of none, but that he would not expect such an effect to occur. My own expectations were the reverse at the time, but informal observa-tions on a few test figures that I constructed after returning home seem rather to support his prediction. If there is any strong tendency to perceive depth consis-tent with symmetry, the dot-pattern in Fig. 1.3 should be seen as symmetrical in an oblique plane. Little or no such effect occurs in normal viewing. It is perhaps a little stronger with viewing through a reduction tube, but hardly such as to argue for a special Symmetry kinship in the present system. The fact remains that ambiguous triangles tend to be seen as symmetrical in depth (Attneave, 1968, 1971), but this phenomenon shows peculiarities of its own, and may have alter-native interpretations. More experimental evidence on the symmetry-and-depth issue is clearly needed.

Some years ago Frost and I (Attneave, 1972; Attneave & Frost, 1969) ob-tained results consistent with the hypothesis that figures tend to be seen oriented in depth in such a way as to make *angles* equal. In our experiments, however, equal angles were also right angles, and it remained an open question as to whether the critical determinant of the goal state was equality or orthogonality (or both). I now believe that it was most likely orthogonality, though a global Law of

Prägnanz would suggest otherwise. The special status of right angles in tridimensional perception is shown by the experiments of Perkins (1972) in which subjects were able to judge rather accurately whether three lines converging at a point could be the projection of a "cubic corner," and by the fact that an ambiguous triangle attains one of its stable states when perceived as a right triangle in depth (Attneave, 1968). Most directly relevant to the present issue is an experiment recently reported by Shepard (1981), in which subjects were again well able to identify possible projections of a rectangular corner, but were relatively poor at identifying possible projections of the corner of a tetrahedron, which is made up of equal 60 degree angles. In any case, we could not incorporate a kinship based on equality of angles into the present dipole system even if we wished to, because at least three points, that is, a trigon, would be required to represent each angle. On the other hand, a preference for (7) *Orthogonality* can be implemented merely by introducing additional mutual facilitation between neighboring coplanar dipoles that are at right angles to each other.

Our consideration of Symmetry and Orthogonality leads to some interesting generalizations on the nature of the present system. This system—though a soap bubble system in the best Gestalt tradition—does *not* enforce any global or unitary Law of Prägnanz; rather we have found it necessary to fractionate Prägnanz into a number of more specific principles that have to be individually implemented. Thus we are under no compulsion to postulate mutual facilitation based on Symmetry, for example, if in fact symmetry is irrelevant to depth perception. In the case of Orthogonality, it would be difficult to maintain that we

FIG. 1.3. A dot pattern symmetrical about a vertical axis was subjected to a 2:1 compression on a 45 degree diagonal to produce this figure. It is therefore the orthogonal projection (disallowing "linear perspective") of a symmetrical pattern rotated 60 degrees from the picture plane. Do you see the pattern in depth—with or without a reduction screen? The symmetry-in-depth becomes much more obvious with the cooperation of additional factors, for example, when the pattern is framed with a parallelogram compressed (into a trapezoid) in the same manner as the dot pattern. Incidentally, the symmetry is perfectly obvious when the pattern is made *retinally* symmetrical (approximately), because "linear perspective" is inappropriate) by viewing the figure at a 60 degree slant on the opposite diagonal.

are still employing the principle of ''like facilitates like'' with which we started: lines at right angles are not alike, but merely in a special relationship, and we could as easily have mutual facilitation between dipoles related by 27 degrees or 106 degrees if it were desirable. Accordingly I have used the term ''kinship'' in preference to ''similarity'' or ''likeness.'' It is evident, however, that the definition of this term turns out to be essentially circular: kindred dipoles are simply dipoles that facilitate each other; thus kinship is whatever we wish to make it.

I alluded earlier to Mach's principles of Economy and Probability, the former of which anticipated the Gestalt Law of Prägnanz. Mach never explained clearly how he supposed these principles to be related to each other, but the distinction between them becomes fuzzier, I think, the longer one contemplates them. Whatever might underly an economy principle could hardly be expected to survive (in either the individual or the race, as the case might be) unless economical (simple, regular) interpretations of the input were more probable than uneconomical (complex, irregular) interpretations, and therefore more likely to lead to adaptive behavior. The comparable assumption on which the present system is based is that, for a given retinal pattern, a possible distal source that contains certain regularities or singularities (reflected by kinships between dipoles) is more probable than one that does not, or one that contains them to a lesser degree. This is virtually axiomatic if the discrepancy is great: it is obviously unlikely that stimulation from a random distal array could have an interpretation consistent with a highly regular array. In the case of weaker regularities or singularities, ecological probabilities become important: for example, what is the probability that two lines (or n lines) are parallel in external 3-space if the proximal constraints are such that they might be parallel? Accordingly we may suppose that the specific bases for mutual facilitation between dipoles reflect ecological contingencies, as a result either of evolutionary pressures or of associative learning in the individual. If the latter, systems of interfacilitating dipoles are identifiable with Hebb's (1949) cell-assemblies, and intercultural differences of the sort that have been claimed (dependent on the prevalence of parallel lines, right angles, etc., in the environment) would be expected.

In the remainder of this chapter I shall discuss several matters bearing on the plausibility of the system, and how seriously I would have the reader take it.

1. Dipoles

I concede without argument that the dipole may be a neurological fiction. The essential point is one that Julesz (1978) has made: that a dipole analysis within a given region yields the same information as a power spectrum analysis done by some other mechanism. What various possible mechanisms for spatial frequency analysis have in common is that they obtain ''second-order statistics,'' dependent on the joint states of elements considered two at a time, as is immediately obvious in the case of the dipole. Julesz's heuristic use of the dipole in his treatment of texture segregation has made for an admirable clarity that would have been difficult otherwise; following his example I have found the dipole to have great advantages of conceptual convenience in the development of the present system, although my dipoles differ from his in a variety of important ways. My assumption is that this system could be reformulated, with little or no change in its functional properties, in terms of alternative descriptors or analyzers in the spatial frequency domain that may be more justifiable on neurological grounds.

2. Neuroeconomy

It is reasonable to ask whether a system like this is within realistic bounds in the quantity of neural machinery that it would require. The answer will obviously depend on the grain or resolution of the system, but a fairly coarse grain may be tolerable for two reasons: one is that many situations will present highly redundant information about depth and orientation, in which case accuracy will be improved by the averaging that occurs in the system; the other is that, as Perkins points out (in Chapter 4), people can perceptually solve rather complex problems in projective geometry but their solutions are rarely precise ones. In any event the arithmetic involved in calculating neural requirements can be made clear. We have supposed that each dipole requires one unique neuron, exclusive of its two end-points in the tridimensional manifold. Earlier we saw that the dipoles can vary in six independent ways. If we take the magical number 7 as the average number of discriminable values on each of these 6 variables, the total number of dipoles is $7^6 = 117,649$. For 10 discriminable values the number is 10^6 or a round million, which is still a very modest fraction of the neurons in the visual cortex. Note that increasing the varieties of kinship, or bases for mutual facilitation, does not change the number of dipoles but only the number of interconnections between them; indeed, the complexity of the system is largely a matter of its interconnectedness. However, since the average number of synapses per cortical neuron is estimated to be as great as 40,000 (Cragg, 1975), and since we suppose that connections are restricted to neighboring regions, it is unlikely that our requirements are excessive in this respect.

Thus encouraged, we might wonder whether we have been too timid in restricting ourselves to dipoles. What if trigons were allowed? Trigons in a 3-space have 9 degrees of freedom; therefore 7 discriminable values per variable would require (under minimal assumptions) 7^9 or 40,353,590 neurons, and 10 values 10^9 or a billion neurons. These figures are at least great enough to give us pause, and make us suspect that third- and higher-order configurations would have to be handled by some other system. Note Julesz's comparable conclusion that textural discriminations based on differences beyond the second order require a system involving focal attention and sequential processing, and the more direct evidence of Beck (1972) and Beck and Ambler (1973) that focal attention is in fact critical to such discriminations.

3. Kinships Between Dipoles

The types of kinship postulated, such as Collinearity, Parallelism, and Orthogonality, correspond to special cases that have a great deal of perceptual saliency, as evidenced both phenomenally and by the accuracy with which their presence or absence is judged. The case for collinearity is particularly strong: people are very good at mentally extrapolating a straight line, in 3-space as well as in the frontal plane (Attneave & Pierce, 1978).

One is also reminded of certain experiments on stabilized retinal images by Pritchard, Heron, and Hebb (1960) and others. The tendency of collinear and parallel elements to disappear and reappear together during stabilization strongly suggests mutual facilitation (in addition to a process of fatigue or adaptation). The report of Pritchard et al. that parallel planes likewise fade in and out together (in a Necker cube or similar figure) would seem to demand something of the order of mutually facilitating trigons, since no individual dipole can define a plane. It is possible, however, that parallelism between *edges* might account for the effect, since it appears that the edges of one plane were parallel to those of the other in the cases observed. If this interpretation is correct, parallel planes with nonparallel edges, as in a regular octohedron, would not necessarily cohere.

The relevance of research on textural discrimination and similarity grouping (Beck, 1966; Julesz, 1975; Olson & Attneave, 1970) has already been indicated, but with rare exceptions (e.g., Beck, 1975; Rock & Brosgole, 1964) such work has dealt with grouping and segregation in two rather than three dimensions.

4. The Tridimensional Manifold

If the system works properly, it will produce what Marr and Nishihara (1978) have called a "2½ D sketch" of the visual field; that is, a model reflecting the distances and orientations of *visible* surfaces as seen from a particular vantage point (somewhat like a relief sculpture or stage set) but not representing occluded surfaces or objects in the round. I have supposed that the manifold or medium is tridimensional, but that it settles upon a single distance value (that of the nearest surface) in any particular direction from the observer.

A similar idea has taken various forms in theories of stereoscopic vision going back at least as far as Boring's (1933) proposal that the inverse of binocular parallax occurs in the nervous system, different directions and degrees of retinal disparity being fused at different "depths" in a neural manifold. The discovery of disparity-specific units in the cortex by Barlow, Blakemore, and Pettigrew (1967) lent a good deal of support to theories of this type. To identify the disparity fusion medium with the manifold that I am proposing is obviously tempting, but encounters some serious obstacles, a major one being that the former represents depth relative to convergence distance, whereas the latter is supposed to represent distances from the observer. Another is Hochberg's important demonstration (1963, illustrated and discussed by Julesz, 1971) that a Necker cube the lines of which are produced entirely by a constant degree of disparity in a random-dot stereogram will still be seen as a cube and will reverse in depth in the ordinary way: the paradox is that the lines could not vary in perceived depth if they owed their existence to constancy of perceived depth. How these pieces fit together I do not know, but any accomodation of the present system to the implications of Hochberg's demonstration will at least require that the "sameness of state" between paired points which activates a projective set of dipoles be defined in terms of variables more complex than luminance, including, say, the presence or absence of local discontinuities in disparity.

The manifold may well be supposed to receive inputs from various sources other than those discussed, and to constitute the medium in which visual images are constructed from information (probably digital in form) in memory. The present system seems quite compatible with the model embodied in a computer simulation of visual imagery by Kosslyn and Shwartz (1977), and further developed by Pinker (1979, 1980) who points out that visual imagery has phenomenally a "2½ D" character, but that some tasks such as mental rotation must draw upon a level of representation independent of vantage point and encompassing arrangements of occluded as well as visible (or visualized) surfaces. Dealing with perception rather than imagery, Marr and Nishihara (1978) suggest that beyond the "2½ D sketch" there is a fully 3-D representation in terms of "object-centered" instead of "viewer-centered" coordinates.

In the system outlined here—which is by no means supposed to be the whole perceptual system—the representation is not only viewer-centered, but also specific to the momentary fixation-point of the eyes. (The same limitation applies to most theories of stereoscopic vision.) Granting that a fully invariant representation of external space can occur only at a higher level, the more modest question remains: what happens in the manifold when the eyes move? It is fairly well established that movement is perceived (i.e., attributed to external objects) only when there is a mismatch between an "efferent copy" of the command to the eye muscles and the consequent "reafference" from the retina (von Holst & Mittelstaedt, 1950). The nature of the matching process has never been altogether clear, however. At the simplest, it might be conceived as a match, on only two variables, between the efferent and reafferent movements vectors. An alternative much more complex, but also more interesting, is that the efferent copy directs a translation of the whole image to the location that would be anticipated as a result of the eye movement, where it interacts with the reafferent image essentially as if the eyes had not moved. If the medium in which such translations occurred were the tridimensional manifold of the present system, they would have the still more basic function of preserving information from one fixation to another, so that the organizational process would not have to be repeated *de novo* after every saccade. The tridimensionality of the medium would be of special importance in the case of *head* movements, which produce movements in the retinal image contingent upon distance. (This point is dramatically demonstrated in the Mach-Eden folded paper illusion.) I shall not speculate at this time on the nature of the neural machinery that might serve to translate images, or on whether the translation might better be accomplished within the manifold itself or via a higher representational level, but it is evident in any case that continuity of appropriate connections with the higher level would need to be maintained; see my earlier conjectures (Attneave, 1974) about a hierarchy of "place-markers" linking analog with digital representations. The compatibility of the present suggestions with the Kosslyn-Shwartz account of shifting "fixation" in the viewing of a mental image should be particularly noted.

A word about *transparency* may be in order at this point. The assumption that in every projective set one dipole must become dominant and suppress all its rivals (which establishes the "2½ D" form of the representation) would seem to deny the possibility of perceiving two surfaces in the same direction, one *through* the other. To accommodate the fact of perceived transparency, we could perhaps modify the system so as to allow two or more dipoles in a set to remain simultaneously active at equilibrium. Rather, however, I am inclined to doubt that two surfaces *can* be perceived in the same direction at the same moment, and to suggest that instead they are perceived successively, with alternate dominance of corresponding dipoles. The changes in dominance might be effected "from above" by some attentional mechanism, or by "fatigue" of the dominant dipoles themselves (cf. the case of ambiguous figures that reverse in depth) or by both. In the situation devised by Kolers (1970) involving simultaneous presentation of a front and a rear view by means of a half-silvered mirror, it seems clear enough that the two are perceived successively. Even more dramatically, Norman Mackworth (1972) has shown that when vertical strips sliced from two different photographs are spatially alternated in a composite picture, one of the scenes in effect disappears when the other is perceived.

5. But Will It Work?

In a system like this, involving complex, recursive interactions, it is exceedingly difficult to follow in detail the flow of events that would follow from presentation of any particular stimulus array. It is therefore possible that the system proposed contains some fatal flaws, outside the scope of my insight. Further assurance that it is workable will, I believe, require computer simulation.[3] In any such simula-

---

[3]The simulation may pose a formidable problem, however, in its demands on computer time and capacity, because of basic structural differences between existing digital computers and the system to be simulated: the computer is not inherently a soap bubble system; its units are not each provided with 40,000 built-in connections to other units; and the simulation would be a ridiculous undertaking if its aim were merely to program a computer to achieve the end-result of spatial organization in as efficient a manner as possible. One could hardly find a better example of divergence between simulation of an intelligent system and pure artificial intelligence without regard for simulation.

tion, a great many system parameters about which I have been vague will have to be specified, if only on a trial-and-error basis. It will surely be necessary to abandon our simplifying pretense that a projective set is activated by equivalence of *luminance* at two retinal *points*. If the system is to work on real scenes of reasonable complexity it should more plausibly take its input from a level entailing contour detection and related processes, somewhat like the "primal sketch" of Marr (1976). At the very simplest level of preprocessing worth investigating, each of the neurons in a retinal pair might be a unit characterized by center-surround antagonism in its receptive field; immediately the size of the receptive fields, both absolute and relative to their separations, would become an important consideration.

6. But Is It True?

The postulates of the system, though requiring additional specificity for computer simulation, are quite specific enough to be wrong. In view of the considerable element of the arbitrary in their choice, it is a practical certainty that many if not all of them are indeed wrong, in terms of correspondence to neural structures and functions, whatever their utility might be in artificial intelligence devices. (That is approximately equivalent to an admission that I am not divinely inspired.) The question of interest is whether an important component in spatial organization is a system similar in its general nature to be the one outlined here as an example. This I view as a hypothesis that is neither confirmed or disconfirmed by present evidence, but a serious possibility which has received less attention in recent years than it deserves.

It is somewhat paradoxical that Prägnanz does not figure as a unitary principle in the present system (despite the Gestalt origins of the system), whereas the alternative possibility that perception corresponds to the interpretation of the input that can be most compactly described (in a symbolic system comparable to Leeuwenberg's) does employ a unitary principle of economy. This distinction tends to fade, however, when we consider that the descriptive system might take cognizance of some but not all varieties of redundancy in the stimulus, and that its assumed capacities for information reduction could be limited in particular ways to match the performance of the organism. A more important difference is that a soap bubble system seems restricted, by considerations of neuroeconomy, to the use of stimulus features of a rather low order, whereas a sequential descriptive system would not be so restricted. To what degree the perceptual organization of tridimensional space can be explained merely in terms of second-order elements (as in the present dipole system) is an empirical question that has not been adequately investigated. (For other purposes, notably object identification, higher-order features are unquestionably abstracted.)

Leeuwenberg's descriptive system is an outstanding intellectual achievement, impressive in both its predictive power and its internal elegance. As mentioned earlier, the difficulty with any such economical-description approach is in conceiving plausible mechanisms (in either neurological or artificial-intelligence terms) whereby the most economical description could be discovered and identified as such. However, soap bubble and economical-description (or, indeed, probable-description) models, are not mutually exclusive, and it is possible that a combination of the two, operating in tandem with various types of feedback, might constitute a more plausible system than either alone.

Some of my friends seem to feel that it is no less than shameful to suggest a theory that one is not prepared to defend tooth-and-nail; I do not agree with them. At the very least, exercises like this one have the effect of revealing important gaps in the factual information on which a tenable theory must be based: our uncertainty about the role of symmetry is only one specific example. This exploration of theoretical possibilities has been instructive to me in a variety of ways, but the degree of resemblance between the mechanisms I have suggested and those inside the head remains to be determined.

ACKNOWLEDGMENT

The preparation of this chapter was supported by USPHS Grant MH 20449-06.

REFERENCES

Attneave, F. Some informational aspects of visual perception. *Psychological Review*, 1954, *61*, 183–193.

Attneave, F. Triangles as ambiguous figures. *American Journal of Psychology*, 1968, *81*, 447–453.

Attneave, F. Multistability in perception. *Scientific American*, 1971, *225*, 62–71.

Attneave, F. Representation of physical space. In A. W. Melton & E. J. Martin (Eds.), *Coding processes in human memory*. Washington, D.C.: Winston, 1972.

Attneave, F. Apparent movement and the what-where connection. *Psychologia*, 1974, *17*, 108–120.

Attneave, F., & Frost, R. The determination of perceived tridimensional orientation by minimum criteria. *Perception and Psychophysics*, 1969, *6B*, 391–396.

Attneave, F., & Pierce, C. R. Accuracy of extrapolating a pointer into perceived and imagined space. *American Journal of Psychology*, 1978, *91*, 371–387.

Barlow, H. B., Blakemore, C., & Pettigrew, J. D. The neural mechanism of binocular depth discrimination. *Journal of Physiology*, 1967, *193*, 327–342.

Beck, J. Perceptual grouping produced by changes in orientation and shape. *Science*, 1966, *154*, 538–540.

Beck, J. Similarity grouping and peripheral discriminability under uncertainty. *American Journal of Psychology*, 1972, *85*, 1–19.

Beck, J. The relation between similarity grouping and perceptual constancy. *American Journal of Psychology*, 1975, *88*, 397–409.

Beck, J., & Ambler, B. The effects of concentrated and distributed attention on peripheral acuity. *Perception and Psychophysics*, 1973, *14*, 225–230.

Boring, E. G. *The physical dimensions of consciousness*. New York: Century, 1933.

Cragg, B. G. The density of synapses and neurons in normal, mentally defective, and aging human brains. *Brain*, 1975, *98*, 81–90.

Gibson, J. J. *The perception of the visual world*. Boston: Houghton-Mifflin, 1950.

Gogel, W. C. The organization of perceived space. *Psychologische Forschung*, 1973, *36*, 196–247.

Hebb, D. O. *The organization of behavior*. New York: Wiley, 1949.

Hochberg, J. *Talk at fourth meeting of Psychonomic Society*. Bryn Mawr, Penn., 1963.

Hochberg, J. *Perception*. Englewood Cliffs,: Prentice-Hall, 1968, 1978.

Hochberg, J., & McAlister, E. A quantitative approach to figural "goodness." *Journal of Experimental Psychology*, 1953, *46*, 361–364.

Hochberg, J., & Brooks, V. The psychophysics of form: Reversible-perspective drawings of spatial objects. *American Journal of Psychology*, 1960, *73*, 337–354.

Holst, E. von, & Mittelstaedt, H. Das Reafferenzprincip. *Die Naturwissenschaften*, 1950, *20*, 464–476.

Julesz, B. *Foudations of cyclopean perception*. Chicago: University of Chicago Press, 1971.

Julesz, B. Experiments in the visual perception of texture. *Scientific American*, 1975, *232*, 34–43.

Julesz, B. Perceptual limits of texture discrimination and their implications to figure-ground separation. In E. L. J. Leeuwenberg & H. F. J. M. Buffart (Eds.), *Formal theories of visual perception*. New York: Wiley, 1978.

Kanizsa, G. The role of regularity in perceptual organization. In Giovanni B. Flores d'Arcais (Ed.) *Studies in perception: Festschrift for Fabio Metelli*. Milan: Martello-Giunti, 1975.

Koffka, K. *Principles of Gestalt psychology*. New York: Harcourt Brace, 1935.

Köhler, W., & Wallach, H. Figural after-effects: an investigation of visual processes. *Proceedings of the American Philosophical Society*, 1944, *88*, 269–357.

Kolers, P. A. The role of shape and geometry in picture recognition. In B. S. Lipkin & A. Rosenfeld (Eds.), *Picture processing and psychopictories*. New York: Academic Press, 1970.

Kosslyn, S. M., & Shwartz, S. P. A simulation of visual imagery. *Cognitive Science*, 1977, *1*, 265–295.

Lashley, K. S., Chow, K. L., & Semmes, J. An examination of the electrical field theory of cerebral integration. *Psychological Review*, 1951, *58*, 123–136.

Leeuwenberg, E. L. J. A perceptual coding language for visual and auditory patterns. *American Journal of Psychology*, 1971, *84*, 307–349.

Mach, E. *The analysis of sensations*. New York: Dover, 1959 (5th ed., orig. 1906).

MacKay, D. M. Quantal aspects of scientific information. *Philosophical Magazine*, 1950, *41*, 289–311.

Mackworth, N. H. *Talk at 68th annual meeting of Society of Experimental Psychologists*. Stanford, Calif., 1972.

Marr, D. Early processing of visual information. *Philosophical Transactions of the Royal Society*, 1976, *B.275*, 483–524.

Marr, D., & Nishihara, H. K. Representation and recognition of the spatial organization of three-dimensional shapes. *Proceedings of the Royal Society of London*, 1978, B *200*, 269–294.

Musatti, C. Forma e assimilazione. *Archivio Italiano di Psicologia*, 1931, *9*, 61–156.

Olson, R. K., & Attneave, F. What variables produce similarity grouping? *American Journal of Psychology*, 1970, *83*, 1–21.

Perkins, D. N. Visual discrimination between rectangular and nonrectangular parallelopipeds. *Perception and Psychophysics*, 1972, *12*, 396–400.

Pinker, S. A. *The representation of three-dimensional space in mental images*. Unpublished doctoral dissertation, Harvard University, 1979.

Pinker, S. A., Mental imagery and the third dimension. *Journal of Experimental Psychology: General*, 1980, *109*, 354–371.

Pritchard, R. M., Heron, W., & Hebb, D. O. Visual perception approached by the method of stabilized images. *Canadian Journal of Psychology*, 1960, *14*, 67–77.

Rock, I., & Brosgole, L. Grouping based on phenomenal proximity. *Journal of Experimental Psychology*, 1964, *67*, 531–538.

Shepard, R. N. Psychophysical complementarity. In M. Kubovy & J. R. Pomerantz (Eds.), *Perceptual organization*. Hillsdale, N.J.: Lawrence Erlbaum Associates, 1981.

Tuijl, H. F. J. M. van. Perceptual interpretation of complex line patterns. *Journal of Experimental Psychology: Human Perception and Performance*, 1980, *6*, 197–221.

2 Coding Theory as an Integration of Gestalt Psychology and Information Processing Theory

Frank Restle (*deceased*)
Indiana University

The purpose of this chapter is to integrate parts of Gestalt theory with information processing theories through the use of coding theory.

CODING THEORY

When a person sees a situation or event, the information received is generally somewhat ambiguous, at least in principle. For example, when I look at a display such as that in Fig. 2.1, it can be seen as a smaller square behind a larger one, or as a large square up against a smaller L-shaped figure. These are two different meanings or interpretations of the same display. As one walks through a forest, one possible interpretation is that there are real, stationary trees and one is moving. Another possible interpretation would be that one is not moving but that the forest is moving under one's feet in a kind of treadmill. It is possible that extremely clever new photographic techniques have been developed to simulate the scene perfectly, or, of course, it is possible that one is imagining or dreaming the experience. I do not assert that all of these interpretations are equally plausible, or even that it is possible to experience all of them, merely that they are possible. The point is that any experience can be interpreted in more than one way.

Any such interpretation can be the basis for coding, generally as illustrated by Leeuwenberg's coding system (see the appendix to Chapter 3). That is, it is possible to enumerate the parts of the stimulus so that all lines, angles, and other features are mentioned in a way that permits reconstruction of all the essential characteristics of the display. Such a representation is here called a

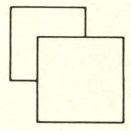

FIG. 2.1. One square in front of another, or a mosaic of square and L-shaped figure.

"primitive code." One interpretation may give rise to many different primitive codes; for example, starting at different places in the figure, constructing parts in different orders, and so on. These different codes are different in a technical but not a material way.

A primitive code can be reduced by the application of various rules of simplification. In analysis of line drawings, for example, Leeuwenberg will simplify a code by taking out repetitions. If A is some segment of code and the code of a display contains AAAA, this can be replaced by 4*A. Now, AAAA has four times the information load or complexity of A, whereas 4*A has the information load of A(once) plus one more unit of information representing the number 4, telling how many times to repeat A. Leeuwenberg also takes out interspersals, making aAaB into <a><AB>. He also takes out symmetry, making aMbNNbMa into Σ(aMbN). Notice that these simplifications act on the code, and are well-defined logical or mathematical-type operations on strings of characters.

A given figure can give rise to many interpretations, each interpretation can be given several primitive codes depending on starting place and the like, and a given primitive code can be simplified in many different ways, using logical operators in many ways. The task of finding the most economical code is therefore something like solving a chess problem, except that in application of coding theory one does not know which player wins or in how many moves.

Simplifying a code reduces its information load, but exactly what is information load? A simple analogy will suffice for the nontechnical purposes of this paper. Imagine that coding a display is equivalent to writing a computer program to reconstruct the essential properties of the display. To reproduce the figure one needs a program, and then certain data. A primitive code corresponds to a computer program that is very simple in structure, for it says something like "move the first length, turn the first angle, then move the next length, then turn the next angle." To make the figure, however, such a program would need a complete list of lengths and angles, which would be quite a bit of data. If a certain length is repeated, the program could be given an instruction saying "repeat the previous length," along with some control to ensure that the given length is repeated the correct number of times. Such a program would need the length (as an item of data) only once, and therefore would use less data than the previously described program.

In the Leeuwenberg theory, the "information load" of a code is the number of data points needed. Thus, to reduce a code is to shift responsibility from the list of data to the structure of the program.

Similarly, in my recently published model of motions (Restle, 1979), I dealt with points that appear to move relative to a larger moving system. There I argued that if the same amplitude, phase, frequency, curvature, or direction of motion is shared by a system and also something moving relative to that system, then the code (i.e., the program to generate the perceived motion) need not handle this numerical value twice, as two data points, but can mention in the program that the same parameter operates in both systems, and therefore reduces the number of data points, which we call the information load.

The experimental prediction, in all such analyses, is that the observer will experience and report that interpretation having the simplest code. Leeuwenberg (1978), however, used the term "prominence" in a most useful way. Suppose that when we compare the information load of various interpretations, one is much simpler than any competitor. Then the subject will accept that interpretation as his perception, the perception will be vivid and clear, and the observer will use phrases like "I really *see* it." If, in contrast, one interpretation is most economical but others exist that are only slightly more complex, then the perception will be much weaker and more ambiguous, and the subject may use phrases like "well, I *think* it is there, but I don't really see it."

Notice that this application of coding theory fits closely with the phenomenological method of experimenting. Coding theory does not immediately tell us the process that goes on in percpetion, and is not a theory of reaction time, fine sensory discrimination, or even quantitative ratings. It asks what we will see, given a certain physical display, in the sense of the interpretation given after due deliberation and inspection of the display. If it is true, as one might suppose, that the process of finding a minimum code in a morass of competitors might take some time, then the subject's *first* response to an ambiguous stimulus would not be particularly interesting, and we should let the observer inspect carefully. An unpracticed and unskilled observer might have difficulty developing all possible interpretations, and might never even consider the "best" interpretation, whereas such oversights would be less likely if the observer is experienced in perception, and particularly if the observer has artistic sensitivities. The subject's response is not usually a simple choice, but instead is a description that serves to distinguish his interpretation from other possibilities. This means that subjects are given free rein to describe their experiences, as in phenomenological studies. For this reason, Coding Theory may serve to analyze experiments and observations that belong to the Gestalt tradition.

CODING THEORY AND GESTALT LAWS

My thesis is that the Gestalt laws, in the main, can be shown to be consequences of Coding Theory as described in the foregoing. That is, I do not propose that Coding Theory competes with Gestalt theory, and that we should seek an *experimentum crucis* to decide between them. Instead, I shall argue that the Gestalt laws, as commonly used, become clearer when rephrased from the point of view of coding theory, and what is more important, Coding Theory explains how to relate the apparently conflicted Gestalt laws.

Wertheimer's Laws Of Grouping

Normally, gestalts arise from well-organized and continuous fields, but Wertheimer argued that even when the field consists of isolated and nearly punctate parts it is drawn into organization. The basic organizing factor was that points near one another tend to form groups, and I must admit that though this seems an obvious fact, I do not have a very good coding-theoretic interpretation. Wertheimer's three other laws of organization have natural interpretations in Coding Theory, however.

Consider first that similar points tend to be grouped together. If they are seen as separate, however, each having code X, then the code would be XXXX . . . for all n points, and if I(X) is the information load of each point, then I(XXX . . . n times . . . X) = nI(X). If instead they are grouped then the code of that group becomes n*X, having an information load of 1 + I(X). This is surely less than nI(X) provided that n is greater than 2 or I(X) is greater than 1. The only grouping of similar parts that would not be stable, then, would be a grouping of two very simple points.

"Good continuation" is particularly difficult to specify in Gestalt theory. It refers to a set of dots lying along a perceptible line or curve, but the difficulty has always been in specifying the imaginary curve. Leeuwenberg would code such a figure a curve, plus the spaced dots on that curve. The total information load is I(curve) + I(dots). If, instead, the dots were seen as separate, then the code would be nI(dots). If the "curve" can obtain a fairly simple code, and if there are a fairly large number of dots, then the figure is most simply seen as a curve with dots on it. This model gives a general specification of the kind of curve that will be sufficient, and then of how many dots must be on it, for the principle of "good continuation" to apply. Obviously, a straight line is the simplest "curve" in coding theory, so it is also the most robust way of "demonstrating" good continuation.

The last of Wertheimer's laws of grouping is "common fate" or common motion. Johansson (1950) made an elaborate investigation beginning with this law of Wertheimer, and found that (a) points need not have a common motion, only a related motion, to be grouped; and (b) many things besides grouping emerge when detailed experiments are done. This whole body of observation is analyzed closely in my earlier work (Restle, 1979) and I have shown that an appropriate coding theory can predict Johansson's experiments on moving dots.

In summary, Coding Theory has been applied to many of the data derived from Wertheimer's laws of grouping, and gives a good account of them. Instead of laws of grouping, however, Coding Theory sees these laws simply as applications of certain effective ways of making a code more economical.

Forces And Field Theory

In the chapter on binocular disparity and perception, Zanforlin (Chapter 13) describes fields of "force" in phenomenal fields, and says that binocular disparity sets up forces or tensions that "force" the perception from two to three dimensions. Let me discuss these ideas, and one or two of his demonstrations, from the point of view of Coding Theory.

First, one requires a basic force that will produce binocular fusion when the same display is shown to the two eyes in a stereoscope. If the left eye sees field X and the right eye also sees X, then the code is XX. If the two fields fuse into one perception, the code is X. Clearly, fusion produces a simpler code.

Now suppose that as in a standard stereogram, the subject can easily fuse most of the two displays, but then there is left a disparity in some part of the field. Suppose that the common part of the fields is coded as X and the two disparate parts as Y' and Y''. Then the code is XY'Y''. If an interpretation can be made, using a three-dimensional structure, which permits fusing of Y' and Y'' into, say, Y, then the new code is XY, surely shorter than XY'Y'' unless the new spatial arrangement is much more complex to code. Thus, by Coding Theory, the disparity produces a "force" in the sense that the code of Y'Y'' is relatively complex. The perception is "forced into the third dimension" in the sense that the three-dimensional structure, by permitting fusion of Y' and Y'' into Y, shortens the code.

The principle of simplicity, attempting to perceive the display using the simplest interpretation in terms of information load, is somewhat similar to a force theory. In Gestalt theory, it was often argued that the good gestalt would have a simplest-possible form which might correspond to a balance of forces, an equilibrium. If the perceptual field should, for a moment, contain an unnecessary complexity, this would be thought of as an excess force. The "force" analogy seems to imply that simplicity is achieved by a continuous and automatic process, whereas coding theory, though actually silent on this point, suggests that the process may be discontinuous and, to some degree, guided by a psychological process. It should be noted, however, that according to Coding Theory, the subject may not know anything about the process of coming to the minimum code, and normally would not be conscious about any but the minimum code.

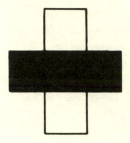

FIG. 2.2.   Zanforlin's figure (one-eye view).

At its present stage of development, all Coding Theory does is to specify the final or asymptotic state of the process of reducing codes, without spelling out the detailed process itself. Therefore, it is different from "force" theories only in unknown and, perhaps, irrelevant ways.

In one particularly interesting demonstration, Zanforlin showed two scenes in a stereopticon in which the usual, two-dimensional interpretation is opposite to what is required for stereoptic fusion (see Fig. 2.2). Disparity is such that the white squares should be seen as closer to the viewer than the black rectangle. If all were on a plane, however, this is a clear example in which the black rectangle would be seen to occlude a white rectangle, and would be in front. Clearly, according to force theory, this demonstration should result in a large excess force.

Consider interpretations of such a figure, from the point of view of Coding Theory. To begin, I have attempted to code the display interpreted as two rectangles, and found that this requires only five information units, whereas when it is seen as one rectangle plus two squares, it would require seven information units. Clearly, it would be seen as two rectangles, if there were no conflicting disparity. But what is to be done with the disparity?

Notice that disparity, in such a figure, affects only left and right edges of homogeneous textures. Therefore, one possible solution is to place the white squares forward in space toward the observer, place the ends of the black rectangle farther away, and then see the rectangle as curved in the "third dimension," bending out toward the observer in the middle so as to lie in front of the white rectangle. Some impression of such an interpretation is shown in Fig. 2.3.

FIG. 2.3.   Curved interpretation of Zanforlin's figure.

Such an interpretation is more complex than a flat back rectangle in front of a white rectangle, but only by the information in the curvature of the black figure. The simplest way to obtain such a curve would use a single angle of curvature so that the black rectangle would be seen, in effect, as bent along the arc of a circle. Several observers, who achieved this interpretation all agreed that the apparent curvature of the rectangle was as smooth as possible.

Notice that in such an interpretation, all vertical edges are placed in depth so that disparity is resolved. The smooth curvature of the black rectangle would result in disparity if it were not homogeneous. As it is, it appears that the bent rectangle, as seen in Zanforlin's demonstration, is the optimal interpretation of this display, with the most economical code.

As to process, Zanforlin's display does not seem to result in an immediate, effortless perceptual process. Several observers did not see his interpretation at all, and it was delayed, perhaps by as much as a minute, in the observation of others. If the perceptual process were "hunting" for a best interpretation, the process might well be slow and uncertain.

Prägnanz Or The Good Gestalt

The principle of simplicity used in Coding Theory was first stated as the Law of Prägnanz in Gestalt theory. As described by Kanizsa (1975), "The degree of Prägnanz is usually considered equivalent to the degree of simplicity, regularity, stability, balance, order, harmony, homogeneity, etc. But this definition allows for a great deal of uncertainty" (p. 48). The difficulties with the good Gestalt are (a) exact definition and measurement of the factors, and (b) a formula for combining the various sources of good or poor Gestalt.

Four of the more objective factors in Prägnanz are simplicity, regularity, symmetry (or balance), and minimum energy. Each of these is represented, in an easy way, in Coding Theory. I shall take examples from an analysis of figural completion by Buffart, Leeuwenberg, and Restle (1981).

Consider first Fig. 2.4, in which panel A presents the figure shown to the observer. Panel B shows the usual "interpretation" completing the square be-

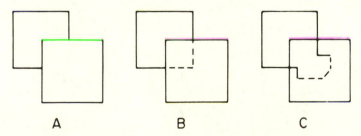

A   B   C

FIG. 2.4.   The principle of simplicity eliminates the interpretation C.

hind. Panel C shows a more complex possible interpretation, which simply has some unnecessary parts. The principle of simplicity says that one will not see such unnecessary complexity, and it is obvious that a coding theory will find the code for such unnecessary complexity to be longer, and to have a heavier information load, than the code of the simpler completion.

Another principle of Prägnanz is regularity. This seems rather vague, but I shall make it specific by saying that regularity corresponds to the repetition of parts of a code. As was mentioned earlier, repetition of subcode X can be coded as nX, which is more economical than XX . . . X.

The principal of symmetry, in a simple visual sense, usually means that half of the display or figure is a mirror image of the other half. In coding theory of figures (Leeuwenberg, 1978), symmetry is found in the code and means that the symbols in one segment of a code are reversed in order from symbols in another segment. In the Leeuwenberg coding model for line drawings, one would write abccba = Σabc, and then the symbol Σ carries an information load. The reason is that the whole expression contains not only abc but also a reference (symbol) to that same segment, and when a segment gets a second reference, the result is an element of information. What this means is that symmetry, though it is often helpful in simplifying a code, is somewhat less effective than repetition. If one is faced with different possible ways of simplifying a code, it often happens that symmetry is not the best rule to apply if it is possible to apply repetition or simplicity. A typical figure, presented by Kanizsa (1975), illustrates this point. The symmetrical completion into a hexagonal lozenge is not the favored completion (see Fig. 2.5 in which Panel C is preferred over Panel B). Notice that in Panel C there are fewer parts in the completed figure, as it has only 5 instead of 6 sides.

The concept of "minimum energy" was discussed in the previous section. When a physical system arrives at minimum energy, however, it is likely to arrive at a configuration with equal sides and equal angles—other configurations usually bespeak unequal and nonoptimal distributions of energy. But it should be obvious that when the parts and angles of a figure are equal, the code can be reduced by use of the principle of regularity.

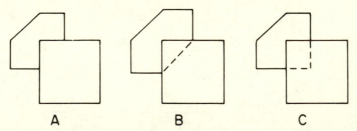

A   **B**   **C**

FIG. 2.5.   Kanizsa's figure, in which C is preferred over B although B is more symmetrical.

In summary, it is here argued that the various subprinciples of Prägnanz are well represented in Coding Theory. Each principle is clarified when we specify exactly what operations may be applied to a code. Measurement is not really a problem, as either one can or one cannot apply a rule to a code. Finally, one does not "add" or "multiply" the effects of such principles. Instead, they are to be thought of as possible ways of simplifying a code that may be arranged in any logical sequence, always seeking that arrangement that results in the most economical possible code. Sometimes simplicity and symmetry, for example, might "cooperate" in that both are used in simplifying a given code. In another instance, one might choose between applying simplicity and applying symmetry, so they "compete." Which will then be chosen is not a matter of intrinsic strength of the principles, but simply a question of which happens to fit into the optimal logical sequence. The end result is the simplest possible code. Notice that this end result, and in fact the entire discussion, is exactly the same as for Wertheimer's factors of organization of disjoint points, and also the analysis of "forces". Whereas these various early attempts to apply Gestalt theory had seemed to result in three different Gestalt theories, our coding-theoretic analysis has shown that they are simply different applications of a unified theoretical process.

NEO-GESTALT THEORY

In defining a category of Neo-Gestalt Theory I follow the usual conventions in naming theories; that is, any theory given the name "Neo-something" is not well defined.

I feel, however, that certain theoretical ideas owe heavy debts to Gestalt theory, but can only with difficulty be attributed to the classic writers. I now turn to an attempt to relate some such ideas to Coding Theory.

Extracting Invariants

From the earlier theory of perceptual constancies, explaining why as one approaches an object it does not seem larger, or as one walks around it, the object does not change shape, or as one brightens the light the color of the object does not change, there has emerged a more recent formulation in terms of "invariants." The idea is that the perceptual system is designed to select some characteristics of the incoming information and respond to them, whereas other properties are discarded.

The most detailed and coherent theory of invariants is probably the theory that the visual system extracts the projective invariants in perceiving an object. If one looks at a square table from the usual angle, the image on the retina is a fairly general quadrilateral, and is only square if one looks straight down at the table.

The table is seen as square; however. Johansson (1974) and others have argued that the visual system does not respond directly to the "Euclidean" form on the retina, but instead would see the resulting image as intrinsically ambiguous. If the observer's point of regard, relative to the table, is moved, however, the shape and dimensions of the quadrilateral on the retina change. What remains invariant through these transformations of viewpoint are the projective invariants of a certain fixed quadrilateral out in space. As one walks around, one does not see the quadrilateral change shape, but instead sees a fixed table in space.

The transformations, in this case, involve all the perspective transformations, all the changes in image that can accompany moving the point of regard around the object, or closer or farther away. The invariants constitute the shape of a rigid, three-dimensional body.

One might think that a limited set of points of regard might leave some residual ambiguity. For example, suppose that I look at the square table from one position, then move my head only a few centimeters in each direction. In all of these viewpoints, the retinal image will always be a foreshortened quadrilateral. Will I be able to see that it is a square, or is this "going beyond the evidence" of the visual system: This question has recently been answered by Ullman (1979) in a geometrical analysis, who showed that if one can identify four particular points on the object in as many as three different viewpoints, one has sufficient visual or geometrical information to specify the three-dimensional shape without ambiguity. There is no need to make infinitely many, or highly varied observations, nor in any way to go beyond the visual information available.

Palmer (Chapter 5) deals with transformations of dilation and shrinkage, rotation on the picture plane, and translation of image. Johansson includes also transformations that accompany rotating the object relative to the line of regard. If the visual system receives a sequence of images corresponding to some systematic motion of object or viewer, we might think of them as being coded separately as V_1, V_2, ... V_n, the n views of the situation. Alternatively, the same situation might be coded as some more complex physical situation Φ and some motion of the observer, M. One would then say that the observer would extract invariants (the code Φ) provided that the code of $\Phi+M$ is simpler than the code of V_1+V_2+ ... $+V_n$, and the vividness of the impression of three-dimensional stability would correspond to the advantage in efficiency of the code of $\Phi+M$ over the separate images. If the stable physical situation is extremely complicated relative to images, or the motion is utterly incoherent, there can be situations in which the invariants would not be extracted. In general, however, as one moves freely about in the world, any interpretation of visual experience as a sequence of images becomes enormously complex, whereas the interpretation of locomotion in a rigid environment gains information load, if at all, only very slowly. The more "natural" the viewing conditions, the less ambiguity.

Thus, it is not necessary to assume that the visual system contains a special mechanism or process for extracting certain invariants. By applying the principle of simplicity, as stated in Coding Theory, it is possible (given an adequate way of coding the particular class of materials) to separate the information in the display into different structures, which may economize in coding. According to such an approach, for example, a rotating object could be coded as the three-dimensional object, plus its path of rotation. The "object" is then, in Neo-Gestalt Theory, seen as the "invariant" and the motion as the variable. An observer, however, can perfectly well be interested in the path of rotation, in which case the same dissection of the total event is performed, but not for the purpose of "extracting the invariant" and discarding the remainder.

A problem in this sort of Neo-Gestalt Theory, sometimes not adequately considered, is that the information coming to the eye might be analyzed in more than one way. It is not sufficient to show that one logically *could* pick out certain invariants, or even to show that some perceptual experiences correspond closely to certain invariants.

Such demonstrations do not show that the visual system is designed to extract these invariants, but merely that it is possible for the visual system to analyze a situation so as to isolate those interesting properties. According to Coding Theory, if another analysis would lead to simpler codes, then another set of invariants would be extracted.

In fact, even in the most familiar instances of extraction of invariants, there are empirical details that have not been well explained. Johansson (1974) has discussed how the eye extracts projective invariants of motion. If one looks, however, at a single point moving in an elliptical orbit that would be a tilted projection of uniform circular motion, there is no impression of such circular motion, or of tilt. If two points are put on the elliptical path 180° out of phase, a good impression of tilt is obtained and the points seem to be the ends of a rigid rod. If the points are only 90° out of phase, the impression is ambiguous but no clear judgment of tilt is possible. Three points, 120° out of phase, make up a rigid triangle and yield a clear impression of tilt. Now, the interesting fact is that all of these displays are somewhat ambiguous and could be interpreted either as circular orbits viewed at an angle, or as elliptical paths of objects that are not rigidly joined. The visual system does not always extract the possible invariants, but seems to be following a higher principle. My conjecture is that the principle is one of simplicity of code.

It is less clear that similar principles apply in the extraction of invariants of surface color under changes or gradients of illumination, as in Bergström (Chapter 18). Notice, however, that his "vector analysis" of illumination involves separating a gradient of illumination, having a simple form, from a relatively complex set of reflectances. If the particular reflected colors are analyzed at every point, it appears that this would require a surface of great complexity, whereas if the same reflected light is analyzed as a gradient of illumination plus a stimulus object, the object can have a much simpler color structure, consisting of patches of homogeneous color. Without a good coding theory for such surfaces,

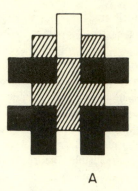

A

B

FIG. 2.6. Transparency through form, as shown by Leeuwenberg.

any hypothesis is a mere conjecture, but it appears that a principle of simplicity might well apply to such displays. It is interesting, in this context, that Bergström, like Land (1964), gets such results more clearly when he uses a more complex display. If one merely had a gradation, across the field, from red to green, this could equally well result from a gradation of illumination or of surface color. With such a simple display, the system would have no basis for choosing one or another interpretation as simpler. When a complicated display is used, there is more opportunity for economies of coding, and it is more likely that a given interpretation will be preferred.

Using simpler displays, Metelli and his associates have studied the phenomenon of transparency, particularly the light that must come to the eye from each area of a display in order to indicate transparency (Metelli, 1974). I have not attempted a coding model for such displays and therefore cannot make any useful contribution to the facts. It is clear, however, that these experiments emphasize a fact that has not been fully discussed in Gestalt theories of Prägnanz, and is an important property both of Neo-Gestalt, invariance-extracting theories and of Coding Theory. That is that a code must be in agreement with the information given. It appears that principles of good continuation, closure, and so on, can *distort* perception, so that the principle may override reality. A Neo-Gestalt Theory, however, states that the visual system extracts certain invariants, and it cannot extract invariants that are not there. It might be simple to see a motion picture as a rotating cube, but if the display is not consistent with such an interpretation, a cube cannot be seen. Metelli has, in effect, emphasized the stimulus conditions that must be satisfied for an interpretation of transparency.

It is natural and efficient to consider only colors in such an experiment, but as has been shown by Leeuwenberg (1978), a strong impression of transparency also depends upon the shapes involved. The displays shown in Fig. 2.6 differ widely in their impression of transparency even though no care has been taken to control whiteness of the sub-areas. Here, seeing two forms, one viewed through the other, leads to very much less information load than seeing the figure as a mosaic of small pieces, and this gain is so great that the eye will overcome some discrepancies of color. It seems important, for future experimental work, to vary both formal and color properties in the investigation of transparency, to determine exactly what properties are extracted, and how this more complex coding system is to be understood.

Going Beyond Sensory Information—Completions

The place of "completion" demonstrations in Gestalt psychology is somewhat ambiguous. On the face of it, and in such interpretations as those of Bruner (1957), such a process of "going beyond" is a direct observation of cognitive processes that supplement perception. Conversely, Gestalt Theory places emphasis on the perceptual character of the experience of the table continuing beneath the book, and particularly of the figure-ground arrangement.

The fundamental idea in figure-ground is quite simple: one can either perceive the table behind the book, the usual completion, or one can imagine a hole in the table, just covered by the book. Each is a possible interpretation or meaning of the scene displayed. If one possibility, when coded, yields a lower information load than others, it will be seen. In most of the figure-ground demonstrations, it is obvious that a continuous ground is simpler to code than a ground "cut out" as it were, to make a mosaic around the figure.

If subjects are shown a display like that in Fig. 2.7 and asked to say what they see behind, they have more than one possibility—they might see any of several different things behind the occluding figure. The idea of such ambiguous completions comes to me from Kanizsa (1975). A very detailed analysis of a number of such figures, from the point of view of coding theory can be found in Buffart, Leeuwenberg, & Restle (1981). Our basic method is to suppose that there are several possible interpretations of a figure, and that one sees that interpretation having the simplest code. Many of the figures used by Kanizsa are difficult to code in the sense that several quite different approaches to the code result in

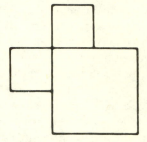

FIG. 2.7. Example of a figure permitting several completion or mosaic interpretations.

almost the same information load. In a number of his figures, in fact, we calculated that two different interpretations would have exactly the same information load, whence there would be perceptual ambiguity, some subjects would see the figure one way and others would see it another way, or the same experienced observer might notice both interpretations.

In a typical figure involving amodal completion (i.e., seeing part of one figure occluded by another) there is no direct visual information to contradict any interpretation, just so the hidden part of the figure would lie completely behind the occluding figure. Thus, the perceptual system is free to "complete" the figure any way it wants, and the principle of simplicity is free to operate in an unusually direct way. Although Kanizsa originally formulated these figures as a challenge to the principle of simplicity, interpreted in the usual Gestalt theoretic fashion, it turned out that the Leeuwenberg coding model for line figures, along with the general ideas of Coding Theory I have presented here, were able to make strong and accurate predictions of response to such figures.

It is interesting that whereas Kanizsa and Gerbino (Chapter 9) suggest perceptual and cognitive completion processes, with the resulting complexities of whether cognitive processes can feed back into the perceptual process on which they are built and so on, the coding-theoretic approach makes no such distinction. In simplest terms, coding theory considers all "interpretations" to be on the same level, and the perceptual process selects one interpretation on the basis of analysis, simplification, and the principle of simplicity.

In Chapter 14, Vicario presents some original and interesting observations in the auditory realm, in which sequences of notes, when partly obliterated by bursts of noise, display many of the same perceptual patterning effects shown by analogous visual displays. Is it possible that such sounds can be analyzed using a coding model for sounds? Some elements of a coding model for sounds have been published (Restle, 1970, 1975; Restle & Brown, 1970; Simon & Kotovsky, 1963; Simon & Sumner, 1968) in which, for example, trills and runs are particularly simple structures. Vicario uses both of these structures in his experiments, and produces something like amodal completion using runs and arpeggios, and a hidden figure using trills. Unfortunately, I have not yet been able to reanalyze this coding model in conjunction with coding theory, so it is not possible to say whether Vicario's results can, in coding-theoretic terms, be said to make a strict analogy with the corresponding phenomena in visual perception.

ECOLOGICAL PERCEPTION

The position of J. J. Gibson, as represented in his recent book (Gibson, 1979) and in his contribution to this book, has some historical affinities with Gestalt psychology but is unique. Whereas Gestalt psychology and the neo-Gestalt theories say that the visual system groups entities, follows laws, seeks Prägnanz, minimizes energy, or extract invariants, Gibson takes the surprising position that the visual system *sees the outside world*. A Gibsonian observer is an active searcher in a complex environment. Generally, Gibson gives us an idea of what would happen in a psychophysical experiment if the observer were to escape from the chin rest and peek around behind the reduction screen to see what is really there.

For the purposes of my chapter, the question is whether the active searcher who sees a stable world of objects, is violating the principle of simplicity.

First, it must be realized that the active observer, looking around and moving in a complex environment, produes a stream of information that is enormously complex. The actual level of complexity is not a matter of concern for coding theory, however. All we are concerned with is selecting that interpretation that yields that simplest interpretation. Whether that interpretation itself has an information load of 1 or 1000 is less important than the fact that it is the simplest interpretation of what is seen. Suppose that I walk about in a room, lecturing, changing my position, my head orientation, and the direction of my eyes. The visual fields from moment to moment are changing, and a code simply reflecting the content of such visual patterns would be enormously complicated, and in fact it would gain complexity with each glance. If we were to suppose that the brain receives all such images, stores and computes on them, then to perceive clearly I should slow down, hold still for a while, and reduce the implosion of information.

Consider, however, a code having a stable outside world, with the viewer moving around in it, turning eyes, and the like. This code is not simple, but as the observer moves around, the code gets more complex only very slowly, as it takes some account of the personal motions. Meanwhile, an alternative interpretation gains information load very rapidly—the interpretation that what I see is a cleverly projected, always-changing image. Parts of such an image slew about, shrink or enlarge, appear and disappear, twist with projective transformations, and even undergo nontopological tearings. In other words, veridical perception as suggested by Gibson's ecological psychology may also be the most economical interpretation possible.

What is wrong with studying pictures, as perceptual psychologists have done for many years, and Gibson execrates? One difficulty, of course, is that the picture *is* one thing and *represents* another, so experimenter and subject may have difficulties in communication. But from the point of view of coding theory, pictures often fail to give a full specification of the situation represented. As Gibson points out, when one moves with respect to an object, parts of the background slide behind the object, and on the other side, parts of the background come into view. If we attempt to present the three-dimensional situation in a picture, then it is no longer possible (except with motion-picture or computer-controlled display techniques) to hide and uncover parts of the background.[1] Therefore, a picture does not serve to burden alternative interpretations with heavy information load, and therefore a picture is ambiguous, or at least more nearly ambiguous than the real situation. Because it is easy to generate ambiguity in pictures, an experimental psychology based on pictures will concern itself with resolution of ambiguities that do not arise in "normal" perception of the situations depicted. For example, certain pictures that depict one object partly hidden beind the other yield ambiguous perceptions of what is hidden. It is possible to make close analyses of such displays and their perception, without coming close to how we really see partly hidden objects. From the coding-theoretic point of view, for certain purposes, that very ambiguity is convenient, since it permits analysis of theoretical questions that would rarely, if ever, arise in the perception of objects. At the same time it should be realized that in real life the active, searching observer would rarely be bothered by the problems that are analyzed in the perceptual laboratory.[2]

My main conclusion however, is that the strong "overdetermination" of perception, characteristic of the active searching observer, is actually to be explained by the principle of simplicity. The perceiver selects the simplest interpretation, without regard for any absolute value of simplicity. The active observer so complicates every false or unreal interpretation that he soon is forced to a unique simplest interpretation.

What is the nature of that interpretation? It can be described as an interpretation that is not dependent on special limitations of observation, and that discards any aspects of perception that could depend on conditions of observation, illusion or delusion, dreams, memories, and so on. But limited views, delusions, and

---

[1]Computerized displays by progressive deletion or accretion of texture can produce a strong impression of one surface sliding behind another. Gibson does not comment on the fact that such a display is very unnatural and nonecological.

[2]The general point is worked out in detail by Buffart, Leeuwenberg, and Restle (1981). Buffart and Leeuwenberg are preparing a theoretical analysis of how the visual system resolves ambiguous scenes. This analysis assumes that the subject imagines relative displacements of the front and back surfaces.

dreams, upon further inspection, may be expected to require complex explanation, and to fall away by the principle of simplicity. What is left? It appears that under these conditions, the observer will see the physical world, or, perhaps more exactly stated, the objective world. Subjective interpretations of perceptual data will, with more and more observation and inspection, become more and more complex and will eventually be at a great disadvantage in comparison to objective interpretations. What is left, the interpretation of our surroundings that is not contaminated by "subjectivity," is the objective physical world. It is a deep question, of some philosophical interest, whether this objective world is "really" to be found merely by taking the simplest interpretation of experience. However, I do not think that Gibson himself gives any explanation of why perception does, or would, perceive the real world. The information is there in the ambient array, but why can we use it correctly? The principle of simplicity is at least a possible explanation as to how we select information from the available pool.

INFORMATION PROCESSING

This book contains several chapters on information processing models of perception. It is not easy to say just what such theories have in common, and they do not seem to be apposite to Gestalt Theory. A central concern in the perception phase information-processing models seems to be with a process by which perception can arrive at its preferred interpretation, with emphasis on processes that can be realized by computer technology and are relatively efficient. The models of perception put forward in this book concentrate on the process by which perception can occur, but they can be related to the kind of coding theory I have outlined.

The "earliest stage" of coding of a line drawing or figure is the extraction of line and angles. Rosenfeld (Chapter 6) discussed a general model progressing from a scene (external to the system, the source of information) converted into an image, which in turn is digitized into an array, usually of numbers, corresponding for example to brightnesses or colors at various points on the image. This array is then segmented, and various features such as borders, regions, and so on, are extracted. By a process of comparisons, specific properties or relations are then defined and identified, and from this the information is related to "models," such as sun, clouds, trees, buildings, road systems, etc. Finally the information is used to yield a particular example or instantiation of the model.

Rosenfeld argued that though it is common to analyze such a system in the direction from scene to image and so on up to model, in fact the system must be prepared to go back from a "higher level" and reconsider lower level decisions. For example, if analysis of an aerial photograph should indicate a road network, but one "line" should turn out to be anomalous, then it might be appropriate to return to the feature extraction stage and reassign parts of the digitized array so as to eliminate or change that line.

The difficulty with any such "looping" procedure, of course, is the danger that it may so revise the input array, attempting to arrive at a coherent model or interpretation, that it may confabulate, leading the computer to "see" what it only expected and did not find the information provided in the image. The description of "models" consists more of names of particular common objects or conditions, than of anything closely related to perception. It appears to me that one could move from the digitized array to lines, regions, textures, or other primitive coding elements, and then could extract "codes" from those elements, simplify them according to acceptable logical rules of simplification (which are computer-compatible and in fact have been programmed by Buffart and Collard at Nijmegen), and search for the simplest code.

In the process of coding, is it possible to go back and revise a primitive code? One difficulty is that, given a primitive code, it is not easy for the perceptual system to estimate whether the resulting information-load is so high that it would probably be beneficial to revise the primitive code. This seems to be a problem in the information-processing problems of computer vision, also. One possible approach is that suggested by van Tuijl (1980), that a simpler primitive code is itself an advantage. This would be an application of "good continuation" directly, because a simple primitive code generally comes about by a straight or uniformly curved line, a uniform texture, and the like.

This is not to say that Coding Theory solves the problems arising in computer vision, discussed by Rosenfeld, but only that coding theory seems to be a development of the later stages of computer vision, from the description of the image in a primitive code, up to selection of an interpretation. The idea of an interpretation and its code is, I think, superior in some ways to the idea of a model and its instantiation. In coding theory, a code in its usual form would correspond roughly to a model, but it would include less cognitive elaboration (that is, interpretation as houses, trees, etc.), and would lie closer to the perception itself. It seems, in Rosenfeld's outline, that computer-vision theory may hurry to a process of *identifying* objects before it has given a good enough account of perception. The "instantiation of the model" would, in coding theory, correspond to the code expression with particular numerical values inserted. That is, a square may be coded as continued repetition of an angle α and a length L, and this is the sort of code that corresponds to a model. To say that the code is continued repetition of an angle $\alpha = 90°$ and a length L = 3 meters, corresponds to an instantiation of the model.

The question whether coding theory would be an improvement on existing programs for computer vision, is moot. It is interesting and heartening, however, to notice that models for artificial computer vision, intended more to replace than to imitate the human perceiver, correspond in general outline and in many details to a model intended to describe human perceptual processes.

Although Leeuwenberg's coding model for line drawings, and the general applications of the principle of simplicity, are quite well developed, the main unsolved problem in coding theory is the question of the process by which coding is carried out. How is the primitive code constructed, how is it simplified, how does the system extricate itself from "local minima" and arrive at optimal perceptions, and so on. The methods used by human theorists to compute codes are relatively laborious and seem to draw rather heavily on "intuition," like the process of inventing a mathematical proof. Some attempt is now being made to expedite and automate the process, with the hopes that such computational improvements will reflect human perceptual processing. The question whether such computational advances will simulate perception, however, may be separate from the question whether they will be useful in artificial perception (computer perception) applications.

Rosenfeld's summary of concepts in computer perception suggests that the levels of processing in computer perception are not entirely different from those postulated in coding theory, and that it may be possible to adopt some of the Coding Theory ideas to improving computer perception. In particular, some of the (to me) vague concepts like regions, features, and models may usefully be replaced by coding-theoretic concepts like lines, angles, and various simplifications of larger codes. Also, the concept of an "interpretation" as used in coding theory may be a useful supplement of the end results of Rosenfeld's analyses, which he described as graphs, assertions, and constraints.

In his discussion, Perkins (Chapter 4) concentrated to some extent on "hill-climbing" procedures, that is, simple processes for improving perceptual performance by a "feedback" mechanism. To implement a hill-climbing process, one needs to specify (a) the space in which one is moving, and (b) which way is up hill. In Coding Theory, the space is one of possible codes, and for types of perception having well-developed coding models, it is quite clear what possible strings of symbols are well-formed specifications of a code, and what are not. Therefore, the set of possible codes is well defined. Furthermore given a primitive code, the various possible steps for reducing it form a tree, and therefore it is possible to say just what limited set of codes of a given display can possible be tried. This makes a delimited, connected space within which to climb hills. The notion of "information load" is well defined in all existing applications of coding theory, and therefore one knows that the hills are made of information load, and furthermore that the process is not hill-climbing but mine-delving, that is, one is seeking a minimum information load.

Perkins also emphasized the conflict between interpretations of local parts of a display, and the extended implications of such local configurations. This presents a problem in most perceptual theories, which have difficulty reconciling the detail that is usually perceived with the large-scale patterns that are also seen, and taking account of such peculiarities as the Penrose impossible figures. Coding theory begins with a primitive code that consists entirely of a close analysis of local details of the display, and in the course of simplifying that code, seeks larger-scale regularities, what Perkins called "implications". The two do not conflict; in fact, it seems apparent that any proper perceptual theory must handle both levels, and Coding Theory provides a coherent way of treating both detail and gestalt, each in an appropriate way.

The experimental findings of Metelli on transparency are challenging (see Chapter 11). Because I do not have any coding theory of surface color, it is impossible to give a serious discussion of transparency from the coding theoretic point of view. Let me take Bergström's "vector analysis" (1977) however, as the basis of a possible coding theory, adding to it the idea that uniform areas of reflectivity should have simple codes, and that it might be simpler to have a few areas of uniform substance with variable illumination (presuming the illumination varies in a simple way) rather than graded changes in substance or reflectivity. With such an approach, the question in a "transparency" experiment is whether four patches of light are consistent with two uniform regions (the black and white square) and a third transparent round object lying in front of them, the round object being uniform in transmission and in reflectance. The theoretical analysis must begin by considering other possible interpretations of the display. For example, one interpretation would be a simple "mosaic" in which the four areas are coded as four different colors, none transparent. This would use four color parameters. Metelli's formula for transparency shows that the transparent interpretation also uses four color parameters, a, b, α, and t. On this basis it is difficult to see why the transparent interpretation would even be made. Notice, however, that if the circular disk is a single shape, then there are only three shapes in the field, two rectangles and a circle, whereas in the mosaic interpretation there are four, two rectangles and two semicircles. Thus, in such experiments, discrepancies in color from the allowable or "optimal" colors must be sufficient to override a difference in the information load of two shapes. Such experimental results should, if properly interpreted in a coding-theoretic frame of reference, have the singular value of comparing information-load from shapes with information-load from surface colors. This sort of "calibration" between two realms of information load, if possible, would be of singular value.

Coding Theory, therefore, in this instance does not solve any theoretical problem, but it helps to focus part of the significance of the "transparency" problem, and to provide a specific quantitative hypothesis for test.

Foster, (Chapter 16), emphasizes three assumptions: (a) that representations are discrete; (b) that a stimulus is probabilistically assigned to a representation; and (c) that the probability of discrimination of stimulus A from B depends on the probability that they receive different representations. Notice that in Coding Theory, structurally-different codes can be said to be discrete, certainly in the sense that there is usually no sequence of intermediate codes stretching from one interpretation to another. Coding Theory is helpful in distinguishing between codes in the usual sense, which have variables or parameters like angle α length

L, and the same code with particular values inserted for α and L. There are small continuous changes possible in α, for example, but these would all be thought of as fitting in the same structural code, or else might result in a complete restructuring. If two codes have the same information load, then subjects are observed to choose one or the other, and at least initially it is natural to say that the choice is probabilistic. The third assumption of Foster, however, is not already in Coding Theory but points to a possible strong experimental method for verification of particular codes. Foster says that a subject can discriminate two stimuli only if they receive different representations or codes. If this is true, at least under appropriate experimental conditions, then it is possible to answer questions regarding interpretations and codes by use of psychophysical experiments measuring discrimination. This last proposal, unfortunately, is not yet securely verified. In Coding Theory it seems possible that subjects could discriminate two patterns that receive the same abstract code, but differ only in parameters; for example, subjects can discriminate a large from a small square though both receive the code *αL* and differ only in the value of L. Furthermore, all regular polygons have the code *αL*, admitting various values of α that give rise to triangles, (120°), squares (90°), pentagons (72°), hexagons (60°), and so on. Such shapes are, of course, discriminable. Therefore, for stimuli to be indistinguishable, it is necessary that they have the same code and (almost) the same metric parameter values for the variables. From this it appears sure that Foster's idea of a "representation" must contain much more metric information than Leeuwenberg's "code," or else Foster's conjecture that discrimination depends upon the stimuli receiving different representations, is only a conjecture and will turn out to be erroneous.

Palmer develops a Gestalt-oriented information processing theory, and this places him in the same general value system as coding theory. In Palmer's theory, going from real world to retina to reference frames to perceptual codes to memory codes, it would appear that "reference frames" correspond rather closely to the primitive codes of coding theory. If this interpretation is correct, then in relation to coding theory, Palmer's problem is close to that of Rosenfeld—the problem of turning a raw "image" into the kind of collection of lines, angles, and other elements from which a perception can be made, that is, from which regularities can be extracted.

One problem that especially concerns Palmer is the fact that in some experiments, subjects appear to see "global" or large-scale features before, and perhaps more easily than, details. To handle this, Palmer introduces a set of reference frames, differently located and of different levels of "resolution" (i.e., large- and small-scale, like high- and low-pass filters in a spatial-frequency model). A given stimulus pattern will fall on a large-scale reference frame, from which global shape properties will be extracted, and may at the same time fall on small-scale reference frames, giving rise to detail information. It is as if Palmer had many different primitive codes, at various levels of resolution, and then his system would process them all in parallel, sending their results up the perceptual-coding level. Leeuwenberg, in dealing with arrangements that have both global and detailed structure, uses a hierarchical code. It seems that the possibilities of such hierarchical codes must occur within the primitive code, so if primitive codes are generated by reference frames, as suggested by Palmer, then the idea of several "levels" of reference frame is appropriate for coding theory. Perkins's mention of Penrose impossible figures raises an interesting problem for Palmer. As Perkins analyzes it, an impossible figure looks all right at each corner, at a small scale, and also looks all right as a whole—it is just that the identifications of lines at the two levels are incompatible. If the two levels are seen independently by different reference frames, how is the discrepancy to be noticed? Leeuwenberg's hierarchical coding system puts both detail and overall structure into one code, and at least in principle can deal with an impossible figure.

An improvement might be made in Palmer's approach in another way. He argues that the "patterns" on a frame of reference can be transformed by being moved left or right or up or down, by change in orientation or "sense," or by changes in "resolution." He gives some elements of the algebra of such transformations. He does not specify however, what patterns can be the subject of such transformations. In discussion of coding of serial patterns, I at one time took the position that the elementary patterns, that could be transformed, must themselves be the product of such transformations on elementary units (Restle, 1970). That is, in Palmer's theory, a pattern itself would be produced by sliding something around, rotating it, or changing its resolution. Simple patterns could be constructed by concatenation of a few such operations, whereas complex patterns would require more complex processes of generation.

Leeuwenberg appears to use this same principle of coding, in that he begins only with elementary angles and line lengths and constructs all possible figures from them. A simple pattern can be constructed from a small number of such angles and lines, or else by simplifying the code of a figure with many parts.

Thus, although at this time Palmer's efforts are independent, his results bear a definite resemblance to coding theory, and it is to be hoped that active cooperation and debate will lead to a theory incorporating the strong points of both approaches.

Attneave's (Chapter 1) approach to the principle of simplicity has, as one goal, an effort to specify an automatic mechanism or process that would arrive at certain very simple interpretations of stimulus patterns. For this purpose, he supposes that the visual system may attempt to maximize certain properties in the representation. A partial list of such properties includes:

1. Equal length.
2. Coplanarity.
3. Parallelism.

4. Collinearity.
5. Overlap or coincidence.
6. Connection.
7. Probability or familiarity.

In general terms, each such property is to be maximized by a process that produces competition or mutual inhibition between two stimulus elements that are unequal, on different planes, not parallel, and so on, and mutual facilitation between stimuli that are equal, coplanar, parallel, and so on.

The properties chosen by Attneave to maximize are, to a considerable extent, properties which would simplify a code in Leeuwenberg's system. Equal lengths, obviously, permit simplification of the code. Coplanarity and parallelism should usually simplify codes, and collinearity (i.e., having a zero angle, which has no information-load) and overlap clearly simplify coding. Being connected permits two line segments to be joined by an angle, in the usual coding process, rather than being named separately or connected by an invisible line. Probability and familiarity, usually referred to under the heading of "context" in coding theory, refer to the fact that if a pattern appears elsewhere or at an earlier time, it can be incorporated into the final code merely by iteration, symbolization, or some other simplified coding procedures. For this reason, data that support Attneave's model will, in all probability, also support a standard coding-theory analysis.

One serious problem in Attneave's model is that his "soap bubble" process is trying to maximize a number of different factors that may conflict. If a figure on a display screen is made to change from a square by having one corner move toward the middle of the figure, the observer might either change the equal lengths of the perceived sides, or might keep the sides of equal lengths and violate coplanarity. If all of the "maximizing" processes go on at once, automatically and in parallel, then such conflicts may be resolved by chance, or in favor of the larger stimulus variable, and so on. Experience with Coding Theory suggests that it is important to develop a rather delicate logic, a way of combining the various simplifying properties, so as to take account of the more subtle methods used by the visual system to extract information.

As has frequently been mentioned, however, a serious unsolved problem in Coding Theory is that of the "process" by which cues are formulated and simplified. At present, Coding Theory emphasizes the end result without knowing much about the approach to that end result, and it is possible that the actual perceptual process, at least in ordinary viewing circumstances, is more nearly automatic than presently envisaged. If so, then models like Attneave's, which attempt to specify automatic or "soap bubble" processes, are most applicable. It might be argued, however, that such a theory should address itself to a defensible theory of the end result. A possible criticism of Attneave's theory is that it probably does not arrive at a correct theory of perceptions. For one thing, it appears that if the subject moves around inspecting the environment, As Gibson emphasizes, he would not arrive at the kinds of properties stipulated by Attneave. Attneave's final space is too rigidly attached to the viewer's eyeballs to be realistic. A second criticism is that the processes of maximizing equal length, coplanarity, and so on, must lead to serious distortions of perception, and might lead to a theory that a person, no matter what he looks at, will see a tile floor. The restraints, imposed on Coding Theory by the requirement of preserving the primitive code, must be introduced into Attneave's soap bubble process so as to keep it at least approximately veridical.

CONCLUSIONS

The purpose of this chapter has been to survey Gestalt, Neo-Gestalt, and information-processing approaches to some of the central theoretical questions in perception, seeing each of these theories and questions from the point of view of Coding Theory.

It was argued that the plethora of Gestalt laws, though undoubtedly a great stimulus to designing new and interesting stimulus displays, has led to a kind of theoretical stagnation. Although Gestalt laws can suggest new demonstrations, they are not capable of telling whether such a demonstration makes a new and important theoretical point, or is merely a new illustration of an old principle. The difficulty is that there are too many old principles, which sometimes contradict one another, and which in no case can be fitted together into a tight and seaworthy theoretical vessel. It was argued that coding theory takes account of many of the principles of Gestalt theory and fits these principles together into a coherent and logical structure.

Neo-Gestalt theories, perhaps in an effort to overcome the excessive richness of the Gestalt bill of theoretical fare, tend to concentrate on single properties that the perceptual system is said to extract. It is argued that such theories usually suffer from incompleteness, considering only one or two properties at a time. An attempt was made to show how Coding Theory can support such Neo-Gestalt theories, by offering boundaries when a certain property will and will not be selected as the perceived invariant. Basically, my hypothesis was based on the principle of simplicity: a given invariant will be extracted if it leads to a simpler code than any other invariant.

Gibson's ecological perception tells us something about the perception of an observer moving and looking around in a real stable environment. Because this process seems very complicated in terms of images, Gibson suggests that it cannot possible be controlled by a principle of simplicity. In my discussion, I tried to show that the principle must be one of *relative* simplicity. Gibson's example of one texture disappearing at its juncture with another texture (an indication of one thing behind another when the observer is moving) can actually receive more than one possible interpretation—one of the substances might melt or disappear right at the juncture, or it might slip behind the other. If the "melting" interpretation is more complex, then the "occlusion" interpretation is preferred. The active observer, by inspecting an object, piles a very heavy information load on every wrong interpretation while adding only a little to the information load of the physically-correct interpretation. For this reason, the correct interpretation gains a tremendous advantage and is clearly perceived.

Finally, it was argued that several of the information-processing models had close theoretical affinities to the Coding Theory, and might be improved by consideration of some of the results of Coding Theory. The information-processing theories tend to be concerned with the mechanism or process by which perceptions are constructed, whereas Coding Theory is more concerned, at present, with the end result. For this reason, it can be hoped that Coding Theory and information-processing models will be complementary and will interact. Coding Theory can in some cases specify the end result of the perceptual process and therefore set a goal for proposed information processes. By the same token, known information processes may set limitations on the likely forms of coding theory, and may help to either support or refine the principal of simplicity. It is quite possible that under ordinary viewing conditions, the viewer may *not* arrive at the simplest possible code but may follow a more automatic process of simplification and be trapped into a nonoptimal interpretation.

As was discovered at this conference, Gestalt theory and information processing are not really opposed theories, but seem more to be complementary approaches to the questions of perception. In this chapter I have attempted to emphasize ways of fitting the two kinds of theory together, and have used Coding Theory as an instrument for this kind of theoretical interconnection. The success of this effort will be better known some time in the future, when our many conjectures have been put to the test of decisive experimentation.

ACKNOWLEDGMENT

The research on which this paper is based was carried out during the author's tenure as a Guggenheim fellow, 1977–78.

REFERENCES

Bergström, S. S. Common and relative components of reflected light as information about the illumination,colour, and three-dimensional form of objects. *Scandinavian Journal of Psychology,* 1977, *18,* 180–186.

Bruner, J. S. On perceptual readiness. *Psychological Review,* 1957, *64,* 123–152.

Buffart, H., Leeuwenberg, E., & Restle, F. Coding theory of visual pattern completion. *Journal of Experimental Psychology: Human Perception and Performance,* 1981, *7,* 241–274.

Gibson, J. J. *The ecological approach to visual perception.* Boston: Houghton Mifflin, 1979.

Johansson, G. *Configurations in event perception*. Uppsala: Almqvist & Wiksell, 1950.

Johansson, G. Projective transformations as determining visual space perception. In R. B. MacLeod & H. L. Pick (Eds.), *Perception: Essays in honor of J. J. Gibson*. Ithaca, N.Y.: Cornell University Press, 1974.

Kanizsa, G. The role of regularity in perceptual organization. In G. B. F. d'Arcais (Ed.), *Studies in perception: Festschrift for Fabio Metelli*. Milano: Martello-Giunti, 1975.

Land, E. H. The retinex. *American Scientist*, 1964, *52*, 247-264.

Leeuwenberg, E. L. J. Quantification of certain visual pattern properties: Salience, transparency, similarity. In E. L. J. Leeuwenberg and J. F. J. M. Buffart (Eds.), *Formal theories of visual perception*. New York: Wiley, 1978.

Metelli, F. Achromatic color conditions in the perception of transparency. In R. B. MacLeod & H. L. Pick (Eds.), *Perception: Essays in honor of J. J. Gibson*. Ithaca, N.Y.: Cornell University Press, 1974.

Restle, F. Theory of serial pattern learning: Structural trees. *Psychological Review*, 1970, *77*, 481-495.

Restle, F. Structural ambiguity in serial pattern learning. *Cognitive Psychology*, 1975, *8*, 357-381.

Restle, F. Coding theory of the perception of motion configurations. *Psychological Review*, 1979, *86*, 1-24.

Restle, F., & Brown, E. R. Organization of serial pattern learning. In G. H. Bower (Ed.), *Psychology of learning and motivation*, Vol. IV. New York: Academic Press, 1970.

Simon, H. A., & Kotovsky, K. Human acquisition of concepts for sequential patterns. *Psychological Review*, 1963, *70*, 534-546.

Simon, H. A., & Sumner, R. K. Pattern in music. In B. Kleinmuntz (Ed.), *Formal representation of human judgment*. New York: Wiley, 1968.

Tuijl, H. F. J. M. van. Perceptual interpretation of complex line patterns. *Journal of Experimental Psychology: Human Perception and Performance*, 1980, *6*, 197-221.

Ullman, S. The interpretation of structure from motion. *Proceedings of the Royal Society of London*, 1979, *203*, 405-426.

3 Metrical Aspects of Patterns and Structural Information Theory

Emanuel Leeuwenberg
University of Nijmegen

INTRODUCTION

The description of a pattern involves both structural and a metric aspects. Structural properties of a pattern refer to the components of a description reflecting qualitatively different features of the pattern. The Appendix summarizes the principal coding rules for the structural description of patterns, proposed by Leeuwenberg (1971), and gives examples of how simple figures are encoded. Metric properties of a pattern refer to the actual numerical values of descriptive components, that is, the actual sizes of lines, angles, and surfaces of a pattern.

It is true that the metric properties of each feature are representable within structural codes, but they do not play an effective role, because they do not affect the "information load" of the code. Whatever the length of the side of a square may be, the structural information for defining a square remains constant. Structural information accounts only for the equality of length's and the equality of angles. Thus the Gestalt law of proximity, which is based on the distance between the elements of a pattern does not have a ready interpretation in terms of structural information theory (Beck, 1967).

The present chapter proposes a metric information measure. This approach, which suffers from the defects inherent in an initial attempt, starts from the dynamic nature of information. This nature is, in our opinion, common to both structural and metric information. The perceptual relevance of the metric information measure will be demonstrated mainly in connection with the Müller-Lyer illusion.

Consider a potter working a piece of clay. Imagine he first wants to make a flat circular disk. Probably he will place the clay in the middle of his wheel and flatten it with a plank. Following this he will steady a knife at a fixed distance from the centre and then allow the wheel to turn, thus producing a flat disk. He can make a more complex form by turning the wheel very slowly and using a stick to press against the thin edge of the disk at regular intervals. This produces a sort of toothed-wheel made of clay. Each succeeding operation carried out by the potter makes the shape of the clay more complex. The complete series of consecutive operations determines the shape of the clay product. Now a similar series of operations forms the structural code of a pattern. But although such structural operations are syntactic (see Appendix) and therefore hardly remind us of the dynamic operations of the craftsman, they really do refer to these and were even probably derived from them. In this sense, a structural code may be understood as being dynamic in nature. This makes it understandable that structural "code theory" although primarily developed for to the description of static patterns, may be applied to "motion patterns" without substantial modifications. Hence Restle (1979) has demonstrated that the perceptions of the simple harmonic motions, employed by Johansson (1969), are accurately predicted on the basis of their structural codes.

Reminiscent of Dember's note (1965) in which any sort of information refers to "change," we will attempt to develop a metric information measure in dynamic terms, such as force, energy or impulse. This last term is regarded as useful for producing specific moving patterns: a ball can be guided to trace any desired pattern when the right number of impulses are exerted at the right places. In the same way should a rocket deliver exactly the same impulses at the same places into the outside world, then it will trace a pattern identical to that of the ball. We will assume that the information content of a pattern is expressible in terms of the independent pieces of data necessary to reproduce the pattern. Attention will be focused on a moving point tracing a single continuous line, without branching. For the moment, the moving object may be conceived of as a rocket flying in resistance-free empty space. With respect to the Müller-Lyer phenomena it is further assumed that the rocket is propelled with constant force, thus giving rise to constant acceleration. The totality of the impulses necessary for application to this moving rocket in order to generate a given pattern, will be equivalent to the metric information load of the path so traced.

Consider a rocket starting to fly in free space and let us focus on the additional impulses applied to this rocket in order that its trajectory will be that shown in Fig. 3.1.

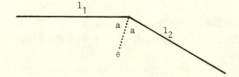

FIG. 3.1. A path traced by an accelerating rocket.

The rocket starts at the left-hand side. At the moment it has passed l_1 its speed is v_1. The rocket, having a mass m, now requires a push to the side, otherwise it will carry straight on. The impulse of this push is equal to $2 mv_2 \cos a$. (a is half angle θ). The rocket is now moving along l_2. At the end of l_2 the rocket having a speed v_2, requires a second push in order to be stopped. If the impulse of this push were $2 mv_2$ the rocket would move in the opposite direction. Therefore, only half of this impulse value mv_2 will be necessary to stop the rocket. The total impulse P of both pushes will be:

$$P = 2 mv_1 \cos a + mv_2$$

Assuming the rocket is propelled forward with constant force, its speed at the end of a trajectory of length 1 is proportional to the square root of 1. If the shortest length of line (l_1) in the figure, as well as the mass and acceleration of the rocket are all normalized to 1, the total value of impulses involved in the trajectory of Figure 1, equals:

$$P = 2 \cos a + \sqrt{2}$$

This value is as a measure of the metric information load of Fig. 3.1.

Notice that according to this metric measure the sharper the angle (the greater the angular deviation) and the longer a line with respect to some shortest line the more the information load. The use of impulses might seem to suggest that some actual eye movement or some sort of internal motion track has in fact preceded the coding of a pattern. But this would be incautious, and it is more reasonable to regard the concept of an impulse as a pure computational tool. The impulse measure need not be restricted to the accelerating rocket model, but may be applied to other models also. In the case of Müller-Lyer illusions, the rocket model seems to be the most appropriate.

MÜLLER-LYER ILLUSION

Müller-Lyer data have been collected by Restle and Decker (1977). We attempt here to predict those data using the impulse measure. The illusion is usually evoked by a line having pairs of "wings" at each end. Restle and Decker have also shown that it can be induced by a line with only one wing at each end (see Fig. 3.2). In their experiment the test line x was 7 mm, and the wing lengths (w) as well as the angle θ were varied independently. Subjects were instructed to match a variable line y to the test line x. The length of the variable line matched to a control test line having no wings is given by y_0. If $(y - y_0)/x$ is positive, then the test line x was over-estimated.

The first step in predicting the overestimation of x using the proposed metric information measure is to assess the metric or impulse load P(T) of a total

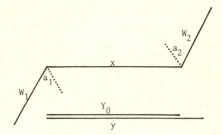

FIG. 3.2. Müller-Lyer pattern, used by Restle and Decker (1977). y_0, which is equal to x, has to be adjusted, so that the length of y is perceived equal with the length of x. $W_1 = W_2$ and $a_1 = a_2$, each being an half angle θ.

Müller-Lyer pattern as presented in Fig. 3.2. According to the above method of computation:

$$P(T) = 2 \cos a_1 \sqrt{w_1} + 2 \cos a_2 \sqrt{w_1 + x} + \sqrt{w_1 + x + w_2}$$

In the Müller-Lyer patterns used in the experiment $a_1 = a_2$ and $w_1 = w_2$. The shortest line (w or x) is treated as the basic unit of length 1. In Fig. 3.2: $w_1 = w_2 = 1$, $x = 2$, $a = 60°$. For this figure: $P(T) = (2 \cos 60) \sqrt{1} + (2 \cos 60) \sqrt{1 + 2} + \sqrt{4}$. Our interest, however, is concerned with x and not with the total Müller-Lyer pattern. If the wings are substracted from the total Müller-Lyer pattern, x will be left over. The impulse load of the wings P(w) equals:

$$P(w) = P(w_1) + P(w_2)$$

The w values are equal to those used in the assessment of P(T). In other words, if they are the shortest lines in the total Müller-Lyer pattern they are equal to 1. In Fig. 3.2: $P(w) = \sqrt{1} + \sqrt{1}$.

Although the difference $P(T) - P(w)$ refers to x, this impulse load should be completed with an additional constant C for normalizing purposes.

Let us therefore look at Fig. 3.3 and consider an extreme deviant of the pattern in which $x = 0$, $a = 0$, and $w = 1$. In this limiting case:

$$P(T) - P(w) = 3.41$$

In our opinion, however, the impulse load which refers to x should be zero when $x = 0$. An impulse load measure $P(x_0)$ is proposed which refers to x in the context of two wings and takes $C = 3.41$ as a point of reference:

$$P(x_0) = P(T) - P(w) - C$$

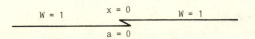

FIG. 3.3. Assumed is that for the limiting case ($x = 0$, $a_1 = a_2 = 0$) no metric information is involved in x in the context of the wings (W).

In this chapter impulse load is identified with metric information but not with perceived length. Interest is here directed toward the latter, however. Certainly impulse load and perceptual length are related. As is mentioned above:

$$P(1) = \sqrt{1}, \text{ so } 1 = P^2(1)$$

The length of a given line is represented by 1. The same holds for x_0, although $P(x_0)$ is not only a function of length's but also of angles, hence:

$$x_0 = p^2(x_0)$$

We now have to consider the role of x_0. However regarded, it must stand for a perceptual estimation of the length of x, considered in the context of the wings. Nevertheless there are two points of view remaining with respect to x_0. Either it refers to the final perceptual estimation or to an intermediate hypothetical construct. We assume that in any estimation task two stages are involved: a context-specified hypothetical estimation and a context-free estimation. If the latter is higher that the first, overestimation will occur. Recall the adaption effect occurring after adapting to light weights. This experience will lead to overestimation of heavier weights. Assuming that x_0 stands for an hypothetical point of departure, we must now find out which is the context-free estimation of x. If this x is greater than x_0 overestimation, ω, will be expected:

$$\omega = \frac{x - x_0}{x}$$

In order to specify the context free x, an extreme deviant of Fig. 3.4 is considered, in which x = 0, a = 90 and x = 1. This extreme case, in which $x_0 = c^2$, coincides with a single x line. We shall assume, however, that neither overestimation, nor underestimation then occurs, so that $\omega = 0$. As a consequence, $x = c^2$. The theoretical overestimation measure will be:

$$\omega = \frac{c^2 - x_0}{c^2}$$

Here c = 3.41 and $x_0 = (P(T) - P(w) - c)^2$, as suggested above. This measure may be regarded as a tentative theoretical equivalent to the previously mentioned operational overestimation ratio, used by Restle and Decker (1977):

$$\frac{y - y_0}{x}$$

FIG. 3.4. Assumed is that for limiting case ($W_1 = W_2 = 0$, $a_1 = a_2 = 90°$) no overestimation of x will occur.

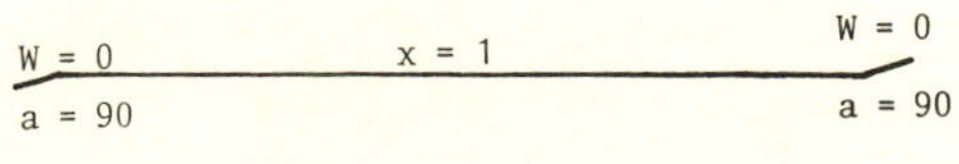

TABLE 3.1
Predicted Overestimations[a]

Wing Length	.25	.5	1	2	4	8
Angle 166°	89	65	12	2	−8	−23
155°	97	83	50	53	58	69
135°	99	92	69	76	86	96
120°	100	98	86	94	100	94
104°	99	100	95	100	96	64
90°	95	99	99	99	82	18
76°	90	96	100	92	57	−54
60°	85	93	98	83	30	−119
45°	80	89	95	71	−2	−196
30°	78	86	93	64	−19	−231
14°	75	85	89	58	−34	−272

[a] The theoretical overestimation values $(x - x_0)/x$ are given for 11 different angles and 6 different wing lengths of Müller-Lyer patterns.

Results

In Table 3.1 the theoretical overestimation values ω are presented ($\chi = 1$), computed for various Muller-Lyer patterns as used by Restle and Decker. In all these patterns the testing x was 7 mm; the wings were varied: w = ¼, ½, 1, 2, 4, 8 times the length of x and the angles varied in 11 steps from 14° to 166°. In the first column of Fig. 3.5 the over-estimation values from the Restle and Decker experiment are shown. Each of the base-lines refer to zero overestimations. The second column yields the theoretical overestimation values ω in an equivalent graphic presentation for several wing and angle values.

Figure 3.5 shows that the theoretical values reveal common characteristics with respect to the experimental data:

1. Values increase with angle θ.
2. Values exhibit an inverted u function of w.
3. The maximum appears at w = x for $\theta < 120°$.
4. A steady shift of the maximum toward shorter wings for greater angles θ.
5. An underestimation of x both for $\theta = 166$ as well as for $\theta < 76$ at w = 4.

The last points, 4 and 5, are not predicted by earlier developed models discussed in the article by Restle and Decker (1977). A bad fit appears where the data show underestimation for short wings and sharp angles θ. The scale of the apparent length and that of the theoretical values also differ largely. This impulse load approach can therefore only be regarded as a suggestive attempt standing in need of further refinement.

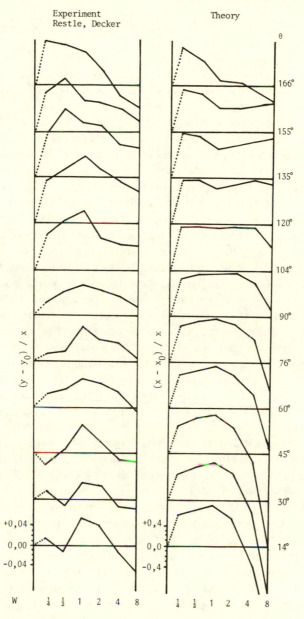

FIG. 3.5. In the left column the experimental overestimation date $(y - y_0)/x$, gathered by Restle and Decker (1977) are depicted for 11 different angles (θ) and 6 different Wing lengths (W) of Müller-Lyer patterns. In the right column the theoretical overestimation values $(x - x_0)/x$ are presented for the same angles and wing lengths.

DISCUSSION

The "accelerating rocket" model is the most compatible with the data for explaining asymmetry in the Müller-Lyer effects. In general, open-end line patterns without bifurcations show slight asymmetries, and it matters at which side the scanning starts. For dot patterns, however, the last model is less appropriate. A better idea would be to think of a jumping fly and to account for the impulses derived from the speeds in jumped projections on the ground. In order to span the distance (λ) between dots the projected speed of a single jump from one dot to another will be $v = \sqrt{\lambda}$, starting with an angle of 45° to the ground. The perceptual relevance of this approach might appear from research on dot clusters.

For closed-line patterns, which are usually conceived of as contours of some surface, neither of the above mentioned models appears useful. A continuously accelerating rocket is at rest at the starting point of the track, but has accumulated a considerable speed by the time it has completed the circuit and returns to the point of departure. A reduced divergence between these two speeds would be more acceptable. A rocket of constant speed might be a useful model-element.

Let us reconsider open-line patterns without branchings. We have distinguished an hypothetical x_0 and an actual x construct. A further audacious assumption that might be entertained is that the process leading to x_0 and also that leading to x, there are again two stages. Before going more deeply into this, it should be noted that whatever the result of this assumption might be, no significant effect should be anticipated in the difference between x and x_0, while it will, in fact, to a large extent be cancelled out by this difference. The effect does not appear from matching tasks, but from less direct methods, resulting in Stevens scales (1974).

It has been assumed that the perceived line length is "born" in the impulse load and the impulse load from the speed. Let us use as point of departure one of Stevens scale functions, so that the perceptual speed $V = v^{1.77}$. At the end of a line (λ) the scanning speed will be: $v = \sqrt{\lambda}$. As a consequence the perceptual speed $V = \lambda^{1.77/2.00}$. This perceptual speed might be the first finger-hold that a line allows. In other words this V might be conceived of as a first underestimate approximation L_1 to the actual length of the line: $L_1 = V$. Feedback information from other than dynamic sources could lead to a correction of the hypothetical L_1 to an improved estimation L_2, such that $L_2 = \lambda$. This would be achieved if $L_2 = L_1^{2.100/1.77} = L_1^{1.13}$. This relation shows a weak overestimation of the first approximation L_1 to the length. It should be noticed that both L_2 and L_1 refer to internal states. The physical length λ does not occur in the latter relationship. Assuming that neither is this a reality in the "psychophysical functions," proposed by Stevens, the above arguments might to some extent clarify the Stevens function: $L = \lambda^{1.11}$. There is no evidence available to contradict the idea that this function reflects a relationship between magnitude estimation and perceptual length, although the last expression does suggest a relation between perceptual length and objective length.

A general question remaining is: how can the metric information load be combined with the structural information load? Whenever the primitive code of a pattern is irreducible by structural operators, the overall information load may equal the metric information load. If, however, final codes are shorter than their primitive codes, angles and lengths will usually be present as discrete components in these shortened codes. In these cases the metric information ought to be assessed for each of these components separately. In other words, the structural code precedes the assessment of metric values. The scale of metric information load with respect to structural information load remains obscure, and this is because there does not seem to be any obvious indication of how to join both types of load into one all-embracing load measure.

From the structural information theory angle, a new approach (Collard, 1982; Buffart, Leeuwenberg, & Restle, 1981) has been attempted, aimed toward a limited specification of metric values. This approach will not be discussed here in detail, but adumbrated by a suggestive example. Attention will be focused on the interaction between two different structural codes of the single pattern, presented at the top of Fig. 3.6.

One code represents two identical polygons, but neither angles nor lengths of the sides are specified (see bottom left of Fig. 3.6). The second code (see bottom right of Fig. 3.6) represents two congruent parallelograms, similarly without specifying their metric aspects. If it is also required, however, that both codes must refer to the one-single pattern, then the angles of the polygon will necessarily be 60° and the sides of the parallelograms in the ratio 1:2. Thus there exist some metric values which are specifiable by the interaction between two codes of a single pattern.

FIG. 3.6.   Two interpretations (bottom) are depicted of the above pattern. Each interpretation is incomplete. In each interpretation neither the angles nor the lengths of the sides are specified, but the angles and lengths become specified if the two interpretations are assumed to refer to a single pattern.

Summary

Quantitative metric values of patterns, such as angle magnitudes and line lengths, seem to give rise to perceptual effects, including grouping overestimation or overaccentation. The same sort of effects are evoked by structural pattern aspects. Structural aspects, however, such as identity or symmetry, do not explicitly account for metric values. A measure for metric information load is proposed, which shares the same foundation as that of structural information. This common basis is the "dynamic nature" of information, giving rise to an impulse load measure for metric values. The new measure is applied to Müller-Lyer-illusion patterns (Restle & Decker, 1977). The impulse load predictions seem to be in sizeable agreement with the experimental data concerning these illusion patterns. It is assumed that the structural code is prior with respect to the metric information assessment. There are also some metric values which can be specified by the combination of two codes of one pattern, but not by either of them separately. In the appendix a synopsis of structural information theory is presented.

APPENDIX

Synopsis Of Coding Theory

The theory has three aspects. Firstly the so-called *coding-language* is specified. It is a formal language of which the alphabet and production rules—also called "coding rules" or "operators"—are defined. These rules can be defined recursively. For the sake of simplicity, we will introduce them below by means of examples.

Secondly, the so-called *code-semantics* are defined. These specify a mapping from the set of codes onto the set of patterns. They will also be introduced by means of examples. A code represents a possible interpretation of a pattern.

Thirdly, many different codes may be able to represent one pattern, or, in other words, can be mapped onto a single pattern by the code-semantics. The difference between such codes is that they do not describe a pattern in terms of the same perceptually independent elements. According to the theory, the perception process tends to select that code exhibiting the *least* number of perceptually independent elements. The number of these elements within a given code is called the structural information (I) of that code.

Perceptual process-constraints and the subject's memory content, both of which will be unknown to the experimenter, may make it impossible for the subject to possess a pattern interpretation that is represented by a calculated minimum code. Earlier results (Leeuwenberg, 1971), however, show a high correlation between experimental results and the context free predictions made.

So, apparently, one can use a static minimum-principle, derived from this minimum-element tendency, as a criterion upon which to base predictions. This principle states that the subject will (almost always) choose that interpretation, which is represented by the code with the lowest structural information: the minimum code. If there are two or more minimum codes he will choose at random one of the different interpretations represented by these codes. In other words, one can predict perceptual ambiguity. The static minimum principle is the formal equivalent of the minimum-principle formulated by Hochberg (1957). Apart from the difference in coding rules it is the minimum principle that is the main difference between Leeuwenberg's theory and the earlier coding systems of Restle (1970), Simon (1972) and Vitz (1968).

Code Semantics 1

The first step in specifying a pattern code is the registration of consecutive lengths (λ μ ν ψ) and angular deviations (α β γ δ), which describe the contour of a pattern (see Fig. 3.7). A series of angles and lengths describing sequentially the contour is called the "*primitive code.*" The structural information of this code is equal to the number of lengths and angles (elements). In principle the commencement of the contour description may be chosen to occur at any arbitrary point on the contour. A primitive code of Fig. 3.7a is λ α ν α λ α ν α (I = 8) and of Fig. 3.7b: ϕ β ν α ν β ϕ β ν α ν β (I = 12). The point of departure and the orientation at the start are indicated by a circle and an arrow respectively in Fig. 3.7.

In cases where two or more lines depart from one point: "Bifurcations" signs ⟦ ⟧ are employed. Figure 3.7c can be described as: ν ⟦ λ ⟧ $\beta\nu$. This code generates: $\nu\lambda$; go back to the end of ν and continue with $\beta\nu$. An alternative description might be: ν ⟦ $\beta\nu$ ⟧ $\alpha\lambda$. This code generates: $\nu\beta\nu$, go back to β and continue with: $\alpha\lambda$.

A series of symbols enclosed by chunk-brackets: { } is handled as one single unitary element. The symbols belong together and do not interfere with outside elements.

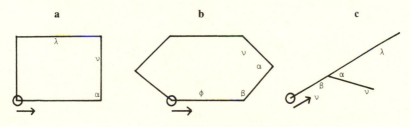

FIG. 3.7.   Examples.

Coding Rules

The second phase of the code-construction is the repeated use of some of the operators in order to minimize the structural information of the primitive code or an already transformed code. Such a transformed code, containing at least one operator, is called a *central code*. If it is impossible to further minimize the structural information of a central code, it will be called an *end code*. The minimum code is the end code with the lowest structural information and will be the result of the applications of various carefully chosen operations, and a selected primitive code. By "the structural information" of a pattern is usually meant the minimum information.

The operations are given below. The *structural information* is indicated by dots placed below the codes.

1. *Iteration:* $3 * [\, (a) \, (b) \,] = a\,a\,a\,b\,b\,b$ $I = 3$
   $3 * [\, (a \; b) \,] = a\,b\,a\,b\,a\,b$ $I = 3$
   $n * [\, (a) \,]$ is sometimes denoted by a^n $I = 2$

2. *Reversal:* $r [\, a \; b \; c \,] = c\,b\,a$ $I = 3$

On this basis two symmetry operations can be defined.

$\Sigma [\, a \, b \, c \,] = a\,b\,c\,r[\,a\,b\,c\,] = a\,b\,c\,c\,b\,a$ $I = 4$
$\Sigma [\, a \, b \, (c) \,] = a\,b\,c\,r[\,a\,b\,] = a\,b\,c\,b\,a$ $I = 4$

The assessment of the structural information will be treated in the next section.

3. *Distribution:*

This rule will be illustrated by an example:

$< (a) > < (b) \, (c) > \; = \; a\,b\,a\,c$ $I = 3$

The procedure stops just before a repetition of the series starts.
For example:

$< (\alpha) \, (\beta) > < (\gamma) \, (\delta) \, (\psi) > \; = \; \alpha \, \gamma \, \beta \, \delta \, \alpha \, \psi \, \beta \, \gamma \, \alpha \, \delta \, \beta \, \psi$ $I = 5$

4. *Continuation:*

The continuation operator is defined as

$\subset \alpha \supset \; = \alpha^\infty \; = \; a, \, a, \, \ldots\ldots\ldots\ldots\ldots\ldots a_\infty$ $I = 1$

The procedure halts if in any pattern another line, or an endpoint of a line is reached (see following).

Structural Information

The structural information of the operations is assessed as indicated in the examples above. In a code, any angle unequal to the zero angle counts for one unit of information. To every part of a code a name can be assigned, and if such a part occurs for a second time it can be represented by its name. Then only the name counts for one unit of information. So the information of

$$\Sigma \, [\, abc \,]$$

can be calculated from its definition

$$\Sigma \, [\, abc \,] = abc \, r \, [\, abc \,]$$

If we assign the name x to abc then

$$\Sigma \, [\, abc \,] = a \, b \, c \, r \, [\, x \,] \qquad\qquad I = 4$$

Code Semantics 2

Usually a short line (with the length of a "dot") is attached to an angle. If the direction of drawing (see Fig. 3.8) and the point in a two dimensional space are given, the semantics of an angle is said to be the drawing of this short line from the point, in a direction relative to the original direction. Such a short line is called a *grain*. For instance, the sequence 90° 0° 0° −90° 0° 45° 0° is a primitive code of Fig. 3.8. A positive angle is a deviation to the left, a negative angle is a deviation to the right. Normally, therefore, a line-segment length is described by an iteration combined with grains of zero angles. Both the zero angle as well as the "zero length," the grain, do not to carry information. The line-length therefore counts for one unit of information: the number of iterations. Usually we *will* name a line with a Greek letter, taken from the second half of the alphabet.

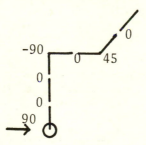

FIG. 3.8. Example.

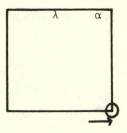

FIG. 3.9.   Example.

Similarly, angles (except zero angles) are represented by a Greek letter taken from the first half of the alphabet.

As an illustration, we construct the codes of a square (see Fig. 3.9).

Here also the starting direction is indicated by an arrow, the point of departure by a little circle; $\lambda = n * [\ (0°)\ ]$ and $\alpha = 90°$, where n is any number.

primitive code: $\alpha \lambda \alpha \lambda \alpha \lambda \alpha \lambda$ $I = 8$
code: continuation: $\subset \alpha \lambda \supset$ $I = 2$

According to the meaning of the continuation rule the repetition of $\alpha \lambda$ will end at the starting point. As another example, see Fig. 3.10.

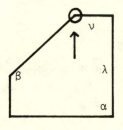

FIG. 3.10.   Example.

primitive code: $\alpha \nu \alpha \lambda \alpha \lambda \alpha \nu \beta \subset 0 \supset$ $I = 9$
distribution   : $< (\alpha) > < (\nu) (\lambda) (\lambda) (\nu) > \beta \subset 0 \supset$ $I = 6$
symmetry   : $< (\alpha) > < \underset{\Sigma}{} [\ (\nu) (\lambda)\ ] > \beta \subset 0 \supset$ $I = 5$
              $\alpha = 90°$
              $\beta = 45°$

The last-mentioned reduced description is regarded as the end code of the above pattern. For another example, see Fig. 3.11.

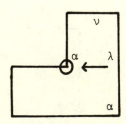

FIG. 3.11.   Example.

primitive code: $\alpha \nu \alpha \nu \alpha \lambda \alpha \lambda \alpha \nu \alpha \nu$ I = 12

continuation   : $\subset \alpha \nu \alpha \nu \alpha \lambda \alpha \lambda \supset$ I = 8

distribution   : $\subset < (\alpha) > < (\nu) (\nu) (\lambda) (\lambda) > \supset$ I = 5

interation   : $\subset < (\alpha) > < 2 * [((\nu)) ((\lambda))] > \supset$ I = 4

$\alpha = 90°$

All visual and auditory patterns can be described in this coding language.

ACKNOWLEDGMENT

I am greatly indebted to H. Buffart and R. Collard for their valuable comments.

REFERENCES

Beck, J. Perceptual grouping produced by line figures. *Perception and Psychophysics*, 1967, *2*, 491–495.

Buffart, H., Leeuwenberg, E., & Restle, F. Coding theory of visual pattern completion. *Journal of Experimental Psychology*, 1981, *7*, 241–274.

Collard, R. *Minimization of structural information: An algebraic approach*. University paper, Nijmegen, Department of Experimental Psychology, 1982.

Dember, W. *The psychology of perception*. New York: Holt Rinehart and Winston, 1965.

Hochberg, J. Effects of the Gestalt revolution: The Cornell symposium on perception. *Psychological Review*, 1957, *64*, 73–84.

Johansson, G. Visual perception of biological motion and a model for its analysis. *Perception and Psychophysics*, 1969, *60*, 17–23.

Leeuwenberg, E. A perceptual coding language for visual and auditory patterns. *American Journal of Psychology*, 1971, *84*, 307–349.

Restle, F. Theory of serial pattern learning: Structural trees. *Psychological Review*, 1970, *66*, 481–495.

Restle, F. Coding theory of the perception of motion configurations. *Psychological Review*, 1979, *86* 1–24.

Restle, F., & Decker, J. Size of the Müller-Lyer illusion as a function of its dimensions. *Perception and Psychophysics*, 1977, *21*, 489–503.

Simon, H. Complexity and the representation of patterned sequences of symbols. *Psychological Review*, 1972, *79*, 369–382.

Stevens, S. S. Perceptual magnitude and its measurement. In E. C. Carterette & M. P. Friedman (Eds.), *Handbook of Perception*, Vol. 2. New York: Academic Press, 1974.

Vitz, P. C. Information, run structure, and binary pattern complexity. *Perception and Psychophysics*, 1968, *3*, 275–280.

4 The Perceiver as Organizer and Geometer

D. N. Perkins
Harvard University

INTRODUCTION

This chapter argues for the reality and importance of a particular strategy in visual processing: the perceiver often resolves the projective ambiguity of stimuli by ''reading in'' certain geometric regularities such as rectangularity or symmetry and deriving a three-dimensional interpretation, one both exhibiting those regularities and consistent with the stimulus. Thus, the perceiver uses regularity assumptions plus a geometric capacity to achieve a spatial encoding of an essentially indeterminate stimulus. To execute this strategy over a range of cases, the visual system must be able to deal flexibly with a variety of geometric regularities and to perform certain geometric computations, either by case-specific or general means. That the visual system indeed does this, and how, are the topics of the following pages.

The discussion focuses on a fairly technical analysis of subjects' performance on certain laboratory discrimination tasks. Therefore, I should say at the outset that the relevant phenomena by no means occur only in laboratory settings or with relatively ''reduced'' stimuli. On the contrary, the everyday world through which we navigate is replete with rectangularities, symmetries, coplanarities, and other sorts of geometric regularities in such objects as books, rooms, vases, and automobiles. There is ample opportunity for the exercise of the organizing perceptual processes discussed here, and some informal observations to be mentioned later suggest that the perceiver takes this opportunity.

In this introduction I want simply to illustrate the approach discussing a special case, the case that inspired the approach in the first place (Perkins, 1968, 1972). Consider the rectangular solid pictured in Fig. 4.1A. The first observation

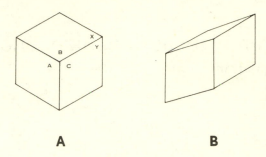

FIG. 4.1.   Box shapes satisfying (A) and not satisfying (B) the geometrical conditions for a rectangular interpretation.

A   **B**

is that we do indeed see a representation of a rectangular solid. It is a familiar point, emphasized by the Ames demonstrations in perception (Ames, 1955; Ittelson, 1952), that such forms are projectively ambiguous, interpretable in principle as any number of odd arrangements in space which project to the given stimulus. That we see a particular shape argues that the viewer adds something—an assumption of rectangularity, or perhaps an anticipation of a form familiar in the environment. Reasons to be given later recommend the former choice.

The second and crucial observation is that not all box shapes built from similar networks of lines appear rectangular. Figure 4.1B is a case in point. Most viewers agree that this figure seems to depict an oblique or skew shape rather than a rectangular one. My conjecture of several years ago (Perkins, 1968) was that perhaps the disposition of edges in such cases was inconsistent geometrically with a rectangular interpretation. In making an oblique interpretation instead, the viewer displayed a respect for geometric realities and revealed a capacity to "do" the relevant geometry in some sense.

A little vector calculus (Perkins, 1968) confirmed that indeed certain box shapes admitted rectangular interpretations whereas others did not. A simple rule governed the distinction. A rectangular interpretation was possible if and only if all three angles A, B, and C as indicated in Fig. 4.1A were greater than 90 degrees.

Informal observations aside, the question remained whether perceivers would systematically respect the geometric constraints over a range of such figures. A formal experiment (Perkins, 1972) confirmed that they would. Under three slightly different conditions, adult subjects viewed a series of drawings like those in Figs. 4.1A and 4.1B from a distance of six feet. Some of the drawings fell well within or well outside the boundary defined by the rule mentioned above, whereas others fell much closer to the boundary. Although of course discrimination was poorer closer to the boundary, overall, subjects classified about 90% of the figures satisfying the rule as rectangular but only about 16% of the figures violating the rule as rectangular.

In the same period, Attneave and Frost (1969) developed a closely related approach to the perception of such figures, an approach that examined whether the human visual system could do the necessary geometry to make accurate slant judgments. When a box shape did satisfy the conditions described above, the constraint of rectangularity plus the angles between the three radiating edges at a corner of the stimulus determined the slants in space of those edges (Attneave & Frost, 1969; Perkins, 1968). The relationship between a rectangular shape and a definite slant can be understood as a special case of the covariance of shape and slant discussed by Beck and Gibson (1955). Given that a shape must yield a certain projection, a particular slant entails a particular shape and, with some ambiguity, a particular shape entails a particular slant. In this case the only ambiguity concerns whether a figure such as Figure 4.1A represents a convex or concave form, a protruding solid or a hollow shell. For either case, the shape-slant covariance determines the orientation.

Again the question arose whether the perceptual system utilized the geometry. Attneave and Frost (1969) conducted an experiment to find out. Their experiment involved three conditions designed to examine the worth of a Gestalt approach to the perception of such forms. In their condition 3, the subjects viewed a stimulus completely consistent with a cubical interpretation, an interpretation highly regular as a three-dimensional shape. That is, the angles, lengths of edges and convergence of opposite edges in the flat stimulus were such as to be fully consonant with the image of an equal-sided rectangular form in space. Condition 2 eliminated the perspective convergence, exhibiting edges parallel in the picture plane. Condition 1 also lacked perspective and the lengths of the edges were adjusted to be equal in the picture plane rather than representing edges of equal length in space. Attneave and Frost utilized an apparatus that provided a monocular view of the stimuli and superimposed on it, with a half-silvered mirror, a binocular view of a wand on a pivot. The investigators asked their subjects to indicate the apparent slant in space of an edge of the stimulus figure by adjusting the wand until it appeared to coincide phenomenally with the edge. The prediction was that in condition 3 when the figure was best organized in space, subjects' slant judgments would fall closest to the geometrical prediction. Condition 1, however, with its "good form" of parallel edges and equal length of edges in the frontal plane, would induce competition between a flat and spatial reading, and subjects would report much less slant. Condition 2 would fall between.

The results fully confirmed the prediction. Attneave and Frost found, however, that even under condition 3, subjects' slant judgments were regressed substantially toward the frontal plane. For example, the regression at 60 degrees was about 21 degrees. This might suggest that the perceptions of the subjects bore little relationship to geometry, but further analysis demonstrated a very strong relationship. Attneave and Frost discovered that in all three conditions, the subjects' judgments varied almost linearly with the correct response. The subjects certainly were using the information for slant implicit in the geometry, although with a systematic ratio of underestimation which varied across the conditions.

In later experiments reported by Attneave (1972), Attneave and Frost's data indicated that under more phenomenally realistic conditions these regression effects lessened somewhat, and with other sorts of stimuli they nearly disappeared. In general, for experiments of this sort, regression effects are a common but not inevitable occurance (for a review, see Perkins and Cooper, 1980). Also, as noted earlier, subjects perform the rectangularity discrimination task imperfectly, though fairly well. It neither seems appropriate to classify the perceiver as a good geometer nor as not a geometer at all, and Perkins and Cooper (1980) attempted to negotiate these extremes by calling the perceiver a "sloppy geometer," as a constant reminder that some conformance to geometry can be expected, but that how much varies considerably.

In summary, the studies of Perkins (1972) and Attneave and Frost (1969) illustrate what is meant here by the perceiver functioning as an organizer and a geometer. Namely, the perceiver attempts to achieve an interpretation of ambiguous projections by imposing geometric regularities such as rectangularity. The perceiver does so with some respect for the geometric implications, for the most part avoiding regular interpretations which are geometrically impossible and perceiving slants roughly matching the geometrically correct slants.

Although the examples illustrate the proposed general theory, they do not justify it. Perhaps the viewer's response to rectangular forms is a very special case, a matter of overlearning of the rectangularities which pervade our urban environment. Perhaps no general Gestalt strategy and no flexible mechanism for doing the necessary geometry operates at all. If indeed some generality in these respects can be demonstrated, then the question of mechanism arises. Just how does the perceiver carry out the seemingly sophisticated geometric computations required? Whether the perceiver in fact employs a range of regularities and whether the perceiver deals with geometric computations flexibly will be the themes of the next two sections. In the section after that, a model will be proposed explaining how the perceiver might carry out these operations. Finally, I will consider the general implications of the present account for Gestalt theories of perception.

THE PERCEIVER AS ORGANIZER

I want to argue here that the perceiver indeed utilizes a variety of geometric regularities in interpreting projectively ambiguous figures. To demonstrate this, one need only produce line drawings which, to the perceiver, fairly unambiguously represent unfamiliar regular three dimensional forms, unfamiliar to exclude familiarity as an explanation rivaling regularity. Figure 4.2 provides a set of examples.

The following organizational principles appear to be at work. Figure 4.2A, picturing an unfamiliar complex form with rectangular corners, demonstrates that

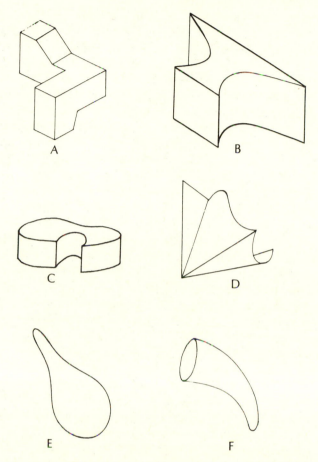

FIG. 4.2.   Projectively ambiguous shapes perceived as specific although unfamiliar three-dimensional forms exhibiting various regularities.

the perceiver's use of rectangularity discussed earlier is "generative" and not
limited to the special case of rectangular prisms. Figure 4.2B depicts a bilaterally
symmetric form, with top and bottom faces perpendicular to the sides, illustrating the perceiver's use of bilateral symmetry as a regularizing constraint. In Fig.
4.2C, symmetry is abandoned, but the perceiver still apprehends a fairly distinct
form; the underlying principle is extension of the shape defined by the top face in
a direction perpendicular to the face. (This constraint in itself does not wholly
determine the object, which could be tilted more or less; the perceiver either
arbitrarily or on the basis of principles not considered here eliminates the remaining degrees of freedom.) Figure 4.2D exhibits a similar principle, except
that the end-shape shrinks into a point along its locus of extension. Figure 4.2E

shifts to another principle altogether, illustrating axial symmetry, or symmetry of rotation around an axis. Finally, Fig. 4.2F shows that, in such surfaces of rotation, the axis need not be straight for a perception based on axial symmetry.

A pencil and paper are all one requires to multiply such artificial examples endlessly. This may be an appropriate place to comment on the function of the perceiver as organizer in more natural circumstances, however. J. J. Gibson has often argued (e.g., Gibson, 1979, pp. 166–168) that the "reduced" stimuli of the experimenter are ambiguous and misleadingly encourage the view that perception routinely involves imposed assumptions. Gibson proceeds to maintain that, in more realistic contexts, the light specifies unambiguously the layout of surfaces in a scene. I have argued elsewhere (Perkins, 1976; Perkins & Cooper, 1980), that even the mobile binocular observer of real scenes depends on assumptions of a sort and that more continuity than Gibson allows obtains between the real-world and "reduced" cases. That theoretical issue aside, however, what role do the specific regularizing phenomena discussed here have in everyday perceiving?

First of all, line drawings are not only the tools of perceptual psychologists but, with all their projective ambiguities, prevalent and important vehicles of communication in many everyday contexts. Accordingly, the sorts of phenomena discussed here get at least that far outside the laboratory. Second, in some cases, the perceiver must deal with fairly "reduced" conditions in viewing real scenes, and there also, the organizing principles discussed here seem relevant. For example, as described in Perkins and Cooper (1980), the John Hancock tower in Boston, Massachusetts, has not a rectangular, but a parallelogram-shaped floor cross-section. Whereas, seen from some angles, the tower appears nonrectangular as indeed it is, seen from others, where the projection happens to satisfy the rule given earlier, the tower looks rectangular. This is evidence that in such circumstances the perceiver resorts to the organizing tactics described here.

Finally, there are informal reasons to believe that these same organizing tactics function in up-close perception. For example, I have observed that the tendency to read a nonrectangular solid block as rectangular, when the projection to the eye satisfies the rule, often rivals motion parallax, and sometimes even binocular information. This suggests that the perceiver is an organizer in perceiving real world scenes close up, where, because corners usually really are rectangular, there normally is no conflict with, but rather reinforcement of, impressions gained through other means like motion parallax.

Although these arguments plea the case of everyday relevance for the processes discussed here, my basic concern in this chapter is the nature of those processes themselves. So far, the examples have demonstrated flexibility in the perceiver as an organizer, but not in the perceiver as a geometer. Only in the case of the rectangular solid has evidence on that point been offered.

THE PERCEIVER AS GEOMETER

In this section I want to describe four experiments that gauge the flexibility of the perceiver as a geometer. Those experiments speak to various combinations of four issues, each issue concerning a way in which the perceiver might be limited in accommodating to the constraints of geometry.

1. *Variety Of Regularities.*   As already demonstrated, viewers are sensitive to the geometric conditions for rectangular corners, and do appear to "read in" various other regularities. Whether they impose other regularities with a sensitivity to relevant geometric conditions remains to be seen, however.

2. *Familiarity.*   Perhaps the perceiver only is sensitive to the geometry of familiar forms. This would suggest that the perceiver is not really doing geometry at all, but perhaps relying on some kind of imagistic memory for the possible cases.

3. *Global Versus Local Regularities.*   In the rectangular forms discussed earlier, the edges at each corner bore an orthogonal relationship one to another, and any corner of the stimulus with three radiating edges could be tested for rectangularity (whereas the rule described applies to the central corner, an equivalent rule applies to the outside corners, where only two faces are visible.) Some other three-dimensional form, however, might involve regularities that obtained among components dispersed rather than clustered at a point. Would the visual system have the flexibility to coordinate information from different regions of the stimulus to do the relevant geometry?

4. *Cartesian Regularities.*   All the edges of the rectangular forms discussed earlier align with a Cartesian coordinate system in the virtual space of the picture—indeed, they practically constitute such a system. As will be seen below, other nonrectangular forms also may distribute themselves in a regular fashion within such coordinate systems. Attneave (1968, 1977) has argued that Cartesian coordinate systems may be involved in a fundamental way in the perceiver's representations of three-dimensional objects in a space. Perhaps the kind of geometric sensitivity shown here only occurs when the perceiver can represent the regularities as aligning with a Cartesian frame of reference.

Each of these issues arises in one or more of the following four experiments, all of which follow the pattern of the rectangularity discrimination study described earlier. In each case, the subjects were asked to look at a series of stimuli with a certain geometric regularity in mind and to judge whether or not each depicted form exhibited that regularity. Some of these stimuli could be projections of three-dimensional forms possessing the regularity, and some could not. The stimuli always were drawn in orthogonal rather than perspective projection and displayed at some distance, so that perspective convergence would not provide an additional information source influencing subjects' judgments. Each experiment included, in random order, a gradation of more and less difficult discriminations, stimuli with measurements barely or decisively satisfying or violating the geometric conditions for the regularity. There was no feedback during the judging. Some combination of verbal instructions, three-dimensional models and one sample stimulus from the regular, one from the nonregular range conveyed to subjects the desired judgment. Subjects were urged to relie on their visual impressions and, questioned about their strategies later, no subject ever reported any conscious geometric strategy for performing the task. Further details of the general methodology can be found in Perkins (1972).

Experiment 1: Skeleton Boxes

In this experiment, 12 subjects each judged four different decks of 48 stimuli in counterbalanced order. Figure 4.3 illustrates the stimuli. Condition A duplicated some of the stimuli from the rectangularity discrimination experiment discussed in the introduction. The other three conditions were constructed by selecting

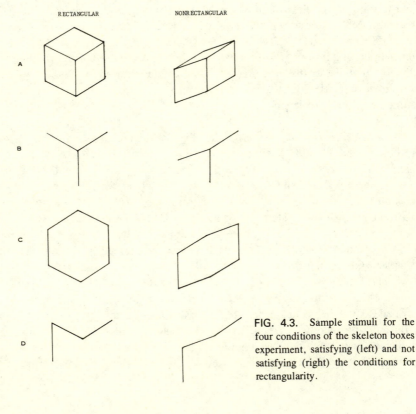

FIG. 4.3. Sample stimuli for the four conditions of the skeleton boxes experiment, satisfying (left) and not satisfying (right) the conditions for rectangularity.

TABLE 4.1
Percentage of Regularities Perceived When Consistent or
Inconsistent With Geometry

Experiment	Condition	% When Consistent	% When Inconsistent	Significance Level of Difference
Original rectangularity experiment (Perkins, 1972)	straight	92	19	.001
Skeleton boxes	A	96	32	.001
	B	92	20	.001
	C	88	46	.001
	D	81	19	.001
Symmetry	—	61	9	.001
Coplanarity	—	66	17	.001
Quadrilateral	A, C as right?	35	38	n.s.
	B, D as right?	60	29	.01
	A, C or B, D? forced choice	57	18	.001

different combinations of edges from the complete box-shape and displaying only those. In each case, the edges included the three edge-directions present in a box shape, so that sufficient information was available to determine whether the pictured edges could represent mutually orthogonal edges in space. The subjects were asked to try to look at the figures in that way, and to report whether they appeared rectangular. As the results recorded in Table 4.1 indicate, subjects proved able to make the discrimination at a high level of significance in all four conditions, although there were significant differences among the conditions, C especially eliciting a less sharp discrimination.

This result bears on the *global versus local* and *familiarity* issues raised above. In conditions C and D, no rectangular corner with three edges occurred, but subjects made the discrimination nonetheless, integrating information from different parts of the stimulus. Also, certainly the rectangularity discrimination in forms C and D could not be said to be familiar to the subjects, although a familiarity explanation still might apply if one supposed that subjects could relate these "skeleton" stimuli to full box shapes, for instance by imagining them to be embedded in such shapes.

Experiment 2: Symmetry

In this study, 12 subjects examined pictures of wedge-shaped forms like those in Fig. 4.4 and judged whether or not they appeared bilaterally symmetric. The stimulus deck, which included 128 pictures, was an exact analog of that em-

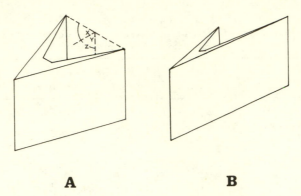

A   **B**

FIG. 4.4.   Sample stimuli from the symmetry experiment, satisfying (A) and not
satisfying (B) the conditions for symmetry.

ployed in the original rectangularity discrimination experiment (Perkins, 1972).
Mathematically, the symmetry case reduces to rectangularity, because, as indicated in Fig. 4.4A, a wedge-shape is symmetric if and only if it contains an
implicit rectangular corner given by the axis of symmetry, the vertical direction,
and the lateral direction. Again, subjects performed the discrimination with
significant accuracy, as shown in Table 4.1. The subjects, however, did not
differentiate as sharply as with the box shapes, often not classifying as symmetric
forms which could be symmetric.

This experiment demonstrates geometric sensitivity to the new regularity of
bilateral symmetry, new phenomenally although mathematically equivalent to
rectangularity as indicated. Besides speaking to the *variety* question, the experiment also involved an unfamiliar stimulus shape. Finally, as with the skeleton
figures in the previous experiment, information permitting a judgment of symmetry was distributed across the figure in the vertical and horizontal edges, rather
than concentrated at a vertex.

Experiment 3: Coplanarity

The 44 stimuli for this experiment were of the form illustrated in Figs. 4.5A and
B. The 16 subjects were asked to try to look at these stimuli as representing two
tilted rectangles in space, the smaller lying flat against the larger. A geometric
rule best described in the context of Experiment 4 below specified when this was
geometrically possible. As in the previous studies, the subjects achieved a significant degree of discrimination.

This result gives evidence of sensitivity to the relevant geometry with a new
regularity, coplanarity, in accompaniment with the rectangularity. It speaks
again to the *global-local* issue, because the discrimination requires taking into
consideration both shapes. Finally, and for the first time, the result bears on the

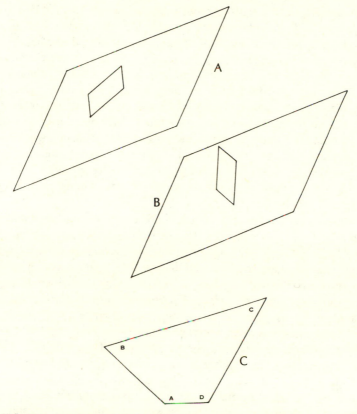

FIG. 4.5. Sample stimuli from the Coplanarity (top) and Quadrilateral (bottom) experiments. A satisfying and B not satisfying the conditions for coplanarity.

Cartesian question. The skeleton figures, Experiment 1, when they meet the rectangularity condition, permit an orthogonal relationship among their edges, which would then align with a Cartesian coordinate system. The wedge-figures of Experiment 2 which allow a bilaterally symmetric interpretation are disposed symmetrically about a Cartesian coordinate system, as indicated in Fig. 4.4A. The present stimuli, however, involve two parallelograms whose corners are not parallel with one another. Therefore, both parallelograms, seen as rectangles, cannot occupy the same Cartesian frame of reference with their edges aligned with its axes. Nonetheless, subjects made the discrimination.

Experiment 4: Quadrilaterals

As the symmetry experiment involved stimuli that were mathematically related to the box shapes of the rectangularity experiment, so this study involved 22 stimuli that were mathematically related to those in Experiment 3. Indeed, Experiment 4 was performed with the same subjects at the same time. Figure 4.5C illustrates the stimuli. Here, under one condition, 8 subjects were asked whether they could see the quadrilateral as a quadrilateral tilted in space such that angles a and c were both rectangular. Another condition asked 8 subjects to consider corners b and d. Finally, in a condition added after the first four of the 16 subjects and always administered last, the subjects were instructed that one or the other pair of opposite corners could be seen as rectangular. They were asked to indicate which. (Although subjects' experience earlier in the experiment might be thought to help them with this condition, order has generally been controlled in Perkins' series of studies and significant order effects have never appeared. In any case, the principle question is whether subjects exhibit the discrimination, even given a little practice without feedback.)

Both this and the prior experiment depended on the same mathematical question: could two angles given in projection be right angles lying in the same plane in space? The condition describing when this is possible can be expressed most readily in terms of quadrilaterals, such as Fig. 4.5C. There will be a common plane in which angles a and c are both right angles if and only if either angle a + b is less than 180 degrees and angle a + d greater than 180 degrees, or, alternatively, angle a + b is greater than 180 degrees and angle a + d less than 180 degrees. When quadrilaterals do not have parallel sides, this condition will hold either for one pair of opposite angles or the other pair. The condition is applied to nested rectangles as in Figs. 5A and B by constructing a quadrilateral from two adjacent sides of one parallelogram and two adjacent sides of the other.

Subjectively, the quadrilateral discrimination proved difficult for the participants and indeed, in one of the conditions without a forced choice, subjects did not discriminate significantly. In the other, however, and in the forced choice condition, a significant degree of discrimination did appear, as shown in Table 4.1. Thus, the findings add yet another regularity to those which the perceiver can handle, introduce a discrimination not only unfamiliar, but somewhat bizarre, require the integration of dispersed features to make the judgement, and finally provide another case which cannot align with the axes of a Cartesian coordinate system.

The discriminations achieved in these four experiments were far from perfect. All four experiments, and especially the last, illustrate again that the human perceiver must be considered a "sloppy geometer." Nonetheless, significant agreement with geometry did appear in all cases. Collectively, the cases argue that the perceiver's geometric capacities are general and flexible so far as the four possible limitations described at the outset are concerned.

TOWARD A MODEL OF GOOD FORM PERCEPTION

The prior characterization of the perceiver as an organizer and as a geometer has been reached without discussing how the perceptual system might accomplish its

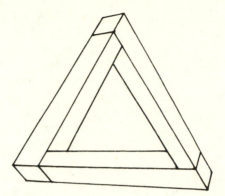

FIG. 4.6. The Penrose triangle
(Penrose & Penrose, 1958).

feats of geometry. Although a well-supported theory will have to await further experimentation, this section attempts to answer that question in a partial and exploratory way. To forecast the conclusion, the circumstances suggest that two distinct processes are at work, one responsible for extending partial determinations of shape and slant over the rest of the stimulus, and the other responsible for achieving these partial determinations.

The extension process can be explained in terms of the well-known "Penrose triangle" illustrated in Fig. 4.6 (Penrose & Penrose, 1958). Since the introduction of this anomolous figure, several investigators have considered its implications for a model of perceptual functioning (e.g., Draper, 1978; Perkins, 1976; Perkins & Cooper, 1980; Simon, 1967). An account has emerged of the process of perceiving the triangle as an hypothesis-making, extension, and testing procedure. The viewer begins at a corner, achieving a local interpretation of the corner as having a certain shape and slant. When attention shifts to a second corner, that corner is seen in such a way that the edges and faces it shares with the initial corner preserve the originally derived orientations. Accordingly, the position in space of the second corner relative to the first is determined. This extension process continues as the viewer scans around the figure. The Penroses, however, designed their triangle so that it would not "close." When the viewer comes full circle back to the initial corner, the most recently examined side appears to fall substantially behind the corner, rather than connecting as it should. There follows a moment of confusion, after which the corner reverts to a normal closed corner. The anomolous interpretation has been discarded, a new local determination made, and the extension process begun anew. All this fits well Gregory's (1970, 1972) concept of perception as an hypothesis-making process, where mismatches between expectation and the stimulus function as a signal to revise the hypothesis. Similar kinds of hypothesis-making, extension, and back-up procedures have figured in computer scene analysis (Mackworth, 1973, 1976; Waltz, 1975; Winston, 1972).

The present perspective has this to add to the foregoing account. Here, the hypothesis-making process is seen as dependent on the organizing and geometric capacities of the perceiver. The Penrose triangle presents corners which satisfy the rectangularity conditions discussed earlier, and, as examined by Attneave and Frost (1969) and Attneave (1972), the viewer can thereby perceive the slants of the radiating edges and faces. Furthermore, the extensions to each successive corner are consistent with a rectangularity hypothesis at the new corner. Thus, the extended hypothesis finds what might be called further support. The hypothesis fails only globally, when the otherwise perfectly regular and determined form does not close. Of course, the same extension process functions in perceiving figures that embody no anomaly. Perkins (1976) performed an experiment in which subjects estimated the angles of pictured forms with trapezoidal tops. The subjects tended to take one or the other end of these figures as rectangular, and Perkins showed that subjects' estimates of the angle at the end opposite the one perceived as rectangular conformed roughly to the implications of the rectangularity hypothesis. The subjects had accomplished the extension with fair accuracy.

Draper (1978), however, points out that with cycles of several more beams than the three of the Penrose triangle, the viewer fails to perceive an anomaly. Apparently, such figures outstrip the viewer's capacity to keep track of the relative positions of the corners in making a circuit. Again, it's necessary to remind ourselves that the perceiver is a somewhat sloppy geometer.

It remains to consider the partial determination process which outputs the shape and slant implied by a regularity. According to the present account, this process fulfills three roles, providing a starting point for the extension process, providing further starting points if the extension process does not achieve an interpretation of the entire stimulus (indeed, conceivably more than one partial determination plus extension might operate simultaneously in different parts of a complex stimulus), and, finally, supporting and making more precise the shape and orientation implied by an extension from elsewhere in the stimulus, when that extension is consistent with a regularity in the region extended to.

Now I explain how this partial determination process might work. A quasi-mechanical model will be described in a particular case and then generalized. After that, this model is compared and contrasted with several alternatives to clarify the options and explain the choice.

Consider the problem of interpreting three edges radiating from a vertex as a rectangular corner in space, and suppose the three edges meet the conditions for rectangularity described earlier. Imagine a trial interpretation, a configuration of three segments in space pivoting on a common vertex. The segments and vertex are constrained so that they project to the stimulus configuration. In fact, this could be realized mechanically by having the segments move only in slots extending upward from the surface of the stimulus, and having the vertex move along a wire. So far, nothing in this model favors a regular interpretation of the stimulus over any other, each arrangement of the segments pivoted on the vertex being equally valid. Now assume, however, that three forces operate in this mechanical system, forces between each pair of segments. The force between a pair of segments is zero when the segments stand in a right-angle relationship to one another, and increases as the segments depart from orthogonality. Were it desired, this too could be realized mechanically by appropriate arrangements of springs. The result is a physical system that will tend to relax toward a minimum energy state, a state satisfying the projective constraints. This minimum energy state constitutes the interpretation of the stimulus as a corner in space with mutually orthogonal radiating edges.

Two points complete the description of the model. First, it hardly needs saying that the model does not propose the human visual system operates with pivots and springs. Rather, the mechanical analogy provides an existence proof that this relaxation process can occur and yield the desired results. Given that proof, it matters little how components of the system are realized, whether as springs or electrical or chemical potentials for example. Second, the special case described above illustrates a general principle applicable not just to rectangular corners but to symmetry, parallelism, coplanarity and the other relationships of regularity discussed earlier. One only need introduce forces favoring those relationships. There results what might be called a "relaxation model" of the partial determination process, with reference to the relaxation of a system into a minimum energy state.

Now I want to consider the partial determination and extension processes together, mention certain variants and explain the choice of this particular account. For one point, care has been taken to speak of "partial determination" rather than "local determination." In cases like the Penrose triangle, "local determination" would fit very well, because projections of rectangular corners provide, in the neighborhood of the vertex, the information for their spatial orientation. As emphasized in the previous section, however, the experiments with symmetry and with the subsets of rectangular forms demonstrate that the perceptual system often enforces regularities among dispersed elements in a scene. Accordingly, it's unreasonable to posit solely a local determination and a global extension process even though such a concept would keep the local determination process simpler, avoiding "action at a distance" in the forces operating between elements of the relaxing system.

Because the relaxation process cannot be restricted to local operation, another alternative becomes attractive. Perhaps the entire interpretive process could be left to relaxation, omitting the extension process as a distinct phase. Theoretically, this would work well. For example, given a stimulus image of a rectangular prism, a candidate interpretation in the mechanical analog would be a kind of skeleton of segments pivoted at the joints. The segments and joints would be constrained to project to their counterparts in the stimulus image and forces favoring rectangular relationships between segments at a joint, parallelism between opposite segments of a face, and coplanarity among the segments of a face would be introduced. This system as a whole would then relax into the desired rectangular interpretation with no distinct extension process. The account would apply nicely to the Penrose triangle, which could relax into a minimum energy configuration only if the segments along one of the sides broke so as not to connect to one of the corners—much as the viewer in fact perceives on discovering the anomaly.

The problem with this integrated one-process theory, however, is that it does not describe the viewer's experience in scanning extended figures like the Penrose triangle. The viewer does not discover the anomaly at once, as some one-step system tries simultaneously to realize the rectangularity relationships, but discovers the anomaly only by tracking around the Penrose triangle, as described earlier.

Another alternative concerns the relaxation process specifically. Attneave (1972) and Perkins and Cooper (1980), taking a cue from Attneave, described much the same sequence of events as proposed by the relaxation process in rather different terms, suggesting that the visual system conducted a kind of cybernetic search for a regular interpretation, measuring departures from rectangularity and other regularities and shifting a trial interpretation to approach more closely the target regularities. This "hill-climbing" model would yield essentially the same results as the relaxation model, and, depending on the hill-climbing algorithm, the trial interpretation might even pass through the same intermediate states. Accordingly, my preference for a relaxation process, so long as it will do the job, derives from parsimony rather than evidence. Why posit feedback loops and perhaps a guiding executive of some sort when the same result can be achieved by a system of forces interacting blindly?

Attneave (Chapter 1) displays a similar preference in proposing a relaxation process which, however, operates among more atomistic elements, "dipoles" representing location and direction in space and packed fairly densely to comprise a representation of the three-dimensional object. Attneave's account is attractive because it posits elements closer to a plausible neurological substrate and assumes less global structures in contrast with the whole segments assumed above. The present account, however, is attractive because it makes quite clear how the proposed quasi-mechanical systems would behave. Attneave's intricately interconnected dipoles leave prediction less certain without an actual simulation.

Another phenomenon may recommend the model proposed here. Informal observation suggests that either psychological set or a deliberate act of will on the part of the viewer can lead him to perceive one or another interpretation of ambiguous figures such as the Necker cube or the trapezoidal prisms used by Perkins (1976). The present theory provides a parsimonious way of interpreting this. The forces operating among the segments are not always "on." Rather, stimulus conditions, contextual influences, and the intention of the viewer result in certain of the inter-element forces being "on" in one situation, and others in another. This leads to different relaxations into different interpretations. Without

some such selective mechanism, which regular interpretation a viewer ap-
prehended when a stimulus allowed more than one would depend on the initial
conditions of the system, conditions which plausibly would vary haphazardly as
the viewer scanned the world. Attneave's dipole model, however, does not seem
to allow straightforwardly for such selectivity in the regularities perceived.
Attneave's model proposes that the forces are "on" all the time. Also, because
of its atomistic nature, there seems to be little opportunity to, for instance, turn
off the rectangularity influence between one whole segment and another. At
least, how this would work in the case of the dipole model is unclear. These
points notwithstanding, certainly the dipole model and the present one are in very
similar spirits, and the difference in the end might well reduce to nothing more
than contrasting levels of description.

All the theories outlined so far belong to a general family. All might be called
"convergence theories." That is, whatever the details, in each case the visual
system arrives at a partial or total interpretation through a series of intermediate
interpretations that converge on one possessing the target regularities. A quite
different family might be called "direct computation" theories. Here, the extension process would remain much as described. Partial determinations would be
achieved in another way, however. For example, the spatial slants associated
with the three radiating edges of a rectangular corner might be computed by some
psychological process equivalent to the evaluation of the algebraic formula for
those slants (Attneave & Frost, 1969; Perkins, 1968). Alternatively, some neurological equivalent of a table look-up might occur, various combinations of the
three projected angles in the rectangularity case being associated with the approximate spatial slants for the three radiating edges. Certainly, other similar procedures could be imagined. The general characteristic is that the visual system
reaches an interpretation without intermediate trial interpretations, by taking
advantage of specific information about the class of cases being treated, rectangularity at a corner, coplanarity of nested rectangles, and so on.

What reasons are there to prefer "convergence theories" in general over
"direct computation" theories? Basically, convergence theories explain more
parsimoniously the flexibility demonstrated in the previous section. The processes posited by the various convergence theories are intrinsically general, able
to deal with a wide range of unfamiliar combinations of regularities, including,
for instance, the opposite right angles in the quadrilateral experiment. In contrast, the direct computation theories require information specific to each combination of regularities accomodated. Because some of the cases investigated involve discriminations that would seem to be rather irrelevant to the perception of
real scenes, it's unclear why the visual system should be so equipped.

In summary, the arguments of this section favor convergence theories in
general, and, among them, a "relaxation theory" of achieving determinations of
some shapes and slants, with an extension process extrapolating until further
computations involving a relaxation process are required or until the interpreta-

tion is complete. Of course, certain gaps remain in this theory—perhaps most important: how are the regularities that function on a particular occasion selected? Also, as must be evident, the arguments by no means force the acceptance of a relaxation model. The visual system could be equipped with the necessary information for a direct computation approach, despite the contrary considerations mentioned above. Among the convergence theories, a cybernetic feedback system rather than a relaxation process might ultimately prove to be a better account, or perhaps the extension process posited here, properly interpreted, could be seen as a special case of the relaxation process rather than as a separate partner. The model advanced here, however, does appear to offer a coherent account of the phenomena, an account with the stated advantages.

THE KIND OF GESTALT THEORY THIS IS

The proposed theory provides an occasion to examine the nature of Gestalt theories of perception. Such a theory can involve one or more of several *Prägnanz* principles, each of which aims to capture what is "good" about the good form the viewer tends to perceive. For example, a minimum energy principle defines good form in terms of a system's relaxation toward minimum energy states. An information-processing account, to mention one possibility, may see good form as a consequence of the perceptual system making default assumptions to resolve essentially ambiguous stimuli and arrive at a definite interpretation. A simplicity principle proposes that the mechanisms of perception seek out a simplest interpretation, which often is taken to mean a highly redundant one featuring symmetries, parallelisms and so on. Finally, a minimum encoding principle suggests that the perceptual system strives for representations as compact as possible relative to some coding system.

Although these principles overlap in many ways, they are not identical. Each advances a somewhat different view of perception. This can be seen by relating each to phenomena they all aim to explain, for example the tendency toward symmetric interpretations of stimuli. According to one possible minimum energy principle, the perceptual system gravitates toward minimun energy interpretations, which, because forces are the way they are, often means symmetric interpretations. According to one sort of information-processing account, symmetry is not a consequence but a default assumption. In contrast, a simplicity principle could posit merely that the visual system seeks out symmetric interpretations without implying such functional purposes as the resolution of ambiguity. Finally, according to a minimum encoding principle, another functional purpose applies: symmetry is utilized in the mental representation to make it more compact.

Which principles of Prägnanz figure in the present model? Certainly most explicit is a minimum energy principle, as the relaxation model was characterized in those terms. Even here, however, some qualifications are necessary. First, notice that regularities are not achieved as a consequence of a system tending toward minimum energy states which happen to entail regularities. Rather, the relaxation process is a way of realizing the implications for shape-at-a-slant of target regularities induced by expectation and the stimulus. Second, the previous section explained that the kind of convergence process proposed could just as well be described as a cybernetic procedure involving some sort of feedback and control mechanism, a mechanism of a much more information-processing character. The preference for the relaxation theory stemmed from parsimony, not evidence. Indeed, it is far from clear what sort of evidence would suffice to distinguish the two.

Whatever the resolution there, an information-processing perspective certainly applies when the proposed relaxation and extension processes are considered in partnership. The relaxation process in effect operates as a hypothesis making mechanism, achieving a partial interpretation which the extension process tests by extrapolating its implications.

The experiments described earlier as well as the relaxation and extension processes also reveal a role for a simplicity principle, the third approach to Gestalt theorizing mentioned above. The interpretive process is a teleological one, directed toward apprehending the stimulus as exhibiting a range of regularities such as parallelisms, coplanarities, symmetries, and rectangularities. These regularities all can be expressed as redundancies of one sort and another, and this fits with a simplicity account, with "simple" taken to mean redundant in certain respects.

Can a minimum encoding principle also be found at work here? In this case, the answer has to be a more qualified one. On the positive side, the processes described certainly achieve an interpretation involving many redundancies, as just affirmed. These redundancies could be encoded economically, for instance by the visual system maintaining only one coded orientation for a whole set of parallel edges, or one coded length for a set of edges of equal length. Nothing in the present theory *requires* the visual system to exercise such economies, however.

Furthermore, there is no particular reason why the relaxation plus extension process described should inevitably arrive at a minimum encoding. Whether it does cannot be evaluated definitively without extensively considering examples in light of a particular encoding system such as Leeuwenberg's (1971, and Chapter 3). In general, however, one would expect both the relaxation process and, on a larger scale, the relaxation plus extension processes, to be subject to a limitation called the problem of local maxima—or in this case, minima. That is, in complex situations, a space of alternative states is likely to include more than one local minimum, more than one state all of whose neighbors rate higher on the variable of concern. A process that incrementally minimizes the variable will sometimes arrive at a local minimum which is not a global minimum. In qualification though, minimum encoding could be an important principle involved without expecting the encoding process always to find the global minimum, which on the average might not be worth the more elaborate search required.

In summary, the present relaxation plus extension model explicitly incorporates minimum energy, information-processing, and simplicity principles and it is at least consistent with a minimum encoding principle. All this might seem somewhat disappointing, because we would like "good form" in our theories of good form perception. Good form in a theory means, in part, parsimony, a preference for one principle rather than three or four. The present theory, however, involves as many principles as it does because the evidence and arguments pushed the interpretation in that direction. A close look at the phenomena of perception discussed in these pages suggested that several principles of a Gestalt character most plausibly were involved. Whatever the ultimate fate of the present model, it may simply be a mistake to expect the alternative Prägnanz principles to represent mutually exclusive approaches to a neo-Gestalt theory of perception.

ACKNOWLEDGMENT

I thank Robert Hodgman, Michael Molino, and Ashuk Nimgade for their able assistance with the investigations reported here. The research was performed at Project Zero, Harvard Graduate School of Education, Cambridge, Massachusetts, operating with support from the Spencer Foundation and National Institute of Education Grant No. G-78-0031. The opinions expressed here do not necessarily reflect the positions or policies of the supporting agencies.

REFERENCES

Ames, A. *An interpretative manual for the demonstrations in the psychology research center, Princeton University*. Princeton, N.J.: Princeton University Press, 1955.

Attneave, F. Triangles as ambiguous figures. *American Journal of Psychology*, 1968, *81*, 447–453.

Attneave, F. Representation of physical space. In A. Melton & E. Martin (Eds.), *Coding processes in human memory*. Washington, D.C.: V. W. Winstone & Sons, 1972.

Attneave, F. Cartesian organization in the immediate reproduction of spatial patterns. *Bulletin of the Psychonomic Society*, December 1977, *10*, 469–470.

Attneave, F., & Frost, R. The determination of perceived tridimensional orientation by minimum criteria. *Perception & Psychophysics*, 1969, *6B*, 391–396.

Beck, J., & Gibson, J. J. The relation of apparent shape to apparent slant in the perception of objects. *Journal of Experimental Psychology*, 1955, *50*, 125–133.

Draper, S. The Penrose triangle and a family of related figures. *Perception*, 1978, *7*, 283–296.

Gibson, J. J. *The ecological approach to visual perception*. Boston, Mass.: Houghton Mifflin, 1979.

Gregory, R. L. *The intelligent eye*. New York: McGraw-Hill, 1970.

Gregory, R. L. A look at biological and machine perception. In B. Meltzer & D. Michie (Eds.), *Machine intelligence 7*. Edinburgh: Edinburgh University Press, 1972.

Ittelson, W. H. *The Ames demonstration in perception: A guide to their construction and use.* Princeton: Princeton University Press, 1952.

Leeuwenberg, E. L. A perceptual coding language for visual and auditory patterns, *American Journal of Psychology,* 1971, *84,* 307–349.

Mackworth, A. K. Interpreting pictures of polyhedral scenes. *Artificial Intelligence,* 1973, *4,* 121–137.

Mackworth, A. K. Model-driven interpretation in intelligent vision systems. *Perception,* 1976, *5,* 349–370.

Penrose, L. S., & Penrose, R. Impossible objects: A special type of visual illusion. *British Journal of Psychology,* 1958, *49,* 31–33.

Perkins, D. N. Cubic corners. *Quarterly Progress Report 89* (Massachusetts Institute of Technology Research Laboratory of Electronics), 1968, 207–214.

Perkins, D. N. Visual discrimination between rectangular and nonrectangular parallelopipeds. *Perception and Psychophysics,* 1972, *12,* 396–400.

Perkins, D. N. How good a bet is good form? *Perception,* 1976, *5,* 393–406.

Perkins, D. N., & Cooper, R. How the eye makes up what the light leaves out. In M. Hagen (Ed.), *The Perception of Pictures, Vol. II: Durer's Devices: Beyond the Projective Model,* New York: Academic Press, 1980.

Simon, H. A. An information-processing explanation of some perceptual phenomena. *British Journal of Psychology,* 1967, *58,* 1–12.

Waltz, D. Understanding line drawings of scenes with shadows. In P. Winston (Ed.), *The psychology of computer vision.* New York: McGraw-Hill, 1975.

Winston, P. H. The M.I.T. robot. In B. Meltzer & D. Michie (Eds.), *Machine intelligence 7.* Edinburgh: Edinburgh University Press, 1972.

5

Symmetry, Transformation, and the Structure of Perceptual Systems

Stephen E. Palmer
University of California, Berkeley

INTRODUCTION

The nature of perceptual organization has long been closely associated with the notions of symmetry and transformation. This relationship has been developed primarily within the Gestalt tradition. For example, von Ehrenfels's original formulation of *Gestaltqualitat* was based on the observation that a melody remains the same when all its notes are transposed (transformed in pitch) to a new key. The Gestalt movement followed this lead by developing and investigating the general proposition that perceptual wholes have properties that do not change when they are subjected to uniform transformations. Wertheimer (1912) carried this still further in his classical experiments on phi phenomenon (apparent motion). He showed that the transformation of an object has a phenomenal reality of its own, one which does not even require the actual physical transformation to occur in order to be perceived. This research is often cited as the "birth" of the Gestalt movement, and the fact that it concerned the perceptual consequences of transformations is far from accidental. Indeed, one of the major contributions of Gestalt psychology was to emphasize that many aspects of perception are invariant over a large number of stimulus transformations. This line of thought has been pursued and extended by a number of perceptual theorists, most notably J. J. Gibson (1950, 1966) in his theory of ecological optics. But it was the Gestaltists who first recognized the power and importance of transformations for perception.

A second major theme of the Gestalt approach concerned the proposal that whole figures are not reducible to simple summations of local parts. The notion of figural goodness or "good Gestalt" was central to their argument, and symmetry was offered as the prototype for this concept. Symmetry epitomized a quality of whole figures because, in an important sense, it can only be defined for whole figures. If a part is claimed to be symmetrical, it can only mean that *as a whole* the part is symmetrical. Later psychologists have tried to formulate the basis of figural goodness more precisely (e.g., Attneave, 1954; Garner, 1974; Leeuwenberg, 1971), and all of them have emphasized the central role of symmetry in one form or another.

The present chapter further develops these two lines of thought and brings them together in a new theory of perceptual organization. Symmetry and transformation are inherently related geometrical constructs, and it is argued that both of them play an important role in understanding the structure underlying the visual system. In fact, this structure is conceived entirely in terms of the transformational relationships among its analyzing elements in space and time. It is further argued that the specific nature of the analyzing elements has little bearing on the nature of the whole system. What *does* matter about the analyzing elements is their internal symmetry because this logically determines the kind of structure the system as a whole can have. The theory is developed rather informally, and a number of its implications are explored. Among other things, it is suggested that this structure illuminates the nature of many important organizational phenomena and the relationships among them: figural goodness, grouping effects, emergent properties, perceptual constancies, real and apparent motion of objects in space, and depth perception.

PRELIMINARY REMARKS

Perhaps the best way to introduce the theory itself is through a brief historical review of the role of symmetry and "good form" in perceptual theory. This will provide a background of antecedents to the current theory and introduce the relationship between symmetry and transformational structure. I then outline the theory in its current state of development and describe how it accounts for some pervasive perceptual phenomena.

Symmetry And Good Form

Gestalt theorists were perhaps the first to emphasize the fundamental importance of symmetry as a construct in perceptual theory. Their view is most succinctly stated in Wertheimer's (1923) law of Prägnanz: psychological organization will always be as "good" as the prevailing conditions allow. Although "good organization" was intentionally left undefined, it clearly embraced such properties as symmetry, regularity, and simplicity (Koffka, 1935). Gestaltists proposed that there existed psychological "forces" toward good form, that emphasized symmetries and regularities in perceived figures. These were thought to be especially important in impoverished stimulus conditions such as brief exposure, low intensity, small size, and so forth. Such forces were also thought to operate autonomously over time in memory. Several studies purported to demonstrate that reproduction of previously presented figures tended to become more symmetrical and regular as the retention interval increased (Perkins, 1932). In general, the notion of "good form" of whole figures was a hallmark of the Gestalt approach to perception, and symmetry was its prototype.

The main shortcomings of Gestalt theory were that it never offered an adequate definition of "good" organization and that it failed to provide a reasonable account of how "good" organizations arose in preference to "bad" ones. "Goodness" was, in effect, an undefined primitive to Gestalt theorists. They were apparently content to trust their own intuitions about figural goodness without attempting to analyze its basis except in the vaguest of terms. Without some further analysis, their theories were circular; certain figures were easily perceived and well remembered because they were "good," but one only knew they were "good" because they were easily perceived and well remembered. Much of the progress that has been made in understanding perceptual structure since then has come from attempts to ground the concept of "good form" in more objective measures of stimulus structure.

Information theory provided the framework for the first significant advance. Attneave (1954) and Hochberg and McAlister (1953) independently proposed that "good" figures contained *less information* (i.e., were more redundant) than bad ones in the sense of information theory. All else being equal, for example, symmetrical figures are more redundant than asymmetrical ones because if the figure is divided along the line of symmetry, one half of the figure can be predicted completely from the other half (Attneave, 1954). Because the perceptual system was viewed as an information processing channel of limited capacity, it seemed only reasonable that the less information a figure contained, the more efficiently it could be processed and stored in memory. Thus, a symmetrical figure could be coded more efficiently and economically than an asymmetrical figure by taking advantage of the redundancies. In effect, the information theoretical constructs of redundancy and information grounded the construct of "good form" in an objectively testable and noncircular fashion. Many experiments confirmed that perceptual preferences for alternative interpretations of ambiguous stimuli were highly correlated with various measures of stimulus complexity and/or redundancy (e.g., Attneave, 1955; Hochberg & Brooks, 1960; Hochberg & McAlister, 1953).

A major difficulty with the information theoretical approach was that it was never quite clear how to determine the amount of information in a given pattern. In other words, it lacked a well-defined, theoretically motivated procedure for constructing codes of figures which could then be made more economical by eliminating redundancies. Leeuwenberg's "coding theory" (1971, 1978) can be viewed as an extension of the information theoretic approach in that it overcomes just these objections. Coding theory explicates an effective procedure for determining the amount of (symbolic) information required to describe a pattern in a given perceptual organization. The procedure requires dividing the pattern into molecular line segments whose sequential relationships are to be represented. The redundancies are extracted by eliminating repetitions, reflections, changes of scale, distributions, and the like from this data structure. Coding theory has been used to predict subjective ratings of stimulus complexity and pattern goodness (Leeuwenberg, 1971), subjective preferences for different organizations within the same pattern, and even preferences for alternative organizations of harmonic motions (Restle, 1979).

Symmetry And Holistic Transformations

Both information theory and coding theory appeal to the construct of redundancy in accounting for figural goodness. Redundancy is related to the concepts of identity and sameness. Even in ordinary language we say that something is "redundant" if there exists another sufficiently like it. In what sense, then, can an individual figure be redundant? Attneave (1954) and Leeuwenberg (1971) explored the more obvious possibility that *local parts* within the figure are the same as other local parts. A less obvious alternative—and one I believe to be more consistent with Gestalt lines of thought—is suggested by Garner's (1974) analysis of figural goodness in terms of "rotation and reflection (R & R) subsets." His approach explores the conception that a "good" figure is redundant to the extent that *it is the same as itself in various transformations*. Garner proposed that the number of different figures generated by rotating his dot patterns by 90, 180, and 270 degrees and reflecting them about their horizontal, vertical, and diagonal axes is a monotonically decreasing function of figural goodness. In a series of many experiments he showed that the size of the R & R subset is a powerful predictor of many dependent variables (see Garner, 1974, for a thorough review).

Garner's formulation is important to the present paper for several reasons. First, it is the only theory of figural goodness that is specifically related to transformational structure. In fact, his formulation turns out to be equivalent to a special case of the group theoretical analysis of symmetry to be discussed below. Second, it is the only theory that does not require perceptual analysis to proceed by first breaking a whole figure down into local component parts and then recognizing relationships among those parts. The size of the R & R subset is determined simply by operations on whole figures: transforming wholes and comparing them to each other for identity. It is in this sense that Garner's theory is the closest in spirit to the Gestalt tradition, even though its own theoretical roots are in information theory.

Garner's theory has a number of serious shortcomings, however. First, it is restricted to a very small subset of transformations—just rotations and reflections—among the stimulus regularities that seem to affect figural goodness.

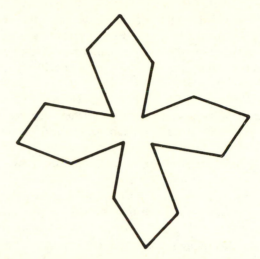

FIG. 5.1. A pattern whose shape and figural goodness vary with perceived orientation (vertical versus diagonal).

Leeuwenberg's theory is far more complete in this respect. Second, it is a theory of "pure stimulus structure" without regard for the observer's potential contribution. By attending in different ways to the same figure, an observer can see it as differentially "good." Figure 5.1, for example, shows a figure which is initially seen as a moderately good "+" shaped form. When one regards it as though it were tilted 45 degrees, however, it becomes an "x" shaped form with far greater figural goodness due to its bilateral symmetry about the diagonal axes. Because both its shape and goodness depend strongly on a perceptual reference frame (cf., Rock, 1973), one cannot ignore the perceiver's contribution in analyzing the nature of perceptual structure. Certainly the figure must have structural regularities, but the observer must be in an appropriate perceptual state to pick up those regularities. Third, the theory is purely descriptive, making no attempt to explain how it is that different figures are perceived. In fact, this is a problem with all the theories discussed thus far. They do not include mechanisms through which perception could actually *happen*. Leeuwenberg's theory, for example, can predict which of several alternative organizations will be seen by most people, but to do so, the theory must be applied to all alternatives in an exhaustive fashion. This is perhaps the greatest failing of theories of perceptual organization: they do not specify how perceptual processing might actually occur. The only serious attempt to do so was the Gestaltist "brain field" theory. This rather vague hypothesis tied their ideas to a physiological mechanism—which was later shown to be inappropriate (Lashley, Chow, & Semmes, 1951)—without ever really specifying the computational nature of the process.

Symmetry In Group Theory

Before turning to the present theory, it is helpful to explicate the mathematical relationship between symmetry and transformations more fully. As will soon become evident, the concept of symmetry that is developed here is broader than the usual idea of bilateral or "mirror image" symmetry. In fact, the present concept of symmetry corresponds more directly to the notion of "good Gestalt" than anything else: regularity and simplicity are part of it as well as strict bilateral symmetry.

The most general mathematical characterization of geometrical symmetry is in terms of its group theoretical structure (see Weyl, 1952). The basic underlying notion is that there are certain geometrical transformations that can, in principle, leave that figure unchanged, and that a set of transformations which does so completely defines the symmetry possessed by the figure. Let us now consider this statement more closely.

In geometry there exists an infinite set of spatial transformations that map space into itself. Each transformation, t, of this set, T, is an operator which assigns to each point, p, its image, $p' = t(p)$, under the transformational mapping. Before going any further it is important to point out that a mathematical transformation is simply a mapping of the elements from one domain into the elements from another domain, or possibly the same one. No assumptions about connected "paths" or "trajectories" are assumed. Only the "starting" and "ending" states are relevant to the transformational mapping.

A certain subset of all such transformations map space into itself such that the entire space is metrically identical before and after the transformation. These are called the "automorphisms" or "similarity transformations." They include operations such as uniformly translating all points in space by a directed distance, rotating them through a given angle about a fixed point, and reflecting them about a single line. There also exist geometrical transformations other than the automorphisms, such as topological deformations, but they do not keep the metric properties of space invariant. It turns out that the automorphisms satisfy the mathematical definition of a *group*. That is, the set of automorphisms: (1) contains a single identity element, i (i.e., no transformation at all), (2) is closed under the composition relation, *, of the group (i.e., if a, $b \in T$, then $a*b \in T$), and (3) is closed under inversion (i.e., if $a \in T$, then $a' \in T$ and $a*a' = i$, where a' is the inverse of a). The composition relation, *, simply represents performing the component transformations sequentially in the specified order.

Global Symmetry.   What all this has to do with symmetry is that it provides an elegant definition for geometrical symmetry: for any pattern, p, the set of automorphisms that leave p unchanged forms a group, S, and this group describes the symmetry of p (Weyl, 1952). In other words, a given transformation, t, is an element in this group if and only if

$$p = t(p), \tag{5.1}$$

where $t(p)$ designates the pattern that results from applying the transformation t to the pattern p. Thus, every figure has a well-defined symmetry group (a subgroup of all automorphisms) for which it is invariant under the transformations of the group and only those transformations. For example, the letter "A" is left unchanged by (1) the identity transformation and (2) "mirror image" reflection about a vertical line through its center. This form of symmetry is usually called "bilateral" or "mirror-image" symmetry and is defined by these two automorphisms and no others. It is the same symmetry possessed by "M," "T," and "W" simply because the same operations (and no others) map these letters into themselves. The symmetry group of the letters "N" and "Z" contains (1) the identity transformation and (2) rotation of 180-degrees about the central point. (Note that central rotation of 180-degrees is always equivalent to reflection through the central point because the "path" of the points undergoing the corresponding real-world motion is not relevant to the mathematical definition of the transformation.) This is sometimes called "centric" symmetry, and it constitutes an example of nonbilateral symmetry. The symmetry group of "X" includes (1) the identity transformation, (2) reflection about a central vertical line, (3) reflection about a central horizontal line, and (4) rotation of 180-degress about the central point. The symmetry group of a perfect circle contains all possible central reflections and rotations, and that of an infinite, homogeneous field (i.e., a Ganzfeld) contains all the automorphisms, including all possible translations and dilations as well as all possible rotations and reflections. Note that translational and dilational symmetries require that patterns extend infinitely in all directions. This is because edges destroy the invariance of any finite pattern over these transformations. (Throughout this chapter we will use the term "dilations" generically to include both radial expansions and contractions.)

Local Symmetry.   The group theoretical analysis given above defines symmetry such that a pattern counts as symmetrical only if the *entire pattern* is exactly the same as itself over a given transformation. We will refer to this condition as *global symmetry*. It is a stringent and seldom achieved requirement. For our purposes, it will be useful to extend the group theoretical analysis somewhat by defining a more restricted notion called *local symmetry*. Local symmetry is, in fact, just like global symmetry except that rather than considering the invariance of the entire pattern over a transformation, we consider that for just a portion of it.

To formalize this notion, we define an operator, *r*, which isolates a local region of a pattern, denoted $r(p)$. This local region is essentially just a subset of the pattern, and there is an infinite number of such local subsets. Now, a pattern is said to have local symmetry over a region, *r*, with respect to a transformation, *t*, if and only if,

$$r(p) = r[t(p)],\qquad\qquad(5.2)$$

where $t(p)$ is just the entire pattern transformed by *t*. One can conceive of the local regional operator as being like a mask—for example, a hole cut in an

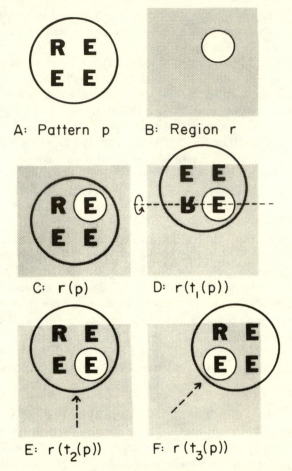

FIG. 5.2. Local symmetries over transformations (t_1, t_2, and t_3) in a region (r) of a pattern (p) with no global symmetries.

opaque surface which covers all but a restricted portion of the pattern behind it. The condition expressed above simply says that a region is locally symmetrical if the given region is invariant over a transformation, even if the rest of the pattern is not.

Let us consider an example. Figure 5.2A shows a pattern composed of four letters which has no global symmetries by the original definition. But if local regions are considered, there are many transformations of the pattern which leave *portions* of it unchanged. These are its local symmetries. For example, consider the region of space depicted in Fig. 5.2B which includes just one of the E's (as shown in Fig. 5.2C). As illustrated in the subsequent drawings, this region is locally symmetrical over reflection about a horizontal line through the center of the E (Fig. 5.2D), over a vertical translation (Fig. 5.2E), and over a diagonal translation (Fig. 5.2F). Similar local symmetries are present in other regions containing Es. In addition, there are also many local symmetries in the homogeneous "background" of this pattern due to the fact that a huge number of transformations will leave such background regions unchanged.

Local symmetries differ from global ones in that they do not constitute a group in the mathematical sense. This is because local symmetries are not closed under inversion or the concatenation operation. That is, if a pattern has local symmetry at a region r under transformations a and b, it is not necessarily the case that it has local symmetry under a' (the inverse of a) nor under $a*b$ (the concatenation of a and b). But the basic notion behind local symmetry is the same as that behind global symmetry. Among other things, local symmetry gives us a common language in which to talk about many different types of pattern regularities, including repeated portions and homogeneous areas.

Relation To Garner's Formulation.   It should be clear that this formulation of symmetry in terms of groups of transformations is closely related to Garner's formulation in terms of R & R subsets. Garner defines the size of the R & R subset as the number of different patterns generated by four rotations and four reflections. Because the transformations in the global symmetry subgroup of a figure are just those transformations that leave the figure invariant, there is a fixed relationship between R & R subset size and the measure of the symmetry subgroup, namely,

$$r = n/s, \tag{5.3}$$

where r is the size of the R & R subset, s is the number of transformations in the symmetry subgroup, and n is the number of transformations used to generate the R & R subset. In the system Garner uses, n is eight because his stimulus set allows only eight possible symmetries. For other types of figures, n could be much larger by including more possible types of symmetry. Otherwise, the basic conceptions of pattern regularity underlying the two formulations are virtually identical. The main difference is whether one focuses on the patterns produced by the transformations (Garner's view) or on the transformations that produce the patterns (the group theoretical view). Another difference is whether the set of transformations is restricted to 90-degree rotations and reflections about horizontal, vertical, and diagonal lines or it includes all automorphisms. There is no reason, of course, why Garner's formulation could not be extended to include any of the automorphisms. A third difference lies in the extension to local symmetries. As we will later demonstrate, this allows the present approach to account for a number of types of pattern structure which Garner's does not. Still, it is clear that Garner's ideas are more closely related to the present approach than are any others. We will now see how these ideas can be applied to construct a theory of perceptual organization.

A TRANSFORMATIONAL THEORY OF
PERCEPTUAL STRUCTURE

With this review as background, I now discuss a framework for a theory of perception which is based on a transformational structure of perceptual analyzers. It seems to be able to account for a wide variety of organizational phenomena with a minimum of assumptions. The reason for this is that it is transparent to just the sort of geometrical transformations an active organism encounters in the environment. It is transparent to these because the analyzing system itself has a similar structure that allows it to "factor out" such transformations in a straightforward manner. The same structure provides a basis for removing redundancies due to pattern symmetries. It is here that the theory makes closest contact with the foregoing discussion of "figural goodness" and the group theoretical treatment of symmetry. The constructs of symmetry and transformation and the relationship between them permeate the entire discussion, however.

Overview

The basic assumption of the theory is that perceptual analysis is carried out in parallel by a multiplicity of *local spatial analyzers* with finite resolution capabilities and a particular sort of transformational structure. This multiplicity is composed of some number of *functional systems,* each of which contains many analyzers computing a single, well-defined function over the restricted spatial region they analyze. Edge-detectors, bar-detectors (Hubel & Wiesel, 1962), directed dipoles (Julesz, 1971), local spatial frequency filters (Campbell & Robson, 1968; De Valois & De Valois, 1980), and the like would each constitute an example of a possible functional system. All spatial analyzers within the same functional system have identical internal structure, but differ in their relationship to the external world and to each other. In particular, they differ with respect to their *position, orientation, sense,* and *resolution,* or some subset of these characteristics. An example would be a collection of two-dimensional edge-detectors of many different resolutions (sizes), in many different positions, with many different orientations of their edges, and including both senses of edge (i.e., both those with the light side on the right of the edge and those with it on the left). For purposes of the following discussion, the specific nature of the function computed by the analyzer is largely irrelevant, as long as it is well-defined with respect to variations in position, orientation, sense, and resolution. Exactly what this means will be discussed more fully later.

The major argument is that the systemic structure implied by these few theoretical statements is sufficient to account for a large number of interesting and important phenomena of perceptual organization, particularly those emphasized by Gestaltists. Perceptual grouping, emergent properties, and pattern goodness can all be understood in terms of the transformational structure of functional systems. In addition, the same structure provides an interesting way to determine various kinds of stimulus equivalence among sets of perceptual objects and to detect motions of rigid objects through a restricted region of space. These issues will be discussed in detail only after the basic assertions of the theory have been discussed more fully.

The Sensory Mosaic

We initially consider a very simple perceptual situation within which to explicate the theory. Consider a two-dimensional perceptual system analyzing a coplanar, monochromatic region of two-dimensional space. Both the perceptual system and the perceptual objects are assumed to be stationary. Later we relax some of these assumptions to consider more interesting perceptual situations such as moving objects, moving perceptual systems, and three-dimensional perception. But for now, these restrictions will simply make it easier to understand the foundations of the theory.

We assume that the input to the system of local analyzers is a fine-grained sensory mosaic of transducers. Their job is essentially to convert continuous information in light into a discrete form usable by later analyses. The only essential properties of this sensory mosaic are (1) that it is discrete, (2) that its spatial resolution is high relative to even the most highly resolved stages of processing that will occur later (but not much higher), and (3) that the intensity resolution (brightness coding) of the elements in the mosaic is at least as high as that required by the later spatial analyzers (but not much higher). In other words, the function of the sensory mosaic is just to transduce spatial structure inherent in light intensity variations without significant loss of information.

The Spatial Analyzers

The transduced output of the sensory mosaic is available as input to the spatial analyzers. These are the backbone of the perceptual system. They compute spatial information by integrating the outputs of the sensory elements according to some finite function over a restricted region of the sensory mosaic. As indicated earlier, the precise nature of this function has little bearing on the present theory beyond the general characteristics outlined below. Further, the way in which the function is computed—its "wiring diagram," if you will—is completely outside the present theory and will not be discussed at all. Thus, for our purposes "spatial analyzer" is a computational abstraction—a "black box" if you will—whose inner workings and physical realization do not concern us. When we discuss "an analyzer," then, we are really talking about a *function* computed over space by a hypothetical device. The device might be a single neural cell, an interconnected set of neurons, or any other biological (or even nonbiological) structure. The idea of an analyzer as a function is developed more fully in a later section.

All spatial analyzers within a single functional system are ''internally'' identical, and they differ only with respect to position, orientation, sense, and resolution. This means that (1) they compute the *same function* over suitably defined (corresponding) regions of space, and (2) they are related to each other by transformations of translation, rotation, reflection, dilation, and their various composites.

Consider the example of a functional system of edge-detectors (à la Hubel & Wiesel, 1962) as illustrated in Fig. 5.3. Spatial analyzer A is an edge detector located in the center of the sensory array with moderate resolution (size) and an orientation of about 45 degrees clockwise from vertical. Analyzer B differs from A only in position relative to the sensory mosaic. In all other respects it is identical to analyzer A and could be generated from it by a pure translation. Analyzer C differs from A in both position and resolution, being just a larger version of the same edge-detector pattern. It is related to analyzer A, therefore, by translation and dilation. Analyzer D differs from A in the orientation of the edge as well as position, and, therefore, it is related to A by rotation and translation. Analyzer E is the same as A except for its sense (and position), being just a reflection of the same edge-detector pattern. In addition to analyzers B through E being transformationally related to analyzer A, they are also transformationally related to each other. In fact, each analyzer is related to every other analyzer within the same functional system by some composite of translation, rotation, reflection, and dilation transformations.

These are but a few examples of the large number of spatial analyzers that constitute the elements within this functional system. As a first approximation, let us suppose that the entire system consists of an orthogonal combination of

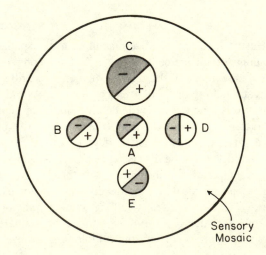

FIG. 5.3. Examples of several ''edge detector'' analyzers within the same functional system which differ with respect to position, orientation, resolution, and sense.

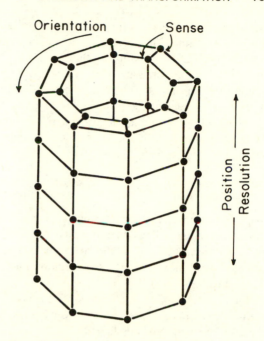

FIG. 5.4. Dimensional structure of
A-space for a functional system.   ANALYZER SPACE

positions, orientations, senses, and resolutions of analyzers. Actually, orthogonal combination poses something of a problem due to the question of whether
the positional representation is in terms of absolute distance on the sensory
surface or in terms of relative distance with respect to the analyzers' spatial
scope. If one postulates a strictly orthogonal structure using absolute distance,
then the high resolution analyzers will be widely spaced relative to their spatial
scope and the low resolution analyzers will be narrowly spaced relative to theirs.
The other possibility, of course, is to postulate that the spacing is constant
relative to the spatial resolution of the analyzer. In this case there will be many
high resolution analyzers whose receptive fields overlap with that of a single, low
resolution analyzer. Note that the latter scheme would require far more high
resolution analyzers than low ones unless it is also postulated that the high
resolution analyzers are restricted to a small central portion of the visual field.

One can conceive of a functional system of analyzers as a five-dimensional
spatial structure within which each analyzer corresponds to a point within this
space. We will call this the "analyzer space" or "A-space" of a functional
system. Its dimensions correspond to X-position, Y-position, orientation, sense,
and resolution. The structure is analogous to a two-sided cylindrical manifold
embedded within a six-dimensional space, where orientation is the cyclic (circular) dimension and sense is the binary (two-sided) dimension. But whereas such a

surface is continuous and infinite, the system of spatial analyzers is necessarily discrete and finite. Therefore, it is more appropriate to conceive of the system as a lattice structure approximating this surface as depicted in Fig. 5.4. Each node corresponds to a spatial analyzer and each arc to a minimal transformation of a single type: translation, rotation, reflection, or dilation. These minimal transformations relate each analyzer directly to its immediate neighbors and indirectly to all other analyzers within the system. (Note that the vertical dimension of the cylinder simultaneously stands for three independent dimensions: x-position, y-position, and resolution.)

Transformational Structure Among Analyzers

We have supposed that the perceptual system consists of one or more functional systems containing local analyzers that are equivalent except for their position, orientation, sense, and resolution (or some subset of these) relative to the sensory mosaic. Let us now define this assumption more precisely and explore some of its implications.

First, let us suppose that each spatial analyzer in the system computes some well-defined, real-valued function over the transducers of the two-dimensional mosaic. The output of this function for a given pattern can be conceived as the degree to which the pattern ''has the feature'' or ''fits the function'' computed by the analyzer, regardless of the specific nature of that feature or function. In other words, we suppose that the behavior of a spatial analyzer can be described by a single valued, numerical function. The value of this function necessarily varies over time, but we are primarily concerned with its asymptotic, steady-state value.

For each possible pattern in the external world, then, each analyzer has some corresponding output. Let us denote all possible patterns as an infinite set, P, and all possible output values for an analyzer as a discrete, ordered set, V. Then the analyzers in the system can be defined as a finite set of functions, A, each of which maps patterns into output values in a many-to-one fashion, denoted $a(p) = v$. The claim, then, is that the computational characteristics of each analyzer are completely specified by its input-output function in response to all possible patterns. Whereas this is obviously not a feasible way to define an analyzer in practice, it serves well enough as a formalization of a theoretical ideal.

We can now define the relationship between any two analyzers in terms of the equivalence of their outputs to the set of all possible patterns. There are two types of equivalence which will concern us: complete equivalence and transformational equivalence. Two analyzers are said to be *completely equivalent* if they have the same (i.e., unmeasurably different) output for all patterns. That is, two analyzers, a_i and a_j, are completely equivalent if and only if,

$$a_i(p) = a_j(p), \tag{5.4}$$

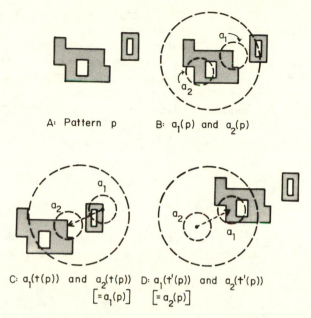

A: Pattern p   B: $a_1(p)$ and $a_2(p)$

C: $a_1(t(p))$ and $a_2(t(p))$ D: $a_1(t'(p))$ and $a_2(t'(p))$
   $[=a_1(p)]$ $[=a_2(p)]$

FIG. 5.5.   Illustration of transformational equivalence for two analyzers (a_1 and a_2) over transformations (t and t') for an arbitrary pattern (p).

for all patterns, p, in P. Given this relation, we can partition the set of all analyzers into equivalence classes of analyzers, each of which has distinguishably different input-output functions. For each such class there will be some number of elementary analyzers within it, not necessarily the same number for all such equivalence classes.

Pairs of analyzers are called *transformationally equivalent* if their input-output functions can be made to coincide after applying a given geometrical transformation to the input patterns of one of them. For example, consider the (arbitrary) pattern shown in Fig. 5.5A and the two analyzers (such as two bar detectors) shown in Fig. 5.5B which differ only in their position relative to the sensory mosaic. The output of the first analyzer to the pattern will be the same as the output of the second if the input pattern is translated by the appropriate distance and direction before being analyzed by the second analyzer (see Fig. 5.5C). It is equally true that the output of the two analyzers will be the same if the input pattern to the first analyzer is translated in the inverse fashion before being analyzed (see Fig. 5.5D).

More formally, we say that analyzers a_i and a_j are transformationally equivalent if and only if,

$$a_i(p) = a_j[t(p)] \text{ and } a_i[t'(p)] = a_j(p), \qquad (5.5)$$

for all patterns, p, in P, where t is the transformation under which a_j is equivalent to a_i and t' (its inverse) is the transformation under which a_i is equivalent to a_j. In general, we will say that one analyzer is "t-related" to another if Eq. 5.5 is satisfied. It should be clear from the foregoing that each analyzer within a functional system will be either completely or transformationally equivalent to every other one. Sometimes the transformational relation will be a "simple" one, such as a pure rotation, and sometimes it will be composite, such as a rotation followed by a dilation and a translation. These transformational relationships are implicit in the structure of A-space as described above.

Functional Systems

Having defined such relations among analyzers, we can partition the system into various equivalence classes according to different types of transformational equivalence. What we have called "functional systems" are, formally speaking, the partitions of the set of all analyzers according to a particular set of transformations: namely, translations, rotations, reflections, and dilations. These transformations constitute a group structure in the mathematical sense (see above). In particular, it is the group of similarity transformations in Euclidean geometry, those which form the basis of "similar" figures about which we all learned in high school geometry. Thus, two analyzers are members of the same functional system if and only if they are computationally equivalent by a similarity transformation of the input pattern.

Note that we have now defined a functional system solely on the basis of its input-output characteristics. The previous examples using edge detectors and so forth were merely illustrations to ground the concepts in concrete examples. Actually, a functional system is a *class* of analyzer systems which is defined by a certain transformational structure. The dependencies between the analyzers themselves and the structure of the system they comprise will be discussed shortly.

Each functional system can be further divided according to various subgroups of transformations. For example, one could partition the set of analyzers into those that are equivalent by rotations alone (differing by just transformations of orientation about a point) or by translations alone (differing by just transformations of position), and so forth. Note that each such partitioning corresponds to dividing the lattice structure described earlier into transformationally equivalent classes of analyzers. For example, if the system is partitioned according to, say, dilationally equivalent analyzers (those that are equivalent except for their resolution), the cylindrical lattice would be divided into a collection of simply ordered, noncyclic graphs corresponding to vertical strips in Fig. 5.4. If it is partitioned according to rotational equivalence, the lattice would be divided into a set of simply ordered cyclic graphs corresponding to the circular sections in the horizontal depth plane of Fig. 5.4.

Such partitions of the set of analyzers correspond to the notion of psychophysical channels. For example, within a dimension such as orientation, there are some number of equivalence classes, each of which corresponds to an orientation channel. Thus, we can think of the present system as the orthogonal combination of orientational, positional, reflectional, and resolutional channels. Across all dimensions, then, a "single channel" would correspond to the equivalence class of analyzers which belong to the same equivalence class for every dimension, that is, to a single node within the analyzer space (which may actually represent a large number of completely equivalent, individual analyzer units). Note also that one can define a relation of transformational distance between any pair of analyzers for any given dimension. The notion of partitioning the set of analyzers in such a fashion and relating them according to their transformational distance will become relevant when we consider modelling attentional processes in perception.

The total system of spatial analyzers is composed of some, presumably small, number of functional systems. Each of these has a transformational structure like that described above except that not all transformational dimensions will necessarily be present for each system. As we see later, the dimensions of a given functional system depend on the internal symmetries of its component analyzer functions. But it is important to remember that there may well be more than one such functional system. This means that the total system is actually a structure of such functional systems. At the present time there is only a little that can be said about the relations among different functional systems. In the following discussion we consider some constraints on their relationships, and later we discuss how higher-order systems can be constructed by comparing the outputs of the functional systems described above.

Systemic Structure And Analyzer Symmetry

We now consider the internal structure of individual spatial analyzers and its relationship to the structure of the functional system as a whole. I have stated several times that the current theory is not concerned with the nature of the particular analyzers which comprise it. We now examine the sense in which this is true. In particular, we want to know what constraints are placed on the nature of the spatial function computed by analyzers in specifying a particular structure for its functional system as a whole. Conversely, we want to know what constraints are placed on the structure of the system as a whole by the internal structure of the analyzer functions which comprise it. Clearly, there must be some significant relationships between the structure of the system at the micro and macro levels.

It should be evident that not all possible spatial analyzers will have an internal structure which is compatible with the set of transformational relationships we have discussed. For example, a classical center-surround receptive field would not have the full transformational structure hypothesized for A-space because many of the elements would be redundant. Pairs of analyzers that are rotationally equivalent would, in fact, be completely equivalent due to their rotational symmetry. Because they are also reflectionally symmetrical, pairs which differ only in sense would also be completely equivalent. This means that center-surround analyzers could not support the dimensions of orientation and sense, and their A-space would be collapsed over these dimensions. Similarly, a system of centered bar-detectors would not support the entire structure of A-space because any pair of analyzers related by 180-degree rotations or reflections about the long or short axis will also be completely equivalent.

Now we see that the relationship between the internal structure of analyzers and the structure of the system as a whole lies in the relationship between the symmetries of the spatial function and the transformational structure of A-space. Formally, we say that an analyzer function, a_i, is *symmetrical* over a transformation, t, if and only if

$$a_i (p) = a_i [t(p)], \tag{5.6}$$

for all patterns, p, in P. Intuitively, this means that a function is symmetrical if applying it to a pattern *always* gives the same result as applying it to that same pattern after it has been transformed by t, regardless of the nature of the pattern. For example, a concentric, circular, center-surround function always gives the same output to a pattern and any rotation of that pattern about the point in the center of its receptive field.

The net result of symmetry in an analyzer function is that the A-space is folded onto itself according to precisely the set of transformations which comprise its symmetry subgroup. In other words, the fact that two analyzers are completely equivalent rather than merely transformationally equivalent means that they will map into the same node of A-space rather than different ones. Therefore, an analyzer function which has no symmetries would support the "complete" transformational structure described earlier, including translations, rotations, dilations, and reflections. An analyzer function that possesses any type of symmetry can support only a "reduced" dimensional structure for the system as a whole. In this way, the internal structure of the analyzer determines the structure of the system as a whole.

For similar reasons, one can specify certain constraints on the internal structure of the individual analyzer functions given a hypothetical structure for the whole system. The constraint is simply that the spatial function computed by the analyzers can *not* be identical to itself (symmetrical) over any transformation postulated to exist within the functional system as a whole. The internal structure of the analyzer functions is not completely determined, of course, because there is an infinite number of different functions that have the same symmetry group.

Given the current hypothesis about the structure of A-space, it is necessary that the internal structure of the analyzers be asymmetrical with respect to translations, rotations, dilations, and reflections. If there is a single functional system, then, it must be composed of asymmetrical analyzer functions. If there were more than one type of analyzer (i.e., more than one functional system), however, the asymmetries could be distributed over a number of different functional systems. In other words, within a total system containing more than one functional system, it is possible for some of them to have, say, rotational symmetry, but only if there are others that are not rotationally symmetrical. This is because if *all* the functional systems were rotationally symmetrical, the total system could not include the orientational dimension postulated to exist somewhere within it.

This is the sense in which it is true that the present theory of systemic structure is independent of assumptions about the internal structure of its analyzers. Given the weak constraints placed by the asymmetry condition, it is clear that whatever results are derived from the theory are due mainly to the systemic structure.

From this perspective, it is interesting to speculate that the precise internal structure of the analyzers themselves may be determined by optimizing the asymmetries they must have. In other words, the spatial functions they compute may be "maximally" asymmetrical with respect to position, orientation, resolution, and sense. This intriguing notion is consistent with the Gestalt conjecture that the properties of parts of systems are determined by their relation to the whole.

Higher-Order Analyzers

The output of the entire system discussed thus far constitutes a representation of the static, two-dimensional, spatial distribution of light over the sensory mosaic. This representation has many desirable properties—as is shortly argued in some detail—but many of them are embedded in the implicit *relations* among these outputs rather than in the individual outputs themselves. The job of extracting these relations is performed by the *higher-order analyzers*. The *second-order analyzers* take the outputs of two (or more) simple, first-order analyzers as inputs, compare them, and output values determined by the relationship between them. It is also suggested that there exist *third-order analyzers* that perform a similar function by comparing the outputs of second-order analyzers. Such higher-order analyzers will turn out to be important for determining perceptual groupings, coding redundancies in figures, and extracting depth information from binocular disparity and motion parallax.

The real role played by these higher-order elements is to extract information about *transformational invariances*. This follows directly from the fact that the first-order units are defined to be transformationally equivalent to each other. Any element whose output is a function of the output similarity of two such related units is, in effect, computing the extent to which some portion of the stimulus is invariant over the transformation that relates the two input units. Such analyzers are potentially related to Gibson's (1966) ideas of extracting invariances and to Goldmeier's (1972) notion of "singularities."

Clearly the higher-order analyzers cannot compare all possible pairs of lower-order analyzers. This would produce a combinatorial explosion. Rather, we assume that only *local* comparisions are made by higher-order analyzers. That is, only relations between analyzers nearby in A-space will be computed, where "nearby" is intentionally somewhat vague. The "nearness" of two analyzers in A-space is defined in terms of transformational distance: the number and type of minimal transformations that separate them within the lattice structure of their functional system (see Fig. 5.4). (Nearness within A-space should not be confused with nearness of receptive fields on the sensory mosaic. There are relationships between the two concepts, but they are not simple.) The proposal that only "nearby" comparisons are made amounts to assuming that there is a low upper limit on the transformational distance between first-order elements which affect a second-order element. Whether these comparisons are made across dimensions or only within them is an open and interesting question. In the extreme, only direct (nearest) neighbors might be compared, effectively computing the minimal transformations of the system. Merely local comparisons will be sufficient for most purposes because significant events in the world tend to be continuous in both space and time. Such continuity means that local comparisons will be able to pick up the relevant information except under quite unusual circumstances (such as in a psychological experiment).

There are many specific ways in which measures of transformational invariance might be computed on the basis of first-order outputs. Correlations and ratios are two obvious possibilities, both of which are probably useful for specific purposes. Rather than specify exactly how the computation is performed, we follow our previous procedure by defining the transformational relations of the second-order system independently of the particular function that might be computed.

Let us assume that (1) the second-order analyzers take the outputs of first-order analyzers as inputs, (2) they compute some single valued function of these inputs which reflects their sameness or difference, and (3) the inputs may be first-order outputs whose temporal difference is zero (simultaneous) or nonzero (sequential). From this type of comparison, the structure of the second-order system emerges as computing transformational invariance over both space and time. The implications of this for the nature of the information second-order analyzers can compute is discussed shortly.

Just as we were able to describe the structure of A-space for a first-order functional system, so too can we describe the structure of A-space for a second-order functional system derived from a first-order one. The second-order space has dimensions similar to those of the first-order space except that it includes time-dependent and order-dependent transformational relations. In particular, the second-order space differs from the first-order space in that (1) the dimensions

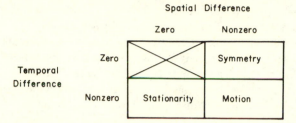

FIG. 5.6.   Types of information computable by second-order analyzers given the orthogonal combination of temporal and spatial differences in their first-order inputs.

are *motions* or, more accurately, *displacements* (translations, rotations, dilations, and reflections) rather than static spatial properties (position, orientation, resolution, and sense, respectively) and (2) these motional dimensions are combined orthogonally with two others, a *rate* or *velocity* dimension (depending on the time lag between the first-order inputs) and a polar *directional* dimension (such as up/down, left/right, clockwise/counterclockwise, and larger/smaller for y-translation, x-translation, rotation, and dilation, respectively). For example, a particular second-order analyzer might be sensitive to small, vertical bars moving rightward at a given rate in one portion of the visual field. Another second-order analyzer might be sensitive to large, horizontal bars rotating clockwise to vertical at a given rate in some other portion of the visual field.

An interesting relationship emerges from the proposed structure for the second-order system. It shows that motion, symmetry, onset, offset, and stationarity information can all be computed by second-order analyzers, depending only on the transformational relationships between the two first-order analyzers whose outputs are being compared. We have supposed that the first-order analyzers compute some function of events over space. Second-order analyzers compare results over some time lag from first-order analyzers whose dimensional distance is not too great. Thus, for each dimension, the two first-order analyzers either have the same value (a transformational distance of zero) or different values (a nonzero distance). Figure 5.6 presents the four possible cases that result from orthogonally combining zero and nonzero distances in the temporal and spatial dimensions. These cases are as follows.

1. If there is no difference between the two first-order analyzers in either the temporal or the spatial dimension, there is no information because there is, by definition, *always* complete invariance between the output of an analyzer and itself at the same time. Presumably this case is not represented in the second-order system because it is useless.

2. If there is no difference between the two first-order analyzers in the temporal dimension but some nonzero difference in the spatial dimension, information about spatial symmetry can be computed. This follows directly from the

definition of symmetry (Eqs. 5.1 and 5.2) in that a pattern has symmetry over a transformation if it is invariant over that transformation. Thus, if a pattern has a symmetry, then the analyzers related by that transformation will have the same output, and any second-order analyzer which compares them will respond to the symmetry of the pattern. The outputs of such analyzers, then, reflect the degree to which local symmetries (as defined earlier) are present in the pattern. Each of the different sorts of symmetry discussed above can be computed by such comparisons.

3. If the two first-order analyzers differ in their temporal properties but not their spatial properties, information about stationarity can be computed. For example, the output of such analyzers could signal changing versus steady-state conditions of the stimulus event at a given position, orientation, resolution, and sense.

4. Finally, if the two first-order analyzers differ in both temporal and spatial properties, information about motion can be computed. Such analyzers are capable of representing translations, rotations, dilations, and reflections. It seems doubtful that reflections are actually computed, however, because they do not occur in the real world. This is because reflections are by nature discrete, discontinuous transformations whereas real motions are continuous. In fact, the only cases of "continuous" reflection transformations ever encountered are those in which it is approximated by rotation in a higher dimensional space. For example, a two dimensional figure can be "reflected" by rotating it about the axis of reflection through the third spatial dimension, but only if its "front" side is identical to its "back" side. Because true, discrete reflections do not occur in the world, it would make sense if they were not represented in the motional system.

The foregoing analysis simply points out the structural relationship among symmetry, motion, and stationarity. It is a logical relationship in the nature of stimulus information which becomes evident in the context of the present hypothesis concerning the structure of the second-order analyzer space. The relationship among these seemingly disparate sorts of information arises naturally within the proposed second-order system.

It is interesting to speculate that there might be a third-order space of analyzers whose derivation from the second-order space parallels that of the second-order space from the first-order one. The development of this idea is too complex to be considered in detail here, but a few things about it should be mentioned. First, if some third-order analyzers compare motion-sensitive, second-order analyzers at the same time in nearby regions of the second-order space, these analyzers would respond to *local motional symmetries*. That is, they would compute invariance of motions. This would plainly be useful for extracting depth information from relative motion parallax (see below). It could also be used to compute motion gradients of the general type discussed by Gibson (1966). If the second-order units differed in rate and time, but not in type of motion, their third-order comparison would be sensitive to *accelerations*. Other sorts of third-order information are undoubtedly useful, but we will not pursue them further here. For present purposes, the foregoing discussion suffices.

RELATION TO PERCEPTUAL PHENOMENA

The theory outlined in the previous section is rich in structure of the sort which is useful for performing perceptual analyses. In the following discussion we consider some of the implications of this structure. It suggests explanations for a number of well-known phenomena simply and parsimoniously. It also provides a suitable framework for computing various other sorts of perceptually useful information. The primary emphasis is on the sort of organizational effects studied extensively by Gestaltists: good form, laws of grouping, emergent features, apparent motion, constancy, and depth perception. Figural goodness is the only domain in which the theory has been developed sufficiently to allow a detailed analysis. For the other topics I merely sketch the way in which they might be handled within the theoretical framework developed above. It is anticipated that the formal theory can be developed to give rigorous accounts of these other phenomena in the future. The following discussion is presented as a preliminary report of work in progress and should be viewed as such.

Pattern Goodness

As mentioned in the introduction, one of the hallmarks of the Gestalt approach to perception was the importance of ''good form'' in visual patterns. Good patterns were those that seemed to be symmetrical, regular, and simple according to introspective intuitions, although the precise properties of such patterns were never explicitly spelled out. The present theory provides a perceptual structure that accounts for pattern goodness in a simple and transparent fashion. The notions are closely allied with Garner's (1974) account in terms of rotation and reflection subsets and with the group theoretical formulation described earlier (Weyl, 1952). They also bear close relationships to Attneave's (1954) application of information theory to perception and to Leeuwenberg's (1971) coding theory. It is perhaps worth restating that the present arguments rely only on the overall structure of functional systems as described above and do not require any assumptions about the internal structure of the component analyzers beyond the symmetry constraints already mentioned.

Global Symmetries.   Consider any arbitrary input pattern presented to the system. We have postulated that it is simultaneously analyzed by many different elements that are the same except for their positions, orientations, senses, and resolutions relative to external space. This state of affairs can be thought of in two different but logically equivalent ways. First, one can think in terms of the external (or retinal) frame of reference. Here we conceive of a single pattern (or many identical patterns) being analyzed by many different analytic functions that are transformationally related to each other. Without specifying anything about the computational function itself, we know that the output of any two such analyzers *must* be the same if (1) their input patterns are identical and (2) the function being computed is the same for both analyzers. It is easy to see that if the pair of analyzers are themselves identical over some transformation, then their outputs must be the same for any pattern whatsoever. In fact, such a pair of analyzers would be classified as completely equivalent.

The second and more interesting way in which to conceive of this situation is in terms of the internal frames of reference provided by the spatial analyzers themselves. It reverses the previous conception in that now we think of *identical analyzers* (or even a single analyzer) processing *many different patterns* that are transformationally related to each other. The idea here is to put oneself in the point of view of the analyzers so that positions, directions, distances, and senses are all defined relative to the spatial function being computed rather than relative to the external world. This situation is illustrated in Fig. 5.7. The ''external frames'' show the patterns and analyzers from the retinal point of view. The ''internal frames'' show the same pattern from the points of view intrinsic to each analyzer. These are defined as though the center of the visual field, its directions (up, down, left, right), and its unit of distance are all specified separately for each analyzer. The result is that the world ''looks different'' within each analyzer's frame of reference. This is in contrast to the external frame of reference in which the pattern looks the same and the analyzers look different.

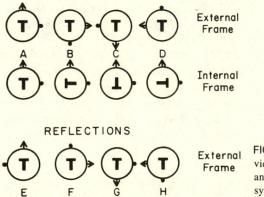

FIG. 5.7. External and internal views of a T-shaped pattern for eight analyzers within the same functional system, related by rotations and reflections. (Arrows indicate the orientation of analyzers and dots indicate their sense.)

Once again, the output of two analyzers must be the same if (1) the input patterns are the same for both and (2) the function being computed is the same for both. Because we know that the latter is true for all analyzers within a functional system (given our current, analyzer-based frame of reference), then output equivalence depends only on the structure of the input pattern. In particular, if applying a given similarity transformation to the pattern results in *the same pattern*, then all pairs of analyzers related by that transformation will necessarily produce the same output. In other words, if the pattern is symmetrical over some transformation postulated to exist in A-space, then the analyzers related by that transformation must produce the same result for that pattern.

The formal definition of functional systems makes this fact abundantly clear. Recall that two analyzers are in the same functional system if and only if,

$$a_i(p) = a_j[t(p)] \text{ and } a_i[t'(p)] = a_j(p), \tag{5.7}$$

where t is any similarity transformation and t' is its inverse. We now add the formal condition for global symmetry (see Eq. 5.1):

$$p = t(p) \text{ and } p = t'(p), \tag{5.8}$$

to reflect the fact that the given pattern, p, is invariant under the same transformations, t and its inverse t', which relate the two analyzers. By substitution of Eq. 5.8 in Eq. 5.7 we deduce that,

$$a_i(p) = a_j(p), \tag{5.9}$$

for pattern p. Clearly this result generalizes for these two analyzers to *all* patterns satisfying the condition of transformational invariance under t. It also generalizes to all pairs of transformationally related analyzers (i.e., all members of a functional system) for patterns that are invariant over the transformation that relates the two analyzers.

The set of patterns that have this structure are the symmetric figures in the expanded group theoretical sense defined earlier. Standard bilateral symmetry (invariance over reflections about a line) is the most obvious case. Because such figures are equivalent to their reflections, the output of any analyzer will be the same as that of another one related to it by reflection in that same line. Note that this is not restricted to analyzer pairs differing only in sense, but includes those that differ in position and orientation as well, as long as they are related by reflection in the line about which the pattern is symmetrical. Thus, the structural regularity of the input figure is mirrored in the output redundancy of the system as a whole. Additional lines of symmetry in the pattern produce further redundancies in the output of the system.

Precisely the same analysis holds for patterns with other sorts of symmetry. Given a figure that is invariant over rotations of n degrees about a point, the output of any analyzer will be the same as that of another related to it by the same rotation. A pattern that is invariant over a translation or a dilation will likewise produce equivalent results for analyzers related by the same transformation, at least in theory. (Translational and dilational symmetries are realized only in infinite patterns, but as we have already seen, they have finite, local counterparts.) In fact, the transformations in the symmetry subgroup of the pattern divide the system of analyzers into some number of equivalence classes within each of which all analyzers have the same output.

Local Symmetries.   The foregoing analysis requires that the symmetries be global—that is, the pattern be everywhere the same before and after the transformation. Local symmetries (in the sense defined earlier) also produce redundancies in the output of the analyzer system, however, without making such a demanding assumption. These redundancies will also contribute to the perceived goodness of figure, and they are just the sort of regularities which Attneave and Leeuwenberg have discussed. Note that they are not covered by Garner's formulation because R & R subsets are equivalent to the analysis of global symmetries given above.

To prove the equivalence of outputs for analyzer pairs given a locally symmetrical pattern we must complicate the foregoing analysis somewhat. First, recall that two analyzers, a_i and a_j, in the same functional system are transformationally related by t (and its inverse, t') if and only if

$$a_i(p) = a_j[t(p)] \text{ and } a_j(p) = a_i[t'(p)], \tag{5.10}$$

for all possible patterns. To make the transition between global and local symmetries, we now define for each analyzer a corresponding *local region* of space which exactly covers the spatial scope of the analyzer. Intuitively, this region is just the smallest region for which the analyzer's output is the same as for the whole pattern across all possible patterns. In other words, we establish a correspondence between analyzers and the local regional operators on patterns discussed earlier so that the computation performed by the analyzer spans exactly the local region of the operator. More formally, the local region, r_i, of an analyzer, a_i, is the smallest region for which

$$a_i(p) = a_i[r_i(p)], \tag{5.11}$$

for all possible patterns. Naturally, there will also be a local region, r_j, for the other analyzer of our hypothetical pair, a_j. (Note that whereas there will be just one local region for each analyzer, there will be many local operators that have no corresponding analyzer.) To these definitions we now add the condition that a given pattern, p, has local symmetry at r_j under the transformation t. This means that

$$r_j(p) = r_j[t(p)]. \tag{5.12}$$

Now, by substitution in Eq. 5.10 we show that,

$$a_i(p) = a_j[t(p)] = a_j(r_j[t(p)]) = a_j[r_j(p)] = a_j(p), \tag{5.13}$$

which is the desired result. Therefore, the outputs of a_i and a_j to a pattern p with local symmetry at r_i and r_j will necessarily be equal to each other if and only if the transformations relating them are the same as the transformations of the local symmetry in those regions.

The net result of our analysis thus far is that the output of the A-space will be systematically redundant for patterns that have symmetry. This is categorically true for patterns with global symmetry. For local symmetry, however, it is only true if (1) the region over which the pattern is locally symmetric happens to be one for which there exists a corresponding analyzer and (2) there exists another analyzer related to the first one by the transformation under which the pattern is locally symmetric. Many such local symmetries will be due to homogeneous regions of brightness, either in the ground or in the figure or both. Such regions will produce local translational, dilational, rotational, and reflectional symmetries, because they are, in effect, "local Ganzfelds." Clearly, such regional homogeneities will drastically increase the redundancy of the whole system's output relative to, say, a random-dot pattern. In fact, these local symmetries are just the sort of structure which underlies Attneave's (1954) "guessing game" analysis of pattern redundancy. The present formulation is preferable because it is far more general and it relates such pattern structure to many other types within a single theoretical framework.

Portions of patterns which are rotationally or reflectionally symmetrical also have local symmetries, as do patterns that include repetitions of elements. The latter contain local translational symmetries of the type shown in Fig. 5.2. Because finite patterns cannot have global translational symmetry, this is the only form one finds in the real world. Lastly, there are local forms of dilational symmetry. These are patterns that have regions that do not vary, at least locally, as a function of diameter outwards from the center. The pinwheel pattern shown in Fig. 5.8A is one example. Naturally, transformations can be combined to form local symmetries of different sorts. For example, Fig. 5.8B shows a spiral pattern which has a combination of rotational and dilational local symmetries. In fact, local symmetries are all that ever really exist anyway. Global symmetry is a convenient mathematical fiction that holds only for idealized patterns conjured up by geometers for simplicity and elegance.

Low Resolution Symmetry. Local symmetry refers to pattern structure in which a local region of the pattern is symmetrical without the entire pattern being

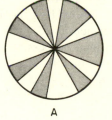

FIG. 5.8. Two further types of local symmetry: transformational invariance for regions over dilations (A) and over the concatenation of rotations and dilations (B).

A   B

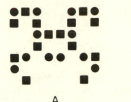
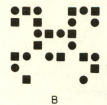

A   B

FIG. 5.9. Low-resolution symmetry: configurations that are completely symmetrical (A) and symmetrical only at a low level of resolution (B).

so. In the system described earlier, this corresponds to its response to symmetry at a high level of resolution independently of asymmetries at a lower level of resolution. Because the system is assumed to be capable of analyzing patterns at low resolutions as well, one wonders whether there should not also be cases of perceived symmetry in which the low resolution analyzers respond to the (approximate) symmetry of the whole pattern even when the high resolution analyzers do not.

One way to realize such conditions is by constructing configurations of elements so that the global, configural structure can be manipulated independently of local, element structure. Figure 5.9 shows two configurations of elements, only one of which (A) is actually symmetrical by reflection about a vertical line. The second figure (B) has what we will call *low resolution symmetry*. Its overall, configural structure is symmetrical in that for each element (square or circle) on one side there is a corresponding element on the other side related by reflection in the vertical line. But the shapes of the corresponding elements are not identical; squares map into circles and circles into squares. Figure 5.9A is essentially the same as B except that the mapping of elements is also symmetrical.

The fact that Figs. 5.9A and 5.9B are perceived to be so similar and that both are perceived to be symmetrical indicates that there is a level of perceptual analysis which is insensitive to the discrepancies between squares and circles. Within the present framework, this level is a low-resolution analysis of the overall spatial structure. We pursue this idea in more detail in the section concerning holism and emergent properties.

Laws Of Grouping

One of Gestalt psychology's most notable and enduring achievements was the discovery and formulation of the "laws of perceptual organization" (Wertheimer, 1923). These laws are essentially a list of stimulus factors that affect the tendency of geometrical elements to be phenomenally grouped together. The impact of each factor was demonstrated under conditions in which the other factors were held constant as much as possible. The major difficulties with the Gestalt approach to such grouping effects are (1) that their laws are purely qualitative and (2) that they never suggested ways in which the different factors could be integrated. For this reason the effects of multiple factors could never be formulated precisely. One would like some overall notion of what is going on in grouping such that all of the factors can be related within some single dimension of "relatedness" of pattern elements.

Within the present theory the natural way to model grouping phenomena is in terms of interdependence: two pattern elements are perceptually related to the extent that they affect the same analyzers. The idea is that for any two pattern elements in a configuration we can, at least in theory, partition the set of all analyzers into four classes: those whose output is determined by (1) neither element, (2) one element alone, (3) the other element alone, and (4) both elements together. It is the relationship between the last set (4) and the previous two sets (2 and 3) which determines the "relative relatedness" of the pair of elements. Intuitively, this relation reflects the extent to which the two pattern elements *interact* during perceptual analysis. Of course, there are gradations of the extent to which both elements determine the output of an analyzer, and this must eventually be considered. But as a first approximation the principle of interactiveness is clear. In fact, it is quite similar to the basic concept of a "Gestalt" (see Köhler, 1920): a system has important holistic characteristics (i.e., forms a "Gestalt") to the extent that its parts are strongly interacting rather than independent.

The rationale for this approach concerns selective attention to the elements within the whole pattern. Grouping is just the other side of the attentional coin from selectivity: if one element cannot be selected out from another, then they are, in effect, "grouped" together to some extent. Thus, if one attempts to attend to one element to the exclusion of another, attention must be selectively directed to those analyzers which are affected only by that element. Exactly how this might be accomplished is not a trivial problem, but it is clear that increasing the relative number of analyzers affected by both components will make the task more difficult. There is an important sense, then, in which the proposal is that "relatedness" of portions of the scene correspond to their "attendability" or "selectability" during processing. The basic proposition is that the structure of the analyzer system strongly determines the ease with which various elements can be selectively attended and that this determines perceived organization in the stimulus.

Both first-order and higher-order analyzers must be considered. In general, a first order analyzer will be affected by more than one element of the spatial pattern if (1) portions of both fall within its spatial scope (i.e., its receptive field on the sensory surface) and (2) they both contain pattern structure to which it is sensitive. It is certainly possible that the first condition might be satisfied without the second one being so. In this case the elements would not interact within that analyzer. For the first-order analyzers, then, the key issue is the "tuning" of the individual analyzer functions for positions, orientations, and sizes.

Second-order analyzers are particularly important for the interaction of pattern elements because they are sensitive to aspects of patterns which are analyzed by independent first-order analyzers. In general, the second-order analyzers will be affected by more than one element of the pattern if (1) they affect independent analyzers whose outputs to them are highly similar and (2) these analyzers are "close enough" in transformational distance within the A-space to be integrated by some second-order analyzer. (Recall that proximity in A-space is not necessarily the same as proximity on the sensory surface.) For dynamic events the same general approach is applicable except that motion analysis first occurs in the second order analyzers. Therefore, these second-order analyzers for motion correspond to the first-order analyzers for static, spatial information and third-order analyzers correspond to the second-order analyzers in terms of responding to similarities of motion.

Proximity.   Spatial proximity is perhaps the most basic organizational factor: elements tend to be grouped together to the extent that they are close together in space (Wertheimer, 1923). This factor arises quite naturally in the present system from the fact that the spatial analyzers vary in position and resolution. Consider three dots that are presented such that two of them, A and B, are closer together than either is to the third dot, C. The A–B pair will fall within the spatial scope of more low resolution analyzers than either the A–C or B–C pairs simply because the former are closer together. Another way of saying the same thing is that the resolution at which the closer dots can be distinguished is higher than that at which the other pairs can be. Clearly the grouping of A and B will be strengthened either by moving them closer together or by moving C further from both A and B. Both will have the effect of increasing the number of analyzers within which A and B interact relative to the number within which A and C or B and C interact. Conversely, the grouping of A and B will be weakened by moving A and B further from each other or by moving C closer to either one of them. These will decrease the relatedness of A and B relative to A and C or B and C (or both) by decreasing the number of analyzers responding to both A and B relative to the number responding to A and C or B and C. These are essential properties of the factor of proximity in perceptual grouping. They are reflected in the present theory quite simply through the dimensions of position and resolution within the analyzer system.

Similarity.   The factor of similarity actually covers a wide range of disparate variables: color, orientation, shape, size, and the like. Simply put, the law of similarity states that, all else being equal, the more similar a pair of elements along these dimensions, the greater the probability that they will be phenomenally grouped together.

The present account of such effects is basically the same as for the law of proximity except that dimensions other than position and resolution are involved. For example, suppose two lines in a configuration have the same orientation whereas a third has a different orientation. To the extent that these different orientations affect the spatial analyzers differentially, the same-orientation pair will affect more analyzers jointly than the different-orientation pair. Whether orientational grouping would dominate proximity grouping is clearly a matter of the relative magnitude of each sort of relatedness. If the orientational difference is small and the positional difference is large, then proximity should dominate. The opposite situation should produce the opposite result.

Similar accounts can be given for the effects of similarity along the other dimensions—color, size, and shape—although we have not explicitly considered color information in the current theory. Similarity of elements along such dimensions will tend to produce interactions within analyzers at both the first- and second-order levels. The shape factor is less clear than the others because it presumably requires a complex analysis including the conjunction of many different dimensions. In point of fact, the conditions under which it is a strong perceptual organizer are not as clear as for the others. For example, Beck (1966) has shown quite convincingly that orientation (upright versus tilted Ts) is a more powerful organizer than shape (upright Ts versis upright Ls), at least for these two shapes and when there are a large number of them in the visual field. In a similar vein, Julesz (1971) has presented extensive evidence that random-dot textures are organized spontaneously in the presence of differences in density, size, and orientation of dots (their first- and second-order statistics) but not for differences in a number of other shape-related aspects.

Common Fate.   Wertheimer (1923) noted that when elements within the visual field are subjected to a common, uniform transformation over time, the moving elements spontaneously organize into a group. This is true for either a sudden discrete shift in position, which produces apparent motion, or a smooth continuous change in position over time. This factor is quite powerful and can be produced easily with a field of random dots. When the dots start to move, a form appears spontaneously whose shape and borders are clear, corresponding to the shape and borders of the moving set of dots. When the dots stop moving, the form that was perceived so easily in motion rapidly disappears.

The present account of this phenomenon is the same as for the preceding ones except that the motion-sensitive, second-order analyzers and their corresponding third-order analyzers are the relevant structures. Those elements that move according to a coherent, unified transformation to which the system is sensitive (translations, rotations, dilations, and their various combinations) will be processed by the same set of motion analyzers whereas the stationary elements will not be. A similar analysis holds for sets of elements moving simultaneously in different directions or at different rates in the same direction. It should be obvious that within the present theory the strength of the resulting group should depend on the similarity of the motions with respect to both direction and rate. Precisely what motions will be perceived is a different question, one that would require a more detailed analysis than can yet be provided.

Continuity And Closedness.   Good continuation and closedness are thought to be further factors that facilitate the grouping of elements within a pattern. Although they are clearly related to the factors of proximity and similarity of orientation, they appear, at least intuitively, to make additional contributions to the grouping of elements.

Continuity is closely related to various local symmetries, particularly those of translation and rotation. For this reason they should have their effects at the level of second- or third-order analyzers. For example, consider a curved line of dots that bifurcates into two branches, one of which has the same curvature as the single line (i.e., has good continuation with it) and the other of which does not. The group formed by the two parts with the same curvature has greater local symmetry in the sense defined earlier than does the group formed by the two parts with different curvatures. In other words, there will be more local regions within which the continuous curve has local symmetries under simultaneous translation and rotation than for the discontinuous curve. Thus, we expect that the parts with better continuation will interact more strongly in these symmetry-sensitive, second-order analyzers.

Closure is more problematic. Closed figures do not seem to possess any special types of local symmetry which are not found in open figures. It is true, however, that closed figures are, by definition, completely connected and continuous. Perhaps it is this additional continuity that makes closedness such a powerful organizer. It is obvious, however, that closed figures also segregate regions of a pattern in a way that open figures generally do not, and this function cannot be fully captured by appealing simply to complete continuity. Just what might be responsible for this effect is not clear. It may be related to depth perception in that closed figures generally correspond to continuous surfaces whose interior regions lie in the same depth plane as its borders, but at a different depth from the surrounding ground.

Symmetry.   One of the most powerful factors of perceptual organization is symmetry in the standard sense of bilateral or mirror-image symmetry. Within the present framework, this particular form of symmetry requires no special explanation; it is but one of the many forms of transformational invariance which are extracted by the second-order analyzers of spatial structure. Pairs of pattern elements that are symmetrically arranged about a line of reflection interact strongly in the symmetry-sensitive second-order analyzers. Such elements, then, will be more closely related in the system than other elements that do not share this relationship of invariance. Different types of symmetry may be differentially powerful as organizers, of course, depending on the number of second-order analyzers that are sensitive to each kind.

In general, the laws of organization are viewed in the present theory as resulting from different degrees of interaction between pattern elements within the system. The output state of the entire system for any given pattern is the result of many such interactions among pattern elements, and different patterns produce different amounts of interaction. For example, two figures of different colors, shapes, and sizes that are widely separated would produce little or no interaction because few, if any, analyzers would respond to both. Two figures of the same color, shape, and size that are close together would produce very strong interaction because most, but not all, of the analyzers that respond to one would also respond to the other. This view of perceptual organization improves on the Gestalt conception in that it provides the structure necessary to integrate qualitatively different factors into the same conceptual framework. Actually doing so would require making many specific assumptions that we are not yet prepared to make.

It is worthwhile to point out once again the crucial role that symmetry and transformation play in the present analysis of laws of grouping. The circumstances under which elements interact strongly within the analyzer system are precisely those in which there are significant symmetries in the sense of local transformational invariance. In such cases, the pattern elements interact in the second-order analyzers to a degree that depends on (1) the degree of invariance over the transformation and (2) the magnitude of the transformation that defines the symmetry. The more complete the invariance and the smaller the transformation (in the sense of transformational distance in A-space), the larger the interaction will be. These two factors provide the quantitative basis for relatedness whereas the transformational dimensions provide the qualitative basis.

It is interesting to notice how similar the present formulation is to the standard Gestalt analysis. Most of the factors they listed (proximity, similarity of orientation, similarity of size, and bilateral symmetry) correspond in a one-to-one fashion with the local symmetries we have postulated to be extracted by second-order analyzers (invariance over positions, orientations, resolutions, and reflections, respectively). It is the overall transformational structure of the system that ties these disparate factors together into a single, coherent, consistent notion of relatedness that cuts across these different factors.

Perceptual Representation

Some of the most intractable problems of perceptual theory concern how patterns are represented perceptually and how they are stored in memory such that they can later be recognized. The issues involved are too complex to be addressed adequately here. But it is important to consider how a system might be used to construct perceptual representations from which patterns could be recognized. After all, identifying objects as instances of known classes is one of the most important functions of perceptual processing, one without which people would not be able to function in their environments.

The basic proposal is that more permanent records of pattern structure are constructed by acts of attention. Attention selects out some subset of the analyzer system in what we will call an *attentional fixation,* and a record is made of both the fixated analyzers and their outputs. A sequence of such attentional fixations is required to describe the pattern in detail, and we suppose that these generally begin at the most global (low-resolution) level and progress to more local (higher-resolution) information. The result is a structural description of the pattern at a number of different levels of detail, each one being related to others within a network-like record of the attentional fixations. Such representations are similar to the sort of networks I have previously suggested to underlie memory for perceptual information (Palmer, 1975, 1977). Elsewhere I have called them "augmented structural descriptions" and have discussed their relationships to other types of representational structures (Palmer, 1978). Now let us consider how such representations might be constructed from the transformational system outlined above.

Attention and Perceptual Reference Frames.   We have assumed that each spatial analyzer within a functional system computes an output for each input pattern. The output of all analyzers within the system for a given pattern, then, constitutes a representation of it which is quite different from its representation at the level of the sensory mosaic. This representation within the analyzer space may be conceived in terms of the cylindrical lattice structure of A-space by imagining the nodes of the lattice being displaced perpendicularly to its surface by a distance proportional to their output levels. The result is a plastically deformed, "lumpy" cylinder in which the peaks and troughs correspond to analyzers with high and low outputs, respectively. We can similarly conceive of the outputs of second- and third-order analyzers in analogous ways within their respective A-spaces.

We assume that this representation in A-space is computed in parallel and is "preattentive." That is, it is the sort of perceptual response which would occur more or less automatically, regardless of the organism's state of attention or even, perhaps, its state of consciousness. It is simply a representation of the input pattern as transduced through the sensory mosaic and transformed by the spatial analyzers. Within the current model, one can think of this process as converting the input pattern into a "lumpy" hypercylinder of a particular shape. We must now consider how this information is analyzed further by perceptual processes and how it might be coded for longer term storage.

The basic mechanism for this further processing, we propose, is an attentional sampling process. Attention is drawn to informative aspects of the input scene, and that information is coded symbolically for storage as a result. The most straightforward approach to modelling attention is to assume that attentional processes select out some compact, connected subset of the analyzers in A-space. The logically limiting case would be if attention were focussed on a single node, reflecting the selection of a particular analyzer class with a specific position, orientation, resolution, and sense. Attention might also select some larger subset of the analyzers—for example, all those with a given position and resolution, but including all orientations and senses. We will take a compromise position and assume that attention is *centered* on a particular analyzer in A-space, but encompasses a large number of neighboring analyzers to a lesser extent. The amount or degree of attention allocated to each analyzer is some monotonically decreasing function of its transformational distance from the centrally attended one. That is, the centrally attended analyzer receives maximum attention, and more distant ones receive correspondingly less. Another way of saying essentially the same thing is that attention is directed toward a single, multidimensional channel, but that its effects spread to nearby channels due to lack of attentional selectivity.

Directing attention toward a particular analyzer establishes what we call a "perceptual reference frame" (or simply *frame*) relative to which the other attended analyzers are specified. This reference frame is critical for the coding of information for storage and its use in further processing. The name "reference frame" is chosen because the attentional fixation includes the same type of background information that characterizes a coordinate system within analytic geometry: a position (origin), orientation (axis), sense (direction along the axis), and resolution (unit of distance). In fact, each analyzer has a different implicit frame of reference, and when a particular one is at the center of attention, its frame becomes the reference frame for all perceptual processing that occurs while attention remains focussed on it.

The reference frame established by an attentional fixation becomes the *transformational base* of the attentional field. This is defined by the position, orientation, sense, and resolution of the central analyzer, that is, by its coordinates within A-space. Each of the other analyzers is then specified relationally by the *transformational distance* between it and the centrally attended analyzer. For simplicity, we assume that the *range* of the attentional field—its spread within A-space—does not vary over different bases. In other words, the set of analyzers within the attentional field and the amount of attention they receive can be specified simply by transformational distances from the base established by the focus of attention.

This means that one can specify an attentional fixation by just two sorts of entities: one specifying the *frame*, and the other specifying the *contents* within that frame. Each of these can be represented by a structured set of real values. The frame itself can be represented by the coordinates of the centrally attended analyzer within A-space, one parameter for each dimension of the space. These coordinates can be either "absolute" (within the A-space) or relative to some previous reference frame or both. The "contents" of the frame are just the outputs of the spatial analyzers within the attentional field. These can also be specified as a structured set of real values—one for the output of each analyzer—where the structure is defined by the transformational relation of each one to the base of the frame. The contents of an attentional fixation can also be specified in terms of absolute or relative outputs or both. We assume that the perceptual code of a whole scene consists of a data structure which stores a sequence of such records of attentional fixations.

Pattern Coding.   In order to make the pattern representation useful for later recognition and classification of new patterns, the descriptions of the frame and its contents must be stored relatively rather than absolutely. This is because it is quite unlikely that the same pattern will be seen again in exactly the same retinal location, orientation, or size. Storing relative information is one obvious way to abstract the representation from its specific parameters. Doing so is particularly easy in the present system because of its transformational and relational structure. Storing a relative description of the frame for an attentional fixation simply requires computing the transformational relation between it and other frames for each dimension. Then the representation of the frame is very much like a relative address in a computer, where the entire address structure can be relocated simply by changing a single, base address.

The contents of frames can likewise be stored relatively. Doing so requires computing the relationships between the outputs of the attended analyzers. This information is readily available in the second-order analyzers whose outputs reflect the comparison of pairs of first-order analyzers. Storing relative descriptions of the contents of a frame, then, can be done by recording the outputs of second-order elements within the attentional field. It is here that redundancies in the first-order outputs can be eliminated by storing together those values that are the same.

Let us assume, then, that both the frame and the contents are represented by relative descriptions. In other words, the analyzers within the attentional field are specified relative to the centrally attended analyzer and their outputs are specified relative to, say, the output of the centrally attended analyzer. Now these two reference points (one for the frame and one for the contents) for recording an attentional fixation can also be described relatively, but they must refer to something outside of the current fixation, namely to the frame and contents of *another* fixation. It makes good sense that each attentional fixation should be related to some more global, superordinate frame. This is because the more global frame defines the space within which the more local one fits. Consider a person's body, for example. The position, orientation, and size of the frame used to describe the shape of the head would be specified relative to the position, orientation, and size of the frame used to describe the body as a whole. Similarly, the frame for an eye or a nose would be specified relative to that for the head as a whole. In general, the interaction between the structure of the stimulus pattern and the structure of the perceptual system will determine which pieces are natural parts. Pieces that affect the same analyzers and interact strongly will tend to be attended together and, therefore, to be stored as a single unit. Pieces that affect different analyzers and do not interact will tend to be attended sequentially and, therefore, to be stored separately as different parts. These natural parts will be coded as local units within more global units of a hierarchical structural description (see Palmer, 1975, 1977).

In general, using other frames as the references for relative descriptions provides a flexible and useful way of storing information. If the analyzers in the attentional field are described as deviations from the centrally attended analyzer, and if the outputs are described relative to some standard (e.g., the output of the centrally attended analyzer), then the whole stored record is coded as a relative description except for the two references. These, in turn, can be specified relative to their more global attentional fixations. The net result is that such representations will be accurate pattern descriptions that depend on their retinal position, orientation, or size only in the absolute reference parameters. Such absolute parameters are thus factored out of the representation as free variables.

Attention As The Mind's Eye.   It is worth noting that attentional transformations within A-space bear a striking resemblance to possible transformations of the eye relative to the world. Just as one can change the position of the eye by a translation (either by moving the eye or turning the head), one can also change the attended position by shifting attention from a given analyzer to one related to it through a translational transformation. Similarly, changes in head tilt correspond to attentional shifts in the orientation domain. In real life, of course, such shifts in attention are generally accomplished by overt muscular movements rather than by purely internal transformations within A-space. With exposures so brief that such overt movements cannot be made, however, purely attentional transformations do seem to occur. At least phenomenally, one seems to "scan" an iconic memory image even though it is fixed in retinal position. Such scanning would correspond to attentional shifts along the positional dimensions of A-space. It may also be true that purely attentional translations occur routinely before actual eye movements are made (cf. Posner, Nissen, & Ogden, 1978).

Perhaps more interestingly, moving the eye closer to an object in order to perceive it in greater detail corresponds to attentional shifts in resolution through dilation transformations. These are probably executed quite frequently in the course of normal perceiving. One often needs finer-grained spatial information than is available initially, and it usually can be obtained without actually moving closer to the object simply by "focussing attention" on a restricted portion of the visual field. For example, attentional shifts in resolution would occur when an observer attends specifically to the pattern or texture of the cloth of a garment after first processing its overall shape, or when an observer "zooms in" on a single small object after briefly surveying the whole scene in which it appears.

The close relationship between the transformational structure of A-space and the transformations that result from movements of the sensory system is far from coincidental. As we see soon, this correspondence of structure makes it possible for the visual system to compensate perceptually for motions of the sensory apparatus through space. This can be accomplished by factoring out the transformation of the eye through the *inverse* transformation within A-space. It may also be important that the attentional transformations discussed here are closely related to operations people can perform on their visual images. For example, Kosslyn and Schwartz (1977) have discussed operations akin to translations, rotations, and dilations ("zooming") in their simulation of visual imagery processes.

Emergent Properties And Holism

The doctrine of holism—the whole is more than (or different from) the sum of its parts—is probably the most central and best remembered tenet of Gestalt theory. It has various meanings, not all of which will be addressed here. Among them, however, is the assertion that perceptual wholes have "emergent properties" that arise when a set of elements interact in space and time. The essence of this claim is that a whole figure is perceived to have properties that are not shared by or even predictable from its parts in isolation. For example, a single point has only positional attributes, but when a number of points are configured into a line, the whole line has attributes of length and orientation. The points of which it is composed have neither of these properties, even as they participate in the configural line and determine its holistic properties.

In the present theory, emergent features of wholes arise naturally as the result of analyzing patterns at different levels of resolution. Each attentional fixation produces a representation for the region of space encompassed by the analyzers within the attentional field. This representation is, in a sense, holistic in that it characterizes just that region of the perceivable world as a single entity. Whereas it is true that this representation is coded in terms of the output of a number of different analyzers, it is also true that the analyzers themselves are holistic in the sense that they compute a function over the entire region rather than just a portion of it. Thus, if one were to attend just to a small region containing a point in a configural line of dots, it would produce the perceptual representation of a filled circle, whatever that might be. But by attending to the line of dots as a whole, a lower level of resolution would be utilized in which the representation would be essentially that corresponding to a line of the appropriate length and orientation, but with lower contrast (cf. Ginsberg, 1971). Hence, there is always a duality inherent in such a system: a pattern can simultaneously be represented as a whole, unitary figure through an attentional fixation at low resolution and as a collection of parts through a sequence of attentional fixations at higher resolution, each of which represents only a portion of the figure. Each level of analysis shows aspects of the complete whole that are, in a very real sense, different from and independent of those at other levels. For example, the dots could be replaced by squares of similar size without substantially affecting the line-like representation of the low resolution analyzers. Low resolution symmetry (see Fig. 5.9) is another example of an emergent property that can be found in the output of the low resolution analyzers.

Naturally, this complete separation of elements and their configurations will not always hold true, especially when there are few elements that are large with respect to the whole configuration (see Goldmeier, 1972). In such cases, the representation at a low level of resolution will respond to characteristics of the geometrical elements as well as those of the whole configuration. Only when there are many small elements will there be a complete separation between the analysis of the configuration and that of its elements. In such cases, the separation results from the fact that the spatial characteristics of the pattern will be analyzed by separate sets of analyzers, the configuration at a low level of resolution and the elements at a high level.

Recent evidence has suggested that low resolution (global) information is processed more rapidly than high resolution (local) information (Navon, 1977). While there clearly must be limiting conditions for this assertion (as Kinchla & Wolfe, 1979, have shown), it is nevertheless an important finding. It supports the Gestalt claim that the emergent properties of the whole are perceptually more salient than those of its parts, at least for a wide range of normal viewing conditions. This, in turn, strongly suggests that there must be a global, low-resolution analysis of patterns which occurs prior to and at least partly independent of the smaller parts of which it is composed (see also Broadbent, 1977). The resolution structure in the present theory and the notion of sequences of attentional fixations suggest obvious possibilities for accomplishing this type of processing. Global pattern information could be extracted by an attentional fixation at a low level of resolution, and local information by subsequent attentional fixations at higher levels of resolution. This also fits with the idea that relative descriptions for attentional fixations are specified with respect to more global attentional fixations.

Another aspect of holism that is captured by the theory is, of course, symmetry and good form in general. These are properties that can only be defined for wholes. They have their representation in the output of the second-order analyzers for spatial properties and in the third-order analyzers for motional properties.

Perceptual Constancy

One of the major puzzles of perception is that of constancy. How do people manage to see a given object as constant in its properties of shape, size, color, and so forth, when they view it from many different perspectives, distances, lighting conditions, and the like? Gestalt theorists saw this as one of the critical problems of perception, and one for which the theoretical constructs of structuralism were hopelessly inadequate. The Gestalt approach centered around discovering *relations* that are invariant over the various transformations to which

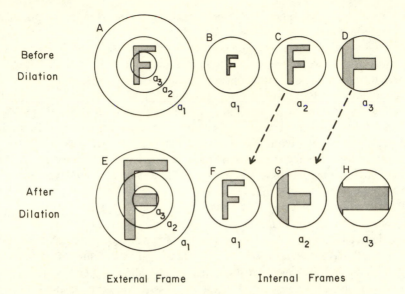

Before Dilation

After Dilation

External Frame   Internal Frames

FIG. 5.10.   Illustrations of constancy in analyzer views (dashed arrows) over a dilation transformation for three analyzers of different resolutions.

the objects might be subjected. Gibson (1950, 1966) has significantly extended this line of theorizing since then.

In this section I argue that the transformational structure postulated in the present theory is particularly well suited to extracting and tracking the invariant properties of objects. This is true both when the object moves and when the observer does. In large part this capability is due to the fact that the systemic structure is itself based on the same set of transformations to which images of objects tend to be subjected: translations, rotations, and dilations (from motions in depth).

To illustrate how the system can be used to compensate for transformations of objects, consider the example shown in Fig. 5.10. Figure 5.10A shows an F-shaped pattern in relation to three dilationally equivalent analyzers. These analyzers are in the same functional system, but at different levels of spatial resolution. Figures 5.10B, C, and D show the pattern as it is "viewed" by these analyzers within their own internal frames of reference. Now suppose that the pattern were dilated, say, as a result of its motion toward the observer (Fig. 5.10E). After this transformation these same three analyzers "view" the pattern differently than they did before. This is obvious when one compares Figs. 5.10B, C, and D (before the transformation) with Figs. 5.10F, G, and H, respectively (after the transformation). Hence, their outputs will change as a result of the transformation. Note, however, that the pattern viewed *before* the transformation by some analyzers is the same as that viewed *after* the transformation by other analyzers. This is indicated in Fig. 5.10 by the dashed arrows. In fact, for nearly every analyzer viewing the original pattern before the transformation there will be another analyzer viewing the pattern after the transformation whose output is exactly the same. This mapping of analyzers whose outputs are identical over the transformation, then, could support perceptual constancy processing.

The transformational relation between the pairs of analyzers whose outputs are the same is just the transformation that has been applied to the pattern. It is easy to see, for example, that in Fig. 5.10 the equal-output analyzers are related by a dilation of the same magnitude as that which relates the original pattern to its transformation. This fact can be generalized to any transformation that is supported by A-space, including any combination of translations, rotations, dilations, and reflections. Thus, constancy is easily maintained over a given transformation on an object simply by tracking the mapping of analyzers onto corresponding analyzers under the transformation that has been applied. How the nature of the transformation can be determined in order to specify the mapping is a problem we will discuss shortly.

The output equivalence of pairs of analyzers before and after an object is transformed follows directly from the definition of transformational equivalence. Once again, recall that two analyzers are related by a transformation, t, and its inverse, t', if and only if,

$$a_i(p) = a_j[t(p)] \text{ and } a_j(p) = a_i[t'(p)] \qquad (5.14)$$

for all possible patterns. This definition explicitly states that if a transformation, t, is applied to a pattern, and if there are analyzers within a functional system that are t-related, then the outputs of the analyzers before the transformation will necessarily be the same as those of their transformationally related homologues after the transformation. This is exactly the situation required for maintaining object constancy through a transformation of the object.

From this it also follows that the system will be able to compensate for transformations (motions) of the sensory surface with respect to the environment. As an observer moves about in the world, the images projecting onto the retina are transformed in the same manner as when the objects move in the opposite way. When the head tilts clockwise with respect to the environment, for example, the sensory images tilt counterclockwise with respect to the retina. When the eyes move rightward, the images move leftward. The previous discussion makes it plain that the present transformational structure allows the object to be tracked through such transformations. The only difference between a moving object and a moving sensory system is that the appropriate compensatory transformation is the *inverse* of the motion for the sensory system. This follows simply from the fact that moving the sensory system according to a particular transformation results in the inverse transformation of the image on the retina.

Naturally, for such a scheme to be of any use in maintaining object constancy, one must somehow *know* what the transformation is. There are two main ways of obtaining this information. First, there can be outside sources of relevant information that specify the nature of the transformation to the visual system. For example, the vestibular system provides independent information about changes in the orientation of the head relative to gravity. This can be (and presumably is) passed on to the visual system to specify rotations of the sensory surface. Another example comes from eye movements. Efferent command signals specify planned eye movements. These signals could affect visual analysis such that the inverse transformational mapping compensates for the sensory changes that occur as a result of the movement.

The second way to gain knowledge about spatial transformations is by direct perceptual analysis. In the present theory such information is provided by the motion-sensitive, second-order analyzers. They look explicitly at transformational invariances over time, detecting exactly the sort of output equivalence that results from uniform transformations of significant portions of the image. Thus, the perceptual system itself can provide the information needed to maintain object constancies as Gibson (1966) has suggested.

Generally speaking, these two sources of knowledge are used in different situations. Indirect knowledge from outside sources seems to be generally available only about transformations of the sensory system itself. Various different systems have evolved in an interrelated manner to provide each other with pertinent information. Direct information from within the perceptual system itself, therefore, is generally the only source of information available about transformations of external objects. Of course, to the extent that information from transformationally sensitive mechanisms in different modalities eventually comes together in an intermodal system (as surely it must), then there is converging evidence from different perceptual sources about the specific nature of the transformation occurring in the world.

Motion Perception

It is clear that the basis for motion representation in the present system lies in the second-order analyzers. These compute transformational invariance over time for three types of motions: translations, rotations, and dilations. As discussed earlier, the space of motion analyzers would include representation of rate and direction as well as type of motion. By the relative outputs of such analyzers it is possible to specify rigid motions of real objects in a simple and logical manner.

Real Motion.   One interesting implication of the proposed theory for motion perception is that translations, rotations, and dilations are equally fundamental forms of motion. There is a tendency to think that translational motion is the basic type of motion and that other motions are "built" out of molecular translations. Whereas this is certainly possible, it is not necessarily the case.

It is true, however, that rotations and dilations will produce translational motion in the higher resolution analyzers. For example, an enlarging square would produce outward translations in the high resolution analyzers responding to the edges of the square. At the low-resolution analyzers, however, the motion analysis would be in terms of a dilation. Perhaps it is this low-resolution component that "organizes" the local translational motions into a holistic size change transformation. (This could also be interpreted by some later process as a change in depth, of course.) Such integration could be performed by higher-order analyzers such that the most global motion (in this case, the dilation) is integrated with the appropriate translations at higher resolutions. A similar analysis would presumably be required for holistic rotations and translations. It is not too difficult to imagine that large-scale integrations over much of the visual field might be able to specify the complex sorts of motion gradients Gibson (1966) has described.

This same structure for motion analysis has the potential for giving rise to the phenomena studied by Johansson (1950) and modelled recently by Restle (1979). Briefly, Johansson found that harmonic motions of multiple dots were perceived quite differently when they moved synchronously in different directions than when they moved in isolation. Whole groups of dots tend to be seen as moving together, if possible, with subgroups moving relative to each other within this framework. The global motional framework would, in the present theory, result from the output of the low resolution, motion sensitive analyzers. High resolution analyzers could then respond to residual motional components relative to the global frame. Precisely how this might be accomplished is not clear, but the theory provides a computational structure in which such organizations of motions might arise naturally.

Apparent Motion. Since Wertheimer's (1912) early studies of phi phenomenon, apparent motion has been of great interest to perceptual psychologists. Critical issues concern whether the basic processes underlying apparent motion are the same as those underlying real motion and how other factors affect it, factors such as shape, size, grouping, and so on (Kolers, 1972).

According to the present theory, the basic processes of apparent motion are the same as for real motion. Both are supported by the second-order analyzers that respond to output identity of first-order analyzers differing in spatial and temporal properties. The fact that the processes are the same does not necessarily mean, however, that the *effects* of real and apparent motions will be the same in all cases. It is entirely possible that differences such as have been noted (see Kolers, 1972) can be understood in terms of the differences between the effects of real and apparent motion on the second-order analyzers. For example, the "jerky" motion perceived when the discrete positions of apparent motion are too far apart may arise from the lack of continuous evidence of motion. That is, the motion sensitive analyzers may respond to the discrete presentations, but only a small subset of them will do so, and even those to varying extents over time. So it is not implausible that real and apparent motion are supported by the same analyzer systems, despite their differences in overall effect.

Depth Perception

Thus far we have restricted the perceptual domain to two-dimensional patterns. This tactic side-steps some of the most important problems of perception: namely, the analyses of depth information. Perceiving depth is problematic because of ambiguities resulting from the projection transformation that occurs when light from three-dimensional objects strikes the two-dimensional receptor surface. The human visual system has evolved numerous processes for disambiguating such information. These procedures rely on the well-known "cues" to depth: binocular disparity, motion parallax, and linear perspective, to name but a few of the most important ones.

The purpose of the following discussion is to suggest lines along which it seems possible to extract depth information within the present transformational structure. Although the details have not been worked out, the system seems to have a structure appropriate for computing certain kinds of depth information.

Binocular Disparity.   Perhaps the most direct and compelling information about depth arises from binocular disparity. The two eyes record slightly different views of the world because of their spatial separation. The difference between these two views can be translated quite directly into information about relative distance in depth. The basic facts of binocular disparity and stereopsis are given in most perceptual textbooks and need not be restated here.

In order to extract depth information from binocular disparity in the present theory we must, first of all, add a second sensory mosaic. We must also add a second system of analyzers, identical to the first, that operates in parallel with it. Given that the visual fields of the two mosaics overlap, it is fairly straightforward to compute binocular disparity. One simply needs second-order analyzers that respond to output identities between first-order analyzers from the left and right A-spaces. When these disparity analyzers signal identity of two retinotopically corresponding regions, the left and right images are fused in depth on the horopter. When they signal identity of disparate regions, their output represents depth relative to the plane of fusion. The direction of the disparity (crossed or uncrossed) corresponds to depth toward or away from the observer relative to the fused plane, and the amount of disparity corresponds to the distance in depth.

Once again, not all possible comparisons must (or even should) be made to extract this depth information. In fact, it should be sufficient to compare analyzers from the left and right A-spaces only for pairs of analyzers differing in horizontal displacement. That is, different resolutions, orientations, senses, and even vertical positions need not be compared. Further, such positionally related analyzers are presumably compared only over a relatively small neighborhood of retinal disparities. Thus, the number of second-order disparity analyzers does not need to be very large.

Computing retinal disparities is only part of the problem, of course, as Julesz's (1971) random dot stereograms have made quite clear. Whereas there may be only one globally optimal solution, this arises from locally ambiguous information. Dev (1975), Nelson (1975), and Marr and Poggio (1976) have independently proposed similar cooperative network algorithms to achieve global stereopsis from merely local interactions. The present system has nothing to add to these theories except for whatever advantage might be gained by the presence of the resolution and orientation dimensions. These properties should add significant constraints on the nature of the global solution by greatly restricting the number of ambiguous correspondences.

Motion Parallax.   A second, exceedingly important source of information about depth arises from movement. When an observer moves about in the world and fixates on a point in three-dimensional space, the images of objects at different depths move at different rates and directions over the sensory surface. Because motion is inherently relative, the same sort of parallax information is available from moving objects.

In a computational sense, the depth information in relative motion parallax is almost the same as that in binocular disparity. The only real difference is that binocular disparity is computed by comparing two spatially separated views at the same time whereas relative motion parallax is computed by comparing two spatially separated views at different times.

This correspondence immediately suggests an appropriate computational structure for motion parallax. The motion-sensitive, second-order analyzers discussed earlier compare the outputs of spatially separated first-order analyzers over time. The resulting space of motion analyzers includes rate and direction of motion for each position, orientation, and size channel in the first-order space. Thus, regions of the image which are moving at the same rate will have the same motional representation. This invariance of motion will be responded to by the third-order analyzers that compare the outputs of second-order analyzers for equivalence. It is not difficult to imagine that planes and surfaces could be located in depth from this sort of motional information within the present transformational structure. Some higher-level process is needed to interpret direction and rate of motion as depth information, but the job is made much easier given the motional analysis performed by the second- and third-order analyzers.

CONCLUDING REMARKS

The foregoing discussion sketches some applications of the present theory to a disparate set of perceptual problems and phenomena: figural goodness, grouping, pattern representation and recognition, emergent properties, constancy, and depth perception. In many cases the proposals simply suggest ways to approach the problems within the framework of the theory. But perhaps the most impressive thing is that the theory seems to apply so naturally to such a diverse set of problems and, at least in some cases, to shed new light on them.

It is too early to be sure that the theory can give a rigorous account of all of these perceptual phenomena. Among the more critical needs are more precise formulations of (1) the higher-order analyzers, (2) the effects of attention, (3) the structure of stored representations, and (4) the way stored representations interact with early analyses during the process of perception. These are difficult issues, to be sure. But the way in which they might be solved is, I suspect, already highly constrained by the structure of the theory as developed thus far. Certain assumptions are natural in the present theoretical context whereas others are strained and awkward. Much of what remains to be done is to explore the natural alternatives and their implications more fully. The last two issues are ones I have discussed at length previously (Palmer, 1975, 1977). The suggestions I made at that time are surprisingly compatible with what I have said here. In fact, there is a real sense in which the present theory can be considered a new "front end" for the memory representation and pattern recognition processes I suggested previously.

Even in its present state of development the theory has touched on a number of potentially important and intriguing possibilities. Here are some comments on five implications of the present theory that I consider to be especially relevant for perceptual theory in general.

1. The critical aspect of the theory is the *overall systemic structure* it hypothesizes for the visual system. There seem to be many perceptual phenomena which may be accounted for simply on this systemic basis, without making strong assumptions about the components of the system. Figural goodness is the best example, perhaps only because it is the one most fully developed. One wonders how much of perception could be accounted for in such abstract, systemic terms. Among other things, this "systemic" approach suggests that certain molecular aspects of the system may be quite irrelevant for understanding important aspects of perception. For example, the current controversy over whether cells in visual cortex are better described as "edge and bar detectors" or as "spatial frequency filters" (see De Valois & De Valois, 1980) may add little to the understanding of many perceptual phenomena. This is not to say that such questions are irrelevant in general, but only that many aspects of "higher-level" perception may *not* depend critically on such "low-level"

sensory details. The current systemic view also suggests that some of the most revealing physiological studies for understanding the nature of perception are those concerning the "functional architecture" of the visual system, its overall structure and interconnections (see De Valois & De Valois, 1980).

2. Along the same general lines, the present theory suggests that significant and rigorous theoretical statements about perception can be made by talking about abstract correspondence between real-world structure and perceptual structure. For example, the definition of a functional system was precisely stated in terms of the real-world transformations required to make the analyzer outputs equivalent. In doing so, many unnecessary assumptions were avoided, assumptions such as those about the nature of the analyzers and, particularly, about the way in which the analyzers achieve their computational results. It seems to be a natural level at which to construct abstract theories about whole *classes* of possible mechanisms. Given the unnecessary and misleading assumptions that often appear in perceptual theories (see Palmer, 1978, for a discussion), this approach is particularly useful.

3. Thinking about perception in terms of *transformational structure* suggests ways to unify sensory modalities. Real-world events consist of physical transformations of objects. Such events generally affect more than one sensory modality at the same time. In a sense, then, the sensory systems split the transformations of events into modality-specific, component transformations, each of which is often ambiguous by itself. For example, suppose an object makes a constant noise as it comes closer to an observer. This situation will cause both a visual dilation and an increase in loudness to take place relative to their respective sensory backgrounds. Now the visual dilation could be the result of either the object getting bigger or the object moving closer. Similarly, the auditory change could result either from the object making a louder noise or the object moving closer. When the two transformations co-occur in space and time, however, the interpretation of an object making a constant noise as it approaches clearly dominates. It is the "simpler" alternative because it alone can account for both component transformations with a single real-world transformation. Thus, if the two transformations converge in intermodal perception, they jointly can specify the real-world event much more completely than either one alone. *The structure of this intermodal perceptual system is just the transformational structure of real-world events.* It is coupled to each separate sense by the corresponding types of modality-specific transformations produced by that type of event. "Getting closer," then, is an intermodal event transformation that has various correlated transformations in each sensory modality. As the foregoing discussion illustrates, transformations provide a useful language for talking about all levels of these processes. The fact that the present theory has such a transformational structure suggests that it could be extended to intermodal perceptual systems quite naturally.

4. In addition to integrating sensory systems with each other, a transformational approach suggests fundamental links between perception and action. As discussed earlier, the current transformational structure is able to compensate for movements of the observer relative to the environment. This is possible because the transformations are fundamentally linked to the results of actions: namely, motions. Turning the head to the right causes images to move to the left, and moving forward causes images to enlarge. It also follows that if an observer wants a better look at an object in the right visual field, the head should be turned rightward in order to move the image toward the center of the field. If the observer wants a closer look at fine detail, he or she should move forward in order to cause the enlargement of the image. Such links between perceptual transformations and the effects of behavioral actions suggest that the kind of theory advocated here would be a good one in which to construct perceptual-motor schemas to guide behavior.

5. Finally, the theory suggests a way in which three dissimilar approaches to perceptual theory can be integrated: Gestalt, Gibsonian, and information processing. The basic approach is plainly within the information processing tradition, although the theory itself is not typical. Whereas it does not assume electrical fields in the cortex as Gestaltists did and does not assume "direct" perception as Gibson did, it nevertheless manages to capture at least some of the flavor of these approaches as well. It supports and extends the Gestalt contention that "good" figures, emergent properties, and laws of organization are critical aspects of perception. It also supports the general idea that the structure of the whole system may be far more important than the nature of its component parts.

From the Gibsonian point of view, the present theory suggests ways in which complex patterns of stimulation might be analyzed computationally, albeit indirectly rather than directly. It stresses the importance of transformations in perception and the invariances to which those transformations give rise. Further, as suggested in the immediately preceding comments, this transformational approach suggests ways in which various different perceptual modalities can be integrated with each other and with actions. Bringing these three approaches together was not in any sense a goal of the theory. It simply happened as the implications of the proposed structure were explored. Perhaps this accomplishment is more remarkable than anything else.

ACKNOWLEDGMENTS

This research was supported in part by Grant 1-R01-MH33103-01 to the author from the National Institute of Mental Health. I would like to thank Nancy Bucher, Ruth Kimchi, Andrew Phelps, and Lynn Robertson for stimulating discussions and their comments on ideas presented in this chapter.

REFERENCES

Attneave, F. Some informational aspects of visual perception. *Psychological Review*, 1954, *61*, 183-193.

Attneave, F. Symmetry, information, and memory for patterns. *American Journal of Psychology*, 1955, *68*, 209-222.

Beck, J. Effect of orientation and shape similarity on perceptual grouping. *Perception and Psychophysics*, 1966, *1*, 300-302.

Broadbent, D. E. The hidden preattentive processes. *American Psychologist*, 1977, *32*, 109-118.

Campbell, F. W., & Robson, J. G. Application of Fourier analysis to the visibility of gratings. *Journal of Physiology*, 1968, *197*, 551-566.

De Valois, R. L., & De Valois, K. K. Spatial vision. *Annual Review of Psychology*, 1980, *31*, 309-341.

Dev, P. Perception of depth surfaces in random dot stereograms: A neural model. *International Journal of Man-Machine Studies*, 1975, *7*, 511-523.

Garner, W. R. *The processing of information and structure.* Hillsdale, N.J.: Lawrence Erlbaum Associates, 1974.

Gibson, J. J. *The perception of the visual world.* Boston: Houghton Mifflin, 1950.

Gibson, J. J. *The senses considered as perceptual systems.* Boston: Houghton Mifflin, 1966.

Ginsberg, A. P. *Psychological correlates of a model of the human visual system.* Unpublished doctoral dissertation, Air Force Institute of Technology, 1971.

Goldmeier, E. Similarity in visually perceived forms. *Psychological Issues*, 1972, *8*.

Hochberg, J., & Brooks, V. The psychophysics of form: Reversible-perspective drawings of spatial objects. *American Journal of Psychology*, 1960, *73*, 337-354.

Hochberg, J., & McAlister, E. A quantitative approach to figural "goodness." *Journal of Experimental Psychology*, 1953, *46*, 361-364.

Hubel, D. H., & Wiesel, T. N. Receptive fields, binocular interaction, and the functional architecture in the cat's visual cortex. *Journal of Physiology*, 1962, *160*, 106-154.

Johannson, G. *Configuration in event perception.* Uppsala: Almqvist & Wiksell, 1950.

Julesz, B. *Foundations of cyclopean perception.* Chicago: University of Chicago Press, 1971.

Kinchla, R. A., & Wolfe, J. The order of visual processing: "Top-down," "bottom-up," or "middle-out?" *Perception and Psychophysics*, 1979, *25*, 225-231.

Koffka, K. *Principles of gestalt psychology.* New York: Harcourt Brace, 1935.

Köhler, W. Die physischen Gestalten in Ruhe und im stationaren Zustand, Eine naturphilosophische Untersuchung, Erlangen, 1920. Translated in W. D. Ellis (Ed.), *A sourcebook of Gestalt psychology.* New York: Harcourt Brace, 1938.

Kolers, P. A. *Aspects of motion perception.* New York: Pergamon Press, 1972.

Kosslyn, S. M., & Schwartz, S. P. A simulation of visual imagery. *Cognitive Science*, 1977, *1*, 265-296.

Lashley, K. S., Chow, K. L., & Semmes, J. An examination of the electrical field theory of cerebral integration. *Psychological Review*, 1951, *58*, 123-136.

Leeuwenberg, E. L. J. A perceptual coding language for visual and auditory patterns. *American Journal of Psychology*, 1971, *84*, 307-350.

Leeuwenberg, E. L. J. Quantification of certain visual pattern properties: Salience, transparency, and similarity. In E. L. J. Leeuwenberg & H. F. J. M. Buffart (Eds.), *Formal theories of visual perception.* New York: Wiley, 1978.

Marr, D., & Poggio, T. Cooperative computation of stereo disparity. *Science*, 1976, *194*, 283-287.

Navon, D. Forest before trees: The precedence of global features in visual perception. *Cognitive Psychology*, 1977, *9*, 353-383.

Nelson, J. I. Globality and stereoscopic fusion in binocular vision. *Journal of Theoretical Biology*, 1975, *49*, 1-88.

Palmer, S. E. Visual perception and world knowledge: Notes on a model of sensory-cognitive interaction. In D. A. Norman & D. E. Rumelhart (Eds.), *Explorations in cognition*. San Francisco: Freeman, 1975.

Palmer, S. E. Hierarchical structure in perceptual representation. *Cognitive Psychology*, 1977, *9*, 441-474.

Palmer, S. E. Fundamental aspects of cognitive representation. In E. Rosch & B. Lloyd (Eds.), *Cognition and categorization*. Hillsdale, N.J.: Lawrence Erlbaum Associates, 1978.

Perkins, F. T. Symmetry in visual recall. *American Journal of Psychology*, 1932, *44*, 473-490.

Posner, M. I., Nissen, M. J., & Ogden, W. C. Attended and unattended processing modes: The role of set for spatial location. In H. L. Pick & I. J. Saltzman (Eds.), *Modes of perceiving and processing information*. Hillsdale, N.J.: Lawrence Erlbaum Associates, 1978.

Restle, F. Coding theory of the perception of motion configurations. *Psychological Review*, 1979, *86*, 1-24.

Rock, I. *Orientation and form*. New York: Academic Press, 1973.

Wertheimer, M. Experimentelle Studien uber das Sehen von Bewegung. *Zeitschrift fur Psychologie*, 1912, *61*, 161-265. Translated in part in T. Shipley (Ed.), *Classics in psychology*. New York: Philosophical Library, 1961.

Wertheimer, M. Untersuchungen zur Lehre von der Gestalt. II. *Psychologische Forschung*, 1923, *4*, 301-350. Translated in W. D. Ellis (Ed.), *A sourcebook of gestalt psychology*. New York: Harcourt Brace, 1938.

Weyl, H. *Symmetry*. Princeton, N.J.: Princeton University Press, 1952.

6 Relaxation Processes for Perceptual Disambiguation in Computer Vision

Azriel Rosenfeld
University of Maryland

COMPUTER VISION

The goal of computer vision is to generate descriptions of given scenes, which are input to the computer in the form of images. An image of the scene is obtained by some type of sensor, such as a TV camera. For input to the computer, the image is converted into a discrete array of numbers, representing scene brightnesses at a closely spaced grid of small spots. This process is called *digitization;* the resulting array is called a *digital picture,* its elements are called *pixels* (short for "picture elements") or *points,* and their values are called *gray levels.* (In the case of a color image, we would convert each color component of the TV image into an array; but we assume here that the image is black and white.) A typical digitized TV picture is a 500 by 500 element array, in which each value is represented by an 8-bit number (i.e., 256 shades of gray are represented).

Scene descriptions almost always refer to objects, surfaces, or regions that are present in the scene. Thus the first step in the description process is segmentation of the picture into parts, ideally corresponding to the appropriate regions. This is most commonly done by classifying the pixels into various categories. For example, if the categories are gray level ranges, the resulting segmentation divides the picture into patches of different brightnesses. (The problem of how to choose a good set of categories is not discussed here.) As another example, if we measure the rate of change of gray level at each point, we can classify each pixel as to whether it lies on an edge, based on whether its gray-level gradient is high or low. Using processes such as these, we extract from the picture a collection of local features (e.g., spots, corners, borders or curves, and regions).

Given a segmentation into parts, the next step is to measure various properties of and relations among the parts. For example, we can measure properties that describe the texture of a region (e.g., first- or second-order statistics of its gray levels), or properties that describe its size and shape (area, perimeter, elongatedness, etc.). We can also determine relations among regions, for example, adjacency, relative position, and the like. This information can be stored in a relational structure, such as a labelled graph, in which the nodes represent the picture parts. Each node is labelled with that part's property values, and the arcs represent relations between pairs of nodes.

Finally, we compare the specific relational structures generated in this way from a particular scene with general relational structures that constitute models for classes of scenes. For example, a model for an outdoor scene might involve properties of and relations among objects such as sky, sun, clouds, houses, trees, bushes, grass, and so on. (Note that both the specific and general structures are likely to be hierarchical, that is, the parts consiste of subparts, and so on.) The

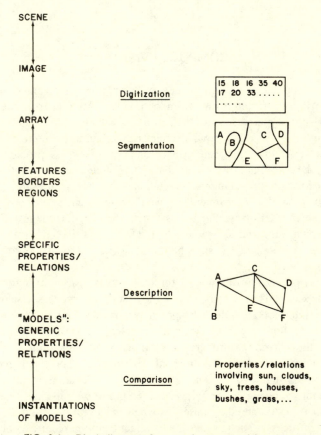

FIG. 6.1.   Block diagram of a general computer vision system.

aim is to establish a correspondence between the specific and general structures, so that the scene can be described in terms of the objects referred to in the model. (The problem of how to choose a good set of models for a given scene is not addressed here.)

A block diagram of the scene analysis process is shown in Fig. 6.1. For a general introduction to the subject, see Rosenfeld and Kak (1976).

CLASSIFICATION PROBLEMS

Classification decisions play important roles at several stages of the computer vision process. As we have already seen, segmentation usually involves classification of pixels. Regions may also need to be classified, based on their shape or textural properties. In addition, at the model-matching stage, when we seek to establish correspondences between graphs describing specific scenes and graphs defining models for classes of scenes, we are in effect classifying the scene graph nodes, using the model nodes as classes.

If individual classification decisions about pixels or nodes are made independently, they can be made very fast, if parallel computer hardware is available to handle large numbers of them simultaneously. This is important because of the very large number of decisions that must be made. As we saw, a TV image contains about $500^2 = 250,000$ pixels; and in matching two graphs having, say, 10 nodes each, there are $10! \doteq 3,500,000$ possible combinations. Unfortunately, when decisions are made independently, they may have a high error rate, because they must be based on a small amount of information—for example, we classify a pixel based on its gray level or local rate of change of gray level, without regard to how other pixels, even nearby ones, are classified.

If we want to make decisions that are reliable and not "noisy," we should examine combinations of pixels or nodes, and try to make optimal joint classifications or matches. Unfortunately, this means that we can no longer make the decisions independently, and so they cannot be made in parallel. Heuristic search or mathematical programming techniques can be used to speed up the decision process, at some cost in optimality. It is still basically a sequential process, however, and thus is inherently slow.

In the next section we briefly describe a recently developed iterative "relaxation" approach to classification which makes joint decisions in a parallel fashion. This approach thus allows relatively reliable decisions to be made rapidly. More important, it initially makes these "decisions" fuzzily or probabilistically, thus deferring commitment, and uses iterative methods to reduce the inconsistencies among these decisions and thus reduce their ambiguity. It is called "relaxation" because it resembles a class of iterative processes by that name that are commonly used in numerical analysis.

RELAXATION

The basic idea of the relaxation approach is as follows. 1. Initially, we classify each object (pixel or node) "probabilistically." In other words, we estimate a probability p_i that it belongs to each of the classes. (If this is not a forced-choice situation, these "probabilities" need not add up to 1; the object may belong to none of the classes.) These classifications are done independently and so can be done in parallel. 2. We now adjust the p_i's for each object to make them more consistent with the p_i's for related objects—for example, neighboring pixels in the picture, or neighboring nodes in the graph. This adjustment process is performed independently for each object; it can thus be done in parallel, hardware permitting. 3. The adjustment process can be iterated several times. Typically, this rapidly leads to a mutually consistent set of p_i's that are all close to 0 or 1. Thus, after a few iterations, it is quite easy to make final classification decisions.

To illustrate how this process works, we give two examples, one relating to pixel classification, the other to graph matching.

Our first example is that of deciding which pixels lie on edges. We could do this independently for each pixel, by measuring the rate of change of gray level and deciding whether it is sufficiently high. This will yield noisy results, however. It will occasionally call edge points nonedge and nonedge points edge because it makes no use of context. We could largely eliminate the noise by "tracking" edges from point to point, moving in the direction perpendicular to the gradient; but this sequential approach would be slow. In the relaxation approach, we proceed as follows: 1a. assign an initial "edge probability" p to each point based on the magnitude of the gradient at that point; 1b. adjust the p's based on those at neighboring points according to the following rules:

1. The no-edge probability 1-p at a point reinforces the no-edge probabilities at all its neighbors.
2. The edge probability at a point reinforces the no-edge probabilities at the neighbors "alongside" it; for example, if the edge runs vertically, the 1-p's are reinforced at the horizontal neighbors.
3. The edge probability at a point reinforces the edge probabilities at the neighbors, provided the two edges smoothly continue one another; for example, the p's at two vertically neighboring points reinforce each other provided the two edges are in near-vertical directions.

The algebraic details of this process will not be given here. In fact, the quantitative definition of the reinforcement scheme does not seem to matter much, as long as it fits the qualitative description just given. After a few iterations of the process, the edge probabilities are close to 1 on smooth borders, and close to 0 elsewhere, so that the edge/nonedge decision has become trivial.

In graph matching, we need to decide, for each scene graph node, which model node it might represent. If we did this independently for each graph node, we would make many errors; but if we had to search for optimum combinations, it would require much time. The relaxation approach to this problem is as follows: 2a. to each scene graph node, assign probabilities $p_1, \ldots, p_m$ that it is each of the model nodes, based on the similarity of its associated properties to those of each model node; 2b. adjust these probabilities based on those at neighboring nodes in the graph. For example, let p be the probability that scene node n is model node m. If it really is m, there should be certain other nodes $m_1, \ldots, m_k$ in certain relationships to it, as specified by the model. Reinforce p in accordance with how high the probabilities of $m_1, \ldots, m_k$ are at neighbors of n (in the scene graph) that stand in the proper relationships to n.

Again, the quantitative details are not too important. After a few iterations, the p_i's representing incorrect matches are generally close to 0, so that only a small number of combinations need to be examined to find the desired match.

DISCUSSION

The relaxation approach was first introduced in Rosenfeld, Hummel, and Zucker (1976), where it was suggested that such processes might play a role in the perception of ambiguous and impossible three-dimensional objects. It has since been applied to a variety of picture segmentation and processing tasks; some of these are reviewed in Rosenfeld (1978). The graph matching application is treated in Kitchen (1980). Similar processes have been applied by Marr and Poggio (1976) to the parallel computation of stereo disparity, and by Barrow and Tenenbaum (1976) to the classification of regions in a picture with respect to a scene model. The relaxation approach is now being used by a growing number of computer vision researchers.

It would be premature to suggest that relaxation processes are involved in human vision. However, these processes do provide a highly parallel method of reducing the ambiguity and enhancing the consistency of an initial set of classification decisions. It is hoped that perception psychologists will find some use for these ideas in visual system modeling.

ACKNOWLEDGMENTS

The support of the National Science Foundation under Grant MCS-76-23763 is gratefully acknowledged, as is the help of Kathryn Riley in preparing this chapter.

REFERENCES

Barrow, H. G., & Tenenbaum, J. M. *MSYS: A system for reasoning about scenes*. Technical Note 121, Artificial Intelligence Center, SRI International, Menlo Park, Ca., 1976.

Kitchen, L. Relaxation applied to matching quantitative relational structures. *IEEE Trans. Systems, Man, Cybernetics,* 1980, *10,* 96–101.

Marr, D., & Poggio, T. Cooperative computation of stereo disparity. *Science,* 1976, *194,* 283–287.

Rosenfeld, A. Iterative methods in image analysis. *Pattern Recognition,* 1978, *10,* 181–187.

Rosenfeld, A., Hummel, R. A., & Zucker, S. W. Scene labeling by relaxation operations. *IEEE Trans. Systems, Man, Cybernetics,* 1976, *6,* 420–433.

Rosenfeld, A., & Kak, A. C. *Digital Picture Processing.* New York: Academic Press, 1976.

7 What is Involved in Surface Perception?

James J. Gibson (*deceased*)
Cornell University

INTRODUCTION

The theory put forward in *The Ecological Approach to Visual Perception* (1979) begins with the properties of surfaces instead of the traditional qualities of objects: color, form, location, and motion. What properties of a surface are perceivable? The following proposals extend what was said in Chapter 2 of that book. I can think of at least nine such surface properties. Most of them have been noticed by phenomenologists, but I assume that they are also real.

Several facts about surfaces as distinguished from objects should be noted. First, a surface is not discrete like a detached object and thus surfaces are not denumerable. Instead, a surface is nested within superordinate surfaces. Second, a surface does not have a location as an object does, a locus in space. Instead, it is part of what I call the environmental layout; it is situated relative to the other surfaces of the habitat underlaid by the ground, the surface of support. A Newtonian body has location relative to the three coordinate axes of mathematical space but these axes are not perceived; they are thought of. Hence the problem of how we perceive space is a false problem, and the unsolved puzzle of how we might perceive locations in space (on the basis of cutaneous or retinal "local signs") is a false puzzle. Third, a surface does not have a color in the sense of that term employed in physical optics, and does not have a form in the sense of that term used in plane geometry.

An object, in this theory, is only a surface that stands out from the rest of the surface layout, the ground, because it is bounded by an occluding edge. This is an ecological fact, to which the figure-ground phenomenon is incidental.

What perceivable properties does a surface have? Here is a partial list: hard to soft, luminous or reflecting, illuminated to shaded, high to low reflectance, uniform to speckled reflectance, smooth to rough texture, opacity to transparency, dull to shiny, and hot to cold. Note that some of these are accessible to both the visual and the haptic system in collaboration, some are accessible only to vision, and the last is accessible only to the skin system.

1. *The Property of Being Rigid, Viscous, or Liquid.*   This is observable by palpating, prodding, or pounding the surface without seeing it, by seeing the "impact-character" of a collision without feeling it, as has recently been shown by Runeson (1977), or by both together. This distinguishing of rigidity-viscosity and firmness-softness is a good beginning basis for later differentiating the variety of substances in the environment, and babies seem to do so at an early age (Gibson, Owsley, & Johnston, 1978; Gibson, Owsley, Walker, & Megaw-Nyce, 1979; Walker, Owsley, Megaw-Nyce, Gibson, & Bahrick, 1980).

2. *The Property of Being Radiant or Reflecting.*   A luminous surface emits light; an ordinary surface only reflects illumination. How are they distinguished visually? If heat accompanies the light the source can also be detected by turning one's skin from side to side.

3. *The Property of Being Weakly or Strongly Illuminated.*   If any surface in a layout is illuminated all of them are illuminated, and there are ambient optic arrays at all points in the air. But some faces of the layout are relatively lighted while some are relatively shaded, and this fact is independent of the amount of light in the air. It depends on the inclination of the surface to the direction of the source, for one thing. How do we see whether a surface is in weak light or in strong light? A surface in weak light during the morning will be in strong light during the afternoon, and vice versa. Ratios of luminance among the visual solid angles of the ambient array must have something to do with it. You cannot tell by touching a surface, of course, whether and how much it is illuminated.

4. *The Property of High to Low Reflectance of the Incident Light.*   The reflectance of a reflecting surface is intrinsic to the substance, that is, the kind of substance it is. Reflectance is a diagnostic ratio, a fraction. The relative reflectances of all the surfaces in the layout are also invariant. How do we see them despite all the fluctuations of terrestrial and artificial illumination? I suggested in my new book (Gibson, 1979, p. 86) that a persistent structure in an ambient optic array underlies the changing structure caused by the movement of the sun across the sky and the resulting interchange between surfaces that are lighted and shaded. Perhaps in this way one can see *both* the relative slants of surfaces in the layout and their relative reflectances. They are what persist; shadows fluctuate.

The fact is that we can see the convexities and the colors of the surface layout underneath the shadows.

5. *The Property of Having Uniform or Nonuniform Reflectance.*   The reflectance of a surface may be uniform or the surface may be speckled, spotted, patterned, pigmented, variegated, or the like. It is not enough merely to say that a surface has an intrinsic "color." A substance is often a conglomerate. The natural spotting of a surface characterizes the substance that underlies it, as does its texture (below). But that fact is complicated by the presence in the human habitat of artificially spotted flat surfaces like drawing pads and canvases, walls, screens, and writing paper. The original surface can often be recognized. The spots, traces, or deposits are manmade. Apart from what we call stains or dirt they are said to be graphic. And apart from those we call purely decorative they stand for something other than the surface itself. Hence they may induce a mediated awareness of this "other" along with the direct perception of the surface. These complex facts tend to confuse everybody, and the study of this kind of mediated perception is full of perplexities. But most of the experiments that illustrate Gestalt theory were carried out with manmade tracings on a surface.

6. *The Property of Being Smooth or Rough and, If the Latter, Whether the Texture is Coarse or Fine and, In Either Case, What Form it Takes.*   This property, especially the form of texture (rippled, pebbled, granular, ridged) is very characteristic of the underlying substance. It can be seen with exactness whenever the illumination has a prevailing direction, or is "glancing," but not so well when it is equal from all directions; then the illumination is said to be "flat." The smoothness, fineness, and roughness of a texture can be detected by rubbing it, as Katz showed (Katz, 1925; Gibson, 1966, p. 126).

7. *The Property Of Being Dull Or Shiny (Lustrous).*   This property is related to its being unpolished or polished (specular). Luster seems to depend on the presence in the optic array of "highlights" on the surface. The property of being polished can be observed by rubbing the surface with the tips of the fingers. Is this the same as the property of being lustrous?

8. *The Property Of Being Opaque Or Transparent.*   The ordinary substances of the habitat transmit none of the incident light (they reflect some portion and absorb the rest). Their surfaces are opaque. A few natural substances transmit some or much of the light. Their surfaces, if the interface is a flat plane, are said to be transparent, more exactly semitransparent. There is refraction at the surface, that is, the rays of radiation are bent, but if a surface of pure water is unrippled, or if a sheet of clear glass is polished, the visual solid angles of an

optic array have essentially the same structure and are not "distorted" by the surface. I think this is what is meant by saying that the still surface of a pool or the parallel plane surfaces of the glass plate are transparent: one can perceive the essential properties of another surface behind it or, as we say, one can "see through it." Note that a translucent sheet (ground, pebbled, or diffusing) allows the passage of light but disrupts the structure of an array. An opaque sheet or screen blocks both the light and its structure. The edge of a transparent sheet does not hide or conceal but the edge of a translucent sheet does, as much as the edge of an opaque sheet. There can also be semitransparent sheets that are only partially concealing or blurring, as some of Metelli's demonstrations seem to suggest (see Chapter 11 by Metelli).

9. *The Property Of Being At A Higher Or Lower Temperature Than The Skin.*   What we call hot, warm, neutral, cool, or cold "to the touch" is relative temperature. Psychologists have emphasized the sensation, but the useful perception of the state of the substance is what matters (Gibson, 1966). It is based on the direction and amount of heat flow into or out of the tissue. You cannot see this; you can only feel it.

PERSISTING AND NONPERSISTING SURFACE PROPERTIES

We can now observe that the most persistent properties of a surface are those numbered 4, 5, 6, 7 and 8, reflectance, natural spotting, texture, shininess, and transparency. The most changeable property of a surface is number 3, that of being lighted or shaded. This is because the general illumination in the medium fluctuates with day and night, with white light at noon and red light at sunset with the sun going behind and coming out of a cloud, with the flickering of firelight or torchlight. Also the incident illumination on a surface fluctuates with the change from morning to afternoon, with the dappling of light under the trees in a wind, with the shifts of lighting as one carries a torch at night; and of course with the arbitrary "ons" and "offs" of artificial illumination. So transient is the illumination on a surface that one might even question whether or not it should be considered a "property" of the surface.

A somewhat more persisting property is number 9, the temperature of the surface and its substance. Number 1, solidity, is quite stable at the ordinary temperatures of terrestial substances, except for ice, which melts at a not unusual level. Number 2, being-luminous, depends on a very hot substance (apart for the exceptional case of luminescence).

The perception of the properties of the persisting substances of the habitat is necessary if we are to know what they afford, what they are good for. But substances change with aging, fermenting, ripening, cooking, and melting. We can see the change in the surface. Persistence is not permanence. The widely accepted assumption that the child learns to apprehend the ''permanence'' of objects when he acquires the ''object concept'' is misleading and unnecessary. The question is this: how do we perceive which properties of a surface are persisting, which are fluctuating, and which are changing irreversibly?

FLUCTUATION IN THE AMBIENT OPTIC ARRAY

Substances change and surfaces undergo periodic changes of illumination but neither can be seen without a specifying change of some sort in the ambient optic array at a point of observation. Fluctuations of the shadow structure of an array have not been studied experimentally under controlled conditions; only an unchanging shadow structure has been so studied.

For example, you can see the surface of a lamp or a lighting fixture as luminous when it is radiating and nonluminous when it is not, in relation to the other surfaces of the room, with a steady-state optic array. If, however, the luminosity fluctuated like the surface of a flame, would not this discrimination be more exact and the perception more vivid?

You can see a shadow cast on a flat surface as a shadow if it has a penumbra, but as a stain on the surface if you eliminate the penumbra with a drawn line (the ''ringed'' shadow of Hering). Moreover, an artificial penumbra will convert a real stain into a shadow (MacLeod, 1940). But the apparent stain with a ring around it will be converted back into a shadow if the latter comes and goes, that is, fluctuates, according to my observation. Similarly a patch of light that looks like a spot of white will be seen for what it is if it fluctuates.

You can see the convexities and concavities of a nonflat surface (the relief), by means of the stationary pattern of light and shade in the array, but only with some ambiguity. The convexities and concavities reverse if you are able to make the illumination seem to come from the opposite direction. If, however, the light source is actuallly moved back and forth over the layout so that the lighted and shaded surfaces interchange, and the shadow structure of the array fluctuates, the relief is no longer ambiguous and does not reverse. So I conclude on the basis of informal motion picture studies.

You can see the dullness or luster of a surface in a fixed array according as highlights are absent or present (see Beck, 1972). But it seems to me that the luster becomes more evident when you move the vase (or your head) and thus cause the highlights to shift relative to the texture.

You can see the transparency of a surface with an unchanging optic array, and this can be simulated experimentally, as noted above. But it can *also* be simulated when some of the interspersed spots of an array have one coherent motion and the remaining spots have another. This change involves permutation of adjacent order. Two separated surfaces are vividly seen, the superposed surface being transparent.

The experiments reported in Chapter 9 of my book (Gibson, 1979) suggest that the optical information for seeing surfaciness is density in the array, a variable of fixed pattern. But the experiment mentioned above on interspersed random textures (see also Gibson, 1979, Chapter 10) and Kaplan's experiment on the gain or loss of texture on one side of a contour (Chapter 11) suggest that the information for seeing the unity or coherence of a surface has to do with changing pattern in time, not with fixed pattern; a persisting property revealed by consistent change. I suggested (1979, p. 179ff.) that what counts for surface perception is the preservation of adjacent order, that is, the continued nonpermutation of order. Consider that the Brownian movement of spots in a microscope is what specifies a nonsurface, a group of particles. Then the continuous unbroken connectedness of a true surface at the ecological level of reality is specified by what I can only call the absence of Brownian movement!

Note that a persistently unchanging pattern of a natural optic array specifies a great deal about the surfaces surrounding an observer. It also specifies that they do not change during the period of observation. A changing pattern of the natural array specifies still more about the surfaces: how they change during the period of observation and how the observer moves. Possible ambiguities are eliminated. The artificially arrested pattern of the peculiar optic array coming from a picture is a different matter; you cannot always tell whether the state of a pictured surface is a persisting one or is only the instantaneous cross-section of a changing state.

THE ECOLOGICAL LEVEL OF REALITY

A surface is the interface between a substance and the medium. The notion of a substance and of degrees of substantiality should not be confused with the physical concept of matter; it is connected with the complicated "states" of matter, the gaseous state being wholly insubstantial and the liquid to solid states being increasingly substantial (for terrestrial animals). Continuous substantial surfaces are not real for physics, but they are primary realities for ecology and for the kind of psychology founded on it.

Animals perceive surfaces and their properties, because animal behavior must be controlled by what the surfaces and their substances afford. (They also perceive the *layout* of surfaces and what the invariants of layout afford, but that is not the main concern of this essay.) There is a need to study the perception of surfaces with a realistic attitude as well as with a phenomenological attitude. The approach advocated is much closer to Gestalt theory than it is to input processing theory ("information" processing, so called). It is a sort of ecological Gestalt theory.

REFERENCES

Beck, J. *Surface color perception.* Ithaca, N.Y.: Cornell University Press, 1972.

Gibson, J. J. *The senses considered as perceptual systems.* Boston: Houghton-Mifflin, 1966.

Gibson, J. J. *The ecological approach to visual perception.* Boston: Houghton-Mifflin, 1979.

Gibson, E. J., Owsley, C. J., Johnston, J. Perception of invariants by five-month-old infants: Differentiation of two types of motion. *Developmental Psychology*, 1978, *14*, 407–415.

Gibson, E. J., Owsley, C. J., Walker, A., & Megaw-Nyce, J. Development of the perception of invariants: Substance and shape. *Perception*, 1979, *8*, 609–619.

Katz, D. *Der Aufbau der Tastwelt*. Leipzig: Barth, 1925.

MacLeod, R. B. Brightness constancy in unrecognized shadows. *Journal of Experimental Psychology*, 1940, *27*, 1–22.

Runeson, S. *On visual perception of dynamic events*. Doctoral Dissertation, University of Uppsala, Sweden, 1977.

Walker, A. S., Owsley, C. J., Megaw-Nyce, J., Gibson, E. J., & Bahrick, L. E. Detection of elasticity as an invariant property of objects by young infants. *Perception*, 1980, *9*, 713–718.

8
Contrasting Emphases in Gestalt Theory, Information Processing, and the Ecological Approach to Perception

Eleanor J. Gibson
Cornell University

THE ECOLOGICAL APPROACH

The title of the Conference, "Processes of Perceptual Organization and Representation," implies its concern with Gestalt theory on the one hand and information processing theory on the other. The concern is also reflected in the introduction to the book. Gibson called his talk "The Ecological Approach to Perception: An Extension of Certain Features of Gestalt Psychology."[1] As this title implies, he was sympathetic to certain themes of Gestalt Psychology and some of them influenced his own views considerably.[2] But this does not mean that the ecological view of perception (his view) was merely an extension of Gestalt Psychology—, far from it, since, as will become clear, it differs profoundly, in some very fundamental ways.

He began his discussion with Köhler's concept of "physische Gestalten" (Köhler, 1920), which he referred to thereafter as "Gestalt physics." He understood Köhler's need to appeal to a rather special brand of physics, because he himself felt it necessary to invent a new branch of physics, which he called ecological optics, to describe appropriately the information in the light that specifies the surfaces, substances, objects, and events in the world. His new optics, however, has little in common with Köhler's physische Gestalten except that the physische Gestalten were described not as random arrangements of particles but as units displaying order, regularity, and relational properties in their own right.

---

[1]This paper was reconstructed from notes that James Gibson had prepared for his discussion at the conference, supplemented by my own knowledge of his thinking.

[2]See, for example, his paper "The legacies of Koffka's *Principles*" (Gibson, 1971).

Natural laws of a dynamic nature accounted for these relations and the holistic character of the "Gestalten." They were in the world, not imposed by the physicist. Gibson agreed that there are holistic entities related to one another in an orderly way in the world, as distinguished from assemblages of particles, but he considered the best exemplars of orderly relations in the world to be the world's surfaces and substances, its places, objects and events, not soap bubbles and the like. The optics necessary for their description in a lighted physical medium (ecological optics) has as its chief concept the "ambient optic array." Such an array is structured by the layout of the world's surfaces, and thus carries relational information about the surfaces, and the like, that it specifies.

Wertheimer's "laws of organization" (Wertheimer, 1923) insofar as he retained any aspect of them, were reformulated by Gibson and assigned to another realm. It has been customary to think of these laws as principles accounting for unification of elements of an array. Gibson was concerned with our perception of the surfaces of the world as unbroken planes in various structural relations to one another. The laws should be considered, he thought, as *pictorial* expressions of the information in light that specifies a continuous surface instead of an aggregation of unrelated points. Proximity, similarity, and good continuation can be so thought of. The "grouping" of elements and the segregation of groups is not a process in the brain, but a fact of the optic array coming from a textured surface. These laws are appropriate for describing static pictured surfaces, as the Gestalt psychologists in fact used them. "Common fate," unlike the first three principles, extends to transformations in the array. It is a kind of dynamic continuity, going along with change in the array, but specifying structure that persists and underlies the change. The law of Prägnanz ("good Gestalten") he considered unnecessary. To state these conclusions another way, he agreed with the rejection of local phenomena by Gestalt psychologists without assuming that local spots of sensation have to be organized in the brain, that is, that Gestalten have to be constructed by brain processes. Unitary structures and orderly arrays exist in the world, as do invariants and transformations in the ambient array that specify (are information for) unity and structure of the world's layout and furnishings.

The figure-ground phenomenon (Rubin) he agreed was also important, but not the prototype of all perception. It is, he thought, the *pictorial expression* of information for a detached object in the environment (even at that, it is in itself equivocal, for it might be a hole in the background, not an object). What it depicts is stationary superposition, the momentary hiding, screening or occluding of a portion of a surface. But it is ambiguous, like any still picture; the unfailing information for an occluding edge is progressive occluding. Michotte's "rabbit hole" and his "tunnel phenomenon" are examples of the information for occlusion in progressive occlusion at an edge. The experiments of Kaplan (1969) and the demonstrations in Gibson, Kaplan, Reynolds and Wheeler (1969) show further that progressive deletion and accretion specify covering and uncovering by an occluding edge.

To state it simply, stationary Gestalten, as exemplified in pictures and line drawings, are not a sufficient basis for perception. It would be better to say that temporal Gestalten are the basis, but actually, it is invariants under changes in the array that are necessary for perception, providing information for the underlying persisting structure beneath the changing perspective structure.

Koffka (1935) emphasized the distinction between the proximal and the distal stimulus. This distinction is not uniquely associated with Gestalt psychology (it was basic to Brunswik's thinking, for example), but it was taken over by Koffka. The "distal stimulus" referred to aspects of his geographical environment, but was not itself the stimulus for receptors on sensory surfaces. I think that this distinction influenced my husband very much at one time, but by the 1970s he had given it up, as he gave up speaking of "stimuli" (a term which carries with it the implication of unstructured particles or aggregations of them). Instead, he distinguished between the surfaces and substances of the world (themselves structured) and information for them in the ambient array, the information structured by the underlying surfaces. His book, *The Ecological Approach to Visual Perception* (1979), is organized to explicate this distinction: Part I is about the media, substances and surfaces of the environment; Part II is about the information for them; and Part III is about perceiving them. In Part II, a chapter on "The Relationship Between Stimulation and Stimulus Information" makes clear the difference between the concepts of proximal stimulation and information.

Finally, a theme of Gestalt psychology which influenced him greatly was the hypothesis that meanings and values are directly perceived, not imposed on bare sensory impressions. This hypothesis was at the heart of Gestalt psychology, not so much for Köhler (although he wrote *The Place of Value in a World of Facts,* 1938) but for Lewin (1936) and Koffka (1935). Both stressed that the "invitation character" or "valence" of a substance, surface, place, or event is simply perceived. Gibson's concept of affordance reflects these ideas, but with a profound difference. He thought of affordances as being objective, because information for them is there to be picked up, not as subjective contributions of the observer, to wit:

> The concept of affordance is derived from these concepts of valence, invitation, and demand but with a crucial difference. The affordance of something does *not change* as the need of the observer changes. The observer may or may not perceive or attend to the affordance, according to his needs, but the affordance, being invariant, is there to be perceived. An affordance is not bestowed upon an object by a need of an observer and his act of perceiving it. The object offers what it does because it is what it is. To be sure, we define *what it is* in terms of ecological physics instead of physical physics, and it therefore possesses meaning and value to begin with. But, this is meaning and value of a new sort. [Gibson, 1979, p. 138ff.]

For Koffka, the value was a "tension" in the phenomenal field, in the behavioral environment, as he called it, as opposed to what he termed the geographical environment. For Gibson, "the affordances of things are specified in stimulus information. They *seem* to be perceived directly, because they *are* perceived directly" (1979, p. 140).

Gibson's hypothesis of direct perception has often been misunderstood in recent times. It has to do with Koffka's distinction between two worlds, the behavioral and the geographical environment, a dualism that Gibson rejected. Gestalt psychology, like all traditional theories of perception, was based on the assumption that sensations are the result of stimuli impinging on sense organs, and that sensations have to be "processed" in some way to yield perceptions. The processes for Gestalt psychologists were ones of organization and redistribution of forces in the nervous system, but the structure and meaning rose from the operation of these processes on otherwise meaningless and unstructured sensations. Gibson rejected the notion of processing that imposed organization on sensations, because the information in stimulation is itself structured by the surfaces and layout of the world. The goal and the contributioin of his last two books was to show exactly how information in the ambient optic array can and does specify the layout of the world. To say that it specifies it is not to say that it resembles it, however. Köhler's doctrine of isomorphism (Köhler, 1938) between tbe world and psychoneural processes was, obviously, rejected by Gibson. It seems, in fact, a very contrived effort to account for any apparent correspondences between the two worlds, a way out of complete subjectivism.

I would like to make a final comment about a difference between the ecological approach and Gestalt psycholgy, having to do with the Gestalt psychologists' reliance on line drawings and two-dimensional static displays. These displays, frozen and depthless, were the basis for many generalizations about perceived "form" and organization. But, for the ecological approach, perception is frozen only in a picture. In everyday behavior perceiving is continuous and so are the events in the world that we have to monitor in order to guide even the simplest behaviors such as reaching and locomotion. The ambient array provides rich information for events and layout in transformations that take place over time, such as the accretion and deletion via occluding edges that specify covering and uncovering. To neglect such information is to fail to deal with the true problems of perception. Yes, we do perceive a layout, textured surfaces and objects in pictures; Gibson was, in fact, profoundly interested in picture perception. But perception of pictures in no way typifies everyday perception; quite the opposite: it is interesting because we have the problem of accounting for how it can be as good as it is, when it is so impoverished by lack of depth and motion. How is it that we see one thing behind another in a picture, when nothing ever moves, either in the picture or by actions of the observer? How is it that we see a whole thing at all? These are interesting questions and Gibson deals with them in Part IV of *The Ecological Approach*. But the answers do not lead to a picture theory of natural perception.

Many of the participants in the conference assumed that perception involves an internal representation derived from stimulus information; further, that the first stage in constructing a structural representation of a stimulus is the abstracting of pattern features such as length, slope, size of angles, and so on. I will forbear commenting on the inconsistency of terminology that requires "information" and "pattern features" to construct a representation of "a stimulus," and quote from the notes used by Gibson at the conference. "I reject at the outset," he said, "the approach that takes for granted a chain of causal steps in the process of visual perception (a causal chain that can be interrupted)." Such a chain (as he described it in the *Perception of the Visual World* [1950]) has often been thought to be composed of (1) an object radiating light; (2) rays of light to an eye; (3) formation of an optical image in a chambered eye; (4) arousal of a physiological image in a retinal mosaic; (5) transmission of impulses in the optic nerve; (6) excitation of nerve cells in the occipital cortex and the centers of the brain, resulting in visual sensations and other perceptual experiences arising from them by hypothetical processes that are not agreed upon. "What I do accept," he said, "is the hypothesis of an active perceptual system." Such a system was elaborated upon in his book *The Senses Considered as Perceptual Systems* (1966).

It is obvious from these comments that he was not in sympathy with current information processing models that emphasize processing, often referred to as "coding," in a hypothetical chain of causal events that begins as "input" of unstructured energy, and posits experiences of an elementaristic nature (see Treisman & Gelade, 1980) that must then be organized by the perceiver to form a representation. This is a construction theory, and furthermore one that includes the most atomistic assumptions. It was frequently stated during the conference that regularities in perception are "imposed," not found. The experiments called upon as evidence are based on ambiguous stimuli and outline drawings. The regularities are symmetry, coplanarity, and so on, reminiscent of the Gestalt laws of organization.

A word about "representations" might be added. Although James Gibson's notes did not refer specifically to this concept, it was prominent in many of the discussions and typifies the kind of theory with which his contrasts, a "mediation" theory. I would like to sketch my own view about the role (or rather, nonrole) of "representations" in perceiving.

A representation generally implies a likeness of some kind, for example, a picture. Perception does not occur by means of looking at pictures in the head. Why should it entail any kind of representation? Such a process would only be pushing the whole enterprise deep into a black box, and comes close to the "little man in the head" fallacy, that there is a perceiver inside perceiving the representation, itself mysteriously generated without perceiving anything to begin with.

Gibson's theory of perception is a theory of direct perception. The theory entails two important assumptions; one, that there is information for invariants and affordances that specifies the things and events, the substances and the layout, in the world. We do not need to construct something from unrelated pieces and bestow upon them some organization. The relations are present in the information. The second assumption follows logically from the first. Because the information (which is structured) is available in the light (or in some other form of energy, such as acoustic or mechanical) no mediation in the form of a representation or a mental structure is involved in perceiving. Perceiving is a process of detecting (extracting) the information in stimulation which specifies the things, events, and so on in the world.

This information is a flow, continuous over time, and it is available, often, to more than one modality. It must, therefore, be abstract. The changes over time can be considered as transformations that have structure (unity and order of different kinds). What we should endeavor to describe are these transformations, the properties and relations that differentiate them. But, because they are abstract, we cannot draw a picture of them.

Should we think of information as being a "representation" of the distal sources, the objects and events and layout of the world? There is structure in the ambient array. Does it represent the layout and changes in the layout? This might be a kind of compromise with the presentday structuralists. (It brings us right back to pictures, which are a case of mediated perception.) But the word "representation" is not right for direct perception. While the information in the ambient array *specifies* the distal sources, it need not resemble them, or provide a likeness of them. In a sense, it corresponds to them, but not in any point-for-point or element-for-element way. It could not, or we could not perceive the same affordances multimodally, as we frequently (perhaps always) do. The information must be amodal, or abstract. Representations of an abstract nature may indeed play a role in thinking. But perceiving is the process of extracting information from the world in the service of guiding our interactions with events that happen in the world, an active process of obtaining information, not manufacturing it.

One evening of the conference was devoted to a discussion of the agreements and disagreements between the Gestalt and the information processing approaches to perception. For an onlooker (as I was) two points emerged. First, there is one very strong agreement between these approaches. Both are sensation-based theories, making the assumption that perception is constructed, with structure and meanings imposed by the perceiver. The processes appealed to (laws of organization, coding, or whatever) may differ, but, the agreement is a very basic one, making the same assumptions about the nature of the world and man's (or other animals') relation to it. The second point is a fundamental disagreement between them. Gestalt psychology was a revolt against structuralism, the kind inherited from British empiricism and the old associationists, and also against S-R theory, both of them rejected as atomistic and molecular. The arguments raised against structuralism and atomism by Wertheimer, Köhler and Koffka carry as much weight today as they did half a century ago. Most psychologists will agree (superficially at least) that perception is unified. But I think that elementarism is not only still lurking there in the information processing view, but becoming alarmingly prominent. It is a presentday structuralism, it seems to me, seeking ultimate particles as rampantly as Titchener ever did. The particles have different names ("textons," "audions," etc.), but the game is the same. The new elements are generally defended as having counterparts in the nervous system, sometimes called "detectors." The detectors are as hypothetical as the particles, however, and I am not sure that a neurophysiologist would welcome this coalition any more than a Gestalt psychologist would. Along with the atomism there is little attempt to explain the unified character and functional serviceability of perception as it occurs in everyday behavior.

It is everyday behavior that a Gibsonian view is most concerned with. The approach is a functional one and it differs from the other two in its major underlying assumptions—the biological utility of our perceptual activities for keeping us in touch with the world, and its view of man as a part of nature, having reciprocal relations with the world that he evolved in.

REFERENCES

Gibson, J. J. *The perception of the visual world,* Boston: Houghton Mifflin, 1950.

Gibson, J. J. *The senses considered as perceptual systems.* Boston: Houghton Mifflin, 1966.

Gibson, J. J. The legacies of Koffka's *Principles. Journal of the History of the Behavioral Sciences,* 1971, *7,* 3–9.

Gibson, J. J. *The ecological approach to visual perception.* Boston: Houghton Mifflin, 1979.

Gibson, J. J., Kaplan, G. A., Reynolds, H. N., & Wheeler, K. The change from visible to invisible: A study of optical transitions. *Perception and Psychophysics,* 1969, *5,* 113–116.

Kaplan, G. A. Kinetic disruption of optical texture: The perception of depth at an edge. *Perception and Psychophysics,* 1969, *6,* 193–198.

Koffka, K. *Principles of Gestalt Psychology.* New York: Harcourt Brace & Co., 1935.

Köhler, W. *Die physischen Gestalten in Ruhe und im stationären Zustand, Eine naturphilosophische Untersuchung.* Berlin: Erlangen, 1920.

Köhler, W. *The place of value in a world of facts.* New York: Liveright, 1938.

Lewin, K. *Principles of topological psychology.* (Tr. by F. Heider and G. Heider). New York: McGraw-Hill, 1936.

Treisman, A. M., & Gelade, G. A feature-integration theory of attention. *Cognitive Psychology,* 1980, *12,* 97–136.

Wertheimer, M. Untersuchungen zur Lehre von der Gestalt. II. *Psychologische Forschung,* 1923, *4,* 301–350.

9 Amodal Completion: Seeing or Thinking?

Gaetano Kanizsa
Walter Gerbino
University of Trieste

1. SEEING AND THINKING: JUST A PHENOMENAL DICHOTOMY?

You do not need to reflect, calculate, reason—in one word you do not need to *think*—in order to decide that in Fig. 9.1 there are two distinct visual objects; that one of these objects is smaller than the other; that their color and shape are different; that one is above the other; and that the latter is more regular than the former. You do not need to think about it because you can *see* these properties and relationships. And we are not the only ones to see them because, as extensive research has shown, many species of animals can discriminate visual objects on the basis of these attributes. Hence, in perceptual activity there would seem to exist operations of categorization, comparison, and grasping of relationships analogous to those that are evident in real, true thought activity.

Starting from this rather obvious premise we can, however, reach two different conclusions concerning the relationships that exist between perception and thought. On the one hand, owing to the fact that perceptual activity can occur without the intervention of thought processes, you could maintain, and indeed it has been upheld (especially by philosophers), that here we are dealing with two completely heterogeneous kinds of psychic activities. The first is the source of the sensorial world (the deceiving and changing appearance of things) and the second is the tool of construction and rational arrangement of reality on the basis of material supplied by the first.

On the other hand, it could be said that a substantial continuity, if not an actual identity, exists between the two kinds of activities which would represent different levels of a single cognitive process. One level would have the same

FIG. 9.1.   You do not need to *think* in order to conclude that there are two distinct visual objects differing in size, shape, color, and relative location. You simply *see* these properties and relationships.

finality and would be ruled by the same laws as the other. This point of view is suggested by the impression that the simplest perceptual event results from operations of the same kind as intellectual ones.

The hypothesis of continuity and, at the limit, of the practical impossibility of a clear distinction between perception and thought can assume different nuances—from a panperceptual to a panlogical conception of the nature of cognitive processes.

It is well known that the Gestaltists maintained that organization laws valid in perception act in thinking too (i.e., panperceptual). And because they apply a field model to perception, they also tend to consider thought processes, and their organization and restructuring, as being dominated by field laws. Meanwhile many cognitivists believe, like Helmholtz, that perceptual processes take place according to rules that obey the very same logic as inferential thought processes (i.e., panlogical). As is well known, these thought processes comprise unconscious reasonings and judgments. The mechanism of perceptual processes is conceived *as if* it were a computer programmed for effecting a logical kind of inferential operations.

It seems to us that the difference between these two theoretical perspectives is substantial. In the Gestalt approach sensory experience is directly represented by cerebral physical events, which would arise from a transformation of stimulation. The features attributed to these physical events could allow the formulation of predictions about the course of phenomena. According to the cognitivist approach, the physical representation of stimuli is replaced at an early stage by a symbolic representation, sensory experience being regarded as conclusions attained by a sequence of procedures of symbol manipulation. These two theoretical perspectives suggest two different processing models: on the one hand, the dynamic self-distribution in a field (or another model of physical events fitting the phenomenal properties), and, on the other hand, the interpretation of data.

In the light of present knowledge, theorists, generally, are unable to decide which model is better. Yet to us a definitive decision is not urgent at all. It is probably more useful to let empirical research develop along parallel lines in both directions and in an atmosphere of peaceful coexistence, and let the facts speak for themselves.

Personally we prefer the information processing theory for thought, for which we find it difficult to imagine how a physical model could work. A physical model, however, is more convincing in helping us to understand perceptual facts. In general, our choice of theoretical preference is dictated by phenomenological evidence. Thus, in thinking we have the impression that our mind quickly carries out those operations of categorization, formulation, and control of hypotheses, analyses, comparisons, and decisions postulated by an inferential theory. When we look with our eyes, conversely, we directly experience that perceptual events behave as if they were subjected to tensions, vectors, influences, to the play of forces in a field.

Our theoretical preference may be debatable, and in the long run proved wrong, but we think that in principle it is not absurd to be guided by the particular characteristics and properties of the reality under investigation when constructing theories and planning methodological procedures. We are well aware, however, of the asymmetry between the use of physical models and the use of interpretative procedures based on symbol manipulation. The choice of a physical counterpart of a phenomenon is often difficult and exposed to experimental disconfirmation; whereas it seems always possible, in theory, to devise a sequence of logical steps sufficient to account for the occurrence of a phenomenon.

Having stated one personal preference, we admit to another. In the present stage of theorizing in psychology, fixating on an exclusivistic or hegemonic position must be avoided. When a relatively unanimous opinion prevails in the interpretation of only a limited number of facts in face of the widest diversity in the interpretation of most facts, it is useless and perhaps even dangerous to decide a priori what is the best way of understanding phenomena and which concepts and methods would be most adequate for studying them.

Admitting for the sake of argument that the perceptual systems works like a computer, we think it is important not to predetermine the set of rules according to which it is programmed. The job of discovering them can be better left to phenomenological observation and experimental research. This set of rules could turn out to be different from that underlying the logical calculus. Failure to bear in mind this possibility, and to assume from the outset that the two activities are governed by the same rules, incurs the risk of unduly postponing the discovery of the actual laws governing either perception or thought. Prematurely adopting either a panperceptual or a panlogical model could blind us to phenomena that are unforeseen by one model or another, or bring about the elimination, as "exceptions," of those phenomena that have no explanation in the adopted model.

In this regard, it seems to us that *amodal completion* is a noteworthy example of a phenomenon that has suffered from theoretical predilection. The following observations and discussions are dedicated to this phenomenon.

2.   AMODAL PRESENCE:
A PHENOMENON TO BE REVALUED

Amodal presence refers to the completion of part of an object that is not directly visible because it is covered by another object. The true importance of this fact has not been sufficiently recognized. Amodal completion was traditionally called "interposition" or "occlusion," and considered as one of the pictorial depth-cues because painters used it together with perspective and light and shade to increase the impression of three-dimensionality in their pictures, as a suitable means of suggesting a more unequivocal interpretation of front-rear spatial relationships of the objects depicted. Although Metelli (1940), analyzing the conditions determining what moves and what appears immobile in the visual field, had demonstrated situations of extraordinary perceptual presence of objects to which a real presence in the physical stimulation did not correspond (see Fig. 9.2), his observations were considered, as often happened with other visual phenomena, interesting curiosities without attracting the attention they deserved.

Michotte himself, who guided many experimental inquiries on the problem of amodal presence (1962), in a brief note first published in 1952, spoke of the phenomenon as a *new* enigma of perception (Michotte & Burke, 1952). Noteworthy also is the increasing attention Gibson (1950, 1966, 1979) devoted to the role of "occlusion" and related factors in the organization of our visual world.

Amodal completion was therefore late to be recognized as genuinely perceptual reality, and then only partially. Because it certainly had not escaped the notice of psychologists, and artists before them, that our phenomenal world is, in the words of Metelli, "a theater of continual totalizations," the absence or scarcity of interest by perceptual scientists toward this interesting phenomenon is

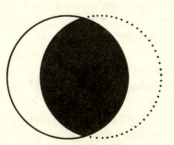

FIG. 9.2.   The black and white disk shown in the figure is made to rotate slowly (the rotation rate can vary from ¼ to 2½ revs per second). The center of rotation is coincident with the center of the arc that constitutes the border between the black and white regions. The prevailing phenomenal outcome is the following: a rotating circular aperture continually covers and uncovers the different parts of an immobile black disk (shown in the figure by a dotted line), which always appears as a complete whole, in part modally, and in part amodally. The part that are present amodally change continually (from Metelli, 1940).

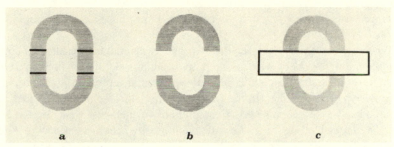

FIG. 9.3.   In a a complete gray ring is seen. In b two gray arches are seen, which can be *thought of* as parts of a complete ring. In c a complete ring is phenomenally present, even if only the same two arches as in b are *modally* present. The parts of the ring occluded by the horizontal bar are *amodally* present.

understandable only as the result of the lack of recognition of its actual perceptual nature. Indeed it has generally been "explained away," that is, eliminated as a problem. Amodal completion was fitted into a preestablished interpretative scheme by considering it as the result of an operation of thought on the perceptual datum. The integration of the hidden part of an object has always been seen as a mental integration, as the contribution of the knowledge of how things are made to the construction of the visual world.

To clarify our meaning in discussion of various kinds of completion and our insistence in distinguishing one from the other, it is useful to illustrate the concepts of mental representation and perceptual presence. In Fig. 9.3, a is an entirely visible gray ring. The two central regions defined by the short horizontal lines have the same perceptual clarity as the two arched regions. Just like the arched regions they are present in visual modality. In b there are only two gray arches. They can, however, be thought of as part of ring a but lacking the two central regions. Even if these two regions are mentally interpolated between the arches to form a ring, they are only "represented," and this mental integration exerts no influence on the aspect of the interruption, which continues to appear as part of the white background. Therefore, their representation is purely mental, having no perceptual clarity. The distinction between this two forms of "presence" presents no difficulties—everyone can recognize the difference between a thing actually seen and one only thought. The situation with c is less simple. Here too the two arches are modally visible. Because they tend to continue spontaneously behind the white horizontal bar, a representation of completion by the perceiver is not necessary. Indeed observers describe c as being like ring a covered by the horizontal bar. In this case, the presence of the two central regions that are not visible modally takes on a different character, one of greater coerciveness. It is no longer a mental representation as in b, but a presence possessing a reality independent of the observer. In the terminology of Metzger (1963) it is an "angetroffen" datum and no longer a purely "represented" datum. Henceforth, we use "encountered" for Metzger's "angetroffen." The name "amodal presence'' is reserved for the ''encountered'' presence of parts not directly visible.

Whereas, as we have said, the distinction between modal presence and mental representation (i.e., between true and proper seeing and thinking in a strict sense) is not very difficult, the distinction between mental representation and amodal presence is not so obvious. In the first place, not all the completions that occur are amodal (i.e., ''encountered'') completions in the sense just referred to. In fact, the majority of the integrations that continually occur in our concrete visual everyday world are representative in character; that is, they are mental integrations. A person who sits in front of us, behind a writing desk, appears to be a complete person, even if the only parts we see directly are the head, arms, and part of trunk. And in the same way the picture, of which we only see the parts not covered by his head, does not have a hole in that spot—it is a complete picture. And this goes for every normal scene, because in a three-dimensional space with bodies in it, it is the rule, from the observer's point of view, for some bodies to be partially covered by others. And yet, even putting aside the interposition of different objects, it must not be forgotten that the visible part of every single body, even when not covered by others, obstructs its rear part from our gaze. In all these cases concerning our every day experience, the integration generally occurs in accordance with our knowledge about the normal shape and color of the more or less familiar objects surrounding us. They are the effects of thought operations on perceptual data.

The validity of such explanation, which would seem universal, should not however, hide from us another equally universal fact. Mental integrations with cognitive bases are almost always accompanied and facilitated by completions of a perceptual nature, of the kind we have called amodal, and which give rise to an ''encountered'' presence.

Let us return to the example of the person sitting behind the writing desk. We have said that he is seen as complete. But complete in what sense? Evidently not in the sense that we would be able to indicate the position of his legs, or the color of his trousers, or the shape of his shoes. The degree of success with which we can infer these things will depend on how well we know the person himself. Guessing them is certainly the result of purely mental operations, however. But in this situation there is something possessing a less vague character, something that imposes itself like a factual datum independent of the observer's contribution. It is the fact that phenomenally the person does not end where its visible part ends—his body continues beyond the edge of the table that forms the border between the visible and covered parts. The ''continuing,'' the ''passing behind,'' has the compelling clarity of the ''encountered'' phenomenon, whereas the shape and color are indefinite and more subjective. The completion of the parts not directly visible would therefore seem to be in this case the result of the simultaneous action of two factors of a different level: one more mental and one more perceptual. The intervention of the perceptual factor becomes evident upon con-

FIG. 9.4. What we see here is a "piece" of a person.

sidering the difference between Fig. 9.4 and Fig. 9.5. The same part of a person is represented in both figures. For the purposes of our analysis the difference between the two is quite considerable. In Fig. 9.4 we have a "piece" of a person, which is enough of a cue to enable us to guess the rest of the body, but it is not quite sufficient to transform its piecemeal or fragmentary aspect, even minimally. In Fig. 9.5 the same configuration is no longer a piece, but the visible part of a whole person, whose invisible part behind the table possesses an "encountered" presence.

Thus, the two situations are, in our opinion, different in essence because in the situation represented in Fig. 9.5 two integrative activities of a different kind are acting together—one tending toward a perceptual amodal completion side by side with a purely mental completion of an inferential kind. The mental factor can be present in Fig. 9.4 in the total absence of the perceptual factor.

We can apply this reasoning not only to the artificial situations in Figs. 9.4 and 9.5, but with even greater validity to the real scenes that continually constitute our concrete visual environment. From the point of view of stimulation, each one of these scenes in our everyday world is usually made up only of a collection of directly visible parts of people and objects. These parts or pieces as such do not have a true phenomenal existence in the actual visual world, however, where we find ourselves in front of whole people and objects covering each other partially. We do not get an impression of integrating "pieces" as in Fig. 9.4, but we see entire objects partially covered as in Fig. 9.5.

In short, amodal completion transforms a collection of pieces into a reality of complete things of a phenomenal "encountered" character. Because amodal completion is an important ingredient in the construction of our daily visual world, rather than being a mere laboratory curiosity, more attention to the

FIG. 9.5. The same pattern of Fig. 9.4 is seen here as the visible part of a whole person.

modalities of its action and a careful study of it under controlled conditions are justified. Once its autonomy and genuine perceptual nature are recognized, that is, no longer "explained away" by being labeled hurriedly as a form of mental integration, amodal completion may become an instrument for outlining the rules, constraints, and tendencies characteristic of the perceptual system. For example, it might be useful in determining whether the "logic" of this system is exactly the same as the "logic" of thought.

In the following sections some observations on the functional effects of amodal completion are outlined. Such effects should serve to reaffirm its peculiar nature as a perceptual mechanism independent of processes that are merely interpretative. Also some areas in which amodal completion can be used as a research tool are indicated.

3.   FUNCTIONAL EFFECTS OF AMODAL COMPLETION

When we spoke of amodal completion as an "encountered" datum, revealing in this characteristic the proof that we are dealing with a phenomenon whose nature is different from that of represented completion, we were referring to the testimony of direct experience, that is, to the impression of being faced with something "objective," independent of us, not influenced by our will or our cognitive set. Indeed, properties such as phenomenal givenness and independence from the observer characterize a perceptual datum and distinguish it from a datum that is merely thought.

In a certain sense, this reasoning might appear circular—amodal completion is a perceptual datum because we have the impression it is perceptual. Other arguments eliminate any possible circularity, however.

Though a perceptual datum is characterized by particular kinds of phenomenal evidence, it has another significant property, namely, it always has a functional effect. In fact, the introduction of a truly perceptual event in a visual situation always produces a functional effect on the aspect or role of the data already present in the situation itself. For instance, consider the so-called geometrical-optical illusions and the effect that a frame of reference exerts on the appearance of a configuration.

Assigning amodal completion to the category of perceptual phenomena should prove more convincing if it can be demonstrated that functional effects exist that lawfully accompany amodal completion and which are absent when the completion is only mental. A number of situations in which the presence of noticeable functional effects of amodal completion seems undeniable are described.

3.1. Anomalous Formation Of Surfaces And Contours

Anomalous surfaces have given rise to theoretical and experimental interest in recent years. Various explanations have been proposed, from those based on

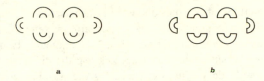

FIG. **9.6.** The attempt to complete by thought the arches in b fails to produce any functional effect. The covering surface, which in a is so compelling, does not appear in b.

physiological mechanisms (lateral inhibition, spatial frequency channels, feature detectors) to those of a cognitive type (inferences based on hypotheses about objects).

Without excluding the possibility that mechanisms of this kind may have an influence, we believe that the most satisfying hypothesis yet formulated was advanced by Kanizsa in 1955. According to him the principal causal factor in the formation of anomalous surfaces is the tendency to amodal completion of lines or surfaces that are perceptually incomplete.

Because it has been sufficiently shown (Kanizsa, 1955, 1974, 1976) that the appearance in the visual field of a modally present surface is a functional effect of amodal completion, we limit our examples to Figs. 9.6 and 9.7. In a (Fig. 9.6) the tendency of the open arches toward completion gives way to an opaque surface clearly distinguishable by brightness from the background, and separated from it by an outline without any corresponding discontinuity in stimulation. In b the outline of the arches is closed and they do not tend toward completion. We

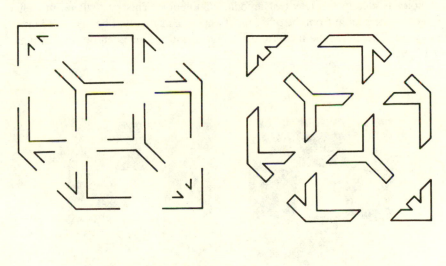

FIG. 9.7.   In b, the eight pieces can be thought as belonging to the Necker cube, which is never actually seen. No anomalous surfaces are formed. In a the incompleteness of the pieces "requires" an amodal completion. The cube's amodal presence produces a functional effect: the formation of oblique opaque bars, visible modally (from Kanizsa, 1979).

can think of completion even in this case, but by no effort can we create a surface with the character of an "external" presence independent of the observer, as happens with the surface formed spontaneously in a. The comparison between the two situations allows us to grasp the difference between "encountered" and thought data. This demonstrates the absolute ineffectiveness of an activity of thought in producing any functional effect on the perceptual aspect of a situation to which it is applied.

3.2. Amodal Completion Increases "Color Quantity"

When a and b in Fig. 9.8 are compared, the impression that there is "more black" in the second than in the first is obtained. This impression is surprising in view of the fact that the directly visible black areas in b are less extended than those in a. The structural difference between the two situations is that in a the black squares and the gray squares appear juxtaposed, there being no tendency for any square to pass behind any of the others. Conversely, there is a very strong tendency toward the completion of the black areas behind the gray ones in b. This results in the increase of the phenomenal quantity of black, despite the decrease of the relative areas of stimulation. Even more convincing instances can be seen in Figs. 9.9 and 9.10. In all these cases, the phenomenal increase of the quantity of color is clearly the result of amodal completion. This particular functional effect is inseparable from the other functional effects that will be discussed later, however. Therefore, the increase of "color quantity" also can be seen in Figs. 9.12, 9.13 and 9.16.

a   b

FIG. 9.8. The black parts tend towards completion under the gray disks only in b. From the standpoint of physical stimulation, the black area are more extended in a than in b. The reverse is true in perception, however.

a   b

FIG. 9.9.   Is there more black in a or in b?

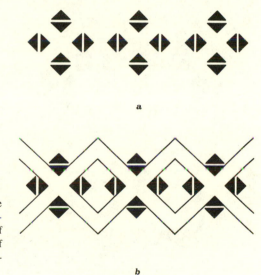

a

FIG. 9.10.   In this case too, in b, the
amodal unification produces an increase in the phenomenal quantity of
black, even though the extension of
the directly visible black parts is identical to that of the triangles in a.

b

3.3. Amodal Completion Creates Different Visual
   Objects

The direction of the completion results in the "encountered" presence of differently shaped visual objects as exemplified by Figs. 9.11–16. At first sight the
four black elements in Fig. 9.11 are unrecognizeable in Figs. 9.12 and 9.13

FIG. 9.11. Four pairs of black sectors. The various mentally possible completions do not affect their identity.

FIG. 9.12. A square with four sector-like appendages as in Fig. 9.14.

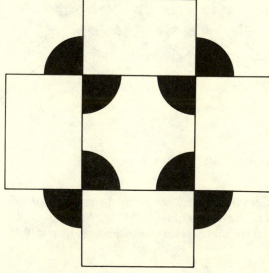

FIG. 9.13. Four disks as in Fig. 9.15.

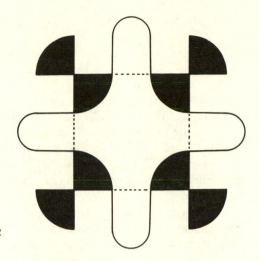

FIG. 9.14. This is how Fig. 9.12 is completed.

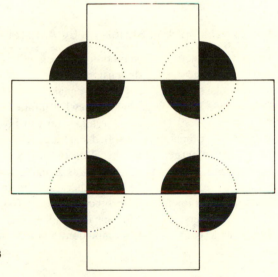

FIG. 9.15. This is how Fig. 9.13 is completed.

FIG. 9.16. Moving from the left top region to the right bottom one, amodal unification of the small triangles occurs in a totally different way, giving rise to totally different structures.

because in these situations the completion is forced to occur in different directions (see Figs. 9.14 and 9.15). This produces the phenomenal emergence of objects with very different shapes.

This effect is so compelling that an observer who is not forewarned typically fails to realize that the modally visible parts, which give rise to two different configurations, are identical in shape and size. This is so true that a perceptual scientist, when faced with these situations, said, "I don't see the problem. If you show me two different things, of course they look different to me." This remark indicates the degree of perceptual clarity that can be achieved by amodal completion. Such a remark would certainly not be said by a person invited to complete either a square or four disks by imagination when viewing the elements in Fig. 9.11. The elements in this case remain what they are, that is, pairs of sectors that touch each other at the tips. On the contrary, the same elements lose their identity as separate distinct units when subserving the configurations observed in Figs. 9.12 and 9.13.

3.4. Expansion And Shrinkage By Amodal Completion

Another influence of amodal completion directly and regularly noticeable in the visual field concerns the dimensions of surfaces which undergo completion. The two semidisks in Fig. 9.17 are of equal size even though the one adjacent to the rectangle seems larger and somewhat inflated. The same applies to the two triangles in Fig. 9.18 and to the trapeziums in Fig. 9.19.

In an experimentally controlled situation, Kanizsa and Luccio (1978) avoided the possible emergence of other illusory factors by using rectangles as test and comparison figures, and the result was an expansion effect of about 8%. Such a result has been confirmed in another experiment conducted with a different psychophysical method by Gerbino (1979) who found an expansion of about 9%. It must be understood that the apparent enlargement refers to the visible part of a surface undergoing amodal completion, and that the effect is clearly of perceptual nature.

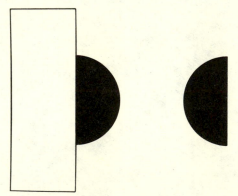

FIG. 9.17.   Even if the two semi-disks are of the same size, the one adjacent to the vertical bar appears larger.

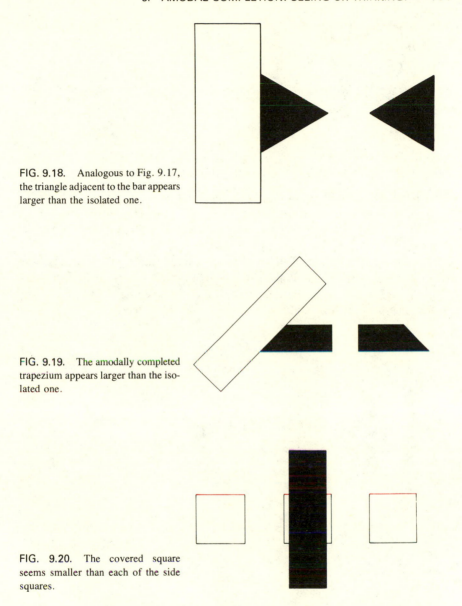

FIG. 9.18. Analogous to Fig. 9.17, the triangle adjacent to the bar appears larger than the isolated one.

FIG. 9.19. The amodally completed trapezium appears larger than the isolated one.

FIG. 9.20. The covered square seems smaller than each of the side squares.

Conversely a shrinking effect is obtained in the dimensions of the covered part, not directly visible but phenomenally present, of a surface of which only two parts are visible (see Fig. 9.20). The amount of such a shrinkage is directly proportional to the width of the covered area (see Fig. 9.21), and can reach up to 5% of the area of the complete figure (for the quantitative data see Kanizsa [1975a] and Tampieri [1979]).

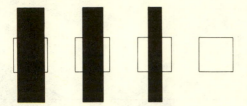

FIG. 9.21.   The phenomenal shrink-age is proportional to the width of the covered area (Kanizsa, 1975b).

3.5. The Afterimage Of An Amodally Completed Figure

A striking functional effect of amodal completion was recently ascertained by Bozzi (1980). When the primary stimulus is similar to the one shown in Fig. 9.22, the complementary afterimage of the pattern to the left of the fixation cross is quite different from the afterimage of the pattern to the right (see Fig. 9.23). Whereas in the afterimage of the right pattern three stable and well-separated greenish rectangles are seen, in the afterimage of the left pattern a whole uninterrupted greenish rectangle is visible. In turn the negative afterimage of the two vertical bars is seen, which alternates with the complete rectangle.

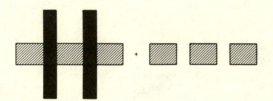

FIG. 9.22.   In the experimental dis-play the textured regions were red. The subject fixated the central cross.

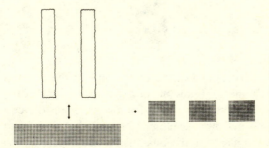

FIG. 9.23.   The portion of the after-image on the right-hand side appears as a stable set of three small greenish rectangles. The portion on the left-hand side appears as a single uninter-rupted greenish rectangle in alternation with the vertical bars.

4.   A TOOL FOR ANALYSIS

Having shown that amodal completion is a perceptual datum, we may mention some observations that indicates its methodological possibilities. Amodal completion allows observation of the way in which principles of organization act in the visual field in those situations free from constraints imposed by stimulation. Indeed, amodal completion occurs in those regions of the field where stimulation merely serves in the formation of the covering surface. The formation of the covered part therefore is not due to the stimulation of the corresponding region. This formation can be conditioned only by the stimulation relative to the adjacent regions. Because the shape assumed by a covered part is not arbitrary, it must depend in some way on the characteristics of the directly visible parts. In other words, the visible part not only possess the tendency to continue but to complete itself in a determinate way and not in any one of the other theoretically possible ways. Conversely, if an interpretative activity were involved, the covered part could assume any shape.

Amodal completion could be a "detector" of such nonarbitrary tendencies. Indeed, observation of the relation between the shape of the completed part and the shape of the visible parts will contribute to specifying the rules governing the functioning of the perceptual system.

In the following paragraphs, amodal completion is used to establish the relative strengths of various principles of organization which have been brought into conflict.

4.1. Simplicity

Considerable efforts have been made to define simplicity, the principle generally considered to be fundamental to all perceptual organization. It is tempting to identify the perceptual simplicity of form with geometrical regularity and maximum symmetry.

Kanizsa (1975a) maintained that such an identification is misleading, and that it probably arises from a belief that perception and thought are regulated by the same "logic." Thought, indeed, is dominated by the search for regularity and symmetry, but this does not imply *ipso facto* that the perceptual system is similarly dominated.

In order to show that the identification was misleading, Kanizsa had recourse to arguments based on figures involving amodal completions. Consider the patterns in Fig. 9.24 and Fig. 9.25. Even though completion in accordance with maximum symmetry is theoretically possible, the actual completion occurs in conformity with the principle of continuity of direction. Thus this principle is the actual decisive factor underlying the obtained completions rather than a hypothetical principle of maximum symmetry. For these patterns at least the ''fate'' of the

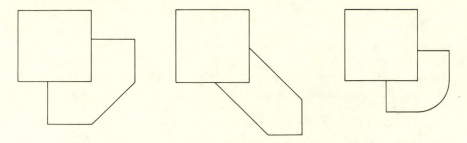

FIG. 9.24. In these situations, the most frequent amodal completion does not conform to the expectations based on a mechanism directed to achieve the maximum symmetry in a configuration.

FIG. 9.25. Amodal completion is so effective that the perceptual outcome is the same as in Fig. 9.24, even if the maximally symmetrical figure is given in stimulation without occlusion.

parts is not determined by the "demands" of the global structure. The example in Fig. 9.26 leads to the same conclusion, where again we see the prevalence of factors acting at a local level against the expectations generated by the global structure. Another example of how amodal completion can act as a "detector" of the actual preferences of the perceptual system was given by Gerbino (1978), one of whose illustrations appears in Fig. 9.27. Regular polygons undergo an obvious phenomenal distortion when each of their angles is covered by a figure with a side that passes through the vertex of the angle. Gerbino interpreted this effect as the result of the tendency of the outline of the polygon to prolong itself under the figure covering it so that the position of the apparent vertex is misplaced. The impression of distortion can be regarded as the consequence of the indifference of amodal completion to those criteria of regularity peculiar to thinking. When "rational" expectations favoring maximum regularity are in conflict with the output of a perceptual mechanism, an impression of irregularity, of deviation from a norm, is produced. This norm is not necessarily valid for perceptual processes, though always valid for rational ones, however.

FIG. **9.26.**   From Kanizsa (1979).

FIG. **9.27.**   From Gerbino (1978).

4.2. Proximity

According to Wertheimer's first ''law,'' grouping in the phenomenal field occurs, other things being equal, so that neighboring elements rather than distant ones come to be seen as members of the same group. In Fig. 9.28 the formation of pairs according to this principle is fairly coercive. Proximity is not a very strong factor of unification, however. Indeed, its action is easily overpowered by other factors, such as continuity and closure. In Fig. 9.29 amodal completion

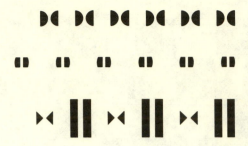

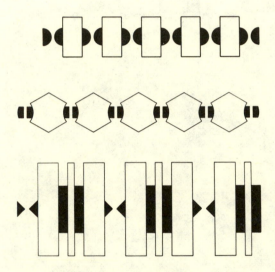

FIG. 9.28. In each of the three rows grouping of elements occurs according to proximity.

FIG. 9.29. Amodal completion allows grouping of distant elements in a manner similar to what happens in Fig. 9.30, where modal interpolations are shown.

FIG. 9.30. With respect to Fig. 9.28, the grouping of proximal elements is overcome by continuity and closure of modally present contours.

186

favors continuity and closure in grouping distant elements rather than near ones. The same grouping of distant elements occurs in Fig. 9.30, where the action of continuity and closure is made irresistible by the modal interpolations.

Evidently the structures formed in amodal completion are equivalent to modal ones. Actual unification behind tbe covering figure is induced by ''forces'' that produce perceptual effects. Of course, the connection of distant elements that is evident in Fig. 9.30 can be executed in thought in Fig. 9.28. But such ''thought'' unifications are difficult and very unstable; so to speak, they ''go against nature.'' But with amodal completion no effort is needed. The unifications in Fig. 9.29 become ''natural''; they are data and not representations.

4.3. The Role Of Familiarity

The tendency to explain all perceptual phenomena as mediated by knowledge, learning, and by past experience derives from the conception that all psychological processes are dominated by the same ''logic.'' Admittedly, the influence of past experience on the mental integration of perceptual data produced by primary processing is enormous. These perceptual data are interpreted, bestowed with meaning by means of inferential processes that are founded to a great extent on our knowledge of the objects in our world. In our opinion, however, the importance of past experience in the interpretation of perceptual data does not legitimize its use as an explicative principle regarding the processes at the basis of the formation of the data themselves. The exclusive emphasis on past experience as a principle to explain the primary data is an optional way. It entails negative consequences, an evident being the ''explaining away'' of interesting phenomena, which means they remain unexplained.

Kanizsa (1969) has given many examples of the inadequacy of knowledge and expectations to overcome the factors that really act in the formation of perceptual data. By observing how the parts of well-known objects complete themselves behind a screen, one can appreciate how the primary processing limits the influence of familiarity (see Fig. 9.31 and Fig. 9.32).

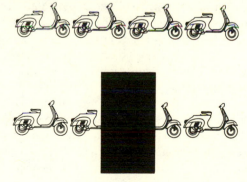

FIG. 9.31.   Despite knowledge about the proper size and shape of scooters, and the fact that many complete exemplars are shown in the picture, an ''anomalous'' scooter is seen behind the bar.

FIG. 9.32.   Knowledge about animal shapes does not prevent one from seeing a "monster" walking behind the vertical bar.

5.   CONCLUDING REMARKS

When an object is partially hidden by another object, the covered part usually possesses the character of thought (or inferred) presence—that is, of representation. The directly visible part is a clue for a cognitive completion, which occurs on the ground of a more or less specific knowledge of an object's shape, color, and so on. Besides these purely mental completions, however, other completions exist which possess the character of perceptual "encountered" presence.

Even if the task of distinguishing between these two kinds of completion is often difficult, our contribution emphasizes the need for and the usefulness of the distinction. As a matter of fact, both kinds of completion have a general relevance because, in ordinary conditions, a phenomenal world without them does not exist. Furthermore represented completions always seem to be accompanied or facilitated by the truly perceptual completion called "amodal."

Two sources of evidence enable one to distinguish one kind of completion from the other. Firstly, phenomenological evidence indicates that an "encountered" amodal presence is a psychological reality different from a merely mental presence. Secondly, the "encountered" amodal completion involves the occurrence of functional effects of perceptual nature. If these effects are taken into account, it becomes evident that amodally completed visual object behaves, to some extent, "as if" it were an object that is modally present in the visual field.

Hence, if we accept a view of perception as a composite product, we can distinguish, on the one hand, the cognitive activities that categorize, recognize, interpret, and attribute meanings; on the other hand, a primary process that organizes the sensory input. From a logical standpoint cognitive activities presuppose the existence of perceptual data. The occurrence of functional effects enables the formulation of the hypothesis that amodal completion belongs to the output of the primary process. It is this output that must be considered as the set of sensory data; such data then are available for successive interpretations. The primary process corresponds to what has been called, according to some popular sketches of information flow in perception, the "preattentive processes" by Neisser (1967) and Broadbent (1977), the "prerecognitive" (Prinzmetal & Banks, 1977), "unit formation" (Kahneman, 1973), "elementary coding"

(Kinchla, 1974), stage, or the stage of "pattern dependent detection" (Uttal, 1975).

Furthermore, the characteristics of the functional effects allows the testing of hypotheses about the set of rules to which primary processing conforms. More specifically, the expansion of the modal part of a completed object proves that invoking interpretative procedures in the explanation of amodal completion is insufficient. The mere interpretation of a given array of regions not as a mosaic but as an object partially hidden by another should not involve modifications of metrical attributes of the directly visible parts. It is a fact, however, that such modifications do occur. Moreover, their existence suggests that the processes of organization leading to amodal completion could be more conveniently represented by those physical events in which the global distribution affects local properties.

We think that just as mental completions can be utilized for study of cognitive activities of the secondary stage, amodal completion can serve as a useful tool for the analysis of the primary process. Though our demonstrations do not exhaust the range of problems raised by completion phenomena, we are confident that they will stimulate additional research.

ACKNOWLEDGMENTS

The preparation of the manuscript has been supported in part by a CNR grant to Walter Gerbino, n°79.00593.08. The authors are indebted to Nicholas Pastore who revised the English translation and offered valuable criticism.

REFERENCES

Bozzi, P. Immagini consecutive e completamento amodale. *Reports from the Institute of Psychology.* Trieste: University of Trieste, 1980.

Broadbent, D. E. The hidden preattentive processes. *American Psychologist,* 1977, *32,* 109–118.

Gerbino, W. Some observations on the formation of angles in amodal completion. *Italian Journal of Psychology,* 1978, *5,* 85–100.

Gerbino, W. Il ruolo della forma nelle modificazioni di grandezza dovute a completamento amodale. *Reports from the Institute of Psychology.* Trieste: University of Trieste, 1979.

Gibson, J. J. *The perception of the visual world.* Boston: Houghton Mifflin, 1950.

Gibson, J. J. *The senses considered as perceptual systems.* Boston: Houghton Mifflin, 1966.

Gibson, J. J. *The ecological approach to visual perception.* Boston: Houghton Mifflin, 1979.

Kahneman, D. *Attention and effort.* Englewood Cliffs, N.J.: Prentice-Hall, 1973.

Kanizsa, G. Margini quasi percettivi in campi con stimolazione omogenea. *Rivista di Psicologia,* 1955, *49,* 7–30.

Kanizsa, G. Perception, past experience and the impossible experiment. *Acta Psychologica,* 1969, *31,* 66–96.

Kanizsa, G. Contours without gradients or cognitive contours? *Italian Journal of Psychology,* 1974, *1,* 93–112.

Kanizsa, G. The role of regularity in perceptual organization. In G. Flores d'Arcais (Ed.), *Studies in perception:* Festschrift for Fabio Metelli. Milan: Martello-Giunti, 1975. a

Kanizsa, G. Amodal completion and phenomenal shrinkage of surfaces in the visual field. *Italian Journal of Psychology,* 1975, *2,* 187–195. b

Kanizsa, G. Subjective contours. *Scientific American,* 1976, *234,* 48–52.

Kanizsa, G. *Organization in vision.* New York: Praeger, 1979.

Kanizsa, G., & Luccio, R. Espansione di superfici da completamento amodale. *Reports from the Institute of Psychology.* Trieste: University of Trieste, 1978.

Kinchla, R. Detecting target elements in multi-element arrays: a confusability model. *Perception and Psychophysics,* 1974, *15,* 149–158.

Metelli, F. Ricerche sperimentali sulla percezione del movimento. *Rivista di Psicologia,* 1940, *36,* 319–370.

Metzger, W. *Psychologie.* Darmstadt: Steinkopff, 1963.

Michotte, A. *Causalité, permanence et réalité phénoménales.* Louvain: Publications Universitaires, 1962.

Michotte, A., & Burke, L. Une nouvelle énigme de la psychologie de la perception: Le "donné amodal" dans l'expérience sensorielle. In *Proceedings and papers of the 13° International Congress of Psychology.* Stockholm: Bröderna Lagerström, Boktryckare, 1952. Republished in A. Michotte (Ed.), *Causalité, Permanence et Réalité Phénoménales.* Louvain: Publicationes Universitaires, 1962.

Neisser, U. *Cognitive psychology.* New York: Appleton-Century-Crofts, 1967.

Prinzmetal, W., & Banks, W. P. Good continuation affects visual detection. *Perception and Psychophysics,* 1977, *21,* 389–395.

Tampieri, G. The shrinkage of amodally completed surfaces in figure-ground situations. *Italian Journal of Psychology,* 1979, *6,* 53–57.

Uttal, W. R. *An autocorrelation theory of form detection.* Hillsdale, N.J.: Lawrence Erlbaum Associates, 1975.

10
How Big Is a Stimulus?

Julian Hochberg
Columbia University

INTRODUCTION

The last few years have seen a great increase in the popularity of organizational approaches to the study of perception, more or less explicitly endebted to Gestalt theory, and of direct or stimulus-informational approaches, explicitly indebted to the work of Gibson (1950, 1979). The mere fact that the appearance of a pattern cannot in general be completely predicted from the appearances of its parts presented in isolation does not by itself provide a basis for reviving anything like Gestalt theory. And the mere fact that what has been called higher-order stimulus information about distal (object) properties are normally provided by the environment, and that such information is sometimes used by the normal viewer, by itself implies nothing whatsoever about the processes of perception. Helmholtz discussed quite explicitly what later was taken by the Gestaltists as the law of good continuation; he discussed at length the importance of motion-produced stimulation, and of active exploration in vision and in touch, as providing what was later to be called the invariant information in the stimulus transformations (Cassirer, 1944; Gibson, 1950, 1979). Moreover, Helmholtz stressed that as far as our perceptions are concerned, the distal properties are usually directly perceived (i.e., we are not aware of the activities of the individual receptors, nor of the processes by which the percepts are constructed). If one is to go beyond (or oppose) Helmholtz in these respects, therefore, it will have to be in terms of evidence about the ways in which larger spans of stimulus information are used, not merely by showing that they are present in stimulation, or that they are used.

That has not yet been adequately done.

I do not see how one can discuss perceptual organization until the phenomena in Figs. 10.1 and 10.2 are dealt with; I do not see how one can discuss any theory

191

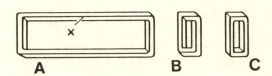

FIG. 10.1.   Although inconsistent as a tridimensional object (i.e., line x must be discontinuous as a dihedral although continuous as a line), A looks tridimensional. The same inconsistent features, in closer proximity (B) look flat, whereas consistent features, equally close (C), look tridimensional (Hochberg, 1968).

of direct response to invariant spatial information until the phenomena of Figs. 10.3 and 10.4 are dealt with; nor do I see how the problem of integrating the information in successive glances can be discussed seriously until the phenomena in Figs. 10.6 and 10.7 are dealt with.

In each case, the phenomena show strong limits on the size of the stimulus pattern that is effective at any time, and imply similar limitations on the duration over which an event can be considered to be a single stimulus. Such limits clearly determine what we can mean by the terms *stimulus information* and *perceptual organization:* if we knew that our visual systems were directly responsive to the changes in light at only one small point over some very short interval of time, it would not seem like much of an explanation to say that "configuration is itself a stimulus," nor that various aspects of the extended visual stimulus (such as gradients of texture and motion) *directly* elicit our perceptions of the world of space and movement. In fact, I believe that many current attempts at perceptual theory seem explanatory and intelligible only because they ignore the question of limits and all of the associated issues that naturally accompany that question.

It seems to me, therefore, that the prudent scientist who is interested in stimulus information or perceptual organization would welcome any indications of relevant sensory limitations, inasmuch as these must help to define the nature of both phenomena and theory. Evidence and arguments to this point abound, but they have been almost totally without effect on those concerned with either organization phenomena or extended stimulus information. The fact is that the general shape and emphases of any theory of perception and of information processing depends strongly on this matter of the size of the effective stimulus. Gibson, at least recognizes that occasions for appeal to enrichment (i.e., occasions in which the organism must contribute what I have called mental structure)

FIG. 10.2.   The intersection at point 2 is reversible despite the interposition at 1 (Hochberg, 1978a; Peterson & Hochberg, in preparation).

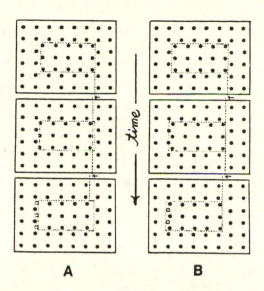

FIG. 10.3. Kinetic occlusion defines a textured moving surface behind a rectangular aperture in a similarly textured surface, at A, and a moving rectangle in front of an occluded surface at B (Kaplan, 1969). The two different arrangements are here distinguished only at the left-hand edge, and only during the left-most moment of the cycle of back-and-forth horizontal motion. If the viewer's gaze is not very near that edge at those times, the viewer cannot distinguish A from B (Hochberg, Green, & Virostek, 1978; Hochberg, Virostek, & Green, in preparation).

arise when stimulus information is inadequate (Gibson, 1951, 1979) or is inadequately picked up, that is, is subthreshold. A substantial change in the way in which we think of perceptual process—that is, a substantial departure from the constructivist theory of J. S. Mill and Helmholtz—can be achieved only if information in an entire extended stimulus array is picked up in some sense to which the word "direct" can be meaningfully applied (cf. Hochberg, 1979b). It is precisely to this point that my present questions are addressed.

The Gestaltists' criticisms of the primitive view of specific nerve energies with which Helmholtz started, and of the list of "primary" sensations of early Associationism, were perfectly well founded, but the physiological speculations and the philosophical edifices that they built on these criticisms were unjustifi-

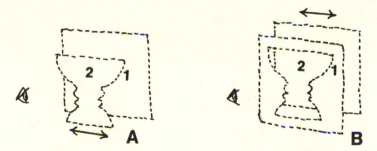

FIG. 10.4. Kinetic occlusion defines the two alternatives of a Rubin figure. In each case, reversal is easier with fixation away from the edge (2) than near it (1) (Hochberg, Virostek, & Peterson, in preparation).

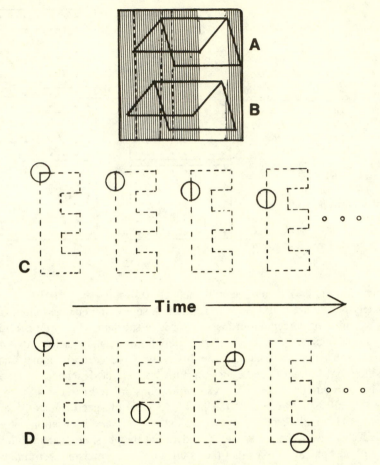

FIG. 10.5. Viewed in successive vertical apertures behind an opaque mask (here shown as a grey screen), the pattern is recognizable in both A and B. At A, however, in which intersections are dissected by the aperture viewing procedure, the object looks flat, whereas at B, in which the intersections are left intact, the object looks tridimensional (Hochberg, 1968). In C and D aperture views are of the same shape in different orders (Girgus, Gellman, & Hochberg, 1980).

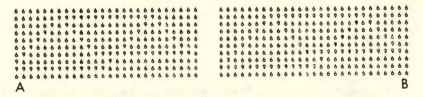

FIG. 10.6. The same shape is delineated by 9s in A and in B, but the 9s are filled in, in B, to increase their parafoveal visibility (Hochberg, 1968).

able. Gibson's attempt to seek out and measure the "higher-order variables" of stimulus information, and the responses that they determine, was probably the most important new attempt since Helmholtz, but is still largely a proposal, with little empirical foundation. Furthermore, even the most inclusive of direct theories will not make the problem of mental structure go away: even if the limits of direct determination by higher-order variables are broad, there still remains the question of where the mental structure comes from that is used beyond those limits, and the acquisition and nature of that structure would not be a minor question in any case. But if the limits of direct pick up are severe—if for much of normal perception the effective stimulus span in space and time is so small that mental structure must comprise a substantial part of the perceptual process—then studying the nature and mechanism of that component become the most urgent task that psychology must undertake.

I briefly review some old and some new demonstrations showing that each individual glance is severely limited in the amount of information that can be picked up, and that these limitations affect the information that can be picked up in sequences of freely initiated and directed glances; then I discuss the implications of these demonstrations for wholistic theories of perception.

(A) THE WHOLE DOES NOT DETERMINE THE APPEARANCE OF THE PART: LOCAL DEPTH CUES AND OTHER LOCAL FEATURES

Figure 10.1a looks three dimensional even though its corners (1, 2) are inconsistent; figure 10.1b looks much more flat. Is this merely a matter of proportion? Not so: Fig. 10.1c looks solid, in the same proportions (Hochberg, 1968). These figures are modified from one of the now-classical Penrose and Penrose (1958) impossible objects. When Jacob Beck called the latter to our attention in 1960, they capped the grave doubts that Virginia Brooks and I had developed about the attempt to devise quantitative models of figural organization (Hochberg & Brooks, 1960). Such attempts continue, but not in my hands, because I now think them misguided: Figs. 10.1a and 10.1b should both look equally (and highly) flat, by any reasonable encoding theory or minimum principle, and they simply do not do so. If this argument seems strained, and insufficient to set against the rich tradition of Gestalt psychology, consider Fig. 10.2 (Hochberg, 1978a). *This is not an impossible object.* The orientation in which the horizontal line looks nearer than the vertical at point 2 is specified by the intersection at point 1 (by the depth cue of interposition, or by the Gestalt "law" of good continuation, terms which I believe to mean the same thing: Hochberg, 1972). In fact, however, if you look at point 2 for a few moments, the perspective will reverse, and the vertical line will look the nearer. (Perspective can also be reversed even while you attend point 1, especially if you try to see it that way, but not as much as at point 2 [Peterson & Hochberg, 1981].)

It is conceivable, of course, that the piecemeal perspective reversals implied by Fig. 10.2 do not occur when both intersections 1 and 2 are ambiguous, that is, when both are unsigned depth cues as they are in the fully ambiguous Necker cube. I cannot think how to test that possibility: note that if the orientation at intersection 1 had not been fixed in Fig. 10.2, the fact that independent reversals occur at intersection 2 could probably not have been detected. Once we recognize that organizations can indeed reverse piecemeal (Fig. 10.2) and that inconsistancies are not immediately evident (Fig. 10.1a) the question of what a perceptual response entails is not clearly answerable. (So the behaviorist's distrust of introspection or phenomenology has yet another good grounding.) I return to this point in my conclusions, in discussing some of the recent experiments that have been taken as evidence for wholistic perceptual process. For now, the point is that the prudent man, faced with this indeterminacy, would assume that if such at least partial independence of part from whole is manifest when that independence *can* be tested, that it is also true of conditions in which it cannot be tested.

Figure 10.1a provides evidence that the corners (as local depth cues) are at least partially independent of the whole configuration in the sense that an impression of their tridimensionality is maintained despite their mutual inconsistency. In Fig. 10.2, the orientation of the ambiguous and unsigned local depth cue at point 2 changes in at least partial independence of the signed depth cue at point 1. And in both cases, where one looks or attends affects what one perceives. I don't see how it is possible, therefore, to subscribe to any theory of perceptual organization that is even remotely like that of Gestalt theory, because these demonstrations reject either the rule that the organization of the whole determines the appearance of the parts, the rule that we perceive the simplest organization that can be fitted to the stimulus, or both rules (see Hochberg, 1981). And I do not see how any alternative organizational theory can be formulated which does not take demonstrations like these into account in some way.

(B) THE LIMITS ON ANY DIRECT THEORY OF SURFACE PERCEPTION

Figures 10.1 and 10.2 dealt with static line drawings, the primary subject matter of Gestalt theory. Figures 10.2, 10.4, 10.6 and 10.7 pertain as well to limitations on any more "ecologically-oriented" direct theory of surface perception.

At the heart of such theories lies the fact that as the relative position of viewer and object change, the invariance of a rigid object or scene will result in invariant relationships within the transformations in the light to the eye that are imposed by the relative motion of viewer and object. This point was first explicitly developed by Helmholtz; the terms of set theory (e.g., invariance and transformation) were introduced to Helmholtz's theory by Cassirer; and the far-ranging discussion of such invariances, and their implications, was of course pursued by Gibson. The nature of one's theory of perceptual organization in particular, and of psychology in general, vary greatly, depending on whether, how, and with what limits one takes such information to be actually used by the organism. No matter how much information there may be in the light reaching the eye, if the organism does not use it, or does not respond to it directly, the psychological consequences remain moot.

Despite the fact that an extraordinary amount has been written about such information, and about how it changes the way in which we must view psychology, the fact is that as yet we know very little about the pickup of such invariances. One particularly simple invariance is the stimulus for surface reflectance. The luminance ratio of object and surround, under changing illumination of both, is essentially invariant. Whether this invariance indeed determines lightness perception has been pursued for well over a century (Hochberg, 1979; Hurvich & Jameson, 1966). A ubiquitous stimulus invariant, one would surely expect it to be a good test case. In fact, it has been almost completely ignored by "direct theorists," and what research there is to this point does not clearly support the contention that reflectance perception is a direct response to luminance ratios (Beck, 1972; Epstein, 1977; Hochberg, 1972).

With respect to the perception of the shapes, movements and spatial disposition of surfaces, we know from the evidence of the robust Ames trapezoidal illusion that kinetic depth information is not exempt from threshold considerations: viewed from a few feet, the rotating and invariant trapezoid, undergoing a continuous and informative transformation in full view of the subject, is nevertheless perceived as an oscillating rectangular surface. Clearly, if thresholds limit the pickup of such higher-order information, the very first task is to explore those limits, and the Ames trapezoid should be a matter of considerable importance to the direct theorists. Instead there has been a remarkable lack of concern with this matter among advocates of this position.[1]

The fact is, that higher-order variables are particularly vulnerable to the question of thresholds, inasmuch as there are two separate levels at which such questions can arise, as I will now attempt to spell out.

---

[1]The only reference by any direct theorist to the Ames trapezoid, that I know, is an acknowledgement by Gibson (1979). In the Ames trapezoid, of course, not only does the static depth cue of linear perspective override the higher-order information specifying an invariant trapezoid undergoing rotation that must be provided by the objects' edges, but a bar thrust through the window and allowed to rotate with it will be perceived to undergo rubbery deformations appropriate to the perceived oscillation that is in turn consistent with the static depth cue. All of this has been known for decades, and immediately raises the question about where such powerful mental structures come from if they are not drawn upon the normal course of perception. The same sorts of questions arise as soon as we think about picture perception (Hochberg, 1978a, 1981b; see section C3b of this chapter).

(1) Carrier Elements And Their Modulations By Higher-Order Variables

In general, higher-order variables are imposed as what we may consider *modulation* on what we may call *carrier elements,* and each of these has its own characteristic thresholds. I will make this point with respect to a particularly simple higher-order variable, that of *texture-density gradient* (Gibson, 1950), but it applies as well to any of the information that is carried by the textures and contours of the visual field.

Imagine each element of texture, for example, each grain on a sheet of sandpaper. If its contrast with the background is too low, or its size is too small, it cannot be individually detected. That is, each texture element has a set of thresholds which must be exceeded if it is to have any effect. Of course, the threshold for the detection of an element in a repetitive or otherwise ordered array will be different from the threshold for the element in isolation, and the threshold for the array of elements will be different from that for each of the elements, but there will nevertheless surely be such thresholds for carrier elements to be effective at all. Now consider the density gradient of the set of textural elements: if the change in density per unit of distance is too small, the texture-density gradient will go undetected, and so will the slant of the surface to which it normally corresponds, that is, the modulation can be below threshold even if the carrier elements are above threshold. This is of course not a new point (cf. Hochberg & Smith, 1955; Smith & Smith, 1963), but it has not been seriously considered by direct theorists. It should be: with this analysis in mind, I will now try to show that the problem of thresholds is indeed a general one—perhaps a critical one—for the question of how, or even whether, such higher-order variables of stimulus information are used at all. The problem is not restricted to such exotic phenomena as the Ames trapezoid.

In the real world of objects and surfaces, information about where one object's surface ends, and a further surface begins, is not carried by lines, but by color differences and by changes in moving texture distributions as well. It is conceivable that the limitations noted in the peripheral use of the line-drawing information noted in connection with Figures 10.1 and 10.2 simply do not apply to the motion-produced patterns of texture-flow that define surfaces and their edges. A primary fact in defining objects visually is that nearer surfaces potentially overlap or occlude parts of further ones. What Gibson calls kinetic occlusion then specifies which surface is nearer. In a and b in Fig. 10.3, a textured surface moves leftward behind an aperture in a nearer surface, or moves as a small rectangle in front of a further surface, respectively. Note that in the third view of both a and b, a column of texture elements is deleted; this information specifies that the physical arrangement is one of a near window and a far surface, respectively. In both a and b, the occlusion and subsequent disocclusion at the left hand edges specify the tridimensional arrangement of the surfaces, and

George Kaplan (1969) showed several years ago that this condition elicits the appropriate perception. A recent series of experiments (Hochberg, Green, & Virostek, 1978; Hochberg, Virostek & Green, in preparation) was designed to discover whether this class of edge formation is less well picked up in peripheral than in foveal vision, or whether the visual system is so attuned to kinetic occlusion that we can afford to ignore the fact that the scene is sampled by a finite number of glances.

In all of these experiments, the display was such that kinetic occlusion might occur only at the left edge (as it does in Fig. 10.3); at the right edge; or at neither. In the last case (and at the unoccluded edge in all cases) the depth information is ambiguous or *unsigned*. When the depth information was signed, the central region could be either nearer or further than the surround. The only depth cues in any cases were those of kinetic occlusion and shear (the latter occurring along the horizontal edges that bounded the central moving set of dots, comprising an unsigned depth cue); of course, no outline between center and surround existed in the displays actually used. In some experiments of the series, fixation points were assigned at different distances from the active edge (e.g., at 0, 1.4, 2, 8, . . . 12.8 degrees from the active edge). Highly significant effects of where one looked were found in several experiments in which task and conditions were varied slightly; detection of depth direction dropped to chance by about 4° from the active edge.

Lest it be thought that the results are not "ecologically representative" because a stationary eye was used in these experiments, let me hasten to add that the same phenomenon holds when the display is viewed by a moving eye executing voluntary saccades: in one of the experiments, whether the active edge specified the central region to be a near or a far surface was changed periodically, in a regular cycle. Above the moving region, a letter was shown at one corner or the other, and what the letter was (e.g., an X or a Y) changed on an erratic schedule. The letter was near the active edge only when that edge specified the center region as being far, whereas at other times the letter was near the corner above the unsigned edge. Below the moving region of the display was a similar moving letter, out of phase with the upper one, and following a schedule that placed it near the active edge only while the latter specified that the center region was near. Subjects were given two tasks: to count the number of changes in either the upper or the lower letter, and to note whether the center region was near or far. When monitoring the changes in the upper letter, all subjects reported the center region to be far; when monitoring the lower letter, the center region appeared near.

It is clear that *the pickup of depth information can depend strongly on where one looks, even with a freely moving gaze*.

There are other ways of talking about these findings, especially in terms of the viewer's intentions (which I discuss later), but none of them that I can think of set aside the main points of this conclusion.

These facts place an upper limit on the extent over which a higher-order variable can be picked up: whenever the higher-order variable that defines perceptual structure is carried by moderately small elements (e.g., by surface texture), the effective radius of pickup of those variables, within each glance, may be so small that perceptual overlap between successive views will not serve as even a *possible* direct basis for perception. We know from research with aperture-viewing (Hochberg, 1968) and motion pictures (Hochberg & Brooks, 1979; Hochberg, 1978c) that people can build up scenes in their mind's eye from views that do not overlap at all. In such cases, the integration of successive glances simply *must* rest on mental structures that bridge that individual glances. Higher-order variables may indeed contribute to our perception of the world through successive glances when the glances overlap, as they normally do. It is clear, however, that mental structures and lower-order variables are important, too, and the perception psychologist's first priority must be to determine the limits of these different levels of determinants, and to discover the mechanisms by which the subject-matter of old and new psychophysics work together.

Concern with molar factors is no license for ignoring the molecular.

A last experiment should be considered before leaving this series. The question is whether the dependence of depth judgment on gaze direction pertains only to perceived edge-depth per se, which makes it of limited importance, or pertains as well to the closely associated question of the perceived shapes of the objects that comprise the content of our field of view.

Several years ago, I proposed that the figure-ground distinction arose as a result of "decisions" as to which side of a peripherally viewed edge was the near surface (figure), and was therefore potentially available to the gaze over its entire extent, and which side of the edge was occludible and background (Hochberg, 1970a); the "laws of figure-ground organization" should then be construed as cues to that decision (Hochberg, 1970a, 1972). This perceptual assumption could not be considered to be merely a single-level matter of perceived depth, however, because figure-ground reversals could occur even when shapes like the vase or faces (alternatives in the Rubin pattern) were so produced as to be unambiguous figures in depth, for example, by using Julesz patterns or by using kinetic occlusion to make one or the other alternative be seen as near surface and the other as occluded background (Hochberg, 1968). For this reason, I argued that the figure-ground phenomenon was not a unitary one, but concealed several separate processes. Julesz (1971) later reported that such figure-ground patterns are nonreversible, but we will now see that that is not true in general, and that the circumstances under which they are relatively nonreversible are directly relevant to the question of the size of a stimulus, and of the inferred response to it.

In the experiment represented in Fig. 10.4 (Hochberg, Virostek, & Peterson, in preparation), an inner set of moving dots defines either a moving vase (Fig. 10.4a), or a moving background as space between two faces (Fig. 10.4b). The stimulus displays actually used dot fields, of course, and not outlines. Subjects were asked to try to see the vase, or to try to see the faces, while they kept their attention and gaze fixed on one of the two fixation points (1 or 2). Summarizing the "vase" responses: when subjects are holding fixation 1, they can see the vase much more readily while watching stimulus A than stimulus B, and when watching stimulus A, they are *forced* by the stimulus information to see the vase more of the time, even when they are instructed to try to see the faces—but this is true only as long as they are fixating point 1. When, conversely, subjects fixate point 2, which is further from the active edge of the moving region, they are more free to see stimulus A as B and vice versa: the edge still defines a potential shape, inasmuch as both alternative responses are still obtained, but the direction of the depth is apparently unsigned at fixation point 2 because of its distance from the edge.

What is important to my present argument in this experiment is the fact that gaze direction and the associated sensory limits determine not only which edge is perceived as nearer, but which *shape* is perceived, even with unambiguously specified stimulus displays. I think these demonstrations (Figs. 10.3 and 10.4) clearly show that there are important limits of pickup of higher-order stimulus information within the individual glance.

Next, I wish to discuss the matter of temporal limits, and how they relate to the spatial limits that I have described.

Direct theorists argue thus: granted that the momentary glance is limited, and that the effective stimulus is smaller in any one glance than the whole configuration or the whole optical expansion pattern being considered: what difference does that make as long as the viewer is free to obtain information from any point in the entire field by shifting his gaze? Indeed, Gibson completely sidesteps the question of the limitations of the momentary glance by considering the entire optic array, subject to a freely exploring gaze, as the relevant stimulus situation. Is this a viable alternative?

I consider that point next, and conclude that such an attempt can only successfully solve the problem under a special set of assumptions that have not been tested.

(C) IMPLICATIONS OF SPATIAL AND TEMPORAL
LIMITS
ON THE PICKUP OF HIGHER-ORDER VARIABLES

Imagine first the contrafactual case of an eye having only a fovea—say, an effective field of vision of about 2°. If a larger shape were presented—say, one of 6°—the eye would have to make several successive fixations in order to encompass the entire pattern, and the viewer's information about the entire shape would have to be integrated from the information obtained from the successive discrete glances. Because these glances are spread out over time, one would think that any account of the perception of the entire shape would have to include some mechanism of memory, storage or expectation—some *mental structure*. An alternative treatment has been offered both by Gestaltists and by direct theorists, however, and we consider it next.

(1) The Notion Of Stimulation Over Time (And Of Timeless/Formless Invariants)

To Wertheimer, the configuration of an entire melodic sequence of notes, or of a succession of visual stimuli in stroboscopic movement, provides the single stimulus event to which the melody or perceived movement, respectively, is the unitary response. The form of the event over time was taken as the direct and essential stimulus for the perceived auditory or visual event. Gibson has similarly taken visual information over time, picked up by the eye in free and active exploration of the optic array, as the direct and essential basis of perception.

(2) The Different Meanings Of The Distinction Between Active And Passive Stimulation, In Constructivist Versus Direct Theories, And Their Relation To The Question of Effective Stimulus Size

Helmholtz envisioned perception (as distinct from sensation, which was not thought by him to be part of conscious experience) as active, and as the result of exploration and expectation. One of his most striking examples is that of active touch: how little can be discerned in response to passive contact, but how the same shape, actively explored by the hand, becomes an organized, perceived object. Gibson and his colleagues have similarly emphasized the importance of active versus passive exploration, indeed using the same example of haptic perception (1962). A different meaning attaches to the two uses of the term, "active," however. This difference is important; is often obscure to those who use the term; and is very closely related to the limits of a direct theory and to the question of the size of the effective stimulus.

To Helmholtz, the purpose of perceptuomotor exploration was to provide the viewer with occasions for mobilizing a schema of expectations about what the results of the next perceptuomotor action would bring, and for testing those expectations (Helmholtz, 1962). Helmholtz, like J. S. Mill, was an early formulator of what is currently called a constructivist theory of perception, and in such theories the function of sensory activity is to test a set of sensorimotor expectations.

To Gibson (the most explicit of the direct theorists in the field of perception), the purpose of sensory activity is to provide for motion of the viewer relative to the object, so as to provide the transformations of the light received which will, by their invariances, provide information about the invariant objects and scenes and layouts in space. Note that by this account, *no* mental structures—no hypotheses, schemas or models of the world—play a role in normal perception. (That is what makes this theory different from Helmholtz's.) The activity has as its purpose the elicitation of informative stimulation, to which the response is direct. Although Gibson may on some occasions distinguish between active and passive presentation of the same stimuli, on other occasions, he does not do so, and *the distinction is in any case without theoretical content in his explanatory system.* I cannot see how in fact the distinction could be maintained without making the direct theory identical to the indirect or constructivist theory (or if it can be done, I have not come across it).

It seems clear to me that the Wertheimer/Gibson theory is at least partially correct: with respect to apparent movement, as early as Exner it was proposed that the entire visual event occurring over some (short) time is the stimulus for the perception of motion; and it is hard to believe that the interval between two or three notes is not indeed a significant stimulus event in the perception of melody. That is, direct sensory responses to stimulus events are surely not restricted to a single point in time any more than they are to points in space. The recent hectic quest for feature detectors, pursued with some success in the field of motion as well as in pattern vision, is testimony of a widespread belief in that point among physiologists and sensory psychologists of varied theoretical persuasions. But questions of temporal limits are as important as those of spatial limits, and indeed as we see later, the one implies the other. In any case, at one extreme, we have the Helmholtzean view of the function of exploratory activity, which by its emphasis on the prediction of sensory events to come, stresses the finite temporal extent of present sensory stimulation; on the other, we have the wholistic approaches, to which a stimulus event that stretches over some unspecified duration comprises the adequate information to which the visual system responds directly. To assume the lower span (i.e., a very brief sensory moment) is, I think, now clearly wrong. Let me try to show why it is also reasonable to assume that there are also upper bounds, and why it is important to determine what they are.

(3) Can The Notion Of Temporally Extended Stimulation Replace The Notion Of Storage (That Is, Of Mental Structure) In Bridging The Limited Momentary Glance?

There are two strong limits that must be placed on the notion of temporally extended stimulation.

(a) *The Elective Nature Of Ballistic Saccades.* Exploration glances are highly elective both as to occurrence and direction, and saccades are programmed in advance and in discrete steps as to when, where and how far the eye will next be sent. That is, after a first glance, the viewer might well elect not to look at other parts of the stimulus display. The act of glancing at some place that has not yet been brought into the field of foveal view requires a very specific decision. In normal vision, in which we are not restricted to a single 2° of foveal vision but enjoy some 180° of total peripheral vision as well, our eyes are moved neither randomly, repetitively nor endlessly: after a few glances at specific places, the perceptual act is normally complete. Visual questions are asked by looking, but are asked only until they are answered to the satisfaction of the viewer acting under some specific perceptual task. I cannot see how we can discuss when the viewer elects to look, where he elects to look, and when he elects to cease looking, without conceding that he possesses some form of mental structure about what he is looking at (some schema, expectation, storage) that guides, sustains and terminates that activity. The activity of the eye is not determined either by the stimulus array, nor yet by the information that the array contains, but by the interaction between these and the viewer's perceptual questions, and by the point at which the latter are answered to his or her satisfaction. The occurrence and duration of pickup thus depends on task and on mental structure, and cannot be defined merely in terms of an array and the free looking that is devoted to it. The point is that the act of exploration is self-limited, and those limits determine both the duration of the temporal event that is considered as a single stimulus, and the kind of theory that we bring to the question of stimulus size.

(b) *When Do "Cue" And "Information" Have Different Implications?* What if the viewer does *not* execute the saccade that brings the next transformation of the field of view, or does not execute the head movement that would disocclude a partially hidden object? Such actions are, after all, elective. (The same question arises, of course, if the effective temporal span of stimulation does not extend beyond the period of the single glance.) These limits are of course imposed by pictures, and Gibson's description of what must then be drawn on is apt (1979, 271f.):

> When the young child... sees the family cat at play the front view, side view... and so on are not seen, and what gets perceived is the *invariant* cat. ... Hence, when the child first sees a picture of a cat he is prepared to pick up the invariants. ... When he sees the cat half-hidden by the chair, he perceives a partly hidden cat, not a half-cat, and therefore he is prepared to see the same thing in a drawing.

The preparation "to see the same thing in a drawing" in response to a picture of a partly obscured cat makes the latter what Woodworth (1938) called a "cue," rather than what Gibson has seemed to imply elsewhere by "information," because it depends upon the past experiences of the child (see the word "hence") and because it is a response to a selected and restricted part of the visual field.

(Elsewhere in the same paragraph, Gibson proposes that the child "pays no attention to the frozen perspective of the picture" and it is hard to see how the interposition of the cat can arbitrarily be selected out from the entire array of information about space of which it is a part unless it is also so used, on sufficient occasions to make an impression, in the course of normal perception of the real world.) The invariant that underlies the transformation that would be produced by a disoccluding head movement is simply not present in the frozen array of a picture, and the only sense in which it can be talked about as being available to the viewer is in terms of what is clearly *mental content* (i.e., "preparation to see") and not in terms of stimulus information in any defined or implied use of the latter phrase; the elicitation of that mental content is attributed to the child's prior experiences with the world ("Hence . . .") in the paragraph quoted above. Moreover, Gibson's use of the notion that the child perceives the invariant cat and not the momentary views, and that the perception of the cat from the frozen view consists in the child's readiness for that invariant to emerge in the course of potential transformations, is identical in content to Helmholtz's view that we do not perceive our momentary sensations but instead perceive the object that generates some anticipated set of orderly sensory consequences to any perceptuomotor exploration we undertake (Helmholtz, 1962, pp. 22f) and J. S. Mill's argument "On the permanent possibilities of sensation"

> The conception I form of the world existing at any moment, comprises, along with the sensations I am feeling . . . the whole of those which past observation tells me that I could, under any supposable circumstances, experience at this moment. . . . My present sensations are generally of little importance, and are moreover fugitive: the possibilities, on the contrary, are permanent. . . . These possibilities, which are conditional certainties, need a special name to distinguish them from mere vague possibilities, which experience gives no warrant for reckoning upon [Mill, 1965, p. 185].

Gibson had already conceded, in 1951, that in the case of pictures, mental structures in the classical sense (e.g., unconscious inference) might be called upon, so his reliance upon what amount to cues and mental structure in the above quotation is no surprise. The question of where these abilities come from, that is, of the circumstances in which the viewer has been called upon to use them outside of the pictorial situation, and of how widespread their use may be, becomes important in assessing the meaning of stimulus information and the content of a direct theory.

The "frozen array" of the picture provides a limiting case of the question that I have been concerned with, i.e., how long a temporal span is needed to convey usable transformation-carried information about the spatial invariants? We know that for some kinds and instances of information, very short bursts of motion will suffice (e.g., Johansson, 1977), but anecdotal descriptions of experiences with distant mountains, rotating radar antennas, and so on, suggests that in other cases longer times—and specific directed effort—are required.

There is another sense in which the succession of glances can be considered as a single stimulus, and that is by taking the sequence (regardless of the fine structure of where the glances have gone, and the number of glances taken) as a single four-dimensional stimulus input. I consider that next.

(c) *The Incomplete Nature Of Visual Storage.*   Only if all of the information provided by the first views of a sequence of views survives through the entire sequence in a form that will affect the final perceptual outcome, could we ignore the limitations of the momentary glance. After all, if the spacing of the texture in the first glance at a sparse gradient, or the direction of a corner in the first glance

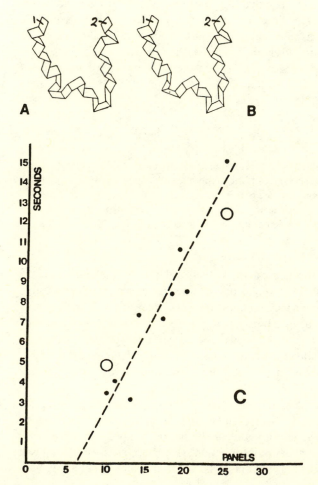

FIG. 10.7. The relationships between an object's surfaces (i.e., its form) are not necessarily directly perceived even when all of the component surfaces are fully visible (Hochberg & Klopfer, 1981).

at some complex pattern, is not retained by the time the next piece of information with which it must be integrated is received (e.g., the spacing of the texture in another glance at the gradient, or the direction of a second corner in the pattern, respectively), then the content of those glances will not have been part of the effective stimulus. Of course, *to the degree that a single invariant is defined over that interval, and to the degree that the perceptual response is indeed based on that invariant, we could ignore the limitations of the momentary glance, and ignore as well the question of how well the information is stored between glances.* In other words, *if* we knew of a set of conditions within which perception were both veridical and predictable from some temporally extended invariant, then we could afford to ignore these questions of momentary limits and interglance storage. We do not, however, have that knowledge, nor do we know that such conditions are at all general. On the other hand, we do know that viewers cannot encode and store all features of each glimpse from one glance to the next, as we see in Fig. 10.1a, and as we will see even more strongly in connection with Fig. 10.7. The prudent man should therefore question the assumption of perfect retention of information between glances as a general rule, and therefore should assume that the span of the event that can be considered to be a single stimulus must depend on the way in which it is sampled, processed, and stored over time (which may indeed in certain cases cover a relatively large duration).

In the previous discussion, I have frequently relied on the limited spatial span of the fovea. One can, however, argue with perfect justice that the fovea is not the sole source of information, that the periphery serves essential functions in perception, and that therefore the argument about perceptual exploration with a small (ca. 2°) fovea is misleading.

Let us consider that point next.

(4) Fovea Versus Periphery, And The "Elementarism" Their Differences Impose

I do not want to argue that the periphery of the eye is useless. Indeed, Fig. 10.6 (Hochberg, 1968) was designed to show that the periphery is as important to the perception of form as I have long believed peripheral vision essential to skilled reading (Hochberg, 1970b). But the fact is that our acuity for the detection of two points, for the recognition of letters, and for the resolution of gratings and texture differences *is* drastically lower at increasing distances from the center of the eye. We do not have to believe in punctiform receptors to recognize this fact. The information carried by specific letters, for example, is detectible in the course of reading text to a distance of about four letter spaces from the fixation point (McConkie & Rayner, 1975). We have seen that there are functional differences in the pickup of signed and unsigned pictorial depth cues (Figs. 10.1 and 10.2) and of kinetic occlusion as signed information about surface-depth (Figs. 10.3 and 10.4), as a function of where one looks.

It is true that we have not as yet separated the factor of attention from that of gaze, in this research, and that we do not know whether the differences between fovea and periphery are all due to failures of acuity, to the greater degree of interference between contours in peripheral than in foveal vision (Bouma & Andriessen, 1973), or to other differences between the two kinds of vision. (There is reason to believe that at least certain kinetic as well as static cues remain unsigned as to which of two regions is nearer until those cues are brought to foveal or near-foveal vision, even though they act to indicate that *some* depth exists even when viewed only peripherally[2]).

In any case, moreover, we know that pickup of most kinds of visual information is poorer in peripheral than in foveal vision, and that the image is not even correctly focused on the retina for normal peripheral vision (Leibowitz & Owens, 1975). To the degree that the pick up of higher-order information depends on resolution, focus or other factors in which peripheral vision is deficient, we indeed have only an exploring fovea (or small region around the fovea) to pick up those aspects of stimulus information. And we next see that this means not only that higher-order information may be limited but that in fact it may be totally unusable under a set of circumstances whose generality and importance are unknown. That is, we have as yet absolutely no knowledge about the set of conditions under which higher-order information can be directly used.

(5) Why The Previous Considerations Might Make Gradients (And Other Extended Stimulus Variables) Generally Unusable

Apply the previous considerations to a texture-density gradient produced by a surface that is slanted horizontally away from the viewer (i.e., with the bottom nearest, as in the ground plane). Some minimum difference in spacing between the top and bottom elements in the field of view must surely be exceeded before the texture-density gradient can provide usable information about slant. Furthermore, it surely must be true that there is some minimum field of view needed to detect that difference, for a given gradient and a given texture-element size, as the following exaggerated limiting case shows: consider a sparse, fine texture, composed of carrier elements that are (a) so small that the usable field of view is only about 2 to 4 degrees, and that the carrier elements become too small to detect except in the region where they are nearest to the viewer (i.e., at the bottom of the optic array); and (b) so sparse that within that region, only two

---

[2]I say this because in the studies connected with Figures 3 and 4, it is clear that the subjects can detect that occlusion is occurring, and the direction in which the occlusion occurs, even at distances from the fixation point at which their depth responses fall to chance levels.

elements fall within a 2 to 4 degree portion of the retina. Under such conditions, more than one fixation would necessarily be needed in order to determine the sense and extent of the difference in texture density between a lower and upper adjacent sample of the optic array.

Now, we do not know whether, and how well, such spacing information is stored from one glance to the next. If such storage is not adequate (and we have no reason at present to think that it generally is), or if the necessary but elective glances are not appropriately sequenced, directed and executed, then the gradient information cannot be used, even with free vision.

Are the considerations evidenced in this exaggerated limiting case so general that they provide a serious obstacle to the use of texture-density gradients and optical flow patterns in real life? I do not know, nor have I seen reason to believe that anyone else does. What research there is, is not particularly encouraging (Gogel, 1977; Johnson, 1972; Smith & Smith, 1977). Certainly, the prudent man would worry somewhat about the matter before either making practical prescriptions to the designers of aircraft displays and landing strips, or building theoretical and philosophical structures on the assumption that such information from extended stimulus arrays is in fact the predominant basis of normal perception.

And in any case, the relevant stimulus questions tend to be obscured by insisting that we ignore the carrier elements and discuss only the modulating information; by ignoring the pickup limitations of the momentary glance; and by disregarding the elective nature of eye movements and of other perceptuomotor behaviors that need motivation and guidance.

(D) PERCEIVED SHAPES AND OBJECTS ARE NOT MERELY LOCI OF POINTS, BUT THEY ARE NOT THEMSELVES FORMS OR OBJECTS, EITHER

To Gestalt theory, the entire configuration determines all of the attributes (e.g., solidity, shape, etc.) of the perceived object, with no clear limits on this assertion (cf. Petermann, 1932). As we noted in connection with Figs. 10.1 and 10.2, this primary claim (that configuration is unitary in the sense that it determines the appearance of the parts) cannot be sustained in view of the effects of gaze direction. There is another part to this claim, however, which requires separate consideration: that when the form falls on different parts of the retina with each change in fixation, the perceptual response remains the same because it is the form of the stimulus to which we are directly responsive and that form has remained invariant regardless of retinal locus (see Koffka, 1935). No provision was made for the limitations and inhomogeneities of the momentary glance. In fact the problem of how the information from successive views is combined, and of how we keep track of the relationship between the successive partial glimpses of any object, has not been directly addressed in a systematic manner by the Gestaltists,[3] nor by any one else, that I know of, save for Hebb (1949), whose view is essentially a physiological phrasing of the constructivist one we discuss later.

A related problem that has received considerable attention, however, is that of compensation for the viewer's eye movements and head movements. This topic has been considered mostly in terms of the perception of motion, and of the partitioning of perceived motion (e.g., into gaze direction changes, framework motion, object motion, etc.). Two general methods of compensation for viewer's movement have been proposed. The first, which goes back to Helmholtz, is that we take the efferent eye movement commands into account. The second, best developed in Gibson's (1957, 1966b) theory of optical kinesthesis and in Johansson's closely related vector extraction model of motion perception, is that uniform transformations of the entire field of view are extracted as a framework against which any residual vectors provide the stimulus for perceived motion. Although these are basically discussions of perceived motion, the relationships between features (or parts of shapes) glimpsed in successive glances can be assigned their relative locations by simple extension: if one feature of the object is centered on the fovea in one glance, and another is centered on the fovea after the eye has made an excursion of, say, 5° to the left, and if that excursion is fully taken into account (i.e., is compensated for either by keeping track of the efferent commands or by pickup of the invariant locus underlying the uniform optic transformation, as Helmholtz and Gibson, respectively, would have it), then the second feature must lie in space 5° to the left of the first.

If we were to stop here in our account of shape perception as integrated across successive glances, however, a great deal of the story would be left out. What these analyses have done *at best* is to preserve the information about the shape as a locus of points in the field, under the transformations supplied by percep-tuomotor exploration, but they have nothing more to say. And there is more to the perception of shape than these compensatory mechanisms for getting the pieces in the correct relationship to each other by cancelling the changes in gaze direction, or by knowing where one is looking at each moment. Let me expand this point briefly.

(1) Form And Shape Are Not Merely Matters Of Spatial Specification

Form and shape are often treated merely as matters of specification: the locus of points in space for which the viewer has different readinesses, that is, that he is prepared to fixate or point to (Festinger, Ono, Burnham, & Bamber, 1967); the

---

[3]Köhler and Wallach (1944) do suggest that retinal anisotropies will be self-correcting as a result of differential satiation, but that explanation could in no way replace the information that is missing in peripheral vision.

invariant distribution of edges and surfaces that comprise an object or scene as they are provided by the changing optic array of a moving viewer (Gibson, 1966b). The specifiable stimulus pattern is just the first step, however, and we do not know the irreducible unit for the various disparate properties that depend on configuration. The following examples show that the perceptual attributes of forms and shapes are not all encompassed by the specifiable locus that comprises such geometrical definitions.

Figure 10.5a shows demonstrations (Hochberg, 1968) that the reversible-perspective figures appear tridimensional only if their intersections are presented in intact form: if the pattern is revealed by successive presentations, either in ways that subdivide the local depth cues (as in a) or that preserve them intact (as in b), the pattern is recognizable as a pattern in both cases, but it looks three dimensional only in b. That is, adjacent egocentric order of small segments is sufficient for shape recognition to occur, but not for perceived tridimensionality; for the latter, the intersections are needed as irreducible features. In Fig. 10.5c (adapted from Girgus, Gellman, & Hochberg, 1980), a moving aperture shows contiguous portions of a concealed pattern (here shown by the imaginary dotted line), whereas in Fig. 10.5d the aperture reveals parts of the same pattern in noncontiguous (random) order. Note that *the shape is equally well specified mathematically as an egocentric locus of small segments in both cases*. Nevertheless, recognition of the shape is much better in condition c than in condition d.

In interpreting the result of the experiment sketched in Figs. 10.5c and d, it should be noted that in both conditions the locus of aperture presentations is such that any eye movements that are made in order to fixate the individual presentations of the aperture would produce strongly overlapping fields of view, and therefore would provide the adjacent order and continuous transformations that are needed in Gibson's theory to specify the locus of points (i.e., the aperture in view 4 of Fig. 10.5b is within 5° of that in view 1.) As far as an efference-readiness theory is concerned, condition d is such as to elicit saccades, whereas condition c is more likely to elicit pursuit movements, and the former are often thought to be at least as well compensated as the latter, if not substantially better. What condition c has that condition d lacks is adjacent order in the presentation of the shape *per se*, and not in its specification of the spatial locus, because the latter is present by any theory in both conditions. This outcome is what one would expect from schema-testing theories of object perception (e.g., Hebb, 1949; Hochberg, 1968, 1970a, 1974a,b; Neisser, 1967), in which shape is viewed as a structure that must be considered in addition to specifying locus.

These arguments may seem abstract, and the demonstrations that I described to support them may be hard to visualize. In any case, the demonstrations lie sufficiently outside what one would take to be the normal conditions of perception that their generality may be questioned. Not so with the next set of demonstrations and experiments.

In both Figs. 10.6a and 10.6b (Hochberg, 1968), a reversible-perspective pattern is delineated by 6s in a matrix of 9s. The carrier elements of the pattern (i.e., the set of 6s) are almost indistinguishable from the background elements (9s) when viewed in peripheral vision. In Fig. 10.6b, we have by filling in the 9s introduced gross contrast differences that make the carrier elements of the shape visible outside of the fovea. *Note that the shape is mathematically equally well specified in a and in b.* In a, we have approximated an aperture-viewing situation that removes much of the effectiveness of peripheral vision, but otherwise preserves the viewer's totally free gaze. That is, in a the viewer is given a glimpse of some portion of the figure only in the center of his vision, but he can receive such a glimpse wherever he elects to direct his eye. Even though the shape is fully specified, and even though free visual exploration is available to the viewer, the shape is not clear: the viewer can with effort (i.e., undertaking the task of tracing out and identifying the shape) recognize and reproduce the pattern as such, but the figure does not look tridimensional, nor does spontaneous perspective reversals occur. In b, the shape is clearly perceptible, with or without effort, and is sufficiently tridimensional in appearance for spontaneous perspective reversals to be reported.[4]

For our present purposes, the main point of this demonstration, which is similar in its basis to those in Figs. 10.3, 10.5c, and 10.5d, is that full stimulus specification and an absolutely untrammeled gaze, are not sufficient in themselves to account for shape perception. The next pair of experiments shows that the same is true of object perception.

The next experiments (Hochberg & Klopfer, 1981) show that full visual information about surface layout, presented to free gaze, does not automatically assure the perception of layout and its relationships. First, I describe an experiment with line pictures, to introduce the problem and method. Subjects were shown figures like those in Figs. 10.7a and 10.7b, with different numbers of panels and twists in different figures. They were asked to judge as quickly as possible, but as correctly as possible, whether the free ends (marked 1 and 2 in the figures shown here, but not in the actual presentations) were the same or different sides of the surface. (They are the same side in a, opposite sides in b). Judgment times are shown in Fig. 10.7c: the solid points show the mean judgment times for pictures of the stimuli having different numbers of panels; note that the times increase fairly regularly with the number of panels. This procedure was repeated in a second experiment, using *tridimensional* versions of the same kinds of twisted objects that had been portrayed in the pictures of the previous experiment. The objects were made of rigid plastic "ribbon," with two different numbers of panels; they were viewed binocularly, and the subjects had free head movement and consequently had full visual information about the corners and

---

[4]It is possible that with sufficient practice, these differences might be overcome, but no hint of that has occurred in our experience with these patterns. In any case, I cannot see how these demonstrations, and the other related work with reading and aperture viewing can be construed as arguing that peripheral vision is unimportant, as it has sometimes been taken to do (cf. Parker, 1978).

edges of the objects before them. The entire visual angle subtended by any object was never more than about 9 degrees. The two empty circles on the graph in Fig. 10.7c show the decision times for the two classes of solid objects used; the results obtained with outline pictures (the solid points) clearly hold as well for freely viewed tridimensional objects.

The point of these experiments is this: although each intersection is fully open to the viewer's gaze, and the stimulus is so compact that one or two glances at most are needed to bring all parts of the entire pattern within foveal vision, whether the two ends are the same or different sides of the surface is not immediately evident. Apparently the viewer needed to parse the figure (perhaps using the fovea much as the unskilled reader uses his finger to "keep his place;" eye movement measurement has not been done with these figures, however, so this description may only be metaphorical).

It is difficult to see what one might mean by the "direct" perception of the object's form or surfaces' layout when the time needed to decide so simple a question as surface orientation increases with increasing number of panels. This point becomes clearer still when we realize that the perception of whether the end panels are same or different, in these figures, is fully elective: if the viewer were to stop at any point short of the final judgment, the relationship between the surfaces, and therefore the specific form of this fully exposed, freely explored, suprathreshold object, mathematically specified as it is and invariant under all of the transformations provided by head and eye movements, would go undetermined.

Form is not a unitary response. A perceived object is not a thing. This point needs some expanding.

(2) Percepts Are Not Objects, Either: The Implications Of These Demonstrations For Wholistic Theories Of Mental Structure

As the opposite side of the tendency to consider that the perception of an object is explained once the locus of points that define its place in space have been specified, the perception of an object is often "explained" in terms of the physical properties of the object being perceived. The temptation is understandable: if we could not count on at least *some* relationships to hold between the potential responses that can be made to any stimulus pattern that elicits the perception of some object, nothing would be gained by concluding that the subject perceives the object. For example, knowing that the subject perceives the leftmost edge of a reversible prism to be nearer, we may predict that the edge will also be judged to appear smaller; the fact that the subject says the lefthand facet appears nearer in Fig. 10.2 would seem to imply that the bottom facet is seen from above. But such interresponse constraints between two parts or attributes of an object, such as the couplings that are often manifest between perceived size and perceived distance, need not be obligatory, nor need we assume that an object must have a definite perceived size during the same perceptual moment that it has some definite perceived distance.

It is true that there has been a resurgence of "wholistic" discussions about shapes and objects, based on demonstrations of context effects (see Cooper, 1980, for a recent review), and on the more demanding mental rotation experiments, but those demonstrations and experiments have not been designed to test how much of the stimulus is effective at one time, nor how consistent and obligatory the interresponse couplings may be. Indeed, the same kinds of limits as were discussed in connection with Figs. 10.3–10.7 in the present chapter can be shown to apply to the mental rotation task (Hochberg & Gellman, 1977).

One must therefore not slide into the implicit assumption that the perceptual response to an object is in any sense an object. Kolers and Smythe (1979) have recently stressed this point with respect to controversies about the nature of imagery, and it is clearly appropriate to the case of perception itself. Figure 10.7 tells us that the perceptual implications of the impossible objects in Fig. 10.1 are not restricted to those anomalous figures: unlike objects themselves, our perceptions of objects are not everywhere dense, and the attributes that we perceive do not in general exist in some internal model of the object, waiting to be retrieved: they are the results of our intention to perceive, and they appear in the context of the perceptual task that calls upon them.

There is a very old theory to this point, that fits all of the demonstrations that I have been describing. I construe these and other demonstrations as providing evidence for the use of local depth cues, and of other local as well as nonlocal features (e.g., gross size or shape), to which we fit schematic maps of objects and events. By schematic maps and events, I mean expectations of what one will see if one looks over there, or moves one's head so as to disocclude whatever is behind that edge. This of course is the approach of J. S. Mill and Helmholtz (see Hochberg, 1979b, 1981, for reviews to this point). This theory can make provision for most of the facts of psychophysics and perception; can explain the figure-ground phenomena and the Gestalt laws in a more plausible fashion than Gestalt theory ever did (Hochberg, 1972, 1974a); and it can embrace Gibson's direct theory without being embarassed by the existence of limits. All of this may well be too good to be true, however, and should not be taken too seriously until we can specify better what is meant by schemas (i.e., by what in Helmholtzian terms would be the premises of unconscious inference), and until we can put limits on this theory as I have been trying to put limits on the other theories of perceptual organization.

ACKNOWLEDGMENT

The new research described in this chapter was assisted by NSF BNS 77-25653.

REFERENCES

Beck, J. *Surface color perception*. Ithaca, N.Y.: Cornell University Press, 1972.

Bouma, H., & Andriessen, J. J. Eccentric vision: Adverse interactions between line segments. *Vision Research*, 1973, *16*, 71–78.

Cassirer, E. The concept of group and the theory of perception. *Philosophical and Phenomenological Research*, 1944, *5*, 1–35.

Cooper, L. A. Recent themes in visual information processing: A selective review. In R. Nickerson (Ed.), *Attention and performance, VII*. Hillsdale, N.J.: Lawrence Erlbaum Associates, 1980.

Epstein, W. (Ed.) *Stability and constancy in visual perception*. New York: Wiley, 1977.

Festinger, L., Ono, H., Burnham, C. A., & Bamber, D. Efference and the conscious experience of perception. *Journal of Experimental Psychology Monograph*, 1967, Whole No. 637.

Gibson, J. J. *The perception of the visual world*. Boston: Houghton Mifflin, 1950.

Gibson, J. J. What is a form? *Psychological Review*, 1951, *58*, 403–412.

Gibson, J. J. Optical motions and transformations as stimuli for visual perception. *Psychological Review*, 1957, *64*, 288–295.

Gibson, J. J. Observations on active touch. *Psychological Review*, 1962, *69*, 477–491.

Gibson, J. J. *The senses considered as perceptual systems*. Boston: Houghton Mifflin, 1966.

Gibson, J. J. *The ecological approach to visual perception*. Boston: Houghton Mifflin, 1979.

Girgus, J. S., Gellman, L., & Hochberg, J. The effect of spatial order on piecemeal shape recognition: A developmental study. *Perception and Psychophysics*, 1980, *2*, 133–138.

Gogel, W. C. The metric of visual space. In W. Epstein (Ed.), *Stability and constancy in visual perception*. New York: Wiley, 1977.

Hebb, D. *The organization of behavior*. New York: Wiley, 1949.

Helmholtz, H. von. *Treatise on physiological optics, Vol. 3*. Originally published 1857. Translated from the third (1909–1911) German edition by J. P. C. Southall. New York: Optical Society of America, 1924–1915; reprinted. New York: Dover, 1962.

Hochberg, J. In the mind's eye. In R. N. Haber (Ed.), *Contemporary theory and research in visual perception*. New York: Holt, Rinehart & Winston, 1968.

Hochberg, J. Attention, organization, and consciousness. In D. I. Mostofsky (Ed.), *Attention: Contemporary theory and analysis*. New York: Appleton-Century-Crofts, 1970. (a)

Hochberg, J. Components of literacy: Speculations and exploratory research. In H. Levin & J. Williams (Eds.), *Basic studies in reading*. New York: Basic Books, 1970. (b)

Hochberg, J. Perception, I. Color and Shape, II. Space and movement. In J. W. Kling & L. A. Riggs (Eds.), *Woodworth and Schlosberg's experimental psychology*. Third Ed. New York: Holt, Rinehart & Winston, 1972.

Hochberg, J. Organization and the Gestalt tradition. In E. C. Carterette & M. Friedman (Eds.), *Handbook of perception, Vol. 1*. New York: Academic Press, 1974. (a)

Hochberg, J. Higher-order stimuli and interresponse coupling in the perception of the visual world. In R. B. Macleod & H. L. Pick (Eds.), *Perception: Essays in honor of James J. Gibson*. Ithaca: Cornell University Press, 1974. (b)

Hochberg, J. *Perception*. Englewood Cliffs, N.J.: Prentice-Hall, 1978. (a)

Hochberg, J. Art and visual perception. In E. Carterette & M. Friedman (Eds.), *Handbook of perception, Vol. X*. New York: Academic Press, 1978. (b)

Hochberg, J. Motion pictures of mental structures. E.P.A. Presidential Address, 1978. (c) [Available from author.]

Hochberg, J. Some of the things that pictures are. In C. Nodine & D. Fisher (Eds.), *Views of pictorial representation: Making, perceiving and interpreting*. New York: Praeger, 1979. (a)

Hochberg. J. Sensation and perception. In E. Hearst (Ed.), *Experimental psychology at 100*. Hillsdale, N.J.: Lawrence Erlbaum Associates, 1979. (b)

Hochberg, J. Levels of perceptual organization. In M. Kubovy & J. Pomerantz (Eds.), *Perceptual organization*. Hillsdale, N.J.: Lawrence Erlbaum Associates, 1981. (a)

Hochberg, J. Pictorial functions and perceptual structures. In M. Hagen (Ed.), *The perception of pictures, Vol. II*. New York: Academic Press, 1981. (b)

Hochberg, J., & Brooks, V. The psychophysics of form: Reversible-perspective drawings of spatial objects. *American Journal of Psychology*, 1960, *73*, 337-354.

Hochberg, J., & Brooks, V. The perception of motion pictures. E. C. Carterette & M. P. Friedman (Eds.), *Handbook of perception, Vol. X*. New York: Academic Press, 1979.

Hochberg, J., & Gellman, L. The effect of landmark features on mental rotation times. *Memory and Cognition*, 1977, *5*, 23-26.

Hochberg, J., Green, J., & Virostek, S. *Texture occlusion requires central viewing: Demonstrations, data and theoretical implications*. Paper delivered at the A. P. A. Convention, 1978. (Available from the senior author.)

Hochberg, J., & Klopfer, D. Seeing is not perceiving: Schemas are needed even when visual information is complete. *Proc. Eastern Psychological Association*, 1981, 148 (Abstract)

Hochberg, J., & McAlister, E. A quantitative approach to figural "goodness." *Journal of Experimental Psychology*, 1953, *46*, 361-364.

Hochberg, J., & Smith, O. W. Landing strip markings and the "expansion pattern." I. Program, preliminary analysis and apparatus. *Perceptual and Motor Skills*, 1955, *5*, 81-92.

Hochberg, J., Virostek, S., & Green, J. *Texture occlusion depends on gaze direction: Fixed and moving eye*. In preparation.

Hochberg, J., Virostek, S., & Peterson, M. *Figure-ground ambiguity and unsigned depth cues*. In preparation.

Hurvich, L. M., & Jameson, D. *The perception of brightness and darkness*. Boston: Allyn & Bacon, 1966.

Johansson, G. Spatial constancy and motion in visual perception. In W. Epstein (Ed.), *Stability and constancy in visual percpetion*. New York: Wiley, 1977.

Johnson, I. R. *Visual judgments in locomotion*. Doctoral dissertation, University of Melbourne, 1972.

Julesz, B. *Foundations of cyclopean perception*. Chicago: University of Chicago Press, 1971.

Koffka, K. *Principles of Gestalt psychology*. New York: Harcourt Brace, 1935.

Kaplan, G. A. Kinetic disruption of optical texture: The perception of depth at an edge. *Perception and Psychophysics*, 1969, *6*, 193-198.

Köhler, W., & Wallach, H. Figural after-effects: An investigation of visual processes. *Proceedings of the American Philosophical Society*, 1944, *88*, 269-357.

Kolers, P. A., & Smythe, W. E. Image, symbols and skills. *Canadian Journal of Psychology*, 1979, *33*, 158-184.

Leibowitz, H. W., & Owens, D. A. Anomalous myopias and the intermediate dark focus of accommodation. *Science*, 1975, *18*, 162-170.

McConkie, G. W., & Rayner, K. The span of the effective stimulus during a fixation in reading. *Perception and Psychophysics*, 1975, *17*, 578-586.

Mill, J. S. *An examination of Sir William Hamilton's Philosophy*, 1865. (On the permanent possibilities of sensation.) Reprinted in R. J. Hernstein & E. G. Boring (Eds.), *A source book in the history of psychology*. Cambridge, Mass.: Harvard University Press, 1965.

Neisser, U. *Cognitive psychology*. New York: Appleton-Century-Crofts, 1967.

Parker, R. E. Picture processing during recognition. *Journal of Experimental Psychology: Human Perception and Performance*, 1978, *4*, 284-293.

Penrose, L., & Penrose, R. Impossible objects: A special type of visual illusion. *British Journal of Psychology*, 1958, *49*, 31-33.

Petermann, B. *The Gestalt theory and the problem of configuration*. New York: Harcourt Brace, 1932.

Peterson, M. A., & Hochberg, J. Perspective reversals that refute both Gestalt and Direct theories of object perception: Measures of local cue strength and attention. *Proc. Eastern Psychological Association,* 1981, 148. (Abstract)

Smith, O. W., & Smith, P. C. On motion parallax and perceived depth. *Journal of Experimental Psychology,* 1963, *65,* 107–108.

Smith, O. W., & Smith, P. C. Developmental studies of spatial judgments by children and adults. *Perceptual and Motor Skills,* 1966, *22,* 3–73.

Woodworth, R. S. *Experimental psychology.* New York: Holt, Rinehart & Winston, 1938.

11 Some Characteristics of Gestalt-Oriented Research in Perception

Fabio Metelli
University of Padua

INTRODUCTION

Are there some methodological characteristics allowing us to label a research in perception as Gestalt-oriented? An authoritative statement seems to suggest a negative answer. In Koffka's obituary, Köhler (1942) referring to the time when Gestalt psychology was emerging, wrote: "We all had great respect for the exact methods by which certain sensory data and facts of memory were investigated, but we also felt quite strongly that work of so little scope would never give us an adequate Psychology of real human beings" (p. 98). Is then Gestalt-oriented research characterized only by the problems studied and not by the method? It would be strange if a body of ideas which proved to be so fruitful in research were not characterized by some—written or unwritten—methodological rules.

This question is also of personal interest to me. Why does a Psychologist think of himself as Gestalt-oriented? There is no Gestalt "creed." The principles of antiassociationism, antiempiricism, and isomorphism (Wertheimer, 1922) are not dogmatic. Isomorphism is a hypothesis, whose function has been to suggest new research, and to formulate testable theories of the neural processes underlying perception. The principles of antiempiricism and antiassociationism represent only critical requirements. Gestalt psychologists refused to accept past experience as a general explanation without proof. The influence of past experience as such has never been denied by Gestalt theorists—the task is to inquire how it acts. Finally, antiassociationism was just a criticism of the concept of association as an arbitrary connection, to which Gestalt theory opposed the concept of "association as an after effect of pair formation in perception" (Köhler, 1967). It is possible, however, to point out some methodological aspects of Gestalt-oriented research by examining how actual research developed and the relevance of the above principles in it. Apart from citing certain classical studies, my examples are chiefly from Italian research. This offers the opportunity to describe and discuss scientific work done in Italy which is not well known to non-Italian scientists.

THE IMPORTANCE OF
PHENOMENOLOGICAL OBSERVATION

I think that the first point characterizing Gestalt research in perception is the requirement of an exact and detailed phenomenological observation and description. For the Gestalt psychologist, phenomenological description is fundamental because, according to the isomorphic hypothesis, the phenomenological datum reflects the neural processes underlying perception (Koffka, 1935). But apart from such theoretical reasons careful phenomenological description must be the starting point of all perceptual research. It provides the data that is the very object of perceptual research. The requirement of a careful phenomenological description is very difficult to follow. It is easy to overlook the necessity of a complete description and to attend only to what is important for one's theory. There is also the difficulty of naive subjects, notwithstanding the instructions of the experimenter, describing not what they perceived but what really "is there," due to the natural attitude of naive realism.

Two important results of good phenomenological observation are the discovery of new phenomena and the solution of previously apparently unsolvable problems. A typical example of the former is the research of Brown (1928, 1931) on motion. He showed that the perception of velocity depends on both the size of the moving object and of the field in which the motion takes place.[1] Brown's research is only one example of the many discoveries resulting from careful phenomenological observation. Not as well-known is the interesting research of Bozzi (1958, 1959, 1961) on the "natural rhythm" of the pendulum and the "natural speed" of an object on an inclined plane. Bozzi analyzed the conditions giving rise to the impression that a pendulum swings freely and does not appear to be artificially speeded or slowed down. The main condition turned out to be the amplitude of the oscillation, whereas it is well known that Galileo showed that the amplitude of the oscillation does not influence the *physical* speed of a pendulum. Bozzi also found that the velocity perceived as natural of an object moving on an inclined plane depends on the size of the moving object, in accordance with Brown's earlier findings.

---

[1]Of course, Brown did not restrain himself in observing these effects, but varied conditions in systematic experiments. However, the starting point was phenomenological observation.

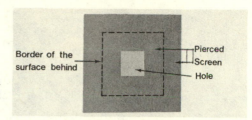

FIG. 11.1. A hole-screen with a homogeneous surface 50 cm. behind the hole.

My collaborators and I (Metelli, Da Pos, & Cavedon, 1977) pointed out that when a screen with a hole is placed at a certain distance (for example, 50 cm.) in front of a homogeneous but differently colored surface (Fig. 11.1), instead of a hole, a piece of colored paper pasted on the screen is perceived; and that in a display consisting of a figure on a ground, both acromatic and homogeneous, seen through a frame, when the albedos of the figure and the ground are very similar, a fog is perceived. Both facts needed careful phenomenological observation in order to be discovered, as they appear fleeting when casually observed in the common perceptual world.

Köhler's research on successive comparison (1923) is an example of how careful phenomenological observation allows a previously unsolved problem to be solved. Fechner (1850) discovered the negative time error. The negative time error refers to the finding that in the successive comparison of two equal sounds the second one is perceived as louder. Sometimes, however, as was known to Fechner, the first sound and not the second sound was perceived as louder. Psychological as well as physiological theories have been proposed to explain these phenomena (Metelli, 1954). No theory, however, was able to predict the direction and the size of errors. In fact, the phenomenon seemed to follow no law (Köhler, 1923; Metelli, 1954). Köhler approached the problem from a detailed phenomenological description. Phenomenological observation revealed that subjects did not compare a perception with a memory image, as it seemed obvious to everybody, but that the second sound was simply perceived as "louder," "equal," or "softer" and no memory image of the first sound was reported. The comparison takes place at a physiological level between a process corresponding to the present sound and a memory trace of the previous sound. Köhler (1923) was able to explain both the negative and the positive time errors. My immediate concern is not with Köhler's theory or with Lauenstein's (1933) development of it. What is of interest is how exact phenomenological observation can suggest the solution of an apparently insoluble problem.

I add another example from my personal experience (Metelli, 1974a; 1975). My own research during the past 10 years has been concerned primarily with the problem of determining the color relationships giving rise to transparency. The perception of transparency does not depend on actual physical transparency. It may be produced by juxtaposing differing reflectances as in Fig. 11.2. In Fig.

FIG. 11.2.   A transparent circle on a bicolor ground is generally perceived. See
text.

11.2, let *a* be the reflectance of the white C-shaped area, *b* the reflectance of the
black reversed-C-shaped area, *p* the reflectance of the half circle contiguous to
the white area and *q* the reflectance of the half circle contiguous to the black
area. Perceptual transparency arises from a splitting of the colors *p* and *q* into the
background colors *a* and *b* and the transparent color *t*. The proportions of which
the colors *p* and *q* are made up of the background colors *a* and *b* and the
transparent color *t* are given by the equations:

$$p = \alpha a + (1 - \alpha)t$$
$$q = \alpha'b + (1 - \alpha')t'$$

In these equations, α and α' are the perceived transparencies of the overlying
colors. The smaller the values of α and α' the less the transparency. These two
equations are solvable only if α is assumed to be equal to α' and t is assumed to
be equal to t', allowing to calculate the values of

$$\alpha = p - q / a - b$$
$$t = aq - bp / (a + q) - (b + p)$$

At the start of my research, I obtained satisfactory confirmations of my theory
in qualitative experiments (Metelli, 1974a, 1975). In quantitative experiments, I
obtained some results that were incompatible with my theory and which caused
me to delay the publication of my work for over two years. After several at-

FIG. 11.3. Partial transparency. The strip in the middle of the figure is only partially transparent. The black of the black squares is perceived through the transparent layer. However, the gray of the gray squares is not.

tempts, among other things, of changing the measurement scale, I resorted to exact phenomenological observation and description of the cases which posed difficulties for the theory. I discovered the very simple fact that these cases belong to a class of phenomena to which my theory did not apply. Those cases which seemed to contradict the theory were always those where either the degree of transparency was not the same in both parts of the figure ($\alpha \neq \alpha'$), or where transparency was perceived only in one part of the figure and not the other ($\alpha = 0$, or $\alpha' = 0$), that is, a case of partial transparency (see Fig. 11.3).

So, in this case also, the lack of exact phenomenological observation hindered the solution of a problem.

AGGREGATION VERSUS STRUCTURE

Whereas phenomenological observation is or should be a prerequisite of all perceptual research, the investigation of perceptual structure has been specific to Gestalt-oriented research. In Gestalt-oriented research a crucial point to be clarified is whether the phenomenon studied has the character of an aggregation or of a Gestalt (i.e., a structure). In an aggregation the presence or absence of a part does not influence other parts. In a Gestalt the presence or absence of a part or changes in size or in intensity influence either other parts or the phenomenon as a whole.[2]

It is perhaps useful at this point to recall an interpretation of Gestalt theory which has always been rejected by its leaders, namely that "everything acts on

---

[2]The distinction between an aggregation and a Gestalt is not absolute. It is not possible to exclude some minimal influence of some item on some other item in perception. But it is important to distinguish the cases where this influence is evident and experimentally testable from the cases where this influence is so slight as to be negligible.

everything'' (Guillaume, 1937). Structural links have to be determined empirically and not assumed. One of the basic problems of Gestalt psychology was to explain a phenomenal world made of distinct entities, that is a world in which there are both natural units where sometimes subunits are perceived, and aggregations, whose members are independent and indifferent to each other.

If in a heap of garbage something is taken or added, the rest of the heap remains unchanged. It is an aggregate. A motor car is parked near a car; the fact that one of them starts and leaves does not seem to exercise any influence on the other. It is perhaps easier, however, to give examples of perceptual units where the presence or the absence of a part influences what is perceived.

1. In the Müller-Lyer illusion, the presence or absence of arrows and their orientation alters the perceived length of the central segment. In this case it is also important to test the effect of other conditions. Does the color of the ground, the thickness of the lines, or the orientation of the figures have any influence? One thing seems to be certain. The presence of another figure, for example, a star does not exercise any influence on the illusion. Figure 11.4a and 11.4b show the Müller-Lyer illusion with and without a star. It is clear that the star is not part of the same structure as the Müller-Lyer figure.

2. Another example is transparency, which can easily be shown to be a non-local phenomenon (Metelli, 1974a). Transparency occurs in Fig. 11.5a but not in Fig. 11.5b. In the configuration giving rise to transparency at least three differently colored surfaces are needed. It is the relationship among these surfaces and not just the characteristics of the region where transparency appears that rules the phenomenon.

3. Another example is the Poggendorff Illusion. The structure established by the oblique lines with the horizontal lines alters the phenomenal position of the oblique lines. These are not longer perceived as parts of the same straight line. If the structure is broken by moving the oblique lines, as indicated in Fig. 11.6, the alignment of the two oblique lines is immediately restored.

It is not enough to establish if a part of the behavioral environment is an aggregate or a Gestalt, or where and among which objects or modalities structural

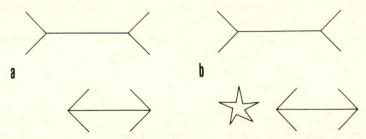

FIG. 11.4.   (a) Müller-Lyer illusion. (b) The presence of a star does not affect the illusion.

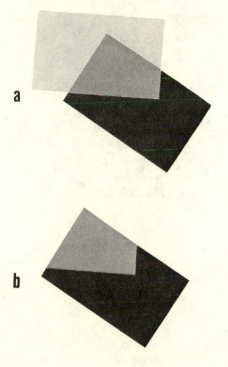

FIG. 11.5. (a) Another example of perceived transparency. (b) The region that was perceived as transparent in Fig. 11.5a, is perceived as opaque.

relations are acting. It is important to establish the degree of their interaction, and how they interact.

4. An experiment of Kanizsa (1970) provides the opportunity to analyze a perceptual organization. In a chessboard whose regular structure is interrupted by a gray circle (Fig. 11.7), what is perceived is a gray circle lying on a black cross, which breaks the regular alternation of the black and white squares of the chess-board. The cross is a sort of break in the continuity of the chessboard and its perception appears to contradict the principle of Prägnanz. It is interesting to

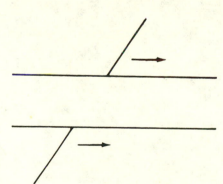

FIG. 11.6. If the two tilted segments are moved together in the direction of the arrows, the illusion disappears.

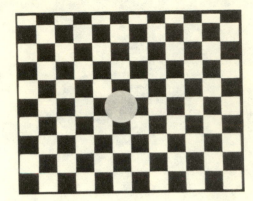

FIG. 11.7. Behind the grey circle a black cross is perceived, breaking the regularity of the chessboard structure (see Kanizsa, 1970).

analyze two hypothetical perceptual "solutions" that could be considered. First the gray circle could be perceived as covering a white square differing in color from the black contiguous squares. In this case, the regular alternation of the chessboard would be preserved. Second, the gray circle can be perceived as covering a black square. In this case, the regular alternation of the black and white squares of the chessboard is broken. The fact that the second alternative is seen indicates that a local Gestalt law (i.e., unification through equality) wins in this case over a global Gestalt law (i.e., uniformity and simplicity of structure). Figure 11.8 shows that the breaking of the regular alternation of black and white of the chessboard occurs also if several squares are covered. In Fig. 11.9, the squares of the chessboard are greatly decreased in size. When this is done, the alternating pattern of the chessboard is not broken but continues behind the gray circle preserving its regularity. Kanizsa (1970) points out that when the squares are made small, we no longer see a chessboard but a texture pattern. How can this effect be explained in terms of organization? One may suppose that a texture is a

FIG. 11.8. A similar effect as in Fig. 11.7 is obtained if several squares of the chessboard structure are covered (see Kanizsa, 1970).

FIG. 11.9.   If the size of the squares is greatly decreased, the microstructure is perceived also behind the grey circle (see Kanizsa, 1970).

strong form of organization[3] and, therefore, global regularity wins over local equality. It seems that becoming more and more uniform the organization becomes stronger and stronger. Should we conclude that a completely uniform surface—that is, a homogeneously colored surface—is the strongest organization? I don't think so. A strong organization shows its character in defending itself against intrusions. A stain is perfectly visible on a homogeneous surface, whereas it is often invisible—or only at times visible—on a textured surface: housewives are well aware of it and very often make use of this knowledge.

PAST EXPERIENCE VERSUS PERCEPTUAL LAWS

A fundamental question in the study of a perceptual phenomenon is determining whether it is the result of past experience or learning. During the first decades of the century this type of explanation was accepted as obvious. Gestalt psychologists, therefore, constructed demonstrations that opposed past experience to the action of the basic laws of perception. These demonstrations showed the greater effectiveness of perceptual laws for determining what is seen. The revival of the empiristic argument by the Transactional psychologists gave rise to a new series of counter demonstrations. Kanizsa (1969) presented demonstrations where it is impossible to see the figure corresponding to past experience. Instead, unusual

---

[3]About phenomenal and functional characteristics of texture, see Metzger (1966, pp. 732–735). Metzger distinguishes between texture and structure, considering them two different forms of organization.

and irregular figures are perceived. These demonstrations have led many to the erroneous idea, which has been difficult to eliminate, that Gestalt psychologists deny the effect of past experience (Kanizsa, 1978), notwithstanding proofs to the contrary (Köhler, 1925). By now, however, the question can be studied without bias; is a perceptual effect due to experience? What is the process through which experience acts?

It is very easy to find examples of research in which this is the primary question. One example is the classical research by Michotte on perceptual causality (1954). I always remember discussing it with a well-known psychologist who considered as evident that the effects studied by Michotte were learned. We always have before our eyes cases of throwing, pushing, and pulling where physical forces are at work. It is not difficult, however, to present examples that are not in accord with past experience. For example, a moving object having been pushed during its motion in the direction of the motion slows its motion instead of accelerating. Though counter to experience, the pushing object is perceived as causing the slowing of the motion. Michotte's phenomena also depend on precise stimulus conditions relating to type of motion, time intervals, and speed. Causality at a distance, without contact between the "active" and the "passive" object, provides further proof that Michotte's phenomena are not due to past experience (Yela, 1952).

But perhaps the most convincing proof that perceptual causality is not a learned phenomenon is given by an experimental study on the perception of attraction conducted first by Kanizsa and Metelli (1961), and then continued by Kanizsa and Vicario (1968). The perception of attraction seems not to exist under natural conditions. Michotte (1954) had observed that when a magnet approaches iron filings, we do not see the filings attracted but the filings appear to jump to the magnet. It is not the magnet but the filings that are perceived as active. Michotte (1954) repeated the experiment using his experimental paradigm. The stimulus display is illustrated in Fig. 11.10. In this experiment, as in the case of the magnet, attraction is not perceived. Michotte, for theoretical reasons as well, denied the possibility of such a perceptual effect. However, if conditions are changed as illustrated in Fig. 11.11 to make the object that is expected to act as a magnet (the first square) jump, and this very quick motion is followed by a very

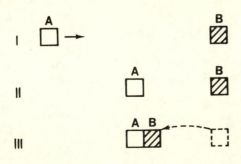

FIG. 11.10. (I) A is moving slowly (3 cm/sec) in the direction of B and (II) stops halfway. (III) B jumps (stroboscopic motion) toward A touching it.

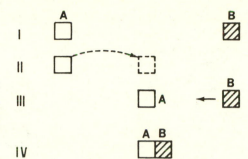

FIG. 11.11.   (I) A and B are motion-less at 7.5 cm. distance (II) A jumps (stroboscopic motion) in the direction of B. (III) B moves slowly (3 cm/sec) in the direction of A until contacting it (see Kanizsa and Metelli, 1961).

slow motion of the second square (which corresponded to the iron filings), the perception of attraction occurs (Kanizsa & Metelli, 1961). The greater speed gives a dominant character to the first square, the magnet-object, whereas the slow speed gives the character of passive (= caused) motion to the motion of the second square.[4] In this case several subjects perceived attraction. An attraction is perceived by almost every subject when, by further altering the stimulus conditions the active, dominant character of the magnet-object and the passive-dependent character of the attracted objects are accentuated. It is evident that an effect that does not exist in nature cannot be learned.

QUALITY VERSUS QUANTITY

One of the more generally known characteristics of Gestalt-oriented perceptual research is that it is mostly qualitative. This is judged negatively by those who are convinced that an essential objective of scientific research is to obtain laws expressed in mathematical terms. There are, however, also psychologists who hold the opposite opinion and who stress that the most original research is often qualitative. Quantitative research, though methodologically correct, is often devoid of originality. The first point of view is shared by the great majority of psychologists and most scientific journals rarely accept papers that are not quantitative. The most authoritative representative of the second point of view was Metzger. His worldwide known treatise "Gesetze des Sehens" (1975) is a mine of experimental data on visual perception, where no place is given to quantitative research. This extreme point of view cannot be considered representative of Gestalt psychology. Koffka (1935) clearly expresses his position. He says "if the qualitative descriptions are correct, it will some time be possible to translate them into quantitative terms" (p. 15). It remains, however, to be established when and why this translation becomes possible. For, not withstanding Koffka's assertion,

---

[4]A difference in size (big square versus little square), acts in the same way, increasing the dominant character of the fast moving square.

which in fact reflects also the thinking of Wertheimer and Köhler, the majority of Gestalt-oriented research remained and remains qualitative.

It needs first of all to be stressed that research in a new field, or research breaking with tradition, is qualitative. Fechner's work is the exception rather than the rule. When a researcher is moving in a "no man's land," when a new phenomenon is observed, the research is confined to nonquantitative conditions. We are tentatively looking for conditions under which the phenomenon appears in a patent way evident to everybody. Then its characteristics are described, its relations with known phenomena, and its necessary conditions studied. Quantification comes later. Sometimes it is a matter of routine work, which the discoverer leaves to somebody else; in other cases the formulation of mathematical laws requires a new idea which appears, maybe, after many years and needs a different mentality and specialization. The Gestalt psychologists have been bearers of new observations, discoverers of new phenomena changing radically the perspectives and the horizon of research. The *Psychologische Forschung,* in the years when it was directed by its founders, is full of such examples. It is then necessary to conclude that a characteristic of Gestalt-oriented research in perception is the qualitative character of such research.[5] Quantification, as a finishing touch, has come afterwards. For example, the quantitative study of Wertheimer's laws began only some years ago and may be considered still going on (Oyama, 1961).

But another no less important point has to be stressed. Quantification is always possible but does not always make sense. As it is well known, correspondence between a particular class of data and the system of natural or of real numbers is not perfect in psychology. Quantifying, that is using numbers in place of data with the enormous advantages that this operation involves, presupposes a meaningful relation between the structure of the data and the structure of the number system. For example, it is well known that in psychological data the determination of an absolute zero, common in physical data, is exceptional. But it has not been sufficiently stressed that often psychological data are a collection of heterogeneous objects, which do not even justify the operation of "counting." In these cases quantification not only gives rise to very poor results (Its presupposition being the identification of really different things or aspects on the basis of a vague common character) and often devoid of sense but risks loosing sight of and concealing much more interesting but at present not quantifiable aspects.

To give an example relating to this last point, I consider an experiment on immediate memory but which is close to perception.[6] The research was not done with homogeneous and meaningless material forming an aggregate of indepen-

---

[5]There are however classical examples of quantification among Gestalt researches in perception (Korte, 1915; Koffka, 1923; Köhler, 1923; Brown, 1928; Duncker, 1929; Lauenstein, 1933).

[6]Only a brief summary of this research has been published in the Acts of the VIII Congress of the Italian Psychologists (see Metelli, 1936).

dent elements, as in the classical type of research going back to Ebbinghaus, but used concrete events with interconnected parts or scenes. The events were presented in the form of a film lasting about one minute, and subjects were asked to write a detailed report of what they saw.[7]

The interest of the research was in the errors in subjects descriptions. The most obvious and simple form of quantification would consist in counting the number of errors made by every subject.[8] What meaning could be given to such a computation? Let us consider three errors: (a) describing erroneously the cap of a child; (b) to say that there were children, without saying how many and without mentioning the sex of each one; (c) describing the action of a person without making any error (in the limited meaning of the word) but giving the event a completely different meaning.[9]

Does it make sense to designate by a number errors of the third kind and by the same number the errors, which do not change the meaning of the event? Clearly not. If errors are divided into different classes (Stern, 1902, 1904), this defect is decreased but not eliminated. But there is something more. Quantifying, that is substituting numbers for data, does not only mean to assert that in one aspect the data have characteristics identifiable with numbers; it also neglects (and therefore often forgets) all the other aspects of data which do not identify themselves, or seem not to be identifiable, with numbers. Quantification implies a drastic impoverishment of the object being studied. So, for example, in the above mentioned research, errors observed in the context of the various descriptions often had a "positive" character, besides the obvious negative one. That is, instead of errors, they could be considered transformations following preferred directions and seeming to have special functions. Some of these transformations appear to be due to processes of equalization among elements of a group, quite

---

[7]The event consisted of a kidnapping of a little girl. First a woman appears, sitting in a park and playing with three children, two girls and a baby boy. A car comes, stops near the group, and a second woman comes out, greets the other woman, and both walk away with the little child. The two girls play together. Suddenly a man comes running, takes one of the girls, brings her into the car, which leaves immediately. The girl who remains alone calls for help, the two women come, and taking the girl, walk together in the direction where the car disappeared. The film belonged originally to a group of four films constructed for a quantitative research on testimony (Musatti, 1933).

[8]This was the way of treating errors, used in the old literature on testimony. For example the degree of fidelity of a witness was given by the formulas $\frac{v}{t}$ or $\frac{v}{t+f}$, where f was the total number of erroneous elements, v was the number of the correctly reproduced elements, and t, the total number of elements. The formulas are due to Stern and Borst (see Musatti, 1931).

[9]One subject describes the event in the following way: there was a lady playing with three children. Then a second lady comes with a car and walks away with the second lady and a child. Then, a man comes and goes away in the car with a second child. Then, the two ladies come again and go away with the third child. It is clear that in this description the structure of the event, centered in the kidnapping, undergoes a radical change: the event splits into three equivalent and repetitive events. It has to be stressed that of about a hundred subjects there has been only this one in which the event was not described as a kidnapping.

analogous to processes observed in perception. Other transformations have the character of a fusion among several elements of a group, and they appear to be extreme or limiting cases of the same process of equalization. Some cases of suppression of elements seem to be, in fact, due to a process of fusion.

The study of the data from this point of view suggested a distinction between peripheral and central transformations. Peripheral transformations appeared to be due to a tendency towards homogeneity and simplicity (two girls and a boy being described as children, or girls). In central transformations, the meaning of the event, or better its subjective meaning, appeared to be the organizing factor causing the transformations. In this case, suppressions have the special character of elimination of disturbances, in order to make the event as coherent and meaningful as possible.[10] In other words, the preliminary result of the research was that an event tends to change in preferred directions. Different errors can represent different stages of the same direction of change.[11]

FACTS VERSUS THEORIES

The complex character and the apparently conceptual vagueness of the Gestalt notion, its connections with Goethe's thinking and with German philosophy brought the superficial reader to an interpretation of Gestalt as a philosophical theory entered into scientific psychology. Also the lack of a precise definition of the concept of "good Gestalt," and the apparently metaphysical character of some assertions ("the whole is different from the sum of the parts") are partly responsible of this erroneous interpretation. A glance at the experimental work published in the first 22 volumes of the *Psychologische Forschung* is enough to show that interpretations of this type are groundless. On the contrary, there is no theory in psychology which has suggested so many researches and which has led to the discovery of new facts in so many fields.

---

[10]A rather common error consisted in describing the arrival of the kidnapper with the car (while the second woman arrived on foot); the man came out of the car, in order to take the girl, put her into the car and left. It is clear that this change simplifies and clarifies the interpretation of the event. In fact it alters the meaning of the event, which is more complex. An interesting point is that the experimenter, who had seen the film several times, seeing it again after some months was surprised by the fact that the kidnapper did not arrive by car. This fact shows how strong the tendency towards a direction of change can be.

[11]It is perhaps worth mention that in the old scientific literature on the subject, the computation of errors had had also the practical purpose of measuring the "reliability" of subjects and the "memorability" of objects or qualities, that is the degree of faith to be put in the memory of a witness, and the degree of probability that a given class of objects or qualities would be remembered in a veridical way. A study of the privileged directions of transformation of events would offer some indications about the reconstruction of an event, independently, or even against the evidence of the majority of witnesses.

Is there anything characterizing Gestalt research in perception which bears on the antithesis between the "elaboration of theories" versus "accumulation of facts?" This point can be treated very briefly because the point of view of Gestalt theory on this topic has been stated in a very clear way in the first chapter of Koffka's *Principles of Gestalt Psychology* (1935). In fact, the classical study of Wertheimer on stroboscopic motion is at the same time a scientific observation of facts and a beginning of a new theory, suggested by facts. It can obviously be considered the model of Gestalt research in general and specifically in perception. But not all, nor the majority of researches, follow this model. Few are the researches that reach the level of providing the foundations for creating the building of a theory. For Gestalt psychologists the purpose of a research is not just to ascertain facts, the relations among facts, the facts conditioning other facts, but the comprehension of facts, which is achieved through hypotheses construction. The hypotheses have to be as concrete as possible (Köhler, 1953), so as to be experimentally testable. These experiments lead to the establishment and discovery of new facts, which confirm, extend, correct, or refute the theory or a part of it. Perhaps not the majority but a notable number of Gestalt-oriented papers in perception follow this rule, avoiding an excess of caution in hypothesizing, which is not suitable for the advancement of the science of Psychology, as well as for Science in general (Köhler, 1953).

ACKNOWLEDGMENT

I am indebted to Dr. Mary Henle for her fruitful criticism and help in editing the manuscript.

REFERENCES

Bozzi, P. Analisi fenomenologica del moto pendolare. *Rivista di Psicologia*, 1958, *52*, 281–302.

Bozzi, P. Le condizioni del movimento "naturale" lungo i piani inclinati, *Rivista di Psicologia*, 1959, *53*, 337–352.

Bozzi, P. Fenomenologia del movimento e dinamica pregalileiana. *Aut Aut*, 1961, *64*, 1–24.

Brown, J. F. Über gesehene Geschwindigkeiten. *Psychologische Forschung*, 1928, *10*, 84–101.

Brown, J. F. The Visual Perception of Velocity. *Psychologische Forschung*, 1931, *14*, 199–232.

Duncker, K. Über induzierte Bewegung. *Psychologische Forschung*, 1929, *12*, 180–259.

Fechner, T. *Elemente der psychophysik*. Leipzig: Breitkopf and Härtel, 1860.

Guillaume, P. *La psychologie de la forme*. Paris: E. Flammarion, 1937.

Kanizsa, G., & Metelli, F. Recherches expérimentales sur la perception visuelle d'attraction. *Journal de Psychologie Normale et Pathologique*, 1961, *4*, 385–421.

Kanizsa, G., & Vicario, G. La percezione della reazione intenzionale. In G. Kanizsa & G. Vicario (Eds.), *Ricerche sperimentali sulla percezione*. Trieste: Università degli Studi di Trieste, 1968.

Kanizsa, G. Perception, past experience and the impossible experiment. *Acta Psychologica*, 1969, *31*, 66–69.

Kanizsa, G. Amodale Ergänzung und "Erwartungsfehler" des Gestaltpsychologen. *Psychologische Forschung*, 1970, *33*, 325-344.

Kanizsa, G. La teoria della Gestalt: Distorsioni e fraintendimenti. In G. Kanizsa & P. Legrenzi (Eds.), *Psicologia della Gestalt e psicologia cognitivista*. Bologna: Il Mulino, 1978.

Koffka, K. Über Feldbegrenzung und Felderfüllung. *Psychologische Forschung*, 1923, *4*, 176-203.

Koffka, K. *Principles of Gestalt psychology*. New York: Harcourt Brace, 1935.

Köhler, W. Zur Theorie des Sukzessivvergleichs und des Zeitfehlers. *Psychologische Forschung*, 1923, *5*, 115-175.

Köhler, W. An aspect of Gestalt psychology. *Pedagogical Seminary and Journal of Genetic Psychology*, 1925, *32*, 691-723.

Köhler, W. Kurt Koffka. *Psychological Review*, 1942, *49*, 97-101.

Köhler, W. The scientists from Europe and the new environment. In F. L. Newmann (Eds.), *The cultural migration: The European scholar in America*. Philadelphia: University of Pennsylvania Press, 1953.

Köhler, W. Gestalt psychology. *Psychologische Forschung*, 1967, *31*, 18-30.

Korte, A. Kinematoskopische Untersuchungen. *Zeitschrift für Psychologie*, 1915, *72*, 194-296.

Lauenstein. O. Ansatz zu einer physiologischen Theorie des Vergleichs und des Zeitfehlers. *Psychologische Forschung*, 1933, *17*, 130-177.

Metelli, F. Transformazioni strutturali di un fatto concreto. *Atti dell 'VIII Convegno degli Psicologi Italiani*, 1936, 85-86.

Metelli, F. L'evoluzione delle tracce mnestiche nel confronto successivo. *Atti del X Convegno degli Psicologi Italiani*, Firenze, Editrice Universitaria, 1954, 1-7.

Metelli, F. Achromatic color conditions in the perception of transparency. In R. B. MacLeod & H. L. Pick, Jr. (Eds.), *Perception: Essays in honor of James J. Gibson*. Ithaca, N.Y.: Cornell University Press, 1974. (a)

Metelli, F. The perception of transparency. *Scientific American*, 1974, 91-97. (b)

Metelli, F. On the visual perception of transparency. In G. B. Flores d'Arcais (Ed.), *Studies in perception: Festschrift for Fabio Metelli*. Milan: Martello-Giunti, 1975.

Metelli, F., Da Pos, O., & Cavedon, A. Some conditions regarding localization and mode of appearance of achromatic colors. *Atti e Memorie dell'Accademia Patavina di Scienze, Lettere ed Arti*, 1977, *89*, 213-221.

Metzger, W. Figurale Wahrnehmung. In W. Metzger (Ed.), *Handbuch der Psychologie*. Göttingen, E. I. Halbband, J. Hogrefe, 1966.

Metzger, W. *Gesetze des Sehens*. Frankfurt am Main: W. Kramer, 1975.

Michotte, A. *La perception de la causalité*. Louvain et Bruxelles: Editions Erasme, 1954.

Musatti, C. L. *Psicologia della testimonianza*. Padova: CEDAM, 1931.

Musatti, C. L. Oblio e arricchimento mnestico nelle deposizioni testimoniali sopra fatti concreti. *Scritti di Psicologia in onore di Federico Kiesow*. Torino: Anfossi, 1933.

Oyama, T. Perceptual grouping as a function of proximity. *Perceptual and Motor Skills*, 1961, *13*, 305-306.

Stern, W. Zur Psychologie des Aussage. *Zeitschrift für die Gesamte Strafrechtswissenschaft*, 1902, *22*, 26-41.

Stern, W. Die Aussage als geistige Leistung und als Verhörsprodukt. *Beiträge zur Psychologie der Aussage*, 1904, I Folge, III Heft, 91-99.

Wertheimer, M. Untersuchungen zur Lehre von der Gestalt I. *Psychologische Forschung*, 1922, *1*, 47-58.

Yela, M. Phenomenal causation at a distance. *Quarterly Journal of Experimental Psychology*, 1952, *4*, 139-154.

12

The Effect
of Perceived Depth
On Phantoms and the
Phantom Motion Aftereffect[1]

Naomi Weisstein
William Maguire
Mary C. Williams
State University of New York, Buffalo

A procedure for producing perception of moving contours where none are present retinally was recently described by Tynan and Sekuler (1975). If a horizontal strip of opaque black tape is used to cover up part of a vertical grating that is moving sideways (Fig. 12.1a), the contours are perceived to continue—clearly, but with lower contrast—in the taped-over region. Unlike other configurations for producing subjective contours (Kanizsa, 1955, 1976), none are seen with this configuration if the grating is stationary.[2] For this reason, Tynan and Sekuler applied a new term, "phantoms," to these movement-dependent contours, to distinguish them from the subjective contours that occur in stationary displays.

Two interesting findings about these illusory contours have come to light. First, the moving phantoms give rise to a compelling motion aftereffect (Weisstein, Maguire, & Berbaum, 1977), just as real moving gratings do. This finding was unexpected, because motion aftereffects have been thought to be a relatively simple and low-level phenomenon, whereas the moving-phantom illusion appears to involve a higher-level, less peripheral process.

---

[1]We would like to thank Charles S. Harris for alerting us to the importance of perceived depth in these displays, and for proposing that we use stereoscopic cues to control perceived depth, as well as for numerous other suggestions and comments. We would also like to thank James R. Sawusch for a careful and insightful reading of the manuscript, and Fanya S. Montalvo for her numerous helpful suggestions. This research was supported in part by National Eye Institute grant NIH 5 RO1 EY 01330 and National Science Foundation grant BNS 76 - 02059 to the first author.

[2]Recently, Genter and Weisstein (1981) have shown that phantom stripes can also be produced with gratings that do not move, simply by flickering the display.

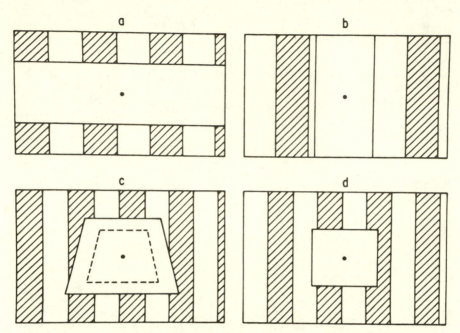

FIG. 12.1.   The displays used to study phantom contours. When the stripes move sideways, phantoms are seen within the opaque regions in a, c, and d but not in b. Figures are drawn to scale.

The second finding is that perception of the moving phantoms has been shown to be affected by perceived depth (Weisstein & Maguire, 1978). What is critical is the depth relationship between the moving gratings and the occluding opaque region. When the opaque region is seen in front of the grating (closer to the observer), the phantoms are not perceived. When the opaque region appears to be in the same plane as the grating or behind it, the illusion is visible. This relationship works both ways: Apparent depth affects the illusion, the illusion affects apparent depth. For example, when the orientation of the occluding region is changed from horizontal to vertical, the impression that a transparent strip lies in the same plane as the moving grating changes to one of an opaque strip hovering an inch or so in front of the grating (Fig. 12.1b). If the opaque strip is truncated in length so that it consists of a trapezoidal or rectangular patch blocking only the middle of the display (Figs. 12.1c and d), the two distinct perceptions alternate (Weisstein & Maguire, 1978). Phantoms are seen only when the patch does not appear to be in front of the moving grating.

The experiments reported here were designed to provide the answers to further questions about the interrelation of moving phantoms, the phantom motion aftereffect, and perceived depth: What effect does monocular versus binocular viewing have on the moving phantoms? If depth cues and other factors increase or decrease the visibility of phantoms, do these factors also increase or decrease the phantom motion aftereffect in the same way?

EXPERIMENT 1: EFFECT OF BINOCULAR VIEWING ON PHANTOMS

In the first experiment, we tested the effects of monocular and binocular viewing on the percentage of time that observers reported seeing phantoms during 60-sec inspection periods. Two sizes of trapezoidal opaque patches (Fig. 12.1c) were used, placed at two different distances in front of the moving display.

Procedure

A square-wave grating, .67 cycles/degree and .8 fL space-average luminance, was presented on a GT-40 display oscilloscope controlled by a PDP 11/10 computer, using Fortran-callable display graphics. The grating was set in motion by an animation technique, which spatially displaced it in small steps. The frame rate was 20/sec; the resulting stimulus moved across the screen with a velocity of 1.8 degrees/sec. The entire display subtended 3.5 degrees vertically and 5.5 horizontally.

Four isosceles trapezoids were constructed from heavy black construction paper. Each contained a small white fixation point at its center. The lower base of each was 1.5 times as long as its upper base; its height was equal to its upper base. Two of the trapezoids measured 1.25 and 2 degrees vertically, when placed .75 cm in front of the screen and viewed from a distance of one meter. A second pair of trapezoids matched the first pair in visual angle when placed 15.5 cm in front of the moving display. Thus, two retinal sizes of opaque patches were presented at two different depths. Each size-depth combination was viewed monocularly in one condition and binocularly in another, yielding a total of eight conditions. These conditions were each presented once, in random order, for 60-sec viewing periods.

Ten observers, naive as to the purposes of the experiment and with normal or corrected-to-normal vision, participated in the experiment. They viewed the displays from a distance of a meter, with head position stabilized by a chin rest. In monocular viewing the dominant eye was used; the other eye was occluded by an eye patch. The observers were instructed to gaze steadily at the fixation point during the viewing period.

At the start of the experiment, phantoms were described to the observers. They were then shown a sample of the moving stripes with one of the trapezoids in front, .75 cm from the screen. All observers reported seeing phantoms, although in other contexts (such as film demonstrations) occasional observers have failed to get the illusion.

The observers' task during the experiment was to indicate when phantoms were perceived, by holding down a switch. They were told to release the switch whenever the phantoms disappeared. The percentage of time that the switch was depressed, during the 60-sec viewing period, was the dependent variable. The illusion tends to come and go during continuous viewing, so most observers pressed and released the switch several times during each viewing period. The computer recorded the time of each switch press and release, as well as the cumulative total time it was held down in each condition.

Results and Discussion

Our main finding was that binocular viewing reduced by one-half to two-thirds the percentage of time phantoms were seen. This is shown in Fig. 12.2, in which

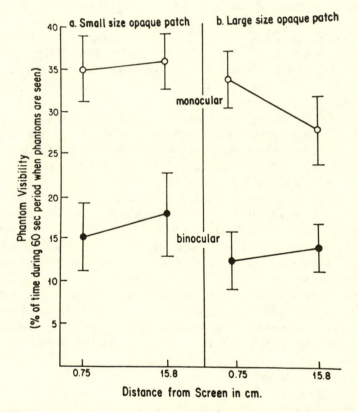

FIG. 12.2.   The results of Experiment 1: The effect of monocular (open circles) and binocular (solid circles) viewing on the visibility of phantoms when the opaque region is physically in front of the moving display by .75 (left) and 15.8 (right) cm. a) Small opaque trapezoidal patch (1.25° high), b) Large opaque trapezoidal patch (2° high). Bars give standard errors.

phantom visibility is plotted as a function of the distance of the trapezoid from the screen, for monocular viewing (open circles) and binocular viewing (solid circles). These points are means, averaged across the ten observers. Figure 12.2a shows results for the small opaque trapezoidal patch, Fig. 12.2b for the larger trapezoidal patch. As the figure clearly shows, binocular viewing decreased the visibility of the phantoms. An analysis of variance (fixed factors, repeated measures) showed that this effect was significant: $F(1, 9) = 8$, $p < .01$. On the other hand, the distance between the opaque patch and the display had no systematic effect on the percentage of time the phantoms were visible. Thus, the stronger accommodation and parallax cues provided by placing the patch a greater distance from the screen did not further diminish phantom visibility.

These results clearly show that binocular viewing diminishes the visibility of phantoms. This adds to the earlier evidence (Tynan & Sekuler, 1975; Weisstein, Maguire, & Berbaum, 1977) that phantoms cannot be attributed solely to local retinal interactions, because such interactions should be present whether viewing is binocular or monocular.

EXPERIMENT 2: BINOCULAR VIEWING AT ZERO AND NON-ZERO DISPARITIES

In the second experiment we tested the effects of monocular and binocular viewing on the visibility of phantoms under two conditions: depth and no depth. In the no-depth condition, the opaque region was part of the graphic display itself. In the depth condition the opaque patch was placed .75 cm from the screen (as in one condition of the first experiment).

Procedure

The trapezoids of the first experiment were replaced by rectangles (Fig. 12.1d), which give rise to less lively impressions of depth but are easier to generate within a computer-driven display. One retinal size of rectangle was used, 1.8 degrees horizontal by 1.5 degrees vertical. The rectangle was either generated on the oscilloscope screen as part of the display, or was made out of construction paper and suspended .75 cm in front of the display. In addition, the display was viewed either monocularly or binocularly. Thus, there were four conditions in all. Each condition was presented four times to each subject, in random order.

Viewing distance, screen luminance, and size and velocity of the grating were the same as in Experiment 1. In order to minimize differences in appearance between the two kinds of rectangles, room illumination was dimmed. The luminance of the two surfaces was .05 fL (zero-depth condition) and .04 fL (depth condition), as measured with an SEI spot photometer.

The experimental procedure was the same as in the previous experiment. Eleven subjects participated, all unaware of the purpose of the experiment and with normal or corrected-to-normal vision.

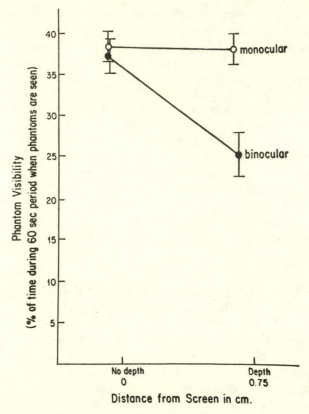

FIG. 12.3.   The results of Experiment 2: The effect of monocular viewing (open circles) and binocular viewing (solid circles) on the visibility of phantoms when the opaque region is either part of the display (no depth, left), or .75 cm in front of the display (depth, right). Bars give standard errors.

Results and Discussion

We found that phantom visibility was considerably reduced under binocular viewing, but only in the depth condition. This is shown in Fig. 12.3, in which mean phantom visibility is plotted as a function of the distance of the rectangle from the screen, for monocular viewing (open circles) and binocular viewing (solid circles). The left-hand points show results for the zero depth condition, when the opaque patch was part of the display itself; the right-hand points show results for the condition where the opaque patch was .75 cm in front of the moving display. As the figure clearly shows, binocular viewing decreased the visibility of phantoms only when disparity cues were present. An analysis of variance showed that the main effects of depth and viewing condition and their interaction were all significant: depth, $F(1, 9) = 9.2$, $p < .05$; viewing condition, $F(1, 9) = 6.6$, $p < .05$; and depth $\times$ viewing condition, $F(1, 9) = 8.6$, $p < .05$. The small reduction in phantom visibility for the depth condition under monocular viewing did not approach significance.

Experiment 1 showed that binocular viewing reduces phantom visibility when the opaque patch is located in front of the moving grating. The second experiment supported that finding, and in addition showed that binocular viewing does *not* reduce phantom visibility when the occluding area is in the same plane as the grating.

EXPERIMENT 3: RELATION BETWEEN PHANTOMS AND THE PHANTOM MOTION AFTEREFFECT

In Experiment 3 we investigated the phantom motion aftereffect. Previous experiments (Weisstein et al., 1977) have shown that reducing phantom visibility by changing the configuration of the display (for example, by using a vertical rather than a horizontal occluding strip) also reduced the phantom motion aftereffect. In the present experiment we tested whether reducing phantom visibility in a different way—by manipulating binocular depth cues—would produce a similar reduction in the aftereffect.

Procedure

The display used to produce phantoms in this experiment differed from the previous displays. It consisted of discrete lines whose luminance modulation approximated a vertical sine-wave grating (1 cycle/degree) moving at a velocity of 1.5 degrees/sec, with a space-average luminance of 3.0 fL. The entire display subtended 6 degrees by 6 degrees. The grating was divided in half, with left and right halves moving towards each other as shown in Fig. 12.4. The relative phases of the left and right halves were symmetrical about the vertical axis. This display was designed to make steady fixation easier, and to reduce optokinetic nystagmus.

Rectangular opaque patches of three different retinal sizes were used: 1 by 2 degrees, 1.5 by 3 degrees, and 2 by 4 degrees, oriented horizontally. These were located in the center of the moving grating (Fig. 12.4), and, as in Experiment 2, were either part of the display itself (zero depth) or were placed 7.6 cm in front of the display. As in the previous experiments, each size-by-depth condition was viewed either monocularly or binocularly on a given trial. Thus, there were a total of 12 conditions. Each observer viewed each condition five times, in random order.

Judgments were made both of the visibility of phantoms and of the strength of the phantom motion aftereffect. As in the previous experiments, observers judged phantom visibility by depressing a key and holding it down for as long as phantoms were seen. Immediately after the 30-sec viewing period, a .5 by 1

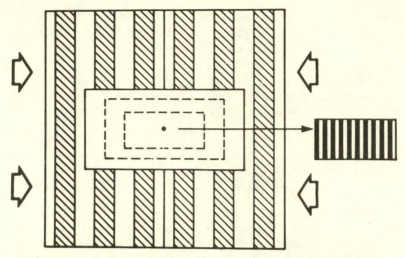

FIG. 12.4. The displays used for Experiment 3. The left and right sine wave gratings moved toward each other as indicated by the arrows. They were adjusted in relative phase so that at each moment in time the display was symmetrical around the vertical axis. Three sizes of opaque rectangle were used, as indicated by the dotted lines. A fixation point appeared in the center. The stationary test patch, displayed after presentation of the moving stripes, is shown at right. The figure is drawn to scale.

degree stationary patch of sinusoidal grating (6 cycles/degree, with a space-average luminance of .6 fL) was optically interfaced by use of a half-silvered mirror so that it appeared in the same plane as the display. The patch appeared in the center of the display for 3 sec (Fig. 12.4). When the phantom motion aftereffect was seen, the left and right halves of the stationary patch appeared to move away from each other, creating a vivid impression of expanding movement. Observers judged the strength of this aftereffect by the method of magnitude estimation, assigning numbers proportional to the perceived velocity of expansion of the test patch relative to a standard (called 10). The standard was the velocity of the moving display. (See Sekuler & Pantle, 1967, and Pantle, 1974, for similar procedures.)

Ten observers participated in this experiment. They were unaware of the purposes of the experiment and had normal or corrected-to-normal vision.

Results and Discussion

Our main finding was that the strength of the phantom motion aftereffect depended strongly on the visibility of the phantoms. A quick inspection of Fig. 12.5a, which plots visibility of phantoms, and Fig. 12.5b, which plots the strength of the phantom motion aftereffect, shows that the measures are highly correlated: All experimental manipulations that decreased phantom visibility also decreased the strength of the phantom motion aftereffect.

Considering first the conditions that decreased phantom visibility, we again found (as in Experiment 2) that placing the opaque rectangular patch physically in front of the moving display dramatically decreased the visibility of phantoms under binocular viewing. This is shown by the bottom dashed curve in Fig. 12.5a. The measure of phantom visibility is again the mean percentage of time (averaged across the 10 observers) that phantoms were visible, this time during 30-sec rather than 60-sec inspection periods. An analysis of variance showed all main effects—depth, size, and viewing condition—to be significant, as well as the interaction of depth and viewing condition ($F[1, 9] = 47.8$, $p < .01$; $F[2, 18] = 4.7$, $p < .02$; $F[1, 9] = 28.8$, $p < .01$; $F[1, 9] = 18.1$, $p < .01$, respectively). Binocular viewing in the depth condition (bottom function, Fig. 12.5a) decreased phantom visibility by as much as 50%, and this condition differed significantly from all other conditions ($p < .01$, Newman-Keuls test). Monocular viewing (middle function) decreased phantom visibility to a smaller extent. Although this difference was not statistically significant, its presence suggests that monocular depth cues (e.g., accommodation, motion parallax) may play some minor role in the reduction of phantom visibility.

Visibility of phantoms was again highest when the opaque patch was part of the display itself (top two functions: open circles, monocular viewing; solid circles, binocular viewing). There is no significant difference between these functions. Maximum phantom visibility in this experiment was higher than in the other two experiments, showing that the use of colliding gratings (which served to reduce optokinetic nystagmus and produce steady fixation) did not diminish phantom strength. Explanations for phantoms based on eye movements therefore seem less likely.

An interesting outcome is the superiority of the intermediate-sized opaque patch in producing phantoms, regardless of the variation in the other parameters. This size effect is statistically significant ($F[2, 18] = 4.7$, $p < .02$). The cause of this nonmonotonic effect is still unclear. However, like the depth effects, it further rules out explanations of phantoms based on local retinal interactions such as eye movements and scattered light, since such interactions would predict strongest phantoms when the opaque patch was smallest.

The results for the phantom motion aftereffect agree in almost all respects with the results for phantom visibility. These are shown in Fig. 12.5b, in which strength of the motion aftereffect (measured as the rated velocity of expansion of the stationary test patch, averaged across ten subjects) is plotted as a function of increasing size of the opaque region within which the phantoms were seen. Again, the size effect was significant ($F[2, 18] = 13.7$, $p < .01$), as was the effect of monocular and binocular viewing ($F[1, 9] = 8.9$, $p < .02$), and the effect of depth versus no depth ($F[1, 9] = 66.5$, $p < .01$). The interaction of viewing condition with depth did not reach significance ($F[1, 9] = 6.8$, $.05 < p$

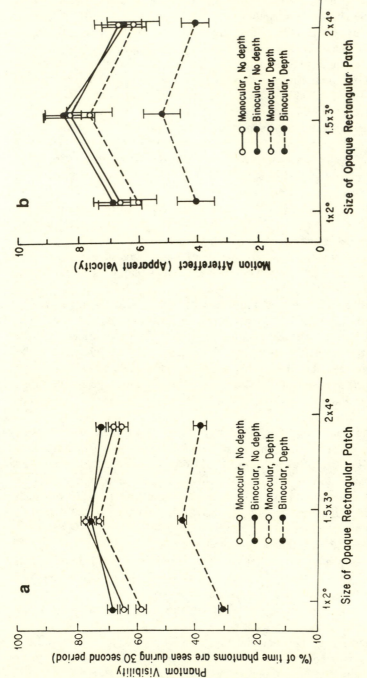

FIG 12.5. The results of Experiment 3: The effect of depth, opaque patch size, and viewing condition on (a) phantom visibility and (b) the strength of the phantom motion aftereffect. In the depth condition the opaque rectangle was 7.6 cm in front of the screen; in the no-depth condition the opaque rectangle was part of the display itself. Visibility of phantoms and strength of the phantom-motion aftereffect were both reduced by the greatest amount when depth cues were present and viewing was binocular. Bars give standard errors.

< .10). However, while this reflects the fact that both monocular and binocular viewing diminish the effect in the depth condition, binocular viewing (bottom, dashed function) clearly reduces the phantom motion aftereffect to a much greater extent. A Neuman-Keuls test showed that the binocular depth condition was significantly different from the three other conditions ($p < .01$). To obtain a more direct measure of the correspondence between the percentage of time phantoms are seen and the strength of the subsequent motion aftereffect, the raw data were analyzed for linear correlation. The overall Pearson r coefficient for the ten subjects together was .895 ($p < .05$); the coefficients for each of the ten subjects individually were .94, .88, .86, .85, .67, .59, .49, .42, .08, and .05. The first eight of these correlations were significant ($p < .05$); the other two subjects showed essentially no correlation. Overall, the data strongly suggest that the motion aftereffect found in the region of the opaque patch depends primarily upon the prior presence of phantoms within that area. As a result, the phantom motion aftereffect is, like the phantoms themselves, affected by depth cues present within the display.

GENERAL DISCUSSION

Comparison with Stationary Subjective Contours and Completion Phenomena

We found that moving phantoms are diminished by depth cues, when these cues indicate that the opaque region within which phantoms are seen is in front of the moving display. Depth cues also seem to play a major role in the formation of stationary subjective contours (Coren, 1972). Stereoscopic depth cues diminish subjective contours if they contradict the depth relations implicit in the configuration (Harris & Gregory, 1973; Lawson, Cowen, Gibbs, & Whitmore, 1974); they *enhance* subjective contours if they support the figural cues to depth (Lawson et al., 1974).

There are obvious differences between stationary subjective contours and phantoms, however. Stationary configurations can produce subjective contours, but in order to produce strong phantoms a configuration must move (or at least flicker[2]). Second, the brightness gradients generated by phantoms are exactly opposite to what one would expect from brightness contrast—they are positives, not negatives—and hence unlike the brightness usually seen with subjective contours (Frisby & Clatworthy, 1975; Kanizsa, 1976). Third, the interrupted stripes, rather than defining an empty region as opaque, appear to continue across it. In this respect phantoms seem more like completion phenomena such as that found across retinal "holes" (Teuber, Battersby, & Bender, 1960), and with stabilized images (Gerrits & Vendrick, 1970). Indeed, elsewhere we have found that when the moving stripes that produce the phantom contours are replaced by columns of X's, the X's themselves will be seen to continue, dimly but unmistakably, in the opaque region (Weisstein & Maguire, 1978; Weisstein & Harris, 1980). However, there are differences between phantoms and other completion phenomena. The opaque region does not disappear or blur when phantoms appear and it does not have to be retinally stabilized or uncoupled with eye movements (Coren & Porac, 1974) for the phantoms to be seen. In fact, a square opaque patch can move harmonically up and down across the display and the phantoms will remain clearly visible (Maguire, 1978).

Nevertheless, all these phenomena—completion, subjective contours, phantoms—have in common strong cues indicating which regions should be grouped by the visual system. This is particularly true of our phantom displays. Besides the figural cue to grouping, which Guzman (1968) calls "matched T's," there is a further cue in the common speed and direction of the components in the moving display. Johansson (1973) has shown that these cues alone can be effective in organizing spatially separate parts of a moving display into perceptual wholes.

Local Retinal Interactions

Our results add to the evidence (Tynan & Sekuler, 1975; Weisstein et al., 1977) that phantoms and the phantom motion aftereffect cannot be accounted for solely by local retinal interactions such as produced by eye movements, scattered light, or spatially extensive "motion detectors" that straddle the empty and filled regions of the display.

Eye Movements.   A motion aftereffect might be produced independently of phantoms if observers moved their eyes away from the empty region to the physically present moving contours during the period of observation. However, there would be little reason to expect that such eye movements would be related to monocular or binocular viewing, or to the size of the empty region. Yet these are the conditions that affect the strength of the motion aftereffect. In addition, colliding gratings facilitated fixation (the fact that the stationary test patch consistently appeared to be expanding rather than moving laterally indicated that fixation was rather stable), but the motion aftereffect obtained with such gratings was as strong as those we have found previously with gratings moving in only one direction (Weisstein et al., 1977; Weisstein & Maguire, 1978).

Scattered Light.   Scattered light within the eye might produce the impression of moving contours in an empty region. However, such scatter should produce stronger phantoms as the empty region becomes smaller, and we found the strongest phantoms with an intermediate-sized empty region.

"Motion Detectors."   Phantoms and a phantom motion aftereffect might arise due to direct stimulation of "motion detectors" that straddle the empty and filled regions of our display. However, to account for our results one would have to assume that fewer of these detectors respond when both eyes are open, and that such detectors respond more for an intermediate-sized region than for a smaller one. Neither of these assumptions seems justified.

Contour- and Motion-Processing Mechanisms not Directly Dependent on Local Retinal Stimulation

Although the strength of the phantom motion aftereffect correlates poorly with any of these local retinal mechanisms, it correlates highly with the strength of the phantoms themselves. It is intriguing that illusory motion is capable of producing motion aftereffects—especially since such aftereffects have been thought to depend critically on local retinal stimulation (Anstis & Gregory, 1965; Masland, 1969; Sekuler & Pantle, 1967; but see Anstis & Reinhardt-Rutland (1976) for a recent interesting exception). Clearly, the appearance of phantoms involves contour- and motion-processing mechanisms that are relatively independent of local retinal stimulation.

Other psychophysical procedures thought applicable only to low-level processes have also been shown to measure mechanisms not directly dependent on local retinal interactions. Weisstein, Matthews, and Berbaum (1974) found that adaptation to an illusory grating reduced tbe apparent contrast of physically present contours, and vice versa. Coren and Theodor (1977) found an increment-threshold difference across an illusory edge, though no differences were found in the interior of the illusory region.

Perceived three-dimensionality has previously been shown to play an important role in processes of this kind. For example, depth-dependent changes in the apparent contrast of a patch of grating have been measured at retinal locations that are sheltered from the direct adaptational effects of a larger grating (Gyoba, 1979; Weisstein, 1970; Weisstein, Montalvo, & Ozog, 1972). The identification of simple line segments has been shown to be aided by a three-dimensional object-like context (Weisstein & Harris, 1974; A. Williams & Weisstein, 1978). The phantom motion aftereffect is another case where psychophysical techniques previously thought to measure rather elementary processes reveal higher-order processes as well. (See Weisstein & Maguire, 1978, and Weisstein & Harris, 1980, for further discussion.)

CONCLUSIONS

There are a number of visual phenomena that have been thought to depend entirely on low-level, relatively peripheral processes. Some of these—for example, identification of line segments, contrast adaptation to illusory contours or gratings, and now motion aftereffects of moving phantoms—have been shown to be affected in important ways by nonlocal aspects of the stimuli, such as apparent three-dimensionality. These findings suggest that there are higher-level contour- and motion-processing mechanisms that may usually elude detection because their output correlates so well, in most cases, with that of the lower-level mechanisms on which they depend. In certain circumstances, however, the higher-level mechanisms can be caught in the act of filtering, enhancing, or overriding the information that comes from the retina. Studying the results of such interactions may provide us with insights into the structure of higher-level visual representations.

REFERENCES

Anstis, S. M., & Gregory, R. L. The aftereffect of seen motion; the role of retinal stimulation and of eye movements. *Quarterly Journal of Experimental Psychology*, 1968, *17*, 173–174.

Anstis, S. M., & Reinhardt-Rutland, A. H. Interactions between motion aftereffects and induced movement. *Vision Research*, 1976, *16*, 1391–1395.

Coren, S. Subjective contours and apparent depth. *Psychological Review*, 1972, *79*, 359–367.

Coren, S., & Porac, S. The fading of stabilized images; eye movements and information processing. *Perception & Psychophysics*, 1974, *16*(3), 529–534.

Coren, S., & Theodor, L. Increment thresholds across subjective contours. *Perception*, 1977, *6*, 107–111.

Frisby, J. P., & Clatworthy, J. L. Illusory contours: Curious cases of simultaneous brightness contrast? *Perception*, 1975, *4*, 349–357.

Genter, C. R. II, & Weisstein, N. Flickering phantoms: A motion illusion without motion. *Vision Research*, 1981, *21*, 963–966.

Gerrits, H., & Vendrick, A. Simultaneous contrast, filling-in process and information processing in man's visual system. *Experimental Brain Research*, 1970, *11*, 411–430.

Guzman, A. Computer recognition of three-dimensional objects in a visual scene. *Project MAC Technical Report*, 1968, *59*, MIT Artificial Intelligence Laboratory, Cambridge, Mass.

Gyoba, J. Differential adaptation to invisible gratings blocked by stereoscopically raised planes. *Tohoku Psychologica Folia*, 1979, *38*(1-4), 29–35.

Harris, J. P., & Gregory, R. L. Fusion and rivalry of illusory contours. *Perception*, 1973, *2*, 235–247.

Johansson, G. Visual perception of biological motion and a model for its analysis. *Perception & Psychophysics*, 1973, *14*, 201–211.

Kanizsa, G. Marzini quazi-percettive in campi con stimolazione omogenea. *Rivista di Psicologia*, 1955, *49*, 7–30.

Kanizsa, G. Subjective contours. *Scientific American*, 1976, *234*, 48–52.

Lawson, R. B., Cowen, E., Gibbs, T. D., & Whitmore, C. G. Stereoscopic enhancement and erasure of subjective contours. *Journal of Experimental Psychology*, 1974, *103*, 1142–1146.

Maguire, W. *Contour completion in dynamic visual displays.* Unpublished doctoral dissertation, State University of New York at Buffalo, February, 1978.

Masland, R. H. Visual motion perception: Experimental modification. *Science,* 1969, *165,* 819–821.

Pantle, A. Motion aftereffect magnitude as a measure of spatio-temporal response properties of direction sensitive analyzers. *Vision Research,* 1974, *14,* 1229–1236.

Sekuler, R., & Pantle, A. A model for aftereffects of seen movement. *Vision Research,* 1967, *7,* 427–438.

Teuber, H. L., Battersby, W. S., & Bender, M. Visual field defects after penetrating missile wounds of the brain. Cambridge, Mass.: *Harvard University Press,* 1960.

Tynan, P., & Sekuler, R. Moving visual phantoms: A new contour completion effect. *Science,* 1975, *188,* 951–952.

Weisstein, N. Neural symbolic activity: A psychophysical measure. *Science,* 1970, 168, 1489–1491.

Weisstein, N., & Harris, C. S. Visual detection of line segments: An object-superiority effect. *Science,* 1974, *186,* 752–755.

Weisstein, N., & Harris, C. S. Masking and unmasking of distributed representations in the visual system. In C. S. Harris (Ed.), *Visual coding and adaptability.* Hillsdale, N.J.: Lawrence Erlbaum Associates. 1980.

Weisstein, N., & Maguire, W. Computing the next step: Psychophysical measures of representation and interpretation. In A. L. Hanson & E. M. Riseman (Eds.), *Computer vision systems,* New York: Academic Press, 1978.

Weisstein, N., Maguire, W., & Berbaum, K. A phantom-motion aftereffect. *Science,* 1977, *189,* 955–958.

Weisstein, N., Matthews, M., & Berbaum, K. Illusory contours can mask real contours. *Bulletin of the Psychonomic Society,* 266, 1974, (Abstract).

Weisstein, W., Montalvo, F. S., & Ozog, G. Differential adaptation to gratings blocked by cubes and gratings blocked by hexagons: A test of the neural symbolic activity hypothesis. *Psychonomic Science,* 1972, *27,* 89–91.

Williams, A., & Weisstein, N. Line segments are perceived better in a coherent context than alone: An object-line effect in visual perception. *Memory & Cognition,* 1978, *6,* 85–90.

Winer, B. *Statistical principles in experimental design.* New York: McGraw-Hill, 1971.

13 Figure Organization and Binocular Interaction

Mario Zanforlin
University of Padua

INTRODUCTION

Since the time of Wheatstone (1838) and Brewster (1847) the stereoscope has never ceased to interest and amuse people in general and psychologists in particular by its ability to evoke the perception of "real" and impressive three dimensionality. But as regards the explanation of stereoscopic perception, differences (or perhaps disparities) of views arose even among the very first investigators (Helmholtz, 1962; Hering, 1865–1868; Panum, 1858). It is easy to observe that the impression of depth arises from some kind of differences or disparities in the stereograms presented to each eye, but an exact definition of the disparities or even of what is meant by disparity is still a problem a century later (Wallach & Lindauer, 1962).

My purpose is not to review the history of stereoscopic perception but to focus selectively on some aspects of the problem that pertain to the controversy between Hering and the Gestalt psychologists on the nature of the underlying processes in stereoscopic perception. A substantial part of this old dispute still lingers on in today's discussion (though the terminology is new and the phenomena under discussion are also new) as can be amply illustrated from current literature (Frisby & Mayhew, 1976; Julesz, 1971; Nelson, 1975; Ramachandran & Nelson, 1976; Sperling, 1970; Wallach & Bacon, 1976).

To outline briefly the two opposing views, we could say that the so-called "elemental" school maintained that depth impression stemmed from a process of binocular point-by-point comparison of the stimulus presented to the two eyes, each with its own fixed depth value of disparity with no preformed monocular

251

"figure" or contour. This theoretical position has been clearly stated by Bishop (1970):

> Because it is not easy to appreciate any change in the appearance of objects when we close one eye, the intuitive conclusion-hardly-surprising- is that form is first elaborated for each eye separately and that stereopsis is added at a subsequent stage by the conjunction of uniocular forms. This view has been widely held. . . Paradoxically the reverse is probably more nearly the case. . . The analyses by which depth discriminations are made, have a mosaic point-by-point or feature-by-feature basis. Line contours of any appreciable length are not required [p. 471].

Julesz stereograms which have been considered demonstrations in support of a point-by-point analysis (Sperling, 1970) are, in fact, usually described as "stereograms without monocular contours" (p. 497).

The exact opposite point of view was held by Gestalt psychologists (Koffka, 1935; Lewin & Sakuma, 1925; Metzger, 1975; Tausch, 1953; Wilde, 1950) although comparatively little research was done on binocular perception, because Gestalt psychologists held that the important things happened at the monocular level. They maintained in fact that binocular interaction does not lie in a point-by-point comparison, but is between organized figures first elaborated in each eye and attracted to each other following the law of similarity and the other grouping laws of Wertheimer. Moreover, according to them, the degree of displacement in depth is not a fixed value but the results of the interaction from all the forces present in the visual field (Koffka, 1935, pp. 273–274). This was the classifical theory, but nowadays things are no longer so clear-cut. Metzger, a leading exponent of Gestalt theory, in a review of the new phenomena that have appeared in recent years, was led to conclude that "interaction between the two eyes does not need the formation of complete formal units" (1975, p. 385). Conversely, in order to explain how it is that the eyes do not "get confused" in choosing which of the many possible "local matches" is the correct one, Julesz (1971) was led to propose a "dipole spring-coupled model" to connect the stimulated points; a physical analog model that would have delighted Köhler (i.e., a Gestalt-type of interaction between "points").

It is true that this "global" process brought in to resolve ambiguities is not considered a Gestalt global process. In fact some authors make the distinction between "low and high spatial frequency" (Frisby & Mayhew, 1976) or between "coarse and fine stereopsis," in both of which a global process plays a part (Julesz, 1976). The tendency is to identify Gestalt with coarse or low frequency stereopsis, whereas "fine" stereopsis is apparently not a Gestalt process. It seems to me that to sustain a point-by-point analysis and to introduce a model of grouping (i.e., interaction between points) in order to resolve the ambiguities derived from the presupposed point-by-point analysis, is in itself contradictory, unless we define the points as visual "units" in the Gestalt sense; Gestalt grouping originated just in order to resolve perceptual ambiguities that the elemental school was unable to explain.

There are, however, also difficulties at the base of the Gestalt theory of binocular interaction. The general hypothesis that there are no substantial differences in the organization of the perceptual field between the monocular and binocular levels implied that: (1) there are binocular Gestalten or units made up of parts presented separately to each eye, in the same way that a group of dots, for example, can be seen as a square at the monocular level. This implication has been shown to be incorrect (Metzger, 1975). I think it is possible to speak of "binocular Gestalten" or units, but not in this sense. (2) Binocular interaction should occur in the vertical as well as in the horizontal dimension. This again is not correct and the difficulty was pointed out first, by Koffka (1935) and later by Zajac (1964). In fact only lateral disparity gives rise to the depth impression and to convergence movements that bring corresponding images together. Thus, if Gestalt grouping forces act at the binocular level, they should act only along the horizontal dimension. Another fact that is not taken into consideration by Gestalt theory is that at the binocular level, figures are not just "attracted," they actually move together and "fuse"; that is, a single image emerges. Thus, there is lateral movement and displacement in depth which can be considered to obey Wertheimer's laws, and there is a "coming together" or fusion that has stricter rules (it at least requires a higher degree of similarity) because it is well-known that rivalry may arise after the figures have been brought together or superimposed. No similar phenomenon is known at the monocular level. Rivalry tends to "separate" the two images and, although it does not completely annul the depth impression, it does hinder it.

I think that Metzger's conclusion quoted above that binocular interaction does not presuppose figure formation, can perhaps be explained on the basis that he adopted Linschoten's (1956) point of view where fusion and rivalry phenomena (see Levelt, 1965) are identified with the depth effect. It is well established now that depth is possible even with rivalry or diplopic figures (Kaufman, 1964; Kaufman & Pitblado, 1969; Mitchell, 1969, 1970). However, as I have already dealt with the problem of the necessary and sufficient conditions to give rise to a depth impression in a previous paper (Zanforlin, 1974), I do not discuss this problem now.

In spite of all this criticism of the classical Gestalt theory, I still consider valid the hypothesis that binocular interaction occurs between monocularly organized figures or structures. I illustrate three examples of how the monocular Gestalten presented to the two eyes interact; that is, how they determine the depth value of the figural elements of which they are composed, and how they are partly modified as result of the interaction. But before doing so, I need to recall some facts and clarify some terms.

First of all, as has been pointed out by Koffka (1935, p. 271), what appears as a "figure" in one eye never interacts with what appears as background (or

FIG. 13.1.   Presenting A to the left eye and B to the right eye (or vice-versa), the two vertical rectangles appear displaced in different planes of depth. The background in between does not partecipate in the displacement. If, instead, C and D are presented, the space between the two rectangles that is now seen as a figure, appears as a tilted surface, that is, it is displaced in depth (from Wilde, 1950).

uniform field) in the other eye, although "corresponding points" may be stimulated. Other authors too have brought evidence on this point. (1) Figure 13.1 (Wilde, 1950) illustrates the first case. When A and B in Fig. 13.1 are presented binocularly, the two recactangles are displaced in depth. The background and the area in between the two figures does not participate in the displacement. But in C and D, where the space in between becomes figure, this space is displaced in depth. (2) In Fig. 13.2 (Linschoten, 1956) figure and ground alternate so that the white or black surfaces are alternately displaced in depth (and indeed both black and white surfaces are displaced when the figure appears as a mosaic). Thus figure-ground segregation at a monocular level is a prerequisite for binocular interaction and what appears as background at a monocular level does not interact nor is it displaced in depth, unless what is called the background is not an "empty space" but a "surface" whose nonhomogeneities (i.e., small figures) are disparate. (3) Moreover the particular characteristics of the figures as determined by monocular organization, can give rise to an impression of depth even though no "real" disparity is present. This is the case in Fig. 13.3 (Law, 1922, 1925) where the different degrees of "illusory" bending of the lines across the two circles creates an "illusory" disparity in the two eyes and the lines appear curved in depth. Thus binocular interaction seems to "come after" monocular organization of the figures.

As regards the concept of "figure" or "perceptual unit," I cannot go into a lengthy digression to remind you of what the Gestalt psychologists meant by it

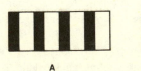

FIG. 13.2.   In both A and B, the black and white stripes alternate beween figure and ground. When presented stereoscopically, only the stripes that appear as figures are tilted or displaced in depth. Sometimes the configuration appears as a "mosaic." In this case the black and white stripes appear tilted in opposite directions (from Metzger, 1975).

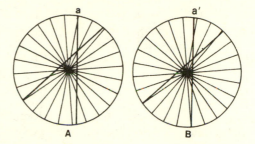

FIG. 13.3. The lines a and a′ are perfectly straight though they appear differently curved in A and B. When the two images are combined stereoscopically, the line appears curved in depth as well as on the frontal plane (from Lau, 1925).

(see Bozzi, 1969, Koffka, 1935; Metzger, 1975 for a clear discussion of perceptual units). It is sufficient here for my purposes to indicate an example to recall that there are "simple" and "compound" or complex, units and that these have different "unitary strengths." A simple straight line is considered to be a very "strong" figure or unit; a line made up of dots is still a figure or unit, but it is composed of subunits (the dots) and as a line it is a weaker unit, it has a weaker force of unitary organization (see A in Fig. 13.4) whereas the dots that go to make up the line are in themselves very "strong" figures.

One way to demonstrate the strength of the unit is to try to destroy it by covering it with, for example, another figure. The impression of continuity of the dotted line under the figure is destroyed in C whereas it is not destroyed in B or in D where the impression of continuity is given by the strength (tendency to complete themselves) of the "elements" that compose the line. If a surface is used instead of a line, the result is just the same (see Fig. 13.5). The surfaces or figures composed of subunits are much weaker than those of uniform colour or contour only.

I think it will be obvious from this distinction that in a stereogram with compound figures, it is possible to have disparity both between the figures as a whole and between the elements composing them. The latter may differ in form, color, and so on even though they go to make up the same whole figure (e.g., a

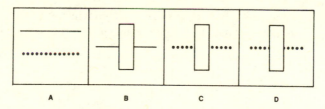

FIG. 13.4. In A both lines appear as units, but the continuous line is perceptually stronger than the dotted line. One way of testing the strength of a perceptual unit is by partially covering it. In B the line appears to continue behind the rectangles, whereas in C the dotted line appears not to continue behind the rectangle; two separate segments are seen. In D, due to the two partially covered dots, the dotted line appears to continue behind the rectangle.

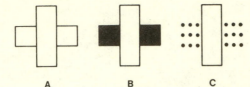

FIG. 13.5. As with the lines, the horizontal rectangles in A and B appear to lie behind the vertical rectangles, whereas in C two dotted squares are seen at the sides of the vertical rectangle.

square) as can be seen from the work of Kaufman (1964), Lawson (1968) and Ramachandran, Madhusudhan Rao, and Vidyasagar (1973). The characteristics of the elements can be changed somewhat independently of the whole figure, but the relationships between the elements both depend on the whole figure and give rise to it.

The assertion that it is the monocularly organized figures that interact in binocular perception does not mean that only the whole figures should interact. If the figures are composed of elements, the elements may interact with those of the other eye and destroy all or part of the monocular organization of the whole figure. Thus when two composed figures interact at a binocular level, the result, that is, the displacement in depth of the whole or of the elements, and the eventual modification of the monocular structure, will depend on attraction forces that tend to bring together or fuse the figures in the two eyes and on the relative strength of the forces that bind the "elements" of the organized monocular figures together.

An example of how composit monocular figures can give rise to the impression of depth and determine the depth value of their elements is provided by Wilde (1950). In A and B in Fig. 13.6 (see also Ramachandran & Nelson, 1976) we see an oblique dotted line, as in C, and not, as in D, a line of coplanar dots plus two displaced dots at the extremities, as an analysis of point-by-point interaction between the elements of the two stereograms would have predicted. In this second case, because all the dots on the shorter line (in A) "correspond" exactly to the inner dots on the longer line (in B), they should not be displaced in depth. Here instead the two whole lines interact and determine the depth value of the single dots.

But this example does not appear to be very convincing (Zajac, 1964 and Linschoten, 1956, declared that they were not able to see it) as it allows the same

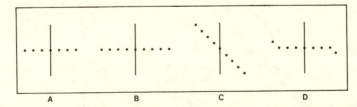

FIG. 13.6.   If A is presented to the left eye and B to the right eye, an oblique line is seen as in C. Only for a moment is the configuration illustrated in D seen.

subjects to see both solutions (C and D). I therefore looked for a clearer example in order to illustrate how the monocularly organized complex figure can determine the depth value of its elements or can be modified by the binocular interaction of its elements.

CASE I

A nice instance of how the whole figure dominated the displacement in depth of its elements or parts, in binocular interaction, occurred to me when observing an old figure used by Prandtl (1917) to illustrate the "Panum minimum case." If A and B in Fig. 13.7 are observed binocularly, the external circle in stereogram A appears to lie obliquely across a smaller one, that is, the inner circle will appear to be on the frontal plane whereas the external circle is rotated around the vertical axis. In C, point a will appear further away than point b and its opposite point on the circle, closer to the observer. In the "Panum minimum case," two vertical lines are presented to one eye whereas only one is presented to the other. The

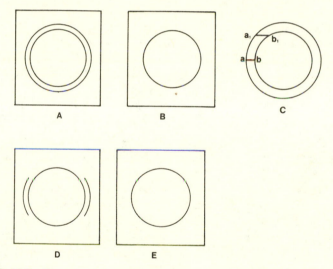

FIG. 13.7.   Presenting A to the left eye and B to the right eye the external circle appears "normal" but laterally tilted or rotated with the left side further away and the right side closer. Considering what should be the displacement of each point of the external circle according to Panum's law, point a_1 should appear further away than a as its lateral distance from point b_1 on the inner circle is greater than that of a (see C). In the tilted circle on the other hand, point a_1 appears closer to the inner circle than a. Panum's law is followed, if two arcs are used instead of a circle as in D and E. The left arc appears farther away, with the two endpoints pointing away from the observer and the right arc closer with the endpoints pointing toward the observer. The two arcs are not seen to complete a circle.

direction and the extent of the shift in depth depend on which side of the fused line the other line lies, and on the lateral distance of the two lines in the same eye. Here the two halves of the circles play the same role as the straight lines and if the inner circles fuse, the two halves of the external circle should be shifted in depth in opposite directions.

At first sight there does not seem to be anything wrong. But on further examination something struck me. If one considers the horizontal distance between the points a and b and a1 and b1 in c of Fig. 13.7, Panum's law will easily predict that point a_1 should appear to be further away in depth than point a, whereas in A and B when the circle appears oblique, point a_1 seems to be much closer to b_1 than point a to b. The demonstration of the functioning of the Panum law is evident if we consider only the arcs and not the whole circle as in D and E. The extremities of the arcs appear much further in depth than the middle; and the right-hand arc faces the opposite direction from the arc on the left hand side, so that it appears that they are not going to meet at all to complete a circle. What is it then that "bends" the arcs to bring them together till we see a complete tilted circle in A and B if not the monocular forces that organize the figure into a complete whole. Displacement in depth of the whole figures dominates, in this case, what should be the displacement in depth of its single component points considered in isolation.

It is true that a line is a very strong unit and we do not perceive the arcs as "elements" of the circle. But we can make the "elements" perceptible as a series of points as in A and B and C and D Fig. 13.8. What we see is still a complete circle tilted in depth in spite of the weaker organizing forces of the complex figure as a whole. The grouping forces that make the dotted circle a unitary figure are still stronger than the binocular interacting force acting on the single points or figure elements of the whole. If we consider that each figure element of the external circle is attracted at the binocular level, to the inner circle present in the other eye, (or to the fused one) and the force of this attraction depends, among other factors, on the lateral distance between the inner circle and each external element, then the attraction should become weaker the further away we move from the horizontal midline of the circles until it becomes zero for the dots above the level of the inner circle. This circumstance may facilitate the unification of the dotted circle as the monocular force will act with quite the same strength around the whole dotted circle.

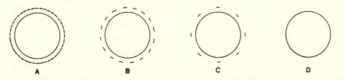

FIG. 13.8.   Presenting either A, B or C to one eye and D to the other eye, a regular dotted circle is seen which is laterally tilted.

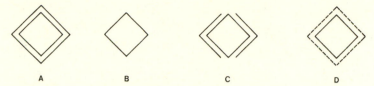

FIG. 13.9.   With B in one eye and A in the other, a tilted diamond is seen. If C is substituted for A, then the external sides appear parallel to the sides of the inner diamond but shifted to different planes of depth. With B, D, a dotted diamond appears broken at the top.

If, instead of a circle, we use a diamond as in Fig. 13.9, where the binocular interacting forces should be constant because lateral disparity along the sides is constant, once again the external diamond appears as a unitary figure, lying obliquely across the smaller diamond, although the elements (lateral side) of the external diamond should appear (as they actually do in C) as parallel and displaced in depth on a different depth plane. Using a dotted figure as the external diamond, the weaker figure tends to be broken at the corner and the view of a unitary dotted diamond sometimes alternates with that of the lateral sides displaced in different depths (D). Here the abrupt switching of direction of binocular force at the upper and lower corners (top and bottom) is more successful in breaking the unity of the monocular figure, particularly when there are no dots in the corner as in D.

To modify further the monocular forces that organize the unitary figure, we can ''cover'' part of the configuration in Fig. 13.10. Covering the external diamond, it loses its unity in binocular interaction and the two sides ''appear'' parallel in different depth planes. The same thing happens with the circle: it loses its unity but a tilted unitary circle sometimes appears when the cover is narrower. This particular configuration gives us the opportunity of showing what I meant when I spoke of nonpossibility of ''binocular Gestalten.'' It is easy to observe in Fig. 13.11 that it is not possible to obtain a unitary circle (line or dotted) made up of parts from the two eyes. In this sense, I say, we do not have a binocular unit or

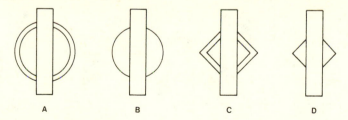

FIG. 13.10.   The configurations shown in Figs. 13.7 and 13.9 are partially covered by a rectangular figure. In both A and B, and C and D, the unity of the figures is broken but less so with the circle.

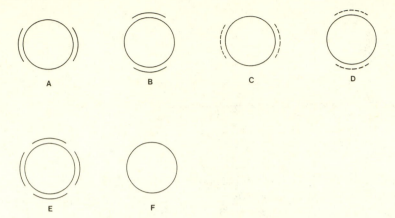

FIG. 13.11. If either A and B or C and D are presented to the left and right eyes, respectively, a circle is not seen. If E and F are combined stereoscopically, a circle is seen.

binocular Gestalten. The direction of the pieces is completely determined by the binocular forces, and no unitary regular circle appears as it does when the "pieces" are presented to one eye only as in E and F. If we can speak of binocular Gestalten then A and B in Fig. 13.7 and Fig. 13.8 are examples of binocular Gestalten.

CASE II

The second example of binocular-monocular interaction is again an instance of Panum's limiting case and resulted from trying to break a straight line by applying monocular or binocular "forces" of different strengths.

If A in Fig. 13.12 is presented to one eye and B to the other, the two rectangles will fuse and the vertical line should break in the middle and the two

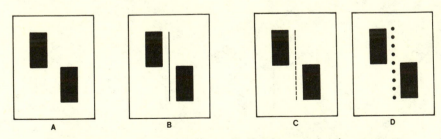

FIG. 13.12. Presenting A to one eye and B, C, D in turn to the other eye causes the line to be seen vertically tilted. Only in D does the dotted line sometimes appear broken into two parts, one closer to the observer and the other farther away.

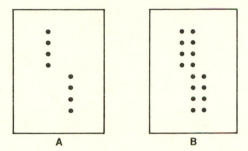

FIG. **13.13.** If A is present to one eye and B to the other eye, the line always appears broken into two parts, and not unitary and tilted, as in Fig. 13.12.

halves be displaced in different depth planes, as they are subject to opposing forces. Instead, what occurs is that the line appears to be tilted in depth and not broken. Thus the monocular forces that bind the line as a unit prevent the binocular forces from pulling the two halves of the line apart. The pulling of binocular forces does not seem to be very strong, because the line keeps its unity even when we use a broken dotted line, as in A and C, and even in A and D with dots. But D is a limiting case, as the dotted line sometimes appears as unitary and sometimes appears to be broken in the middle. But a clear case of a broken line is obtained, if stronger binocular forces are applied, that is, figures with greater similarity with regard to the elements of the central line, as in A and B of Fig. 13.13. In this case the fused dots presented to the two eyes are very effective in pulling apart the two halves of the line that now appears broken, and the two halves are seen in different depth planes. It should be pointed out that not even in this case we can speak of point-to-point interaction as the subunits of the dotted lines are figures in their own right and they can enjoy similarity of form or color whereas the theoretical points should have no form.

In these examples of binocular interaction, modified Panum limiting cases were used, as one of the figures was presented to one eye only and had no counterpart or corresponding figure in the other eye. This technique has been very useful in keeping quite distinct the monocular and binocular forces that interacted. It has therefore been possible to demonstrate how, depending on the relative strength of the interacting forces, the monocular force can modify the displacement in depth of parts and elements of the figure or the binocular forces can modify or break the monocular unitary figure. In the next example more conventional stereograms are used to demonstrate how the visual "properties" of monocular figures can affect binocular interaction or how binocular interaction can modify the visual properties of monocular units.

CASE III

The visual properties of "rigidity" and "nonpenetrability" of the monocular units can affect their displacement in depth in binocular interaction. A nice

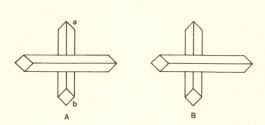

FIG. 13.14. If A is presented to the left eye and B to the right eye, the vertical stick should be seen nearer the observer than the horizontal stick. No displacement does in fact occur, although sometimes the two pieces a and b seem to fluctuate as independent parts, and rivalry is experienced. When the left and right images are reversed the vertical stick appears farther away, as one would expect.

example to illustrate this kind of phenomenon is Schriever's famous stereogram (1924) of the cross made of two wooden blocks one on top of the other. If you reverse the left and right images illustrated in Fig. 13.14, no displacement in depth occurs. Koffka (1935) speaks by analogy of a blocked balance "where one of the factors of interaction (the unity of the sticks) produces a maximum of stability so that the other factor (binocular interaction) may remain completely ineffective" (p. 274). This may indeed be considered an extreme case of "rigid nonpenetrability" of the figure (monocular figure).

In A of Fig. 13.14, the two parts a and b of the vertical stick, although they may be considered as two separate pieces, make up such a strong and rigid visual unit that displacement in depth (toward the observer) of the vertical block when the left and right images are interchanged is impossibile. If these two parts were not a "unit," we would easily see the two independent pieces nearer the observer and the horizontal piece further away. Indeed this is sometimes the case with a simple contour figure, but the configuration is very unstable and the displace-

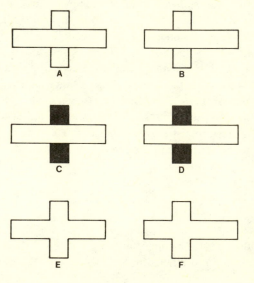

FIG. 13.15. If A is presented to left eye and B to the right eye, the horizontal rectangle appears curved and bent, towards the observer after a short time. If the images are reversed, the vertical rectangle appears behind the horizontal rectangle, which is straight and rigid. The same thing happens with C and D. With E and F, the horizontal rectangle appears bent independently of which image is presented to which eye.

ment in depth very brief and very shallow. But changing the relative strength of the monocular force of organization and the binocular force of attraction, we get all the cases from rigid nonpenetrability to elasticity and complete penetrability of the visual objects.

In A and B or C and D of Fig. 13.15 with similar but flat figures, we still have impenetrability but the surface becomes elastic or flexible under the binocular forces. When, because of the disparity, the vertical rectangle appears to be nearer the observer than the horizontal rectangle, the horizontal rectangle "bends"[1] to allow displacement in depth (near the observer) of the vertical figure. (Occasionally some bending is seen when the covered rectangle should appear further away, as if the two surfaces were glued together.) Sometimes at the beginning of observation, you can see the two pieces of the vertical figure broken for a short while and the configuration very unstable; then the horizontal rectangle bends and the configuration becomes stable. The same thing happens to C and D. In E and F, the horizontal rectangle bends equally easily in whichever direction the vertical one is displaced. In A and B of Fig. 13.16, however, in spite of the fact that monocularly it appears to be very similar to Fig. 13.15, in binocular interaction when the vertical should appear further away, the horizontal stripe no longer appears to be a unit but breaks up into two independent figures as open windows. This I think, happens because in "bending" it is "broken" by the contours of the vertical figures that become "corners" (i.e., double surface contours or contour common to two surfaces).

In the case of C and D when the horizontal rectangle should appear to be nearer than the vertical one, usually it does not break but becomes "transparent"

FIG. **13.16.** Presenting A to the right eye and B to the left, the two parts of the horizontal rectangle appear tilted like windows opened toward the observer. If the images are reversed, the horizontal rectangle appears further away and straight and not like two windows opening away from the observer. In C and D when the horizontal rectangle appears further away, it also appears opaque and behind the vertical rectangle. But when the stereograms are reversed the horizontal rectangle appears nearer, above the black rectangle and transparent. The two lateral "pieces" very seldom appear like a window, as in the previous case.

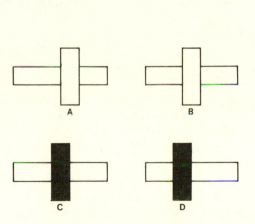

---

[1]Professor N. Pastore has informed me that he reported a similar phenomenon (Pastore, 1974).

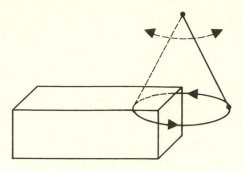

FIG. 13.17. When a pendulum is made to oscillate near a solid surface and a neutral grey filter is put in one eye, according to the Pulfrich effect, the apparent path of the pendulum "penetrates" the solid surface.

with the contours completing themselves across the black surface (provided the black surface is not too wide). It is a case of a strong tendency for a figure even covered to appear as a single surface and thus flat and rigid. Completion of the horizontal contours across the vertical surface is possible because they are the same color. If the vertical surface is a different color, the "crossing" is not possible and the two parts break as in the previous case. It should be noted that in all cases when the "covered" surface is made to appear further away it usually appears as a unitary, straight, rigid and opaque surface; only occasionally it appears slightly bent. Were the two parts not a "unit," they should always appear as two oblique surfaces like a window opening outwards.

Finally, a case of complete penetrability of a "real" solid object can be obtained by the Pulfrich (1922) effect. If a pendulum oscillates near a solid object such as a wooden block (see Fig. 13.17) the apparent circular path of the pendulum can be made to go across the most static solid object. In fact the two monocular figures of the pendulum are so strongly bound together by "common movement" that the resulting displacement in depth is little modified by the static forces that give rise to the perception of the real solid but static object.

CONCLUSION

It has been noted that the two classical theories on visual perception, the "elementaristic" (Hering, 1865, 1868) and the Gestalt (Koffka, 1935) are still at the basis of current discussion of the process of binocular perception, even if the terminology has changed.

The weak points of the two theories have been examined briefly; most of the Gestalt criticism of the elementaristic theory is still valid and even Julesz, whose stereograms were considered to support the theory of point-by-point binocular analysis, finds it necessary to introduce a "grouping" mechanism to resolve the ambiguities arising from such an analysis. As for the Gestalt theory, which was the first to propose a grouping process, it has been pointed out that the classical theory was too general to account for many of the phenomena. If some restrictions are introduced, an explanation can be found for most of the known phenomena. The restrictions follow.

1. At binocular level the grouping process, although very similar to that of monocular field organization and in general obeying the same laws, does not give rise to composite figures from separate "figure-elements" presented to the two eyes. At the binocular level it is not just a question of attraction between the figures in the two eyes, but there is actual movement (besides eye convergence) toward each other and finally fusion in a single percept.

2. Binocular interaction occurs only along the horizontal and not along the vertical dimensions (whereas at monocular level it occurs in all directions).

3. Interaction that gives rise to the depth effect should be considered as distinct from the process of fusion that it precedes. Fusion has stricter rules for combining the figures in the two eyes than the process of depth effect, and "repulsion" of the two figures may ensue if the rules are not met and fusion impossible; "repulsion" may hinder the depth effect if it is not counteracted by other forces.

Within these restrictions, binocular interaction does occur between the two monocularly organized figures presented to each eye. Evidence is brought to show that monocular organization in figure ground is a prerequisite for binocular interaction and the displacement in depth concerns the figure and not the ground. Moreover, "distortion" of some figural element caused by monocular organization does affect binocular interaction and the displacement in depth of the figure. For a better understanding of binocular interaction, it is stressed that at monocular level the unit figure may be simple or composed of separate elements which are themselves figures in their own right and sometimes interaction between each element-figure in the two eyes may be stronger than the overall, complex figure. In these cases a modification or "rupture" of the complex Gestalt may result although this depends on the relative strength of the forces that intervene at monocular and binocular level.

New evidence has here been presented to show how a complex configuration may determine the displacement in depth of its elements or figural components, contrary to the expectation of point-by-point analysis (case I). But weakening the organizing forces of the monocular figure or strengthening the binocular forces in suitable ways, the monocular configuration may be broken by binocular interaction (case II). Evidence has also been brought to show how binocular interaction can or cannot modify the monocular figure characteristics of unity, rigidity (or elasticity), and penetrability, and how displacement in depth is affected according to the relative force that intervenes in organizing the monocular figures or, at binocular level, in attracting them (bringing them together) in the two eyes (case III).

Binocular attraction between the figures in the two eyes in general seems to obey Wertheimer's grouping laws as the force of attraction depends on the relative distance and the figural characteristics of the figure units in the two eyes. Hence a hypothesis such as that of Julesz regarding the dipole spring-model which does not allow for different strengths of the forces of attraction depending on the figural characteristics of the elements, cannot be accepted. But rather than a new theory, greater emphasis is here laid on the need to investigate monocular-binocular organization of the figure in a Gestalt framework, in order to obtain a clearer understanding of both processes. The evidence here presented is just an example to indicate that this kind of analysis could be fruitful.

REFERENCES

Bishop, P. O. Beginning of form vision and binocular depth discrimination in cortex. In F. O. Schmitt (Ed.), *The neuroscience: Second study program*. New York: Rockefeller University Press, 1970.

Bozzi, P. *Unità, Identità, Causalità* (una introduzione allo studio della percezione). Bologna: Cappelli editore, 1969.

Brewster, D. On the knowledge of distance given by binocular vision. *Philosophical Magazine*, 1847, *30*, 315-318.

Frisby, J. P., & Mayhew, J. E. W. Global processes in stereopsis: Some comments on Ramachandran and Nelson. *Perception*, 1976, *6*, 195-206.

Helmholtz, H. von. *Treatise on physiological optics*. New York: Dover, 1962.

Hering, E. Die Gesetze der binocularen tiefenwahrnehmung. *Archiv fur Anatomie Physiologie und wessenschaftliche medicin*, 1865, 79-97, 152-165.

Hering, E. *Die Lehre vom binocularen Sehen*. Leipzig: Engelmann, 1868.

Julesz, B. *Foundations of cyclopean perception*, Chicago: University of Chicago Press, 1971.

Julesz, B. Global stereopsis: Cooperative phenomena in stereoscopic depth perception. In R. Held, H. Leibowitz, & H. L. Teuber, (Eds.), *The handbook of sensory physiology, Vol. VIII*. Berlin: Springer, 1976.

Kaufman, L. On the nature of binocular disparity. *American Journal of Psychology*, 1964, *77*, 393-402.

Kaufman, L., & Pitblado, C. B. Stereopsis with opposite contrast contours. *Perception and Psychophysics*, 1969, *6*, 10-12.

Koffka, K. *Principles of Gestalt psychology*. London: Harcourt Brace, 1935.

Lau, E. Versuche über das stereoskopische Sehen. *Psychologische Forschung*, 1922, *2*, 1-4.

Lau, E. Vezsuche über das stereoskopische Sehen. *Psychologische Forschung*, 1925, *6*, 121-126.

Lawson, R. B. Stereopsis and form disparity. *Psychological Record*, 1968, *18*, 361-368.

Levelt, W. J. M. *On binocular rivalry*. Soestenberg-the Nederlands, Institute for Perception RVO-TNO National Defense Research Organization 1965.

Lewin, K., & Sakuma, K. Die Sehrichtung monokularer und binokularer Objekte bei Bewegung und das Zustandekommen des Tiefeneffektes. *Psychologische Forschung*, 1925, *6*, 203-357.

Linschoten, J. *Strukturanalyse der binokularen Tifewahrnehmung: Eine experimentale Untersuchung*. Groningen: Wolters, 1956.

Metzger, W. *Gesetze des Sehens*. Frankfurt: Woldemar Kramer Verlag, 1975.

Mitchell, D. Qualitative depth localization with diploplic images of dissimilar shape. *Vision Research*, 1969, *9*, 991-994.

Mitchell, D. Properties of stimuli eliciting vergence eye movements and stereopsis. *Vision Research*, 1970, *10*, 145-162.

Nelson, J. I. Globality and stereoscopic fusion in binocular vision. *Journal of Theoretical Biology,* 1975, *49,* 1–88.

Panum, P. L. *Physiologische Untersuchungen über das Sehen mit zwei Augen.* Kiel: Schwers, 1858.

Pastore, N. Binocular depth perception. *American Scientist,* 1974, *62,* 262.

Prandtl, A. Die spezifische tiefen auffassung des Einzelauges und das tiefensehen mit zwei Augen. *Fortschrift fur Psychologie,* 1917, *4,* 257–326.

Pulfrich, C. Die stereoscopie im Dienste der isochromen und heterochromen Photometrie. *Naturwissenschaft,* 1922, *10,* 553–564, 569–574, 569–601, 714–722, 735–743, 751–761.

Ramachandran, V. S., Madhusudhan Rao, V., & Vidyasagar, T. R. The role of contours in stereopsis. *Nature,* 1973, *242,* 412–414.

Ramachandran, V. S., & Nelson, J. I. Global grouping overrides point-to-point disparities. *Perception,* 1976, *5,* 125–128.

Schriever, W. Experimentelle studien über stereoskopisches Sehen. *Zeitschrift fur Psychologie,* 1924, *96,* 113–170.

Sperling, G. Binocular vision: A physical and a neural theory. *American Journal of Psychology,* 1970, *83,* 461–534.

Tausch, R. Die beidäugige Raumwahrnemung. *Zeitschrift für experimental und angewandte Psychologie,* 1953, *1,* 394–427.

Wallach, H., & Lindauer, J. On the definition of retinal disparity. *Psychologische Beiträge,* 1962, *6,* 521–530.

Wallach, H., & Bacon, J. Two forms of retinal disparity. *Perception and Psychophysics,* 1976, *19,* 375–382.

Wheatstone, C. Contributions to the physiology of vision I: On some remarkable and hitherto unserved phenomena of binocular vision. *Philosophical Transactions,* 1838, *8,* 371–394.

Wilde, K. Der Punktreiheneffekt und di Rolle der binocularen Querdisparation beim Tiefensehen. *Psychologische Forschung,* 1950, *23,* 223–262.

Zajac, J. L. Is binocular correspondence and disparity still a dominant factor in binocular depth perception? *Psychological Bulletin,* 1964, *62,* 56–66.

Zanforlin, M. Stereopsis with figures of different form and opposite contrast. In A. A. Vari (Ed.), *Studies on perception.* Milan: Martello-Giunti, 1974.

14 Some Observations in the Auditory Field

Giovanni B. Vicario
University of Padua

1. INTRODUCTION

I present some observations I have made on auditory perception. I do so for the following reasons. First, from a comparison of auditory phenomena and visual phenomena, I hope you will be able to see the similarities in the way the central nervous system processes the output of different sensory channels. Second, acoustic stimuli are simple and precise, and auditory perception is relatively simple (leaving out speech) in comparison to visual perception. Third, auditory phenomena are themselves interesting, without considering the implications for perceptual processing. Fourth, the study of tonal experience—apart from a few illustrations of Gestalt phenomena by Wertheimer (1923), Koffka (1962), Metzger (1975), and Deutsch (1975)—has been neglected. I think that tonal experience is at the same time the proper material and the yardstick for any investigation in auditory field. All the stimulus situations you will hear have been assembled by means of a Moog synthesizer controlled by a microcomputer (Roland Microcomposer MC-8).[1]

2. PHENOMENAL DEPENDENCE

The term ''phenomenal dependence'' refers to the fact that, given a structure decomposable into two substructures, one of them seems to ''belong to'' the

---

[1]All the auditory stimuli here described (numbers in brackets) were actually demonstrated to the people attending the conference.

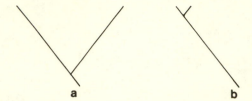

FIG. 14.1.   In *a* there are two lines of equal phenomenal weight. In *b* the small line appears phenomenally dependent on the longer one, as a branch in respect to the trunk.

other. For instance, in Fig. 14.1a you can see two lines that are not dependent on each other; in Fig. 14.1b the smaller is evidently an appendix of the longer (like a branch in respect to the trunk).

In vision, phenomenal dependence can only be described in words. I cannot remember any case in which the "perception" of dependence, in addition to the possibility of an overt description, is accompanied by some perceptual modification of the dependent substructure, such as a change in hue, size, etc. Even in Benary's (1924) triangle or in Fuchs' (1923) cross we have no impression of dependence between the substructures.

We can fill this methodological gap—it is important to "see" the dependence, but it is more important to "show" it—by transposing into the auditory field the stimulus relations illustrated in Fig. 14.1. Consider the following acoustic stimuli:

$$
\begin{array}{ll}
440 \text{ Hz, } 1,600 \text{ msec}—392 \text{ Hz, } 1,600 \text{ msec} & (14.1) \\
440 \text{ Hz, } 800 \text{ msec}—392 \text{ Hz, } 1,600 \text{ msec} & (14.2) \\
440 \text{ Hz, } 400 \text{ msec}—392 \text{ Hz, } 1,600 \text{ msec} & (14.3) \\
440 \text{ Hz, } 200 \text{ msec}—392 \text{ Hz, } 1,600 \text{ msec} & (14.4) \\
440 \text{ Hz, } 100 \text{ msec}—392 \text{ Hz, } 1,600 \text{ msec} & (14.5) \\
440 \text{ Hz, } 50 \text{ msec}—392 \text{ Hz, } 1,600 \text{ msec} & (14.6)
\end{array}
$$

As you can hear, when the first tone is made very much briefer than the second tone, it becomes an appendix of the second tone, that is, the first tone "falls on" the second.

This phenomenon is well known in music, where it is defined as "acciaccatura", a musical embellishment that consists in putting before a note a very short one. The fact that musicians speak of it as a "grace-note" testifies to the existence of dependence. Yet we have here, in addition, the fact that the short note undergoes a very evident perceptual modification. The salience of the note is decreased and it is heard to fall on the second—which we do not notice in the short line of Fig. 14.1b. (Further information on the phenomenon can be found in Vicario, 1960b.)

2.   EMBEDDED FIGURES

Everybody knows Gottschaldt's (1926) demonstration, in which individual figures are masked when embedded in a pattern of lines. The accepted explanation

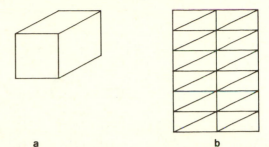

FIG. 14.2. The cube *a* cannot be seen in tesselation *b*, because the elements of the cube become part of the structure *b* (from Gottschaldt, 1926).

a   b

is that the constituent elements go to complete other shapes or figures provided by a stronger structure (see Kanizsa, 1969, for a review of the problem). Figure 14.2 presents an example. A in Fig. 14.2 can not be seen in B because the elements of A become part of the structure of lines defining B.

I tried to find something similar in the auditory field, but I was faced with a difficulty. To add some tones to the left and to the right of a succession of tones—as in a melody—does not mean that we have "embedded" that succession, but that we have constructed another succession, that is, another melody. Returning to visual field, nobody would say that an F is "embedded" in an E, because the horizontal line at bottom simply changes the F in an E. What does "to embed" mean?

I have been not able to answer this difficult question, so I have made two assumptions: (a) the object to be embedded must be easily recognizable by some features other than its musical or tonal content; (b) the embedding structure should share in common with that of Fig. 14.2b some iterative features, as in a tessellation.

I think I have identified the right object in the "gruppetto," another musical embellishment easily recognizable because of its snake-like course. In Fig. 14.3 you can see on the left its musical notation (very expressive) and on the right its most common production. Stimulus 7 presents a gruppetto.

C, 0.1 sec − D,0.1 sec − C,0.1 sec − B,0.1 sec − C,1 sec
(where C = 523, D = 587, B = 494 Hz)   (7)

As you can see, the four notes of the embellishment (C-D-C-B) may be divided in two groups: (C-D) and (C-B). Now, let us add other groups (CD) to the left of the gruppetto, and other groups (CB) to its right. Let us do the thing gradually, in order to see what happens to the gruppetto.

FIG. 14.3. On the left the musical notation of the "gruppetto"; on the right its most common production.

| (each tone=0.1 sec) | CD-CB | (14.8) |

$$\text{CD-CD-CB-CB} \quad (14.9)$$
$$\text{CD-CD-CD-CB-CB-CB-} \quad (14.10)$$
$$\text{CD-CD-CD-CD-CB-CB-CB-CB} \quad (14.11)$$
$$\text{CD-CD-CD-CD-CD-CD-CB-CB-CB-CB-CB-CB} \quad (14.12)$$
$$\text{CD-CD-CD-CD-CD-CD-CD-CD-CD-CB-CB-CB-CB-CB-CB} \quad (14.13)$$

I think I have been able to disrupt the perceptual structure of the gruppetto by means of another perhaps stronger structure, that is the "trill," a truly iterative pattern. In fact, the left half (C-D) of the gruppetto comes to be an element of the trill C-D-C-D-C-D-C . . . , while the right half (C-B) comes to be an element of another trill, namely C-B-C-B-C-B-C. . . . The addition of more and more groups on either side of the gruppetto (CD-CB) leads to a progressive dissolution of the snake-like structure and to the setting up of a stronger pattern. In stimulus (14.10) we can still hear in the melody a sort of writhing, but from stimulus (14.11) on the two trills appear to have absorbed the two parts of the gruppetto.

I think that we could rightfully say that we have "embedded" one of the auditory patterns into the other. The vanishing of the gruppetto has not been obtained through the addition of tones which would resemble the transformation of an F into an E. Rather, just as in Fig. 14.2 one is aware that the cube is present in the lattice, although he cannot see it, the listener presented with stimulus (14.13) is aware that in the point of junction between the two trills all the tones necessary to build the gruppetto are present, yet he is unable to hear it. Perhaps some important feature of the "embedded figure" phenomenon lies in this "hide-and-seek" game. (For further discussion of the phenomenon, see also Vicario, 1980.)

I tried to transfer the described effect to speech perception. In the Italian language there are some words (extremely rare) that simultaneously satisfy the following conditions:

1. They consist of 4 syllables, like the 4 tones of the gruppetto
2. They share with the gruppetto the syllabic structure: A-B-A-C.
3. They give rise, when divided into two halves, to 2 meaningful words not related to the original 4 syllable word
4. They are balanced, both as a whole and in part with respect to their frequency.

The following words are the only ones I could find:

CARICARE (to load) = CARI (dear men) + CARE (dear women)
RIVERITO (respected man) = RIVE (banks) + RITO (rite)
SEMISERI (serio-comic) = SEMI (seeds) + SERI (serious men)

I recorded on a tape repetitions of these words:

... CARICARICARICARICARECARECARECARE ... (14.14)
... RIVERIVERIVERIVERITORITORITORITO ...   (14.15)
... SEMISEMISEMISEMISERISERISERISERI ...   (14.16)

I asked four naive subjects to tell me the words they heard. Not one of them recognized the four-syllable embedded words. After the trial, two of them said: "I heard CARI and CARE ... thinking it over, I could even hear CARICARE ... "

I do not know if the referred observation is a true sign of the possibility of embedding words. The methodological problems are many and subtle: for instance, as soon as the subject passes from the verbal report to the visual representation of the words he has just uttered, the trick is spotted and the trial cannot continue.

3. EMBEDDED ELEMENTS

Let us consider one of the beautiful optical-geometrical illusions of Galli and Zama (1931), where an element of a structure disappears from sight when it is embedded in a stronger structure (see Fig. 14.4).

In addition to the disappearance of the base of the triangle, we notice that the oblique lines appear thicker and darker. Not long ago I began a systematic study of this effect, particularly on some displays which I regard as a simplified version of the Galli and Zama's illusion. Consider Fig. 14.5, where two such displays are depicted: A is an instance of successful embedding and B of unsuccessful embedding.

The embedding effect is not very strong, and I hope that the size of the pictures will not make it vanish. The two possible perceptual outcomes are depicted in Fig. 14.6. When one perceives the stimulus as in b there is no embedding. The crossing line keeps its identity, its thickness, and its color. When one perceives the stimulus as in a, the crossing line loses—inside the column of

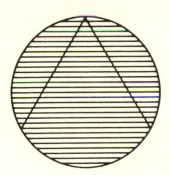

FIG. 14.4. The isosceles triangle cannot be seen because its base is embedded in the structure of horizontal lines (from Galli & Zama, 1931).

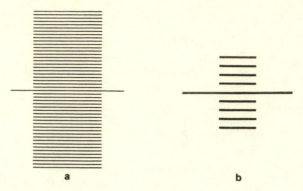

FIG. 14.5. In *a* the longer horizontal line loses its individuality and seems to pass behind the column of shorter lines. In *b* the longer horizontal line keeps its individuality and passes in front of the whole structure.

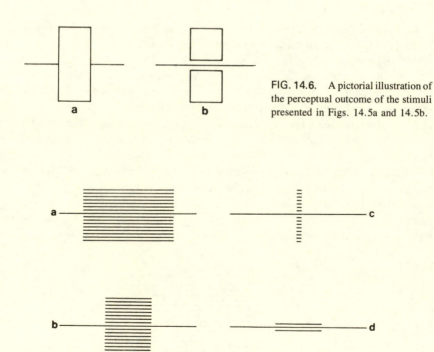

FIG. 14.6. A pictorial illustration of the perceptual outcome of the stimuli presented in Figs. 14.5a and 14.5b.

FIG. 14.7. The embedding of the longer horizontal line depends on the width (*a* and *c*) and on the height (*b* and *d*) of the columns. The embedding is successful in *a* and in *b*, and unsuccessful in *c* and *d*.

short horizontals—its identity and becomes gray and thinner. It is seen to pass behind the column of short horizontals and the parts of the line extending beyond the column are seen as thicker and darker. The main variables affecting the effect are: (a) the thickness of the lines; (b) the spatial frequency of the lines; (c) the height of the upper and the lower column; (d) the width of the columns. I have not yet systematically investigated the effect of these variables. Qualitative observations indicate that the height and width of the column of horizontal lines are important as can be seen in Fig. 14.7.

A similar phenomenon occurs in the auditory field. Consider stimulus (14.17), where a steady 440 Hz tone is mixed during its course with six other tones. The intervals between tones are minor thirds in order not to fall within the critical band. The SPL (sound pressure level) for each tone is 70 dB.

$$
\begin{array}{c}
740 \text{ Hz, } 1.5 \text{ sec} \\
622 \text{ Hz, } 1.5 \text{ sec} \\
523 \text{ Hz, } 1.5 \text{ sec} \\
440 \text{ Hz, } 0.5 \text{ sec} + 440 \text{ Hz, } 1.5 \text{ sec} + 440 \text{ Hz, } 0.5 \text{ sec} \\
370 \text{ Hz, } 1.5 \text{ sec} \\
311 \text{ Hz, } 1.5 \text{ sec} \\
262 \text{ Hz, } 1.5 \text{ sec}
\end{array} \qquad (14.17)
$$

t ⟶

In listening to stimulus (14.17) we notice that the continuous phenomenal presence of the 440 Hz tone is much lessened—or is not heard—especially when we do not pay very much attention to the tone, and we listen globally to the situation. (The 440 Hz tone cannot disappear totally, since another effect takes place here, of which we shall speak later.) When the 440 Hz tone stands alone, it appears noticeably louder, in the same way as the line in Fig. 14.5a is seen darker on either side of the column.

In stimulus (14.18) we reduce the length of the additional tones, by means of an operation that resembles the reduction of the width of the column in Fig. 14.7c.

$$
\begin{array}{c}
740 \text{ Hz, } 0.1 \text{ sec} \\
622 \text{ Hz, } 0.1 \text{ sec} \\
523 \text{ Hz, } 0.1 \text{ sec} \\
440 \text{ Hz, } 1 \text{ sec} + 440 \text{ Hz, } 0.1 \text{ sec} + 440 \text{ Hz, } 1 \text{ sec} \\
370 \text{ Hz, } 0.1 \text{ sec} \\
311 \text{ Hz, } 0.1 \text{ sec} \\
262 \text{ Hz, } 0.1 \text{ sec}
\end{array} \qquad (14.18)
$$

t ⟶

As you notice, we now hear the 440 Hz tone very well. On the other hand, reduction of the height of the columns—as in stimulus (14.19), which is the auditory equivalent of Fig. 14.7d—does not make the 440 Hz tone appear more audible than in stimulus (14.17).

$$523 \text{ Hz, } 1.5 \text{ sec}$$
$$440 \text{ Hz, } 0.5 \text{ sec } + 440 \text{ Hz, } 1.5 \text{ sec } + 440 \text{ Hz, } 0.5 \text{ sec} \qquad (14.19)$$
$$370 \text{ Hz, } 1.5 \text{ sec}$$

t _____→

The difference in results may be due to the problem of consonance. It is hard to hear the 440 Hz tone alone, because, when added to the 523 and to the 370 Hz tones, it gives rise to a chord. We may improve the independence of the 440 Hz tone by mistuning it with respect to the two other tones, and by tuning them to each other at the interval of a major third, as in stimulus (14.20).

$$538 \text{ Hz, } 1.5 \text{ sec}$$
$$440 \text{ Hz, } 0.5 \text{ sec } + 440 \text{ Hz, } 1.5 \text{ sec } + 440 \text{ Hz, } 0.5 \text{ sec} \qquad (14.20)$$
$$360 \text{ Hz, } 1.5 \text{ sec}$$

t _____→

The transposibility of the embedded element effect from the visual to the auditory field—if truly attained—gives rise to a problem. As you will have noticed, I have treated acoustic stimuli as if they were in some way separate, as visual stimuli on the retina are. We know, on the contrary, that a loudspeaker produces only one sound wave from a multiplicity of signals. So to speak, individual tones begin to exist only after the auditory system has resolved the sound wave in its components. As a result, some principles concerning the visual organization—that is the Gestalt principles of proximity, similarity, good continuation, and so on—cannot be applied directly to the complex wave resulting from the summation of simultaneous tones: those principles should take place only after the single tones have been picked out from the complex wave. If the comparison with the perceptual field as modeled in visual perception holds, the auditory system needs another stage of processing in order to produce an output comparable with that of the visual system.

4. OBJECTS IN AUDITORY FIELD

The main problem of auditory experience is the simultaneous presence in the perceptual field of several—if not too many—auditory objects. We have just pointed out that the sound wave is unique—at the eardrum level—for all the sound wave producing sources in the environment, to which tones, noises and voices are phenomenally related. Surely there are theories that solve that problem by means of the analysis of the sound wave resulting from simultaneous acoustic stimuli (see, for example, Nordmark 1978). Nevertheless, I try to demonstrate that something important is passing unnoticed in such theories, because a multiplicity of auditory objects can be obtained even in a purely sequential acoustic stimulus.

Consider stimulus (14.21), where a sequence of four tones is presented in cycle.

A a B b A a B b A a B b A....   (14.21)

A = 311 Hz   a = 1,480 Hz
B = 330 Hz   b = 1,661 Hz
each tone = 0.7 sec

What we hear is a succession of tones alternatively low and high in pitch. Now, let us reduce their duration to 50 msec each. We now hear something new, that is two separate trills: one low in pitch, constituted by the low tones; the other high in pitch, constituted by the high tones. Everything happens as if the strong structure of the trill can overcome the time separation of its components, in the sense that the tonal proximity is more effective than the time proximity. Tone A goes to join tone B, which is nearer in tonal space, than tone a, which is next in time; a joins b rather than B. When Bozzi and I (Bozzi & Vicario, 1960) first described this phenomenon, we stressed factors of unification, pointing out that in audition there are two kinds of proximity: one in time, the other in tonal space, and that they are somehow interchangeable. Our aim was to find in the auditory field something comparable to the principles Wertheimer stated for visual field. Since then, however, I have been very impressed by the fact that a unique chain of stimuli could give rise to two separate chains of events, and successfully tried to translate the effect to the visual field. Let us consider the stimulus situation represented in Fig. 14.8, where 1, 2, 3 and 4 are four neon bulbs lit in cycle in that succession.

If the succession of the stimuli is very slow (duration of each light 360 msec, with interstimulus intervals of 120 msec), we see apparent movements in accordance with the temporal sequence of the lights (1-2-3-4-1-2-...). If, on the

1 o   o 3

FIG. 14.8.   Four neon bulbs flashing in the succession 1-2-3-4-1-2-.... When the rate of flashing is slow, we see apparent movements in the right order 1-2-3-4-1-2-.... When the rate of successive flashing is very fast, we see two apparent movements 1-3-1-3-1-... and   2-4-2-4-2-.... (from Vicario, 1965).

2 o   o 4

contrary, the succession of the stimuli is very fast (duration of each light 105 msec, with interstimulus intervals of 35 msec), we see horizontal apparent movements, that is 1-3-1-3-1 . . . and 2-4-2-4-2. . . . The point is that apparent movement occurs between stimuli which are not contiguous on time axis—as one can rightly expect—but between stimuli which are separate on time axis by another physical event that takes no part in the building of the movement considered. (For more information, see Vicario, 1965. Bregman and Campbell (1971) also discovered the effect, which they call "streaming"; Michon, 1977, speaks of "clustering.")

The conclusion that we can build a multiplicity of phenomenal objects by means of a single chain of physical events is strengthened by another observational fact. The trills of stimulus (14.21) are clearly continuous, with no gaps between one tone and the next. In other words, between any A and B, for instance, we are unable to notice any pauses, that is the tones corresponding to the a's and b's that go to build up the other trill. The perceptual process eliminates the physical gaps present between the notes and what is perceived are two continuous trills.

5.   AMODAL COMPLETION

Put your pencil horizontally so as to cover the cross in Fig. 14.9. You will see a regular isosceles triangle behind your pencil, as the visible parts complete themselves in a simple and regular fashion. It does not matter that you are perfectly aware of the real but partially hidden shape: completion is irresistible. This type of demonstration was devised by Michotte (Michotte, Thinès, & Crabbé, 1964) in order to make clear what he called "amodal perception." That is, a compelling phenomenal presence without sensory stimulation. Michotte showed that neither imagination, nor past experience and expectations can overcome internal (Gestalt) forces of organization in the building of a visual figure.

Amodal completion is, in opinion of many, one of the more important facts for the science of perception. First, it has biological value. We are almost

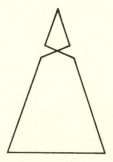

Fig. 14.9.   In covering with a pencil the cross on the triangle, you will see a regular triangle in spite of the fact that you know that there is a cross behind your pencil (from Michotte et al., 1964).

perfectly adapted to a world of physical objects of which we *never* perceive all the parts in the same moment. Second, for its usefulness in research. In controlling the way that properly devised objects complete themselves when partially amputated, concealed, broken etc., we can hope to catch perceptual or cognitive processes at work and thereby discover the underlying processes. (See also Kanizsa, 1970.)

Amodal completion also takes place in the auditory field. Consider stimulus (14.22). Two 440 Hz tones (T1 and T2) are presented. They last 1.5 sec each, and there is a pause (P) of 0.5 sec between them.

T1	P	T2	
440 Hz	0.5 sec	440 Hz	
60 dB		60 dB	(14.22)
1.5 sec		1.5 sec	

There is no doubt about what one hears: two identical tones following each other, or a steady tone interrupted during its course. Now, let us fill the gap between the tones with pink noise (PN), 20dB in intensity above the tones (14.23).

T1	PN	T2	
440 Hz	80 dB	440 Hz	
60 dB		60 dB	(14.23)
1.5 sec	0.5 sec	1.5 sec	

We now have the impression of a single uninterrupted tone. We hear it more or less clearly persisting during the noise, as if the latter "covers" it.

When I studied this phenomenon (Vicario, 1960a), I found that the illusory presence of the tone underneath the noise is linked to certain conditions. First, the noise must be louder than the tone by at least 15–20 dB. If, for instance, the intensity is the same—as you can hear in stimulus (14.24)—the noise no longer "covers" the gap, and the tone is heard as interrupted.

T1	PN	T2	
60 dB	60 dB	60 dB	(14.24)

The phenomenal impression of whether one "hears the tone again" is a very good phenomenological means for deciding whether we "heard" the tone during the noise, or not. Second, the duration of the noise cannot be too longer: the impression of persistence of the tone vanishes. Listen to stimulus (14.25), where T1 and T2 are separated by a PN lasting for three seconds.

T1	PN	T2	
60 dB	80 dB	60 dB	(14.25)
1.5 sec	3 sec	1.5 sec	

The first tone seems to persist for a while underneath the beginning noise, then vanishes, and then comes again. This illustrates the weak point of observations of this kind. The listener is never quite sure whether he really heard the tone, or only imagined it.

Unfortunately, in the acoustical field we have few opportunities for "demonstrations", such the one presented in Fig. 14.9, which "show" that what we perceive is not matter of past experience, nor imagination nor expectations, but of autonomous laws of perception.

I can offer nevertheless a stimulus situation that perhaps attains the same goal. In (14.27) another tone (T3) is added to the noise, namely a 988 Hz. For the purposes of demonstration I first let you hear stimulus (14.26), and then stimulus (14.27) where the extraneous 988 Hz tone is added to the interposed noise.

T1	T3	T2	
440 Hz	988 Hz	440 Hz	
1.5 sec	0.5 sec	1.5 sec	(14.26)
60 dB	60 dB	60 dB	

T1	T3 +	T2	
	PN 80 dB		(14.27)

Now, as you can hear, in stimulus (14.27), we perceive within the noise an illusory 440 Hz tone, and not the 988 Hz tone actually present. In order to make T3 audible, we must lessen PN intensity by at last 10 dB, as in stimulus (14.28).

T1	T3 +	T2	
	PN 70 dB		(14.28)

The phenomenon of amodal completion described here is not unknown. In his chapter on "Auditory Illusions and Perceptual Processes," Warren (1979) puts it among the cases of "illusory continuity of interrupted patterns" that embrace the "picket fence effect" (Miller and Licklider, 1950), the "auditory figure-ground effect" (Thurlow, 1957), the "continuity in alternately sounded signals" (Elfner, 1971), and perhaps a few others. I called it (Vicario, 1960a) the "acoustic tunnel effect" because it resembles very closely a phenomenon investigated in the visual field by Burke (1952), a pupil of Michotte.

In any case, let us now make use of this effect as a tool for investigating the way auditory objects complete themselves "behind" other auditory objects. I would point out that I am at the beginning of such an inquiry, and that the ensuing observations are preliminary in nature. Consider stimulus (14.29), where a two octave diatonic scale is interrupted at its eighth step by Pink Noise. Each tone and the PN last 0.2 sec, and the signal to noise ratio is −20 dB. (Numbers refer to the pitch of the tones. The unit is the semitone, and 33 is the 440 Hz tone.)

24-26-28-29-31-35-35-PN-38-40-41-43-45-47-48   (14.29)

As you can hear, the amodal completion of the diatonic scale is rather good, in the sense that there is a strong illusory presence of the missing central note, note 36.

What happens when the noise lasts too long? In stimulus (14.30) we have a diatonic scale too, but the missing tone is substituted by two steps of noise, as if it had to "cover" two tones.

24-26-28-29-31-33-35-PN-PN-38-40-41-43-45-47-48   (14.30)

To put into words what one has heard is here more difficult. The report of six subjects with a musical education is as follows. Four of them heard the missing tone as repeated (36-36); the remaining two heard a long tone 36 staying still throughout the noise. What happens when the noise does not last long enough? In stimulus (14.31) the diatonic scale stops at its seventh step, then we have 1 step of noise, and finally the scale continues from the 11th step. The hypothesis is that the noise cannot "cover" all the three missing tones.

24-26-28-29-31-33-35-PN-41-43-45-48-50-52   (14.31)

The outcome seems to me very clear. We hear a jump in the course of the scale, and therefore we can conclude that its phenomenal continuity is compromised.

Consider stimulus (14.32), where we have an ascending diatonic scale of 12 steps, then 5 steps of noise, and finally a symmetric descending scale of 12 steps. The duration of each tone is reduced to 0.1 sec in order that the duration of the noise not be overly long. The noise lasts for the exact time necessary for a scale that regularly ascends and descends without gaps.

24-26-28-29-31-33-35-36-38-
-40-41-43-PN-PN-PN-PN-PN-43-41-   (14.32)
(45-47-48-47-45)
-40-38-36-35-33-31-29-28-26-24

Amodal completion of the melody underneath the noise is rather good, but we cannot "perceive" the scales joining at the fifteenth step (note: 48). The subjects report that they "hear" something like a "swarming" under the noise, to which they cannot give definite tonal attributes.

The slope or "speed" of the scales can be varied, as you can hear in the following stimuli. The interval between the tones is 1 semitone in stimulus (14.33), 2 semitones in (14.34), 3 semitones in (14.35), 4 semitones in (14.36) and 5 semitones in (14.37). The actually audible parts of the scale consist of four steps on either side. The missing tones are centered on tone 36 (523 Hz C) and

consist of three steps. Noise is presented in place of the missing tones. The
duration of each step is 0.1 sec.

$$31\text{-}32\text{-}33\text{-}34\text{-PN-PN-PN-}38\text{-}39\text{-}40\text{-}41 \tag{14.33}$$

$$26\text{-}28\text{-}30\text{-}32\text{-PN-PN-PN-}40\text{-}42\text{-}44\text{-}46 \tag{14.34}$$

$$21\text{-}24\text{-}27\text{-}30\text{-PN-PN-PN-}42\text{-}45\text{-}48\text{-}51 \tag{14.35}$$

$$16\text{-}20\text{-}24\text{-}28\text{-PN-PN-PN-}44\text{-}48\text{-}52\text{-}56 \tag{14.36}$$

$$11\text{-}16\text{-}21\text{-}26\text{-PN-PN-PN-}46\text{-}51\text{-}56\text{-}61 \tag{14.37}$$

The subjects told me that the more steep or "speedy" the scale, the stronger the
impression of its continuation underneath the noise.

I stop here bringing instances of amodal completion and phenomenal continuity because I have not yet conducted systematic experiments to ascertain what are the conditions of the phenomenon. The only conclusion one can draw is that there is in auditory field something comparable to the facts already known for visual field. As with visual objects, the completion of auditory objects takes place only when their missing parts are substituted by more prominent objects—in our case, a very much louder pink noise.

REFERENCES

Benary, W. Beobachtungen zu einem Experiment ueber Helligkeitskontrast. *Psychologische Forschung*, 1924, *5*, 131–142.

Bozzi, P., & Vicario, G. Due fattori di unificazione fra note musicali: La vicinanza temporale e la vicinanza tonale. *Rivista di Psicologia*, 1960, *54*, 235–258.

Bregman, A. S., & Campbell, J. Primary auditory segregation and perception of order in rapid sequences of tones. *Journal of Experimental Psychology*, 1971, *89*, 244–249.

Burke, L. On tunnel effect. *Quarterly Journal of Experimental Psychology*, 1952, 4, 121–138.

Deutsch, D. Musical illusions. *Scientific American*, 1975, *233*, 92–104.

Elfner, L. F. Continuity in alternately sounded tonal signals in a free field. *Journal of the Acoustical Society of America*, 1971, *49*, 447–449.

Fuchs, W. Experimentelle Untersuchungen ueber die Aenderung von Farben unter dem Einfluss von Gestalten. *Zeitschrift für Psychologie*, 1923, *92*, 249–325.

Galli, A., & Zama, A. Untersuchungen ueber die Wahrnehmung ebener geometrischen Figuren die ganz oder teilweise von anderen geometrischen Figuren verdeckt sind. *Zeitschrift für Psychologie*, 1931, *123*, 308–348.

Gottschaldt, K. Ueber den Einfluss von Erfahrung auf die Wahrnehmung von Figuren, I. *Psychologische Forschung*, 1926, *8*, 261–317.

Kanizsa, G. Perception, past experience and the "impossible experiment." *Acta Psychologica*, 1969, *31*, 66–96.

Kanizsa, G. Amodale Ergänzung und "Erwartungsfehler" des Gestaltpsychologen. *Psychologische Forschung*, 1970, *33*, 325–344.

Koffka, K. *Principles of Gestalt psychology*. London: Routledge & Kegan Paul, 1962.

Metzger, W. *Gesetze des Sehens*. Frankfurt am Main: Kramer, 1975.

Michon, A. *Perception et estimation du temps*. Report to the XVI Journées d'Etudes de l'Association de Psychologie Scientifique de Langue Francaise. Poitiers, 22–24 Septembre 1977.

Michotte, A., Thinès, G., & Crabbé, G. *Les compléments amodaux des structures perceptives*. Paris: Béatrice-Nauwelaerts, 1964.

Miller, G. A., & Licklider, J.C.R. The intelligibility of interrupted speech. *Journal of the Acoustical Society of America*, 1950, *22*, 167–173.

Nordmark, J. O. Frequency and periodicity analysis. In E. C. Carterette & M. P. Friedman (Eds.), *Handbook of perception, Vol. IV, Hearing*. New York: Academic Press, 1978.

Thurlow, W. An auditory figure-ground effect. *American Journal of Psychology*, 1957, *70*, 653–654.

Vicario, G. L'effetto tunnel acustico. *Rivista di Psicologia*, 1960, *54*, 41–52. (a)

Vicario, G. Analisi sperimentale di un caso di dipendenza fenomenica tra eventi sonori. *Rivista di Psicologia*, 1960, *54*, 83–106. (b)

Vicario, G. Vicinanza spaziale e vicinanza temporale nella segregazione di eventi. *Rivista di Psicologia*, 1965, *59*, 843–863.

Vicario, G. Gottschaldt figures in hearing. *Italian Journal of Psychology*, 1980, *7*, 197–202.

Warren, R. M. Auditory illusions and perceptual processes. In N. Lass (Ed.), *Contemporary issues in experimental phonetics*. New York: Academic Press, 1979.

Wertheimer, M. Untersuchungen zur Lehre von der Gestalt. II. *Psychologische Forschung*, 1923, *4*, 301–350.

15

Textural Segmentation

Jacob Beck
University of Oregon

INTRODUCTION

A visual display is segmented into regions in two ways. It is segmented at loci of abrupt changes in brightness, or color, that is, at contours, and it is segmented on the basis of textural differences. Textures are visual patterns composed of elements repeated over an area so that the pattern as a whole is perceived to have a characteristic lightness, directionality, coarseness, and so on. There are two problem in textural perception. First, how is a display segmented into textural components or regions on the basis of stimulus differences? Second, what determines the perception of specific figures such as produced by stippling in an engraving or etching? The segmentation of a display into textural components does not in itself specify specific figures. The perception of specific figures involves processing beyond that which leads to textural segregation. It requires specifying spatial relationships such as figure and ground, and the grouping of the segmented textural components with respect to each other. This chapter is concerned only with the first problem: how is a pictorial display segmented into textural components on the basis of stimulus differences? The hypothesis is proposed that textural segmentation is based on information about the slopes, sizes, colors, and brightnesses of textural elements and their parts.

Texture is a segmentary variable. That is, like the variables of color, brightness, disparity, and movement, textural differences segment a visual display into components that are necessary, though not sufficient, for the perception of specific figures. In order to provide the empirical background for the hypothesis, the first part of the paper summarizes research that shows that textural segmentation is a function of simple stimulus variables with good preattentive acuity and not of higher-order stimulus relations and transformations. Textural segmentation is a type of acuity and more closely related to the visual processes underlying discriminability than to inferential and organizational processes. Inferential and organizational processes which produce a description of a stimulus through the operation of either a "principle of probability" or of a "principle of economy" play a minimal role in textural segmentation.

EMPIRICAL FINDINGS

1. Ratings Of Similarity Of Individual Figures Do Not Predict Textural Segmentation

Similarity judgments of individual figures are strongly influenced by line arrangement. A T tilted 45 degrees clockwise, for example, is judged to be more similar to an upright T than is an L (Beck, 1966). The mean rated similarity on a scale from zero to nine for a T and an L was 3.8, and for a T and a tilted T, 8.0. When these letters were repeated to form textures, however, changes in the arrangement of the lines which left the component lines vertical and horizontal (upright Ts and Ls) failed to produce strong textural segmentation; changes in the slopes of the component lines to 45 degrees and 135 degrees (upright Ts and rotated Ts) produced strong textural segmentation. Figure 15.1 shows that the pattern of tilted Ts segment themselves from a pattern of upright Ts while the pattern of Ls do not. Figure 15.2 presents another example making the same point taken from an unpublished study. The figures making up the patterns were taken from Mach (1959, p. 107). A cat like figure, its mirror image, and rotations of the cat figure, and of its mirror image were repeated to form three regions. Subjects were asked to indicate for each of nine targets at which of the two boundaries the natural break occurs. In Fig. 15.2, the division may be made

FIG. 15.1. The tilted Ts (a difference in line slope) are segmented from the upright Ts whereas the Ls (a difference in line arrangement) are not.

FIG. 15.2.   The mirror image figures (a difference in overall figural slope) are segmented from the upright figures whereas the inverted figures (no difference in overall slope) are not.

at the transition from the cat figure to its mirror image (right) or from the cat figure to its inversion (left). The procedure was identical to Beck (1966). The results showed that the overall slope of the figures was important for textural segmentation. Figures having the same overall slope tended to be seen as forming a single textural region. Nine of ten subjects divided the target shown in Fig. 15.2 in terms of the overall slope of the figures and placed the boundary between the cat and its mirror image. Mach pointed out that figures which are symmetric about a vertical axis are more readily seen as similar than figures which are not. This was confirmed in the present study. The middle and right figures presented individually were judged by all ten subjects as more alike one another (mean rated similarity 8.2) than the middle and left figures (mean rated similarity 4.5). Textural segmentation occurs strongly as a function of a small set of simple stimulus properties such as brightness, color and slope and not of relational stimulus properties such as line arrangement and vertical symmetry which affect the similarity judgments of individual figures.[1]

The fact that the rated similarity of individual figures fails to vary inversely with textural segmentation is not puzzling. I showed that the similarity ratings of an upright figure and of that figure rotated 45 degrees clockwise were the same for a variety of different figures (Beck, 1973). Judgments of similarity of individual figures were influenced by the sameness of the transformation taking one figure into another. In contrast, the degree of textural segmentation produced by the figures was influenced by the discriminability of the figures. Highly discri-

---

[1]Instead of assuming that textures are compared on a small set of properties, the hypothesis has recently been proposed that similarity judgments of textures are based on the spatial frequency content of the stimuli. Harvey and Gervais (1981), using textural patterns synthesized by combining seven spatial frequencies, have shown that judgments of similarity of stochastically generated textures were predicted by the spatial frequency content of the stimuli. Whether spatial frequency analysis will be useful in describing similarity judgments of deterministic textures or textures composed of elemental figures remains to be seen.

minable figures, such as an upright [and this figure rotated 45 degrees, gave good segmentation. Figures that were not discriminable, such as a C-like curve and this curve rotated 45 degrees, gave poor segmentation. Judgments of rated similarity, however, will predict textural segmentation when the similarity judgments are determined by stimulus differences measured in terms of stimulus discriminability. For example, the mean similarity ratings of lines differing in their slopes and in their curvatures varied inversely with their effectiveness in producing textural segmentation (Beck, 1973). Pairs of lines and curves judged to be equally similar produced about equal textural discrimination. Similarity as it determines discriminability affects textural segmentation; similarity as it is related to the transformations relating two figures does not. Goldmeier (1972) has shown that similarity judgments of individual figures may be based on a wide variety of relations and transformations.

2. Stimulus Properties That Produce Strong Textural Segmentation Are Discriminated Preattentively: They They Do Not Require Attention Though They May Attract It

Recent experiments support the hypothesis of two types of stimulus discrimination: one serial and requiring concentrated or focused attention, and one parallel and occurring without attention or with attention distributed over the visual field. What stimulus discriminations require focused attention and what stimulus discriminations can be made preattentively cannot be answered definitely at this time. Julesz (1962) pointed out that stimulus differences that are picked up with scrutiny and depend on attentional focusing do not spontaneously produce the perception of separate textural components. I have hypothesized that textural segmentation occurs as a function of the conspicuousness of stimulus differences before the focusing of attention (Beck, 1972). Several experiments have shown that the textural segmentation produced by figural differences corresponds to their discriminability when presented extrafoveally in a multielement display in which a subject is uncertain about the position of a target and cannot focus his attention (Ambler & Finklea, 1976; Beck, 1972, 1973, 1974; Beck & Ambler, 1972, 1973). In the experiment of Beck & Ambler (1972), a subject was required to monitor eight display positions. As would be expected, the discriminability of a T tilted 33 degrees clockwise from an upright T (mean errors 19.4) was significantly better than that of an L (mean errors 40.6). When a subject, however, was able to concentrate his attention on one display position, the discrminability of a tilted T from an upright T (mean errors 19.2) was not significantly different than that of an L (mean errors 15). In general, the discriminability of figural differences are not related to their effectiveness in producing textural segmentation when a subject is able to focus his attention. The discriminability of an L from an upright T, in fact, has been found to be often better than that of a tilted T when attention was focused whereas the discriminability of an L from an upright T was always worse than that of a tilted T when attention was distributed (Ambler & Finklea, 1976; Beck & Ambler, 1972, 1973; Beck, 1974). Line slope is the more salient property with distributed attention whereas line arrangement is the more salient property with focused attention. This is what would be expected if focusing of attention increased the sensitivity to line arrangement. The line arrangement of a tilted T and an upright T are the same and would interfere with the discrimination of a tilted T; the line arrangement of an L and of an upright T differ and would facilitate the discrimination of L.

What is suggested is a two stage processing of pattern information specialized for texture and form perception. Textural discrimination occurs relatively early in visual processing and segments a pattern into regions on the basis of nonrelational stimulus properties that are registered automatically and in parallel without attention or with distributed attention. The simple stimulus properties producing strong textural segmentation are also those that attract attention and eye fixations when an individual searches for a target (Engel, 1976). The perception of a specific figure requires specifying, in addition to the slopes and lengths of contours and lines, the positions of these relative to each other and to an external frame of reference. The nonattentional and distributed attentional systems appear to be comparatively insensitive to such relational properties as line arrangement and figural orientation. Discriminations based on line arrangement or figural orientation require, at least in a multiple element textural pattern, focal attention and serial processing. I return to this question in my concluding remarks.

3. Textural Segmentation Occurs On The Basis Of Simple Physically Defined Properties: Examples Are Brightness, Color, Movement, Size, And Slopes of Contours And Lines of Figures

The most important of the properties associated with shape for textural segmentation is slope (Beck, 1966, 1972, 1973; Olson & Attneave, 1970; Schatz, 1977). Differences in the arrangement of lines of a figure that leave the slopes of the component lines the same do not generally produce strong textural segmentation (Beck, 1966, 1967, 1972). Similarly, differences in figural orientation that leave the slopes of the component lines the same do not generally produce strong textural segmentation. Figure 15.3 illustrates the textural segmentation produced by rotating an upright U and an L. Unlike Figs. 15.1 and 15.2, where the segmented figures are contiguous and constitute a spatial region, the segmented figures in Fig. 15.3 are spatially separated. Spatially separated figures embedded in a background pattern provide a purer measure of the effectiveness of different kinds of similarity in producing textural segmentation. When the segmented figures fill a circumscribed spatial area, as in Figs. 15.1 and 15.2, textural segmentation may be improved by the proximity of the figures to one another.

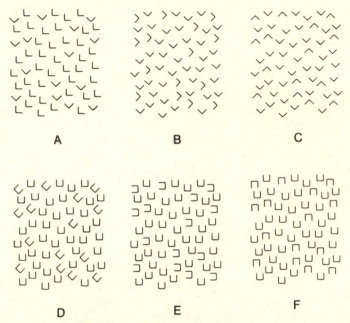

FIG. 15.3.   The displays show the textural segmentation produced by rotating L and U figures. Textural segmentation is strongest in displays A and D, intermediate in displays B and E, and is very weak, if it occurs at all, in displays C and F.

The strongest textural segmentation occurred with a 45-degree rotation (displays A and D), intermediate degrees of textural segmentation with a 90-degree rotation (displays B and E), and little or no textural segmentation with 180-degree rotation (displays C and F) (Beck, 1972). The rotation of the disparate figures in Displays A and D altered the slopes of their component lines from vertical and horizontal to 45 degrees and 135 degrees. The rotation of the disparate figures in displays B and C and in E and F left the slopes of their component lines the same as the background figures. Greater textural segmentation, however, occurred for the sideways disparate figures in displays B and E than for the inverted disparate figures in displays C and F. Rotating an upright U on its side changes the number of horizontal and vertical lines. I proposed that the greater segmentation of the sideways Us is due to the fact that the sideways Us differ from the upright Us in the number of their vertical and horizontal lines (Beck, 1972). The upright Us have two vertical lines and the sideways Us have two horizontal lines. A difference in the distribution of line slopes as well as a difference in actual slope is effective in producing textural segmentation. Marr (1976) has made the same point.

The sideways and inverted Vs have the same slopes of their component lines as the background upright Vs. The greater textural segmentation of sideways Vs than of inverted Vs appears to be due to the overall orientation of the figures (Beck, 1972). The upright V has its greatest extent in the horizontal direction and the sideways V has its greatest extent in the vertical direction. Olson and Attneave (1970) pointed out that in terms of slope analyzers an upright V would most likely stimulate a horizontally oriented receptive field and a sideways V would most likely stimulate a vertically oriented receptive field. One might expect that if the greater textural segmentation of the sideways Vs than of the inverted Vs occurred because the upright and sideways Vs differentially stimulated vertically and horizontally oriented receptive fields, then making the sideways Vs small would improve their segmentation. The segmentation of the sideways Vs is quite sensitive to visual angle. Textural segmentation of the sideways Vs in Display B was found, in fact, to be better than that of the Ls in Display A when the Vs subtended a visual angle of less than 5 minutes (Beck, 1972). Schatz (1977) has suggested an alternative explanation. He proposed that textural segmentation is a function of both the lengths and orientations of virtual lines as well as of actual lines. Virtual lines are imaginary lines inserted between the end points of lines and corners and act as though they were faint copies of physically present lines. They are less effective than actual lines in producing textural segmentation.

It is important to point out that not all changes in slope facilitate textural segmentation equally well. A + rotated 45 degrees to form an X has the same slopes of lines as a T tilted 45 degrees but is segmented less strongly relative to figures with vertical and horizontal lines than a tilted T. For example, the segmentation of Xs in a background of upright Ts is weaker than the segmentation of tilted Ts in a background of upright Ts (Beck, 1966, 1967). Textural segmentation, however, corresponds to the preattentive acuity of an X and of a tilted T in a multielement display requiring distributed attention. At 5.1 degrees of eccentricity, the detection of a tilted T in a four-element display consisting of either all upright Ts or three upright Ts and a disparate figure was significantly better than that of an X (Beck, 1974). When a single figure was presented allowing a subject to direct attention to the figure, the discriminability of an X and of a tilted T from an upright T was the same. One might expect that if the poorer segmentation of X figures is due to their lack of discriminability in the periphery, then making the X figures large would improve their segmentation. An experiment provides corroboration. Subjects were asked to scale the textural segmentation of tilted Ts, Xs, Ls, and sideways Ts in a background of upright Ts. The procedure followed was that of Experiment III in Beck (1972). In Fig. 15.4, the first figure in each pair of figures indicates the background figure in a display, the second one shows that disparate figures. Subjects were instructed to rate on a scale from 0 to 100 how well the disparate figures stood out immediately, as a whole, from the background figures. For line lengths between 2 and 2.8 millimeters (4 to 6 minutes), the mean segmentation ratings of the X figures were statistically worse than that of the tilted Ts ($p < .05$). For longer line lengths, the mean segmentation ratings of the X figures were not statistically significantly worse than that of the tilted Ts.

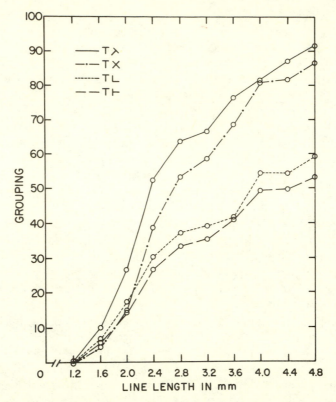

FIG. 15.4.   Mean ratings of textural segmentation as a function of figure size. The displays were like those shown in Fig. 15.3. The first figure in each pair of figures indicates the background figures; the second one indicates the disparate figures.

Another example of physically equal differences that produces differing degrees of textural segmentation has to do with the special status of the vertical and horizontal directions. A texture made up of vertical and horizontal lines gives better segmentation than a texture made up of 45- and 135-degree lines even though the difference between the slopes of the lines is 90 degrees in both instances (Olson & Attneave, 1970). The detection of a horizontal line in a four-element display made up of all vertical lines or of three vertical lines and a horizontal line, was significantly better than the detection of a 135-degree line in a display made up of all 45-degree lines or of three 45-degree lines and one 135-degree line (Beck, 1972). This suggests that the superiority of vertical and horizontal lines in producing textural segmentation has its origin in the greater sensitivity of the preattentive visual system to the difference between vertical and horizontal lines than to the difference between 45-degree and 135-degree lines.

Probabilistically generated dot patterns have provided a useful way of studying textural segmentation. Discrimination of textures differing in dot density or gray level was investigated by Green, Wolf & White (1959). Textural segmentation as a function of higher-order statistical differences has been studied by Julesz and his colleagues (Julesz, 1962; 1978; Julesz, Gilbert, Shepp & Frisch, 1973). Julesz has conjectured that textural segmentation does not occur for textures that have the same global first- and second-order statistics. That is, textures that differ only in third- and higher-order statistics are not spontaneously segmented. For black and white textures, first-order statistics measure the probability that a monopole, such as a dot, will fall on a black point of the texture, and second-order statistics measure the probabilities that a dipole, a pair of dots, falls on black and white points of the texture. Third-order statistics measure the probabilities that a tripole, three dots, falls on black and white points of the texture. The converse, however, is not always true (Julesz et al., 1973). A texture made up of combining L- and 7-like elements is not discriminable from a texture made up by taking their mirror images although they differ in their second-order statistics. The L and 7 elements have dipoles at 135 degrees; the mirror images of the L and 7 elements have dipoles at 45 degrees. Textures made up of upright Ts and sideways Ts also fail to produce strong textural segmentation although they too differ in their second-order statistics (Beck, 1966, 1967). Such findings indicate that textural segmentation, as might be expected, depends on the amount of difference in dipole statistics. The quantitative aspects of Julesz's model have yet to be worked out.

There is a similarity between the hypothesis that textural segmentation occurs in terms of elementary feature analyzers and the hypothesis that it occurs in terms of first- and second-order statistics. Random dot textures differing in first-order statistics, for example, differ in dot density or overall gray level. Random dot textures differing in second-order statistics differ in the spatial distribution of the dots. Two random dot textures with an identical number of black dots but one of which has the property that the minimum nearest neighboring distance is 10 dot spaces have the same global first-order statistics but different second-order statistics. The two textures are readily discriminated (Julesz et al., 1973). The texture with the statistically unconstrained distribution of dots contains irregular clusters of black dots not present on the texture with the constrained distribution of dots. The use of random dot textures does not in itself preclude discriminations being based on locally defined features produced by the statistical constraints. Random dot textures differing in first- and second-order statistics will differentially stimulate cells having receptive fields with different widths and orientations, and which differ in the excitatory and inhibitory action of their center and flanking regions. Purks and Richards (1977) present evidence that the discrimination of random dot textures depends on the differential stimulation of contrast and bar detectors and that the statistical properties per se are not the relevant variables.

According to Julesz (1978) the conjecture that textural segmentation does not occur for textures that have the same first- and second-order statistics is equivalent to the conjecture that textural segmentation does not occur between textures with identical power spectra, that is, have the same spatial frequencies in terms of a Fourier series of sines and cosines. MacLeod and Rosenfeld (1974) have shown that broadly tuned bar-like units having receptive fields with several excitatory and inhibitory regions can account for much of the experimental data that has been interpreted as evidence for narrowly tuned Fourier-like spatial frequency analyzers. Though an explanation based on nth-order statistics and an explanation based on contrast and feature detectors make similar predictions in many instances, the two explanations, as will be pointed out later, are not formally equivalent.

4. Textural Segmentation Is A Function Of The Projection Level Representation Of A Stimulus; Constancy Mechanisms, However, May Reduce Textural Segmentation

Display A in Fig. 15.5 is made up of background vertical lines and of disparate diagonal lines that are tilted 18 degrees clockwise from the vertical. When presented in the frontal plane, textural segmentation is weak. Slanting the display toward the floor produces a compression of the retinal image and increases the differences in slope between the vertical and diagonal lines projected on the retina. This is illustrated by display B in Fig. 15.5, which shows the projection of display A onto the frontal plane when the display is slanted 75 degrees toward the floor. The question is whether textural segmentation will improve even if an

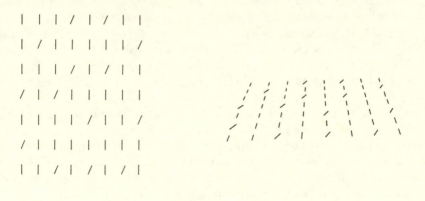

A   **B**

FIG. 15.5.   Display A shows the target consisting of vertical lines and of diagonal lines tilted 18 degrees clockwise from the vertical. Display B shows the projection onto the frontal plane of display A when it was slanted 75 degrees floorwise.

individual does not perceive the changes; that is, even if the retinal changes are not perceived because of perceptual constancy. Floorwise slanting of a display improves textural segmentation despite the occurrence of good size and slope constancy (Beck, 1975). This is what would be expected if textural segmentation is a function of the projection level representation of stimuli. Slanting a display produces several concomitant changes in the projected retinal image: (a) a vertical compression of the retinal image; (b) changes in the retinal lengths of the lines and the spacing between the lines; (c) changes in the retinal slopes of the lines; and (d) a horizontal convergence of the retinal image. The experiment showed that it was the increased slope differences between the retinally projected vertical and tilted lines in a display that was responsible for the improved textural segmentation.

Subjects made magnitude estimations to indicate the strengths of textural segmentation of the disparate diagonal lines. The mean rating of display A (16.6) slanted floorwise was between the mean rating of display A presented upright (9.1) and the mean rating of the retinally equivalent projection of display A, display B, presented in the frontal plane (23.9). Constancy mechanisms which caused the lines on display A to appear veridical when the display was slanted, that is, similar to how they were seen when the display was presented upright, reduced rated textural segmentation. The effect of perceived slope may be due to response bias. That is, the mean ratings may reflect a "corrected judgment" in which observers consciously allowed for the phenomenal similarity of the vertical and diagonal lines in judging textural segmentation. Another possibility is that constancy mechanisms in correcting the perceived slopes of the lines tend to inhibit textural segmentation based on the differences between the projected retinal slopes of the lines.

Head rotation is another instance in which textural segmentation is influenced by phenomenal as well as retinal orientation. Olson and Attneave (1970) performed experiments in which subjects viewed circular arrays in which one quadrant differed. Textural segmentation was evaluated by the time it took to locate the disparate quadrant in the circular array. As in my experiments, differences in line slope produced excellent textural segmentation while differences in figural orientation were ineffective. They also found that textural segmentation of both lines and angles was affected by the orientation of the entire array relative to the vertical and horizontal. That is, vertically oriented lines and angles in an array of horizontally oriented lines or angles gave strong textural segmentation, whereas 45-degree oriented lines and angles in an array of 135-degree oriented lines and angles gave weaker textural segmentation. Head tilt was varied in order to evaluate whether textural segmentation was dependent on retinal or geographic (i.e., gravitational) orientation. They found that for lines and paired dots varying in slope both retinal and graviational orientation had significant effects on textural segmentation. For angles, however, only retinal orientation had a significant effect.

Perceptual constancy may involve both projection level mechanisms and inferential cognitive mechanisms. The various psychological "invariance hypotheses" are examples of constancy based on cognitive inferences. For head rotation, constancy would be the result of a cognitive computation that uses information about head tilt to correct for the orientation of the retinal image. The hypothesis proposed is that textural segmentation occurs at the projection level and precedes cognitive constancy mechanisms based on computations. Constancy resulting from projection level processes, however, may be expected to affect textural segmentation. It is possible that the effect of geographic orientation is the result of feedback from labyrinth cells that cause the orientation specificity of a receptive field to change with head tilt so as to maintain constant geographic orientation. Physiologists have found single cells in the cat striate cortex that responded to the geographic orientation of lines rather than to their retinal orientation (Denney & Adorjani, 1972; Horn, Stechler & Hill, 1972). The fact that textural segmentation of angles is tied to retinal and not geographic orientation would be due to the absence of such detectors for more complex properties. The number of cells in the visual cortex whose receptive fields are modified by head tilt are relatively few (Horn, Stechler, & Hill, 1972). It should be noted that Olson and Attneave (1970) found that the effect of retinal orientation was greater than that due to geographic orientation. In fact, the perceptual grouping of lines under some conditions appears to depend only on retinal orientation (Gillam & McGrath, 1979).

5. Textural Segmentation May Be Interfered With By Extraneous Stimulus Differences That Can Not Be Gated Out Preattentively

An interesting case of interference occurs with a display composed of red and blue diagonal lines and red and blue vertical lines. Segmentation, in terms of line slope, i.e., segmenting the display into vertical and diagonal lines is interfered with by color similarity since there are both red and blue diagonal lines and red and blue vertical lines. Similarly, segmenting in terms of color, i.e., segmenting the display into red and blue lines, is interfered with by slope similarity since there are both vertical and diagonal red lines and vertical and diagonal blue lines. Textural segmentation fails to occur in terms of a conjunction of properties. One can search out and hold in attention red vertical lines, blue vertical lines, red diagonal lines, or blue diagonal lines. However, the visual system can not preattentively segment a display on the basis of a conjunction of color and slope properties.

Shiffrin and Schneider (1977) reported an extensive series of experiments showing that subjects could be trained to detect automatically and in parallel stimulus differences mediating form discrimination. After reading their paper, I decided to test whether practice and training can eliminate the interference produced by color and slope in textural segmentation. I was interested in whether subjects can develop an automatic detection response to a combination of slope and color properties and eliminate their interference with one another.

Two subjects were instructed to count as quickly as they could specified diagonal lines embedded in a background of other lines. The experimental displays consisted of diagonal red lines in a pattern of upright red lines and diagonal blue lines, and diagonal blue lines in a pattern of upright blue lines and diagonal red lines. In these displays either the color or the slope of the nontarget lines interfered with the counting of the target lines. The control displays consisted of diagonal red lines in a pattern of upright red lines, and diagonal blue lines in a pattern of upright blue lines. Comparison of the counting times for the experimental and control displays allowed the effect of the interfering property to be evaluated.

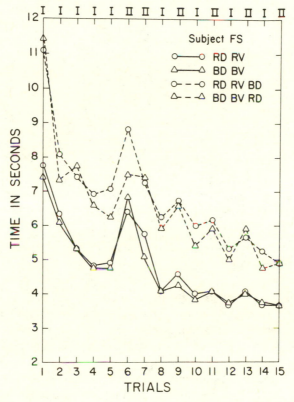

FIG. 15.6. The mean time to count the disparate lines consisting of: (a) red diagonals (RD) embedded in background lines consisting of red verticals (RV), and of red verticals and blue diagonals (RV BD); (b) blue diagonals (BD) embedded in background lines consisting of blue verticals (BV), and of blue verticals and red diagonals (BV RD). Roman numerals I and II show the stimulus set used on the indicated trial.

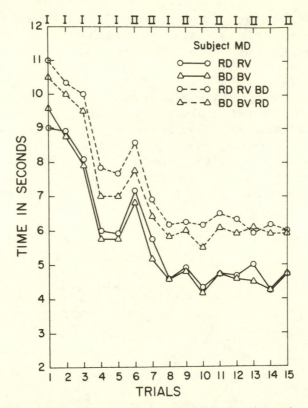

FIG. 15.7. The mean time to count the disparate lines consisting of: (a) red diagonals (RD) embedded in background lines consisting of red verticals (RV), and of red verticals and blue diagonals (RV BD); (b) blue diagonals (BD) embedded in background lines consisting of blue verticals (BV), and of blue verticals and red diagonals (BV RD). Roman numerals I and II show the stimulus set used on the indicated trial.

Six different arrangements of the target and nontarget lines were prepared for each of the four kinds of displays. There were two stimulus displays of 14, 15, and 16 target lines. The lines in a display were 1.27 cm in length and arranged irregularly in seven columns and six rows. Each display contained 28 nontarget lines. The nontarget lines were divided into 14 red and 14 blue lines in the experimental displays and were either all red or all blue in the control displays. The four kinds of displays prepared in the six different arrangements made a total of 24 stimuli. A subject was instructed to count either the diagonal red or diagonal blue lines as quickly as possible without making errors. If a subject reported an incorrect number of target lines the stimulus was presented a second time. The counting times recorded are for stimuli in which a subject responded correctly. The 24 stimuli in a set were presented in a different irregular order to each subject on 15 consecutive days. A second set of stimuli was prepared identical with the first except that the positions of the target lines were changed. These were introduced on trial six. Roman numerals I and II in Figs. 15.6 and 15.7 show the stimulus set used on the indicated trial. On the first day of the experiment each subject was given practice counting each of the four types of stimulus displays. On each succeeding experimental day, each subject was given practice counting one of the four kinds of displays. The practice stimuli differed from those used in the experiment.

Figures 15.6 and 15.7 present the results for the two subjects. They show that counting time decreased with practice. However, the difference in counting times for stimuli in which color and slope interfered with counting the target lines and the control stimuli remained the same. The introduction of a new set of targets on trial six increased the counting times for both subjects. The results, therefore, indicate that though there was an overall improvement with practice, color and slope continued to interfere with counting the target lines even after 15 days of practice. The implication of the experiment is that one cannot focus on a particular pairing of color and slope and filter out preattentively nontarget combinations of these variables. A supplementary experiment showed that the interference was not result of the nonuniformity of the background in the experimental displays.[2] Treisman and Gelade (1980) have reported similar results.

A MODEL FOR TEXTURAL SEGMENTATION

Introduction.   Textural segmentation involves breaking a visual pattern into components which in some sense are internally uniform. It is an example of what Wertheimer called similarity grouping. Wertheimer (1923) proposed a number of principles or laws of organization to describe how the parts of a visual display tend to be grouped. Although our understanding of organizational principles is incomplete, I conjecture that the laws of organization operate on at least three

---

[2]A supplementary experiment was conducted to determine the effect of background uniformity using the same procedure as in the main experiment. The target lines were again diagonal red and diagonal blue lines. The nontarget lines in displays with diagonal red target lines were (a) vertical red lines and (b) vertical red and vertical blue lines. The nontarget lines in displays with diagonal blue target lines were (c) vertical blue lines and (d) vertical red and vertical blue lines. Search through the arrays was not slowed by the nonuniformity of the color of the nontarget lines in the background and the experiment was concluded after six days. The mean counting time averaged over these six days for two subjects was 3.96 seconds for diagonal red lines in a background of vertical red lines, and 3.83 seconds for diagonal red lines in a background of vertical red and vertical blue lines. The mean counting time was 3.86 seconds for diagonal blue lines in a background of vertical blue lines, and 3.88 seconds for diagonal blue lines in a background of vertical red and vertical blue lines. The disappearance of interference argues that the interference in the main experiment was not the result of background nonuniformity but the result of making the discrimination depend on the conjunction of slope and color properties.

levels of visual processing that serve different functions. *One function* is the linking of features into hyperfeatures or elements for textural and figural perception. In an article in 1973, I mentioned in an aside that textural segmentation occurs in terms of a preliminary unitization (Beck, 1973). That is, the features that distinguish textures are features of elements and textural segmentation occurs in terms of these elements. For example, in a pattern consisting of Ls embedded in a pattern of upright Ts, the linking of the vertical and horizontal lines to form Ls and Ts prevent the vertical and horizontal lines from acting as independent textural elements. Thus, the vertical lines of the Ls and Ts are not seen as a separate textural component relative to the horizontal lines. Similarly, short lines are relatively ignored when they belong to long lines. In display B in Fig. 15.8, for example, the short horizontal lines link to form a long line. The length of the long line is an "emergent" feature which makes it stand out from the surrounding short lines. In display A, the horizontal lines are part of the textural elements formed by linking with the vertical lines, and the tendency for the short lines to link into long lines is decreased. Fox and Mayhew (1979) have shown that if a dot is placed near upright and sideways Vs (e.g., figures like those of B in Fig. 15.3), textural segmentation is interfered with. The interference, however, was reduced if the distance between the dot and the V element is increased. One explanation of this finding is that the dot placed near the V becomes part of the

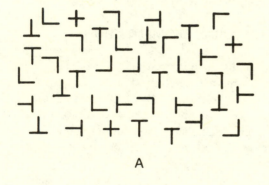

A

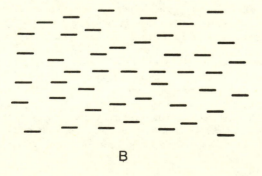

B

FIG. 15.8. Example of textural segmentation in which element formation is important. In display B, the short horizontal lines link to form a long line which is segregated from the surrounding short lines. In display A, the connecting of the short horizontal lines to vertical lines tends to inhibit the linking of the short horizontal lines into a long line.

elemental unit, i.e., the textural element is the V plus dot. Common features between textural elements are assumed to decrease textural segmentation. When the distance between the dot and the V was increased, however, the dot was no longer part of the V textural elements and segmentation improved. Local linking processes form higher-order textural elements prior to textural segmentation. Proximity, good continuation and possibly other grouping processes play a role in these linking processes. There is evidence that some of the overall organization of a figure is encoded at an early stage of visual processing (Banks & Prinzmetal, 1976; Harcum & Shaw, 1974).

A *second function* is the aggregation of textural elements into textural regions or components. Wertheimer (1923) defined similarity grouping as a tendency for like items to band together. He proposed that similarity grouping is an associative process that interrelates like elements. Wertheimer, however, did not systematically investigate the kinds of similarity that are effective in producing strong similarity grouping. As pointed out above, not all kinds of similarity produce similarity grouping equally well. Similarity grouping is strongest for simple nonrelational variables that segment a visual pattern into regions of uniform visual texture. It is, of course, clear that grouping implies the complementary process of segregation. Thus, similarity grouping may be described as a segregative process based on stimulus differences as well as an associative process based on stimulus likeness. Figure 15.9 helps clarify the difference between an associative and a difference model. It shows the grouping of diagonal lines in a pattern of vertical lines. In display A, the diagonal lines all have the same slope and one can hypothesize that they are grouped because they are alike in slope. In display B, the diagonal lines have differing slopes and grouping of the diagonal lines must be ascribed to the dissimilarity between the slopes of the diagonal lines and neighboring vertical lines. Phenomenally, the grouping of the diagonal lines in the bottom display appears to be as good or almost as good as that in the top display. Dissimilarity will be assumed to be the basic factor underlying similarity grouping, in multiple element displays. Similarity grouping in such displays is an instance of textural segmentation and depends on the simultaneous discrimination of stimulus differences prior to a narrowing or focusing of attention.

The *third function* is perceptual disambiguation. As mentioned earlier, the perception of a specific figure involves specifying the relations between the segmented parts of a visual pattern. The linking processes that create textural elements and the processes of segmentation that create textural components restrict the possible organizations of a visual pattern. A unique organization of a visual pattern, however, is not determined and alternative perceptual organizations remain possible. Organizational principles such as closure and symmetry provide a basis for disambiguating the alternatives consistent with a visual pattern. Closure and symmetry are characteristics of the Gestalt Law of Prägnanz or of figural goodness. They reflect the regularities in a visual pattern that enable the perceptual system to recode the information in the pattern in a more efficient

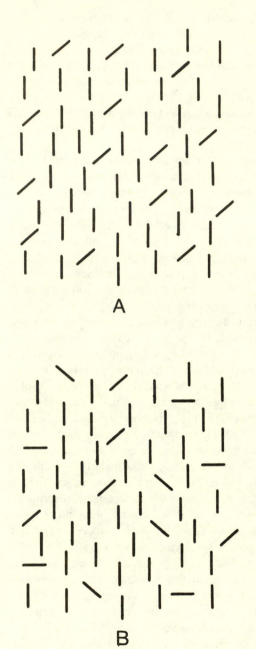

A

B

FIG. 15.9. Illustration contrasting an associative and a segregative model of similarity grouping. In display A, the disparate lines all have the same slope and textural segmentation may be ascribed to associative processes based on the similarity of slope. In display B, the disparate lines have differing slopes and textural segmentation must be ascribed to the dissimilarity between the slopes of the disparate lines and the neighboring vertical lines.

way. The kinds of similarity that are important are not only of physical properties but also of relations and transformations that allow an encoding of information economically (Attneave, 1954; Garner, 1974). Such relations and transformations do not affect textural segmentation.

Principal Assumptions.   The hypothesis proposed is that textural segmentation is the result of differences in first-order statistics of stimulus features of textural elements. The assumptions of the model are: (a) Feature detection occurs in terms of receptive fields like the elliptical receptive fields that physiologists have found in the visual systems of cats and monkeys (Hubel & Wiesel, 1962, 1968; Kuffler, 1953). (b) There is a linking of the features extracted from the retinal array in terms of textural elements that preserve the spatial relations between the elements of the texture. (c) The features belonging to textural elements in neighboring spatial regions are compared and differences encoded. Difference detectors encode the total differences in color, brightness, slope, and size of textural elements in neighboring spatial regions. (The lines of the upright and tilted Ts, for example, in Fig. 15.1 differ in two values of slope.) Differencing operations are assumed to take place with respect to both features detected by elementary feature detectors and the emergent features of the textural elements themselves. The regions used by the difference detectors are of a range of sizes. (d) There are decision units which inspect the degree to which difference detectors corresponding to textural elements are stimulated. The function of the decision units is to segment a display into textural components on the basis of the magnitude and distribution of the difference signals.

Properties Producing Textural Segmentation.   Two hypotheses have been proposed to characterize the stimulus properties producing strong textural segmentation. In 1967, I hypothesized that textural segmentation occurs strongly for stimulus properties extracted by elementary feature detectors (Beck, 1967). In 1972, I attempted to characterize the stimulus properties giving textural segmentation psychologically. I hypothesized that textural segmentation occurs strongly for those stimulus properties that are readily discriminated when presented in the periphery in a patterned visual filed in which an individual does not know where to attend—what I called in that paper peripheral discriminability under uncertainty (Beck, 1972). These are stimulus properties that may be discriminated without the focusing of attention. The two hypotheses are logically independent of each other. They became related if one assumes that only those properties that are picked up by elementary feature detectors are able to be discriminated preattentively.

Magnitude Of Difference Signals.   What variables affect the magnitude of difference signals? Difference signals are proportional to the degree to which feature analyzers are stimulated by textural elements in one spatial region and are not stimulated by textural elements in a neighboring spatial region. Thus, feature differences that fail to strongly stimulate feature analyzers fail to produce strong textural segmentation. For example, experiments have shown that no distinction is to be made between curves and lines. The difference between a curve and line segments that only crudely approximate the curve fails to produce textural segmentation (Beck, 1973). Schatz (1977) has also shown that changes in the slopes of lines made out of dots do not produce as strong textural segmentation as similar changes in the slopes of solid lines. Solid lines may be expected to stimulate edge and bar detectors more strongly than dotted lines.

It is further assumed that the difference signals are decreased by shared features that stimulate common feature analyzers. For example, the magnitude of the overall slope difference signal is a function of the distribution of slopes of the textural elements. It varies directly with the number of slope analyzers that are stimulated by one textural element and not by the other and inversely with the number of slope analyzers that are stimulated by both textural elements. If a feature added to a textural element causes the stimulation of common slope analyzers, the magnitude of the overall slope difference signal is reduced and textural segmentation decreased. Fox and Mayhew (1979), for example, reported that if upright and sideway Vs (figures like those of B in Fig. 15.3) are surrounded by circles textural segmentation is decreased. The fact that the circles stimulated the same slope analyzers would decrease the magnitude of the overall slope difference signal. Another example is the demonstration by Schatz (1977) that a change in the slope of a single line from vertical to diagonal produced stronger textural segmentation than a change in slope of three parallel lines from vertical to diagonal. Multiple lines are blob like and may be expected to stimulate similarly oriented receptive fields and decrease textural segmentation. It is the overall slope difference between stimuli that is also important for discriminating figural differences preattentively. If two diagonal lines differing in slope are surrounded by three lines of the same slope, the preattentive discriminability of the slope difference is decreased (Pomerantz, Sager & Stoever, 1977).

An unpublished experiment shows that differences in line arrangement which in themselves do not give strong textural segmentation may interfere with textural segmentation. The procedure of Beck (1972) was used to assess the textural segmentation of displays in which the background and disparate figures were not all the same but varied. The displays were like those shown in Fig. 15.3. In Fig. 15.10, the figures to the left of the dash indicate the background figures in a display; the figures to the right of the dash indicate the disparate figures. Figure 15.10 shows the mean time it took to count the disparate figures in a display and the mean ratings of textural segmentation. The mean counting times and the mean ratings that are not significantly different from each other ($p < .01$) are underscored by the same lines in Fig. 15.10. The results show that introducing arrangement differences into either the background figures or the disparate figures reduced the segmentation of the disparate figures. For example, a tilted T in

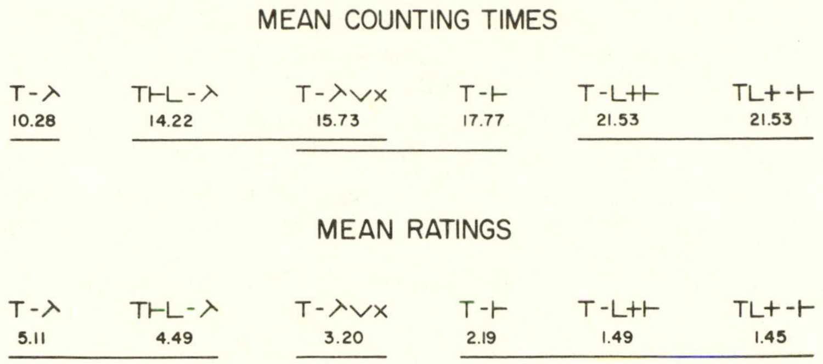

MEAN COUNTING TIMES

T-⅄	T⊢L-⅄	T-⅄∨x	T-⊢	T-L⊬	TL⊣-⊢
10.28	14.22	15.73	17.77	21.53	21.53

MEAN RATINGS

T-⅄	T⊢L-⅄	T-⅄∨x	T-⊢	T-L⊬	TL⊣-⊢
5.11	4.49	3.20	2.19	1.49	1.45

FIG. 15.10.   The mean times to count the disparate figures and the mean ratings for textural segmentation are shown. The left figures in each pair indicate the background figures in a display; the right ones indicate the disparate figures. Pairs of figures underscored by the same line fail to differ significantly.

a background of an upright T, a sideways T, and an L yielded weaker textural segmentation than a tilted T in a background of upright Ts. A tilted T, an X, and a V in a background of upright Ts yielded weaker textural segmentation than a tilted T in a background of upright Ts. The difference between slope and arrangement difference in producing textural segmentation, therefore, appears to be quantitative rather than qualitative. One reason why textural segmentation may occur less strongly for differences in line arrangement than for differences in line slope is that, since the slopes of the component lines of the figures are the same, the figures would tend to stimulate common slope analyzers that would decrease the difference signal.

Difference signals arising from two different features, for example, slope and brightness summate and strengthen textural segmentation. Thus, the segmentation of tilted Ts in a display of upright Ts is enhanced if there is also a difference in the brightness of the lines (Beck, 1967). Textural segmentation was increased by increasing the brightness difference between the background and disparate figures. Though the textural segmentation increased with increased brightness difference, the relative textural segmentation produced was approximately the same for the three different brightness levels. The linear correlations between the mean ratings of textural segmentation for nine disparate figures embedded in a display of upright Ts were .94 (brightness levels 1 and 2), .93 (levels 1 and 3), and .97 (levels 2 and 3).

I have assumed that differencing operations are taken over a range of field sizes. The strength of a difference signal will also be assumed to be a function of the size of a spatial region over which it is taken. The larger the spatial region for which a difference signal occurs, the stronger the textural segmentation. It is also assumed that the greater the number of display locations from which a particular difference signal occurs, the stronger will a display be segmented in terms of that stimulus difference. Thus, stimulus differences that are discriminable in the periphery produce stronger textural segmentation than stimulus differences that are not readily discriminable outside the fovea. For example, an X in a background of +s produces much weaker textural segmentation than a tilted T in a background of upright Ts though the slope differences in the two instances are the same (Beck, 1966, 1967). The eye in the periphery is generally myopic or hyperopic and the image formed by the X figure because of the arrangement of its

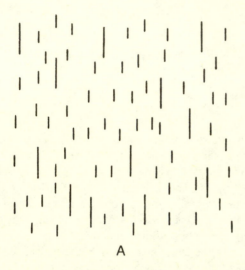

A

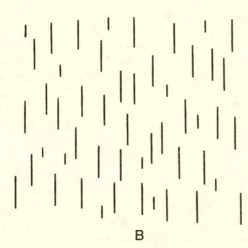

B

FIG. 15.11.   Long lines segregate in a background of short lines better than short lines segregate in a background of long lines.

lines would be less discriminable from a + than would a tilted T from an upright T.

Textural regions are discriminated from each other and it is not meaningful to say that region A is more readily discriminated from region B than is region B from region A. This, however, is not the case when one has to discriminate a figure embedded in a pattern of different figures. One may, therefore, expect textural segmentation in which disparate figures are embedded in background figures to exhibit various asymmetries. Figure 15.11, for example, shows that long lines segregate readily in a display of short lines. Short lines, however, do not segretate as well as a display of long lines. Another example of asymmetry is given in Beck (1973). I showed that textural segmentation is stronger for complete triangles in a field of incomplete triangles (i.e., triangles with the base line missing) than for incomplete triangles in a field of complete triangles. Such asymmetries in textural segmentation appear to reflect asymmetries in discriminability. An experiment using the procedure similar to that of Beck (1974) showed that it is easier to detect peripherally in a four-element array a long (.95cm) line in an array of short (.48cm) lines (mean errors 3.7) than a short line is in an array of long lines (mean errors 6.7), $[t(14)=5.20, p<.01]$. What is suggested is that the visual system is more sensitive in the periphery with distributed attention to the presence of a stimulus property than to its absence. The discriminability of a short line in the periphery is decreased by neighboring long lines; the discriminability of a long line is not as adversely affected by neighboring short lines.

Spatial Arrangement of Difference Signals.   Because textural segmentation occurs in terms of the spatial locations of the elements, an assumption of the model is that the difference detectors keep track of the locations of textural elements that produce the difference signals. The location of a textural element is a function of the locations of the individual features making up the element, for example, the center of the area. The experiments reviewed in section 3 have shown that the relative locations of features, such as line arrangement, gives only weak textural segmentation. It is, therefore, of interest to inquire whether the spatial arrangement of difference signals, for example, whether they form a good figure, facilitates textural segmentation. Figural goodness does not appear to be very important. In an unpublished study, I masked dot targets making up good figures (circles) and poor figures (irregular figures) with a pattern of random dots. The number and proximity of the dots were controlled. The brightness of the pattern of random dots could be varied and observers were asked to reduce the brightness of the random dot pattern until the target figures could be seen. The results indicated that figural goodness had little effect. The amounts by which the masking pattern of random dots had to be reduced in brightness before circles or the irregular figures were seen did not differ significantly. Uttal (1975) found that figural goodness, as defined by Garner (1974), had little effect on the

FIG. 15.12. Textural segmentation fails to occur because of the uniform dissimilarity of lines throughout the display.

detectability of dot figures when the figure was embedded in a pattern of random dots.

Decision Units. The function of decision units is to segment a visual pattern into textural components on the basis of the magnitude and distribution of difference signals. Textural segmentation is hypothesized to occur if the magnitude of the difference signals, for example, slope, between components in a visual pattern is sufficiently greater than those within components. Textural segmentation may fail to occur because there are too many difference signals. Figure 15.12 shows vertical, diagonal, and horizontal lines. There is no spontaneous textural segmentation although attention can be directed to either the vertical, diagonal, or horizontal lines and they can be held in attention. The presence of strong difference signals uniformly throughout the display interferes with spontaneously segmenting the display. Every line produces strong slope difference signals because of its difference in slope from neighboring lines. As mentioned earlier, textural segmentation also occurs in terms of single properties such as slope or color but not in terms of a conjunction of properties such as slope and color. If competing difference signals are present, alternate segmentations occur which interfere with each other. This competition is assumed to occur among decision units.

CONCLUDING REMARKS

Textural Elements. The hypothesis proposed is that the retinal intensity array is transformed into textural elements as a result of a small number of grouping operations such as the Gestalt laws of proximity and good continuation. Textural segmentation occurs as a result of feature differences between textural elements. The hypothesis that textural segmentation occurs in terms of features and properties as components of elements makes the output of feature analyzers not freely available to subsequent processes. Only certain subsets of features are effective in producing textural segmentation. An alternative view is that textural segmentation occurs in terms of the retinal intensity array before grouping into elements. This approach is taken by Julesz et al. (1973) and Schatz (1977). Julesz's conjecture that textures with identical first- and second-order statistics are not discriminable without scrutiny does not restrict the dipole differences to be considered. (The conjecture originally was formulated with random dot textures in which there are few, if any, figural constraints.) Dipole differences across textural elements that break up figures as well as dipole differences between textural elements that retain figural integrity should produce textural segmentation.

Display A, in Fig. 15.13 shows a pattern in which the dipoles in the top 11 rows differ from the dipoles in the bottom 11 rows. Alternate U figures in the

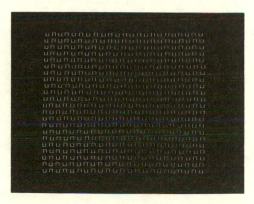

FIG. 15.13. Example in which textural segmentation does not occur though the interfigural dipole statistics differ. In display A, long and short dipoles are found in the bottom 11 rows due to Us in the same columns facing in opposite directions that are not found in the top 11 rows. Textural segmentation, however, does not occur. Textural elements are not restricted to connected figures. In display B, the U figures in the top 11 rows are all upright and aligned. The connecting of the lines into U figures reduces but does not completely inhibit the linking of the base lines of the Us into long lines. These long horizontal lines, as well as the U figures, constitute textural elements. The top half of the display is segmented from the bottom half on the basis of horizontal length differences.

A

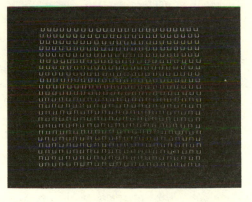

B

same column in the bottom 11 rows are oriented in opposite ways. If one considers dipoles across U figures, the bottom 11 rows have long and short dipoles not present in the top 11 rows. If one restricts the dipoles to the U figures, the upright and inverted Us have the same dipole statistics. Across U dipoles are less salient than within U dipoles and a spontaneous segmentation of the display into two textural regions does not occur. It is important to point out that textural elements are the result of local linking processes and are not restricted to connected figures. In display B of Fig. 15.13, the U figures in the top 11 rows are all upright. Due to both the proximity and alignment of the Us, their base lines are seen to make up long horizontal lines. The connecting of lines into U figures reduces but does not completely inhibit the linking of the base lines of the Us into long horizontal lines. These long horizontal lines, as well as the U figures, constitute textural elements. The top half of the display is now segmented from the bottom half on the basis of length differences. There is also a tendency for opposing upright and inverted Us in the bottom halves of the displays to link. If the opposing U figures are brought closer together, this tendency is greatly increased. When the opposing Us link to form a new textural element, the dipoles between the bases of opposing Us become within element dipoles rather than between element dipoles. The opposing U textural elements in the bottom halves of the displays differ in size or in within dipole statistics from the Us in the top halves of the displays, and textural segmentation is strengthened.

Isodipole Textures.   Julesz and his colleagues have constructed displays that have identical first- and second-order statistics but which give strong textural segmentation. Discrimination in these counterexamples appears to be based on features that would differentially stimulate concentric and elliptical receptive fields. A striking example, taken from Victor and Brodie (1978), is shown in display A of Fig. 15.14. They juxtaposed a disk-like texture with an ellipsoid-like texture. Though the two textures have the same Buffon needle statistics (i.e., the frequency of intersection with line segments placed randomly on either texture are the same), as well as first- and second-order statistics, the textural difference is immediately discriminable. The disk-like and ellipsoid-like texture elements would differentially stimulate concentric and elliptical receptive fields. Similarly, the other counterexamples discovered by Julesz and his colleagues would differentially stimulate bar detectors differing in size and in orientation. Display B in Fig. 15.14 shows another example. It is of particular interest because the dotted lines in the disparate and background figures have the same slopes. Julesz (1980) suggests that textural segmentation occurs because the disparate and background textural elements differ in the number of line ends or terminators. Marr (1976) had previously pointed out the importance of terminators for textural discrimination. Frisby and Clatworthy (1975) have argued that the elliptical-like receptive fields discovered by Rodieck and Stone (1965) would be specifically sensitive to line ends and would respond strongly to their presence.

The statistical approach of Julesz has been valuable for studying textural perception. It has led to both interesting experiments and important theoretical analyses. Nth-order statistics are mathematically more tractable than receptive fields. As noted earlier, there is a similarity between the hypothesis that textural segmentation occurs in terms of elementary feature analyzers and the hypothesis that it occurs in terms of nth-order statistics. First- and second-order statistics

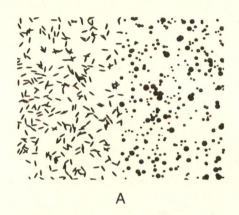

A

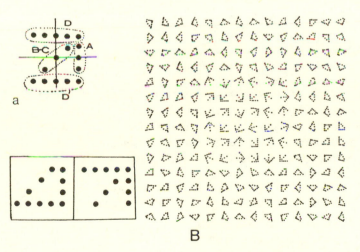

B

FIG. 15.14.   Examples of textural segmentation in which the second-order statistics are the same. Display A is from Victor & Brodie (1978); Display B is from Julesz (1981).

encode properties relating to the sizes, orientation, and distribution of black in a black and white textural pattern. Many of the experimental results can be interpreted in terms of either receptive fields or nth-order statistics and do not support either model relative to the other. The counterexamples found by Julesz and his colleagues, however, show that the two models are not formally equivalent. The fact that differential stimulation of receptive fields of specific sizes, orientations, and shapes explain these counterexamples reinforces my own introspection that it is differences in the first-order statistics of features rather than differences in the nth-order statistics of image points that are important for textural segmentation.

Two Attentional Modes: Preattentive and Focused Attention.   Texture and form perception appear to be mediated by different processes. Line slope is the more salient property for perceiving textural similarity while line arrangement is the more salient property for perceiving form similarity (see section 1). Corresponding to the similarity judgments are the results of experiments on focal and preattentive discrimination. The discrimination of a difference in line arrangement is often better than of a difference in line slope when attention is focused; the discrimination of a difference in line arrangement becomes worse than of a difference in line slope when attention is distributed (see section 2). Foster and Mason (1980) have also found adaptation effects to the slopes of the component lines but not to the arrangement of component lines of a figure. This suggests that two attentional modes with different functional characteristics subserve the perceptions of line slope and of line arrangement. Line slope is a segmentary property, which, like brightness, color, and size, may be picked up preattentively over a large spatial area. In contrast, line arrangement involves a more detailed analysis of spatial relations that requires focused attention.

Treisman (1977) has suggested that focal attention and serial processing are required to integrate the separable attributes of the stimulus registered by independent analyzers. She hypothesized that automatic and parallel processing is possible only when an elementary feature mediates discrimination. It is uncertain, however, whether the perception of spatial relations such as line arrangement or figural orientation always requires attention. Ambler and Finklea (1976), for example, found that a difference in line arrangement could be discriminated as well as a difference in line slope in a four-letter display in the fovea. It is possible that when a form is completely clear and unambiguous, spatial relations may be processed without attention. Attentional processing may only be necessary when a stimulus is degraded such as when it is presented in the periphery or in the fovea when confusing nontargets are near the target as in a multiple element textural pattern. In an unpublished experiment, Ambler and I further studied whether the distributed attentional system is more sensitive to differences in line slope than to differences in figural orientation.

The targets consisted of (a) single letters, (b) four letters located in the corners of an imaginary square, and (c) four letters embedded in a textural pattern. Fifty

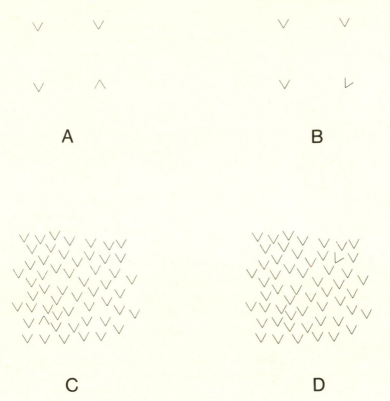

FIG. 15.15. A difference in figural orientation (A) was discriminated as well as a difference in line slope (B) when presented in a four-letter display. A difference in figural orientation (C) was discriminated more poorly than a difference in line slope (D) when embedded in a textural pattern.

additional upright Vs were added so that each of the four corners of the imaginary square where a stimulus letter could appear was now surrounded by upright Vs. The stimulus letter was either a V rotated 30 degrees clockwise or an inverted V. Figure 15.15 shows the two stimulus letters and examples of the four- and fifty-four-letter targets. The two alternative stimulus letters were presented in separate blocks. In the single letter target, a single letter was presented in one of the four corners and a subject was asked to identify whether it was an upright V or one of the stimulus letters. In the four- and fifty-four-letter targets, a subject was required to discriminate between a target containing all upright Vs or a target containing a stimulus letter, that is, three upright Vs and a rotated or inverted V in the fourth corner. Two groups of eight subjects served in the experiment. One group of eight subjects was run with the four-letter targets. A second group of eight subjects was run with the single letter and fifty-four-letter targets. Exposure durations were chosen for each subject to given an error rate of between 10 and

TABLE 15.1
Mean Errors

Display Number	Rotated V	Inverted V
Single Letter	8.6	10.1
Four Letters	8.1	7.5
Fifty-four Letters	8.5	18.9

Note: The means in the single letter and 54-letter targets are based on 48 trials per subject. The means in the 4-letter targets are based on 64 trials per subject.

20 percent for the rotated V stimulus letters for each of the three target types.

Table 15.1 presents the mean errors for each of the two stimulus letters and three target types. The mean errors for a rotated V and an inverted V did not differ significantly in a single letter target [$t(7)=.59$], and in a four-letter target [$t(7)=.56$]. In the fifty-four-letter target, the mean errors for a rotated V differed significantly from the mean errors for an inverted V[$t(7)=3.59$, $p<.01$].

I have hypothesized that textural segmentation occurs for properties that may be discriminated preattentively. The finding that a rotated V was more discriminable than an inverted V in the fifty-four-letter target, but not in a single letter target, is consistent with this hypothesis. In a single letter target, the brightness difference with the background allowed for the focusing of attention on the letter presented. The finding, however, that the discrimination of a rotated V and of an inverted V was the same in a four-letter target poses a problem. In a four-letter target, distributed attention was required since a stimulus letter could appear in any of the four corners and a brightness difference could not direct attention. Textural segmentation, however, fails to occur for an inverted V in a background of upright Vs (see Fig. 15.3). Although no conclusive answers can be offered, there are two possibilities. One possibility is that differences in the effectiveness of different stimulus properties under focused and distributed attention does not reflect a dichotomy in processing, as suggested by Treisman, but reflects a continuum of discrimination difficulty (Beck & Ambler, 1972). A difference in figural orientation may allow for preattentive processing with distributed attention with a small number of figures segregated from the background and spatially separated from each other. When surrounded by a large number of figures, as in a texture, the inversion of a figure is not distinctive enough to allow for nonattentional processing. Multiple adjacent nontarget figures with lines of the same slopes produce feature specific inhibition (Bjork & Murray, 1977) and also increase the chance that a nontarget will be mistaken for a target (Eriksen & Spencer, 1969). Under these conditions, discrimination is not possible without focused attention and textural segmentation does not occur. An alternative explanation is possible which retains the hypothesis that the discrimination of differences in spatial relations such as figural orientation requires focal attention. Shaw and Shaw (1977) have shown that subjects can differentially attend to various parts of the field. The failure to find significantly more errors for an inverted V than for a rotated V in a four-letter display may have occurred because subjects divided their attention among the four possible stimulus locations. That is, a subject may have been able to process one and four spatial locations with equal efficiency. Allocation of attention would not only increase the discriminability of an inverted V but impair the discriminability of a rotated V. As a result of attention, subjects respond not only to line orientation but to the orientation of the entire figure. The discriminability of a rotated V from an upright V would be impaired because both have a downward pointing angle. In a fifty-four-letter target internally directed attentional focusing is not possible. An attempt to focus attention on an individual letter is interfered with by the stimultaneous processing of adjacent letters (Eriksen & Schultz, 1979).

Vertical-Horizontal Superiority.   In section 3 it was pointed out that the difference between vertical and horizontal lines produces greater textural segmentation than the difference between 45-degree and 135-degree lines. Another example of the superiority of the greater sensitivity of the visual system to the vertical and horizontal direction is that a pattern of sideways Vs segments itself from a pattern of upright Vs but a pattern of backward Ls fails to segment itself from a pattern of Ls (Olson & Attneave, 1970). I have suggested that the textural segmentation produced by sideways Vs in a pattern of upright Vs is the result of differentially stimulating vertical and horizontal receptive fields. Why do not an L and a backward L differentially stimulate 135 and 45 degree receptive fields? It may be that there are more vertically and horizontally oriented receptive fields than 45-degree and 135-degree oriented receptive fields. Another possibility is that a vertical-horizontal frame of reference facilitates textural segmentation by lowering the degree of activation that difference signals must reach before they are further processed. That is, sideways Vs in a pattern of upright Vs and backward Ls in a pattern of Ls both produce weak difference signals. A vertical-horizontal frame of reference, however, facilitates the automatic and parallel processing of the difference signals resulting from sideways Vs and upright Vs producing textural segmentation. The difference signals resulting from backward Ls and Ls, in contrast, require focal attention and serial processing that prevents textural segmentation.

REFERENCES

Ambler, B., & Finklea, D. L. The influence of selective attention in peripheral and foveal vision. *Perception and Psychophysics,* 1976, *19,* 518–524.

Attneave, F. Some informational aspects of visual perception. *Psychological Review,* 1954, *61,* 183–193.

Banks, W. P., & Prinzmetal, W. Configurational effects in visual information processing. *Perception and Psychophysics,* 1976, *19,* 361–367.

Beck, J. Effect of orientation and of shape similarity on perceptual grouping. *Perception and Psychophysics,* 1966, *1,* 300–302.

Beck, J. Perceptual grouping produced by line figures. *Perception and Psychophysics,* 1967, *2,* 491–495.

Beck, J. Similarity grouping and peripheral discriminability under uncertainty. *American Journal of Psychology,* 1972, *85,* 1–19.

Beck, J. Similarity grouping of curves. *Perceptual and Motor Skills,* 1973, *36,* 1331–1341.

Beck, J. Relation between similarity grouping and peripheral discriminability. *Journal of Experimental Psychology,* 1974, *102,* 1145–1147.

Beck, J. The relation between similarity grouping and perceptual constancy. *American Journal of Psychology,* 1975, *88,* 397–409.

Beck, J., & Ambler, B. Discriminability of differences in line slope and in line arrangement as a function of mask delay. *Perception and Psychophysics,* 1972, *12,* 33–38.

Beck, J., & Ambler, B. The effects of concentrated and distributed attention on peripheral acuity. *Perception and Psychophysics,* 1973, *14,* 225–230.

Bjork, E. L., & Murray, J. T. On the nature of input channels in visual processing. *Psychological Review,* 1977, *84,* 472–484.

Denney, D., & Adorjani, C. Orientation specificity of visual and cortical neurons after head tilt. *Experimental Brain Research,* 1972, *14,* 312–317.

Engel, F. L. *Visual conspicuity as an external determinant of eye movements and selective attention.* Eindhoven, The Netherlands: Catholic University, 1976.

Eriksen, C. W., & Schultz, D. W. Information processing in visual search: A continuous flow conception of experimental results. *Perception and Psychophysics,* 1979, *25,* 249–263.

Eriksen, C. W., & Spencer, T. Rate of information processing in visual perception: Some results and methodological considerations. *Journal of Experimental Psychology Monograph,* 1969, *79,* (No. 2, pt 2).

Foster, D. H., & Mason, R. J. Irrelevance of local position information in visual adaptation to random arrays of small geometric elements. *Perception,* 1980, *9,* 217–221.

Fox, J., & Mayhew, J.E.W. Texture discrimination and the analysis of proximity. *Perception,* 1979, *8,* 75–91.

Frisby, J. P., & Clatworthy, J. L., Illusory contours: Curious cases of simultaneous brightness contrast? *Perception,* 1975, *4,* 349–357.

Garner, W. R. *The processing of information and structure.* Hillsdale, N.J.: Lawrence Erlbaum Associates, 1974.

Gillam, B., & McGrath, D. Orientation relative to the retina determines perceptual organization. *Perception and Psychophysics,* 1979, *26,* 177–181.

Goldmeier, E. Similarity in visually perceived forms. *Psychological Issues,* 1972, *8,* Monograph 29.

Green, B. F., Jr., Wolf, A. K., & White, B. W. The detection of statistically defined patterns in a matrix of dots. *American Journal of Psychology,* 1959, *72,* 503–520.

Harcum, E. R., & Shaw, M. R. Cognitive and sensory lateral masking of tachistoscopic patterns. *Journal of Experimental Psychology,* 1974, *103,* 663–667.

Harvey, L. O., & Gervais, M. J. Internal representation of visual texture as the basis for the judgment of similarity. *Journal of Experimental Psychology: Human Perception and Performance,* 1981, *7,* 741–753.

Horn, G., Stechler, G., & Hill, R. M. Receptive fields of units in the visual cortex of the cat in the presence and absence of bodily tilt. *Experimental Brain Research,* 1972, *15,* 113–132.

Hubel, D. H., & Wiesel, T. N. Receptive fields, binocular interaction, and functional architecture in the cat's visual cortex. *Journal of Physiology,* 1962, *160,* 106–154.

Hubel, D. H., & Wiesel, T. M. Receptive fields and functional architecture of monkey striate cortex. *Journal of Physiology*, 1968, *195*, 215-243.

Julesz, B. Visual pattern discrimination. *IRE Transactions of the Professional Group on Information Theory*, 1962, *IT-8*, 84-92.

Julesz, B. Perceptual limits of texture discrimination and their implications to figure-ground separation. In E. L. J. Leeuwenberg & H. F. J. M. Buffart (Eds.), *Formal theories of visual perception*. New York: Wiley, 1978.

Julesz, B. Spatial nonlinearities in the instantaneous perception of texture with identical power spectra. *Philosophical Transactions of the Royal Society, London*, 1980, *B290*, 83-94.

Julesz, B. Figure and ground perception in briefly presented isodipole textures. In M. Kubovy & J. Pomerantz (Eds.), *Perceptual organization*. Hillsdale, N.J.: Lawrence Erlbaum Associates, 1981.

Julesz, B., Gilbert, E. N., Shepp, L. A., & Frisch, H. L. Inability of humans to discriminate between visual textures that agree in second-order statistics revisited. *Perception*, 1973, *2*, 391-405.

Kuffler, S. W. Discharge patterns and functional organization of mammalian retina. *Journal of Neurophysiology*, 1953, *16*, 37-68.

Mach, E. *The analysis of sensations*. New York: Dover, 1959.

MacLeod, I. D. G., & Rosenfeld, A. The visibility of gratings: Spatial frequency channels or bar detecting units. *Vision Research*, 1974, *14*, 909-916.

Marr, D. Early processing of visual information. *Philosophical Transactions of the Royal Society, London*, 1976, *B275*, 483-524.

Olson, R., & Attneave, F. What variables produce similarity grouping? *American Journal of Psychology*, 1970, *83*, 1-21.

Pomerantz, J. R., Sager, L. C., & Stoever, R. J. Perception of wholes and of their component parts: Some configurational superiority effects. *Journal of Experimental Psychology: Human Perception and Performance*, 1977, *3*, 422-435.

Purks, S. R., & Richards, W. Visual texture discrimination using random-dot patterns. *Journal of the Optical Society of America*, 1977, *67*, 765-771.

Rodieck, R. W., & Stone, J. Analysis of receptive fields of cat retinal ganglion cells. *Journal of Neurophysiology*, 1965, *28*, 833-849.

Schatz, B. R. *The computation of immediate texture discrimination*. MIT Artificial Intelligence Laboratories, Memorandum 426, 1977.

Shaw, M. L., & Shaw, P. Optimal allocation of cognitive resources to spatial locations. *Journal of Experimental Psychology: Human Perception and Performance*, 1977, *3*, 201-211.

Shiffrin, R. M., & Schneider, W. Controlled and automatic human information processing: II. Perceptual learning, automatic attending, and a general theory. *Psychological Review*, 1977, *84*, 127-190.

Treisman, A. Focused attention in the perception and retrieval of multidimensional stimuli. *Perception and Psychophysics*, 1977, *22*, 1-11.

Treisman, A., & Gelade, G. A feature-integration theory of attention. *Cognitive Psychology*, 1980, *12*, 97-136.

Uttal, W. *An autocorrelation theory of form detection*. Hillsdale, N.J.: Lawrence Erlbaum Associates, 1975.

Victor, J. D., & Brodie, S. E. Discriminable textures with identical Buffon-needle statistics. *Biological Cybernetics*, 1978, *31*, 231-234.

Wertheimer, M. Untersuchungen zur Lehre von der Gestalt. II. *Psychologische Forschung*, 1923, *4*, 301-350.

16

Analysis of Discrete Internal Representations of Visual Pattern Stimuli

David H. Foster
University of Keele

1. INTRODUCTION

How does our capacity to discriminate spatial visual stimuli depend on the way that these stimuli are encoded internally by the visual system? This basic problem is considered here within a theoretical framework that encompasses a number of specific theories of how such stimuli might be internally represented. The intention is to develop a general approach to the experimental investigation of these internal representations and their relationship to visual discrimination performance. This chapter is intended to be nontechnical and a more formal account of the ideas presented here may be found in Foster (1980a, b).

Theories about the visual discrimination of objects or patterns may be divided into two types, depending on whether the internal representation that is hypothesized to occur is *structured* or *unstructured*. An unstructured internal representation describes the object or pattern as an approximately point-for-point "image" of the spatial distribution of the light intensity in the stimulus, and is limited in its fidelity only by visual acuity. These pointillistic representations may be internally compared with each other by applying certain smooth and continuous families of internal spatial transformations that are directed towards bringing the representations into coincidence. Judgments about the similarity of stimuli are assumed to be determined by the overlap of the transformed representations (see, for example, Foster, 1978a; Foster & Mason, 1979; Hoffman, 1970; Marko, 1973; Pitts & McCulloch, 1947; Shepard, 1980). A structured internal representation, conversely, describes how the stimulus is spatially organized, in terms of for instance the lines and regions in the object and how these entities are located in relation to each other. Judgments about the similarity of stimuli are assumed to be determined by the extent to which the components of their descriptions concur (see, for example, Foster and Mason, 1979; Kahn & Foster, 1981; Reed, 1973; Sutherland, 1973).

In principle, these two types of hypothesized internal representation should not behave in the same way in response to a spatial deformation in a stimulus object. An unstructured internal representation should vary smoothly and continuously as the shape of the stimulus is varied. Because the postulated comparison process is also smooth and continuous, visual sensitivity to these changes in the stimulus should vary smoothly and continuously also. For structured internal representations, the situation is fundamentally different. The nature of this difference is examined here for a class of structured internal representations which have the property that they are composed of components drawn from some fixed and finite repertoire. Such internal representations, which form a very large class, are called *discrete*. (Structured internal representations which are not formed in this way have been discussed by Foster [1975].) The class of discrete internal representations includes those hypothesized pattern encodings that make use of "critical" pattern features such as oriented lines and curves (Gibson, 1969; Rumelhart, 1971) and those encodings that specify various global properties or attributes such as symmetry, area, and "jaggedness" (Aiken & Brown, 1971; Mavrides & Brown, 1969; for review, see Sutherland, 1973). It also includes those hypothesized representations based on forming "relational structural descriptions," that is, the listing of local pattern features such as lines and blobs, and the spatial relations that may be defined between these local features, such as "above," "right of," and "joined to." Further spatial relations between these assemblages may be given until the necessary level of detail in the description is achieved (Barlow, Narasimhan, & Rosenfeld, 1972; Foster, 1978b; Foster & Mason, 1979; Kahn & Foster, 1981; Reed, 1973; Sutherland, 1968, 1973).

Independent of the precise character of its composition, we may view the formation of a discrete internal representation from its repertoire of components as constituting a probabilistic process. The rationale for this assumption derives from several considerations. First, there are inevitable small random variations in the physiological state of the nervous processes involved in processing the pattern stimuli. Second, there are more general fluctuations in the observer's attentional state, changes in his attitude, and lapses in memory, all of which serve to impart an apparent indeterminism to the construction of an internal representation. Third, there is an inherent ambiguity associated with some stimuli so that two or more equally appropriate internal representations might be formed, one at a time, in response to presentation of the stimulus. Illustrations of this phenomenon, at a relatively high level of pattern representation, occur with the classical ambiguous figures, like the Necker cube and Rubin's vase-faces illusion. Other examples are provided by ambiguous alphabetic characters that can be assigned more than one letter label with equal probability (Blesser, Shillman, Cox, Kuklinski, Ventura, & Eden, 1973; Naus & Shillman, 1976).

Although the construction of internal representations is to be treated here as being nondeterministic, such an approach does not preclude the possibility of dealing with those pattern stimuli that almost always give rise to the same internal representation. One simply imposes the constraint that the probability of that representation being assigned is sufficiently close to unity.

Given a system of discrete internal representations comprising combinations of components drawn from some appropriate repertoire, one should in principle be able to observe discontinuities in visual performance analogous to those reported in auditory perception. Experiments performed by Liberman and his colleagues (Liberman, Harris, Hoffman, & Griffith, 1957; Liberman, Harris, Kinney, & Lane, 1961) showed that as certain speech-like stimuli were varied in equal steps along an acoustic continuum, the discriminability of adjacent pairs of stimuli was better when the stimuli were located each side of a phoneme boundary than when they fell within the same phoneme category. A similar result was obtained by Cutting & Rosner (1974) for nonspeech auditory stimuli. There are evident differences between the functional processes subserving vision and audition; in particular, we need not suppose that there is a visual analogue to the "motor theory" of speech perception (Liberman, Cooper, Shankweiler, & Studdert-Kennedy, 1967; Stevens & House, 1972); but, at a formal level, there are some similarities between the present approach and these auditory studies, with discrete internal pattern representations or their components taking the place of phoneme categories.

The existence of this analogy between possible visual and auditory encodings does not in itself provide an adequate foundation on which to conduct an exploratory investigation. There are three basic problems. First, there are no dimensions naturally associated with a spatial pattern along which the changes in shape may be measured, like voice onset time for a speech-like stimulus. Second, we have no explicit method for relating the discriminability of patterns to the construction of the hypothesized internal representations. Third, although internal representations may be obtained from a fixed repertoire of components, some of these components may involve quantities that vary smoothly and continuously as the pattern is transformed; for example, a pattern consisting of two points may give rise to an internal representation that contains a component specifying the distance between the two points. Changes in discrimination performance associated with such continuously varying quantities may mask changes in performance due to discontinuously varying components.

To resolve these and other, related problems, it is necessary to contrive a suitable theoretical framework, and this is attempted in the first part of this study. The second part is concerned with experimental applications. In brief, the organization of this chapter is as follows. A more complete description is first put forward for the kinds of internal representation that are to be analyzed. Next a relationship is formulated between pattern discrimination performance and the various probabilities governing the composition of the hypothesized internal representations. The proposed investigatory technique is then set out. This technique rests on the use of a group of spatial transformations smoothly parameterized by a single variable. After this theoretical development, two experimental applications of the technique are considered. One application concerns the encoding of the collinearity or noncollinearity of the points in a pattern; the other application concerns the encoding of the angle between two connected lines. Finally, some observations are made on the general applicability of the technique and its relation to experiments involving the categorical identification of pattern stimuli.

2. DISCRETE INTERNAL PATTERN REPRESENTATIONS

In developing a description of discrete internal representations, it is useful here to draw a distinction between two types of component in the repertoire of components from which the representation might be composed: first, there are components which are used to form a basis for the representation and which merely indicate or denote various parts of the pattern; second, there are other components that designate various properties that may be associated with those pattern parts. This distinction is made more precise below. (Note that although interest is in both two- and three-dimensional visual stimuli, for brevity reference is usually made to just "patterns"; parts of patterns are called "subpatterns".) Assume that there is in the repertoire of components a fixed and finite set of pattern *primitives* that form a basis for the internal representation; typical primitives might denote points, lines, and regions in a pattern. Suppose that associated with each primitive or set of primitives there is available a fixed and finite set of *attributes* in the repertoire. These attributes are variables that can specify properties or characteristics appropriate to those primitives. For single primitives, typical attributes might designate some *position* of a point, some *length* of a line, and some *area* of a region; for sets of primitives, typical attributes might designate some *distance* between two points, some *angle* between two lines, whether a point is *left of* or *right of* a line, and whether a point is *inside* or *outside* a region. Attributes associated with sets of primitives, rather than single primitives, can in particular define "relations" between those primitives, but for the present no distinction need be made between these and other kinds of attribute.

The attributes listed above are seen to be either continuous variables, thus the length of a line can assume any value in an interval of values from zero to infinity, or discrete, thus the attribute designating whether a point is left of or right of a line can assume only one of two values. Although not all continuous and discrete attributes may be typified in this way, these examples are typical of the ones to be considered here. Attributes with other kinds of values, for example functions, are discussed by Rosenfeld (1969). Note that although we have introduced continuous attributes, this does not imply that the proposed description includes the unstructured type of internal representation mentioned in the introduction. Only a finite number of continuous attributes are allowed here.

A discrete internal representation, then, is assumed to consist of a number of pattern primitives in association with certain attributes and their values. For example, a pattern consisting of a point and a line might be given the internal representation comprising two primitives labelled "point" and "line," an attribute that designates the perpendicular distance of the point from the line, and some value of that distance. In view of the comments in the introduction concerning the likely non-deterministic nature of the formation of an internal representation, the selection of primitives, of attributes, and of attribute values will each be regarded as probabilistic processes. Because it is certain that on each occasion that the pattern is presented, one or more pattern primitives are incorporated into the representation, and one or more attributes and their values are assigned, the probabilities specifying the selection of these quantities should sum (or integrate) to unity.

The discrete character of the internal representations considered here is manifested at several levels: in the finiteness of the number of pattern primitives within the representation, in the finiteness of the number of attributes associated with each primitive, and, for discrete attributes, in the finiteness of the number of values each attribute may assume. The technique of analysis to be described relates mainly to the discrete attributes rather than to the primitives. This choice is less restrictive than it appears, however, because variations in the selection of primitives may be re-expressed as variations in the selection of values of a discrete attribute associated with some more fundamental primitive. For example, instead of dealing with the assignment probabilities of primitives labelled "spot" and "line," one could, given a single primitive labelled "figure" and a discrete attribute called "shape," equivalently consider the assignment probabilities of the attribute values "spot-like" and "line-like." Thus the analysis of primitives may be considered as a special case of the analysis of discrete attributes.

3.   PATTERN DISCRIMINATION DETERMINED BY PROBABILITY DIFFERENCES

To relate performance in visually discriminating patterns to the construction of the proposed discrete internal pattern representations, we make the general assumption that pattern discriminability is determined by the differences in probabilities of each of the internal representations assigned to the patterns. The following example helps justify this idea.

In Fig. 16.1, pattern A has probability $p_1(A)$ of giving rise to internal representation r_1, and probability $p_2(A)$ of giving rise to internal representation r_2. An

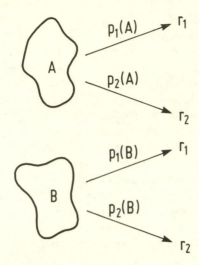

FIG 16.1.   Two patterns A and B and the probabilities governing the assignment of hypothetical internal representations r_1 and r_2 to each.

analagous scheme holds for pattern B. No other internal representations are supposed to occur. Note that one (and only one) representation may be assigned at a time to a pattern; accordingly, the probabilities of the representations must sum to unity for each pattern. It seems reasonable to expect that the more likely A and B are to give rise to different internal representations, the more likely A and B are to be visually discriminated. With this in mind, suppose that the differences (in magnitude) in the probabilities $p_1(A)$ and $p_1(B)$ and in the probabilities $p_2(A)$ and $p_2(B)$ are each large. Then by the above summation condition, $p_1(A)$ and $p_2(B)$ are each close to unity and $p_2(A)$ and $p_1(B)$ are each close to zero, or vice versa. In either case, A and B give rise most of the time to different internal representations. Discriminability should therefore be high. Suppose instead that the differences (in magnitude) in $p_1(A)$ and $p_1(B)$ and in $p_2(A)$ and $p_2(B)$ are each small. If A gives rise most of the time to representation r_1, then so does B, and if A gives rise most of the time to representation r_2, then so does B. Discriminability should therefore be low.

We now apply this hypothesized general relationship between pattern discriminability and assignment probabilities of internal representations to the discrete attributes within the internal representation. Because the investigatory technique to be described involves the visual comparison of patterns that do not differ greatly in their shapes, we suppose that the probabilities governing the selection of pattern primitives and attributes are the same for each of the patterns in the range of patterns under consideration; only the probabilities governing the assignment of the attribute values will be assumed to vary with pattern shape. This assumption causes no great loss in generality (see comments in section 2), and its plausibility is made evident when the method of generating a range of pattern shapes is formulated and some specific applications are described.

The discriminability of two patterns is thus assumed to be determined by the differences in the probabilities controlling the assignment of attribute values; the greater these differences, the greater the discriminability of the patterns. There are a number of ways we can calculate these differences for a given set of possible assignment probabilities, and the details of the computation depend on whether each difference is for a continuous or discrete attribute. The precise choice of metric for these differences is not critical for the predictions of the proposed approach (Foster, 1979, 1980b).

To measure the visual discriminability of two patterns, we might use the percentage of correct responses in a suitable forced-choice discrimination task. It is useful, however, to employ the discrimination index d' which arises in the theory of signal detection (Green & Swets, 1966; Swets, 1973). The index d' increases monotonically with discrimination performance and $d' = 0$ corresponds to the nondiscriminability of the stimuli. The usefulness of d' in the present study resides mainly in the fact that differences in performance for conditions with and without the operation of some hypothesized attribute may, in certain circumstances, be computed to give a "net" discrimination performance associated with that attribute. (Discrimination indices are additive; see Durlach and Braida, 1969.) As is shown, this may simplify the separation of the contributions of discrete and continuous attributes to discrimination performance. In addition, performances for different paradigms may be compared directly; for example, both two-alternative and four-alternative forced-choice paradigms are used here. It should be stressed that the index d' is used only as a computational device; the principle of the technique to be described does not depend on the particular choice of performance measure, providing that the measure increases monotonically with pattern discriminability.

4.   ANALYSIS BY PARAMETERIZED PATTERN PERTURBATION

Suppose that one applies to a pattern a family of spatial transformations T_s, smoothly parameterized by a single variable s. The parameterization should satisfy certain technical conditions, including one related to the group property of the family. These conditions are given in the Appendix.

As the pattern is deformed under the action of the transformations T_s, the probabilities governing the assignment of values to the hypothesized discrete attributes will change. Figure 16.2 illustrates for one discrete attribute a hypothetical dependence of three assignment probabilities for attribute values v_1, v_2, and v_3, as the parameter s runs through its range. (The precise shapes of the curves are not important; see Foster, 1979, 1980b.) For values of the parameter s around the point labelled s_1, the attribute value v_1 is almost always assigned; similarly, for values of s around the point s_3, attribute value v_2 is almost always

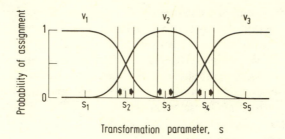

FIG. 16.2. Hypothetical dependence of assignment probabilities on pattern transformation parameter s for three attribute values v_1, v_2, and v_3. Increments in s of $-\Delta s$ and $+\Delta s$ about points s_2, s_3, and s_4 are indicated by the pairs of arrowed vertical lines.

assigned, and for values of s around the point s_5, attribute value v_3 is almost always assigned. Suppose a particular value of s is selected from its range and this value is then altered by small *fixed* positive and negative amounts, $+\Delta s$ and $-\Delta s$, respectively. If the increments $+\Delta s$ and $-\Delta s$ are applied at a point close to s_3, then very little change occurs in the assignment probabilities as the pattern is transformed from "state" $s-\Delta s$ to "state" $s+\Delta s$ (indicated in the figure by the arrowed vertical lines). In contrast, at a point such as s_2, there are large and opposite changes in assignment probabilities as the pattern "state" changes from $s-\Delta s$ to $s+\Delta s$ (again indicated by the arrowed vertical lines).

Suppose that the assumptions of section 3 are valid, and consider the contribution of this discrete attribute to the discriminability of the different pattern shapes caused by the increments $\pm \Delta s$ in s. From Fig. 16.2, one would expect this contribution to be minimum when s equals s_1, s_3, or s_5, and maximum when s equals s_2 or s_4. Whether the contribution of this discrete attribute to discrimination performance proves observable depends on how the assignment probabilities of other possible discrete and continuous attributes change with the parameter s. The conditions that have to be satisfied in order that only one selected discrete attribute gives a varying contribution to discrimination performance with variation in s have been listed in full elsewhere (Foster, 1980b). For the present purpose, we concentrate on two assumptions. The first is that the conditions under which the stimulus patterns are viewed may be chosen to generally favour the use of discrete rather than continuous attributes. Given that there is a limited pattern-encoding capacity of the whole visual system (a capacity lower than that implied by the spatial distribution of retinal receptors), this bias might be achieved if one presented patterns or subpatterns in sufficient numbers or densities in the field so that an encoding by discrete attributes was then forced as the most economical procedure. Recall that from information theory, the information provided by a variable depends on the number of values it can assume; by definition, less information is specified by a discrete attribute than by a continuous attribute. This strategy, of course, presupposes that the encoding process is sufficiently labile to be adjusted in this way. The second assumption is that the scale for the parameter s may be chosen so that, independent of the "reference" point in the range of s about which the increments $\pm\Delta s$ are applied, the same changes occur in the probabilities governing the assignment of continuous attributes. Thus, although the continuous attributes might contribute to discrimination performance, their contribution should not vary with the parameter s. The properties of the family of transformations T_s listed in the Appendix imply that a given value of the increment Δs always corresponds to the same change in the transformation T_s, independent of the value of s. The effect is to secure a "transformational uniformity" (Foster, 1980b) in the continuum of patterns generated by the family of transformations. How these requirements are met in practice is discussed later.

Provided the selected discrete attribute satisfies certain other constraints, it may be shown (Foster, 1979, 1980b) that the results of the example in Fig. 16.2 may be generalized. The following rule then summarizes how the discriminability of patterns perturbed in shape by fixed increments $\pm\Delta s$ in s should vary with the parameter s. *Where assignment probabilities are maximum, discriminability is minimum; where assignment probabilities are changing most rapidly, discriminability is maximum.* Practical applications of this approach to the analysis of discrete internal representations are illustrated in the following two sections.

5. AN ATTRIBUTE DESIGNATING THE COLLINEARITY OR NONCOLLINEARITY OF POINTS IN A PATTERN

The experiment described here is designed to test the qualitative features of the investigatory technique set out in the previous section. The putative discrete attribute chosen for this test is one designating the collinearity or noncollinearity of points in a pattern. Collinearity, or its failure, has been suggested to have a special role in a number of visual operations, for example, in the perceptual grouping of stimulus parts (Prytulak, 1974; Wertheimer, 1923), in the visual detection of targets embedded in noise fields (Caelli & Umansky, 1976; Uttal, 1973), in the discrimination of targets from non-targets (Prinzmetal & Banks, 1977), and in visual acuity for pattern arrangement (Andrews, Butcher, & Buckley, 1973; Bouma & Andriessen, 1968). Clearly, one of the simplest stimuli that can specify collinearity or noncollinearity is a figure consisting of three points; the stimuli used in the present experiment were of this form. Pattern displays consisted of collections of three-dot subpatterns each as illustrated in Fig. 16.3. The action of the selected group of transformations T_s is specified by the deformation angle s shown, the distances between dots 1 and 2 and between dots 2 and 3 being held constant. The task of the subject entailed the discrimination of perturbed subpatterns produced by fixed angular increments $+\Delta s$ and

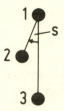

FIG 16.3. Three-dot subpattern. The center-to-center distances between dots 1 and 2 and between dots 2 and 3 are constant and equal. The deformation of the subpattern is specified by the parameter *s*, which measures the angle shown.

$-\Delta s$ about various reference angle values *s*, including zero. The range of *s* was from $-30°$ to $+30°$. Over this range, therefore, the separation of the closest pair of dots in a subpattern did not vary with *s*. The number of subpatterns in each display was four, and in both parts of the experiment, detailed below, subjects had to take into account all of the subpatterns in the display for efficient performance in the task. (The locations of the perturbed subpatterns were randomized.) The number of subpatterns, sufficient to raise pattern-discrimination threshold well above that for conventional spatial acuity, was determined in preliminary experiments (see section 7 for further details). Note that the present experiments are fundamentally different from previous studies on vernier acuity and hyperacuity in which simple arrangements of points and lines were also used (Beck & Schwartz, 1979; Ludvigh, 1953; Westheimer & McKee, 1977).

The rationale of the experiment is as follows. The assignment probability of the proposed attribute value specifying the collinearity of the dots in a subpattern should be maximum when the deformation angle *s* is zero. (Subjects showed no evidence of a nonzero bias.) As *s* increases (or decreases) from this value, the assignment probability of the other attribute value, specifying the noncollinearity of the dots in the subpattern, should increase until it, in turn, reaches its maximum value. If there is no contribution to discrimination performance from any other attribute, the rule stated in the previous section may be applied to give the following prediction. When the reference value *s* of the deformation angle is zero, the discriminability of the perturbed subpatterns should be minimum, and, as *s* increases in magnitude, discriminability should reach a maximum, and then eventually fall again.

Details of the experimental methodology have been described in full elsewhere (Foster, 1979). Stimulus patterns were produced on a display CRT con-

(a)

(b)   (c)

FIG. 16.4. Typical stimulus displays (to scale) for the three-dot subpattern discrimination experiment. The total extent of each display in a, b, and c subtended about 1.83° at the eye.

trolled by an on-line computer which also recorded subjects' responses. Each stimulus presentation interval lasted 80 msec. The experiment was divided into two parts. In part (i), subjects performed a two-interval forced-choice "same-different" discrimination. In each trial, one presentation interval contained a pair of oppositely perturbed subpatterns, one on each side of the field (parameter values $s - \Delta s$ and $s + \Delta s$), along with a pair of identical "dummy" unperturbed subpatterns, one on each side, as in Fig. 16.4a; the other interval contained identical unperturbed subpatterns on each side of the field as in Fig. 16.4b. (The dummy subpatterns were introduced so that the number of stimuli to which subjects had to attend was raised to the required number, as explained above.) The two pattern presentations were separated by a 1.5-sec blank field, the duration of which was too great for apparent motion effects to occur. For any one subject, the magnitude of the angular increment Δs was fixed at either 14° or 18°, so that mean level of correct responses fell about midway between chance and perfect performance. Subjects were required to indicate in each trial the presentation interval in which the subpatterns on the left of the display differed from those on the right. Subjects maintained central fixation throughout the presentation period. (Subpattern positions, orientations, deformation angles, and the ordering of the "same-different" intervals were randomized and balanced over runs.) Neither in this nor in any of the subsequent discrimination experiments were stimuli described to the subject by the experimenter using categorical terms related to the values of the specified discrete attribute.

Figure 16.5a shows the results of this part (i) of the experiment. The discriminability of perturbed subpatterns from unperturbed subpatterns, specified by the index d', is plotted as a function of the reference value s of the transformation parameter about which the increments $\pm\Delta s$ were made. Clearly, the dependence of d' on s has the predicted shape. There is a minimum in performance at $s = 0°$, a maximum each side of this position, and a fall-off at extreme values of s. (There were no significant subpattern orientation effects; Foster, 1979.)

The proposed theoretical scheme does not, however, provide the only possible interpretation of these results. For example, subjects may have employed a discrimination strategy in which they attended only to the strongly noncollinear subpatterns in a display. Because each "different" display had on each side both perturbed and unperturbed subpatterns, with different reference values s (see Fig. 16.4a), such a strategy could have reduced performance to chance levels when the reference value s was zero for the perturbed subpatterns. Alternatively, subjects may have interpreted the terms "same" and "different" used in the description of the task in some special way that resulted in a spurious variation in discrimination performance with s. It is also possible that the reduced discriminability of the perturbed subpatterns which occurs when s is zero is a consequence of a general failure to distinguish mirror images.

Part (ii) of the experiment was designed to resolve these issues. Subjects were now informed of the nature of the perturbations in the subpatterns, and no

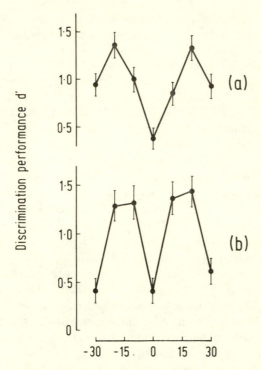

FIG. 16.5.   Performance in discriminating dot subpatterns. The discrimination index d' is shown as a function of reference value s of the transformation parameter. The vertical bars indicate ±1 standard error of the mean. Data are pooled over four subjects. Performances in a and b refer to different versions of the experiment (see text).

dummy unperturbed subpatterns were used in the displays. Subjects performed a highly specific two-alternative forced-choice task involving the reporting of the *direction* of pattern perturbation. (Mirror image confusion was examined in a separate control experiment, described later.) Each trial entailed the presentation of a single display consisting of four vertically oriented subpatterns, as in Fig. 16.4c, in which one subpattern had transformation parameter value $s + \Delta s$, and the other three identical subpatterns each had transformation parameter value $s - \Delta s$. Subjects were required to indicate the direction ("left" or "right") of perturbation of the "odd" subpattern relative to the other subpatterns. (Location of the odd subpattern, direction of its perturbation, and deformation angle were again randomized and balanced over runs.) For the results reported here, the magnitude of the increment Δs was fixed at 10° for each subject.

Figure 16.5b shows the results of this part (ii) of the experiment. The dependence of discrimination performance on the reference value s of the transformation parameter has the same form as in Fig. 16.5a, that is, a central minimum and a maximum each side. Although there are some differences between the two sets of data, the agreement in shape is good in view of the different design of the two experiments. To dispose of the possibility that the minimum at $s=0°$ is an artifact of mirror-image confusion, part (ii) of the experiment was repeated with discrimination performance determined at smaller intervals on the s axis. The previous scale for the parameter s is too coarse to show whether, as would be expected from the proposed scheme, discrimination performance is low for small nonzero values of s for which the subpatterns are *not* mirror images. This control experiment established that performance does indeed decrease when s is made sufficiently small but nonzero. Mirror-image confusion, if it exists here, appears not to be an important factor in determining the shape of the discrimination characteristics (for further details, see Foster, 1979).

There is one other possible interpretation of these results which is critical to the testing of the proposed investigatory technique, namely that, contrary to assumption, the scale for the parameter s is such that there is a contribution to discrimination performance by some continuous subpattern attribute that not only is not constant with s but actually determines the observed characteristics. This interpretation may be regarded as a special case of the alternative view of internal representations and their internal comparison mentioned in the introduction to this chapter. For unstructured pointillistic internal representations, it would not, however, be sufficient to have a single continuous monotonic function of dot separation to measure the deformation of the subpatterns. This is because the selected family of transformations T_s produces a monotonic variation in the separation of one dot from another as s increases or decreases from zero. On such a basis, discrimination performance should show a similar monotonic dependence on s, which has not been observed here. To achieve a measure of discriminability that does vary suitably with s, it is necessary to have at least two continuous functions that depend monotonically on the deformation of the subpattern (Foster, 1979). To determine whether there is a significant contribution to discrimination performance from such hypothesized continuous measures, a further control experiment was performed in which the size (as opposed to the shape) of the subpatterns was varied. Each subpattern was perturbed by increasing or decreasing its size about "reference" values of a size parameter in such a way that the linear displacements of the dots induced by increments in this parameter were equal to the largest of the displacements that occurred in part (i) of the experiment. It was reasoned that if the variation in discrimination performance found with angular deformation were the result of some combination of continuous functions acting over a range of subpattern extents, then one might expect an analogous variation in discrimination performance in the control experiment. Certainly, if the hypothesized continuous measures were sufficiently sensitive to register the displacements of the dots in parts (i) and (ii) of the experiment, they should be sufficiently sensitive to register the displacements in this control. Discrimination performance was, in fact, found not to vary significantly from chance levels for subpattern sizes encompassing those used in the main experiment. Evidently, the displacements of the dots in the subpatterns do not provide an adequate basis for discrimination unless those displacements are organized to constitute a discrete change in the shape of the subpattern.

Given that a discrete attribute designating collinearity or noncollinearity is indeed part of the internal representation of the dot subpatterns, and from the studies cited at the beginning of this section this seems plausible, the results of this experiment appear to provide support for the qualitative features of the proposed investigatory technique. The particular values of the transformation parameter s at which maxima and minima in discrimination performance occur then provide specific data concerning the characteristics of this attribute. Thus, the assignment probability of the attribute value specifying noncollinearity approaches a maximum when the angular deformation reaches about 30°. Between 10° and 20° angular deformation, the assignment probability of this attribute value and the complementary attribute value specifying collinearity are changing most rapidly. It should perhaps be noted that these critical values of the deformation angle are special to the size of the subpatterns, and their distribution in the field. What happens when the number of subpatterns in the field is reduced is discussed in section 7.

6. AN ATTRIBUTE DESIGNATING THE ACUTENESS OR OBTUSENESS OF AN ANGLE BETWEEN TWO LINES

This experiment explores the possibility that in the internal representation of patterns consisting of connected lines there is a discrete attribute that designates whether the angle between two lines is acute or obtuse. From acuity studies concerned with the smallest detectable change in angle it has been shown that visual threshold for angle change increases smoothly and monotonically with angle, providing that the lines comprising the figure are not close to the vertical or horizontal (Hakiel, 1978). Within the present framework, such angular discrimination would be interpreted as being determined by continuous attributes. But, as Goldmeier (1936), Olson & Attneave (1970), and Rock (1973) have

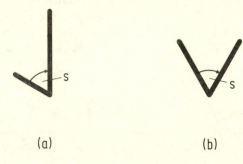

(a)   (b)

FIG. 16.6.   Chevron subpatterns: a asymmetric and b symmetric. The deformation of the subpatterns is specified by the parameter s shown.

FIG. 16.7. Typical stimulus displays (to scale) for the chevron subpattern discrimination experiment. The total extent of each display in a and b subtended about 1.8° at the eye.

(a)   (b)

shown, the orthogonal nature of the angle between two perpendicular lines and departures from orthogonality are most evident when the lines are close to "preferred or singular spatial directions." These directions are usually the environmental vertical and horizontal. It is obviously important not to confound this sensitivity to orthogonality with the general improvement in angular acuity associated with vertical and horizontal axes (Hakiel, 1978; Onley & Volkmann, 1958; Rochlin, 1955; Weene & Held, 1966). By giving several stimulus figures a common alignment, one can, however, define preferred spatial directions other than the vertical and horizontal (Attneave, 1968).

These factors were taken into account in the design of the present experiment, which was performed in two parts with different types of stimuli. Figures 16.6a and b show the two kinds of subpattern used, namely asymmetric and symmetric chevrons. For both subpatterns, the action of the family of transformations T_s is specified by the angle s indicated. Note that the distance moved by each arm due to increments $\pm\Delta s$ in s is constant with s. Figures 16.7a and b show how these subpatterns are arranged in the field. In each of these two figures, one of the chevrons has transformation parameter value $s+\Delta s$ and the other three each have transformation parameter value $s-\Delta s$. The supposed preferred spatial direction is defined in Fig. 16.7a by the common direction of the long arms of the asymmetric chevrons, and in Fig. 16.7b by the common direction of the bisectors of the symmetric chevrons. These preferred directions are not interchangeable: the directions of the bisectors of the asymmetric chevrons are not all the same in Fig. 16.7a, and the directions of one or other of the sides of the symmetric chevrons are not all the same in Fig. 16.7b. In each of the two types of display, the preferred direction is selected from a range of angles starting at 22.5° to the vertical, and increasing by 45° steps up to 337.5°. With this range, the preferred direction does not coincide with the vertical, horizontal, or 45° oblique.

In each part of the experiment with the asymmetric or symmetric chevrons, the task of the subject was to detect the location of the "odd" chevron. Because the preferred spatial direction in Fig. 16.7b does *not* coincide with the arms of the chevrons, and because in Fig. 16.7a it *does,* it is hypothesized on the basis of the observations made earlier that the internal representations of the chevrons in Fig. 16.7b have only continuous angle attributes, whereas the internal representations of the chevrons in Fig. 16.7a have continuous angle attributes and a discrete attribute designating acuteness or obtuseness. If this hypothesis is correct, one should expect from the arguments in section 4, a local maximum in discrimination performance when the reference value s is 90° for the asymmetric chevrons, and no such local maximum for the symmetric chevrons. Note that although we have not assumed that the scale for the transformation parameter is such that the putative continuous attributes give a constant contribution to discrimination performance (see section 4), we have assumed that this contribution varies sufficiently smoothly and slowly with s that it does not mask the contribution of the hypothesized discrete attribute. This assumption of the way in which the continuous attributes should vary with s is supported by the angle-acuity data obtained by Hakiel (1978) mentioned earlier.

The methods for this experiment were similar to those for the previous experiment with the dot-pattern stimuli. In the present case, subjects were required to

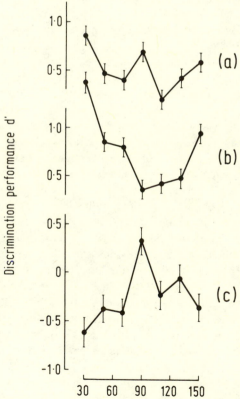

FIG. 16.8.   Performance in discriminating chevron subpatterns. The discrimination index d' is shown as a function of the reference value s of the transformation parameter. The vertical bars indicate ±1 standard error of the mean. Data are pooled over four subjects. Performance in a refers to the asymmetric chevrons, in b to the symmetric chevrons, and in c to the difference of a and b.

indicate the quadrant in which the odd subpattern appeared. Central fixation was maintained as before. The magnitude of the angular increment Δs was fixed at $10°$ for all subjects. The results are shown in Figs. 16.8a and b. The variation in discrimination performance d' for the asymmetric and symmetric chevrons, respectively, is plotted against the reference angle s about which the increments $\pm\Delta s$ were made. For both types of chevron, there is a relatively high performance at extreme values of s. There is a marked difference, however, in performance around the point $s=90°$: there is a peak in d' values in this region for the asymmetric chevrons, and none for the symmetric chevrons. (For further analysis, see Foster 1980b.)

These results are consistent with the predictions put forward above. Significantly, outside the critical region about $s = 90°$, discrimination performance for the asymmetric and symmetric chevrons is similar: each shows a monotonic increase as s moves towards the ends of its range. If the putative continuous attributes determining these performances were the same for the two types of figure, then one might estimate the net contribution of the hypothesized discrete attribute to discrimination performance by subtracting the performance shown in Fig. 16.8b from that shown in Fig. 16.8a. The result of this operation is shown in Fig. 16.8c. The maximum at $s=90°$ is well defined, but the fact that there are negative values of the index d' suggests that there may be an overall shift in the level of contribution from continuous attributes for which some compensation should be made.

The existence of a discrete attribute designating just two angle properties, namely acuteness and obtuseness, does not preclude the possibility of a third angle property, namely orthogonality, being effective under suitable conditions. The stimuli of the present study involved only the first two angle properties: none of the displays required the discrimination of an orthogonal chevron from a nonorthogonal chevron.

7. GENERAL APPLICATION OF THE PATTERN PERTURBATION TECHNIQUE

In the derivation of the rule relating discrimination performance to assignment probabilities of attribute values (section 4), it was assumed that the scale of the pattern transformation parameter s could be chosen so that the contribution to discrimination performance of continuous attributes did not vary with s. In practice, it may not be obvious *a priori* how this constancy should be established. The two experimental applications described in the preceding sections circumvented the problem in different ways. In the first experiment (section 5), concerned with a putative discrete attribute designating collinearity or noncollinearity, the contribution of possible continuous attributes to discrimination performance was assumed to be zero, and this assumption was supported by a subsequent control measurement. In the second experiment (section 6), concerned with a hypothesized discrete attribute designating angle acuteness or obtuseness, it was not assumed that the contribution of continuous attributes to discrimination performance was zero (or merely constant with the parameter s). Instead, the weaker assumption was made that the contribution of continuous attributes varied smoothly and slowly with s relative to the contribution of the hypothesized discrete attribute. In the event, this assumption appeared justified, and by computing the differenced discrimination performance for the two types of chevron stimuli, only one of which was supposed to produce the discrete angle attribute, one could make an estimate of the net contribution of that attribute to discrimination performance.

Alternatively, given the possibility that the contribution of continuous attributes to discrimination performance may be estimated experimentally, as was done for the chevron stimuli, one can test a range of magnitudes of the increment Δs at each value of s, and, by the construction of psychometric functions, arrive at a scale for the transformation parameter s that is uniform with respect to the contributions of continuous attributes. Provided that the contribution of a selected discrete attribute to discrimination performance is not affected by the presence of "uncorrected" contributions from continuous attributes, the above differencing procedure, with a non-uniform scale for s, may be more efficient.

It was noted in section 5 that in the experiment on collinearity–noncollinearity there was good qualitative agreement in the dependence of discrimination performance on transformation parameter in the two parts of the experiment. Each part involved the presentation of displays with four subpatterns in the field. As indicated earlier, when the number of subpatterns was reduced, performance increased markedly. For example, in a replication of the first part of the collinearity-noncollinearity experiment, with just two subpatterns in the field, reliable, smoothly varying discrimination performance over the whole of the parameter range was obtained when the magnitude of the increment Δs was reduced to one quarter the value used in the four subpatterns case. This improvement in performance is consistent with the assumption made in section 4 concerning the existence of a limited pattern-encoding capacity of the visual system. If there were indeed such a limit, then fewer subpatterns in the field would permit more faithful internal representations of each to be established, with attribute values assigned from more finely distributed ranges using more narrowly tuned probability functions. The supposed changeover from discrimination performance determined by "coarse" discrete attributes to that determined by "fine" continuous attributes may be related to the observations by Beck (Beck, 1972; Beck & Ambler, 1972, 1973) concerning some of the differences evident in "distributed" and "focal" attention. Beck suggested that when attention is distributed over a large area, the visual system is preferentially sensitive to simple variables such as the slopes of lines (vertical, horizontal, and 45° oblique), whereas, when attention is focused, there is an increased sensitivity to how lines are arranged in relation to each other. Although the technique proposed here is in principle capable of analyzing the discrete attributes of internal representations produced in focal attention, the separation of these attributes from continuous attributes is likely to be easier when internal representations result from distributed attention.

8. RELATIONSHIP TO EXPERIMENTS ON CATEGORICAL IDENTIFICATION AND DISCRIMINATION

As mentioned in the introduction, there is an analogy between the approach of the present study and that of some experiments in auditory perception concerned with the discriminability of stimuli that may be classified categorically (for reviews see Macmillan, Kaplan, & Creelman, 1977 and Massaro, 1976). Most of these experiments have concentrated on determining to what extent discrimination performance can be predicted or explained in terms of categorically identified quantities when the stimulus is varied along an appropriate continuum. There are fundamental differences, however, between the present approach and these auditory studies. In the latter, the categorical quantities (here actually corresponding to discrete-attribute values) are usually evident *a priori*, and in many cases constitute the salient properties of the auditory stimulus. In the present approach, it is seen that (a) the "categorization" is, in general, only partial, in that both discrete and continuous attributes are assumed to operate, as in the chevron-discrimination experiment (compare Pisoni & Lazarus, 1974); (b) the nature of the discrete attributes may be apparent only after the discrimination experiment has been performed; and (c) the presence of a discrete attribute in the representation may not be necessary for the generation of a reliable categorical labelling of the stimulus in terms of the values of that attribute. To illustrate the last point, in a replication of the chevron-discrimination experiment (section 6) in which subjects were asked to report whether the indicated chevron was acute or obtuse, it was found that identification performance was significantly better than chance for the 80° and 100° symmetric chevrons. There is, presumably, adequate information available in the continuous attributes produced by the symmetric chevrons to enable a reliable categorical labelling to be computed, although such information is apparently not available early enough to assist performance in the pure discrimination task.

An informal result related to the issue of stimulus identification concerns the appearance of the subpatterns used both in the three-dot-discrimination experiment (section 5) and in the chevron-discrimination experiment (section 6). In part (ii) of the first experiment and in both parts of the second, three out of four subpatterns in each display were identical. Nevertheless, subjects reported that frequently *all* of the subpatterns in a display appeared different. The notion of internal representations being constructed in a probabilistic fashion is evidently compatible with this observation.

9. SUMMARY

The approach to the analysis of internal visual pattern representations outlined in this chapter incorporates three basic assumptions:

1. Internal representations contain discrete pattern attributes.
2. The construction of internal representations is a probabilistic process.
3. The visual discriminability of patterns is determined by the differences in probabilities governing the construction of the representations produced by each pattern.

On the basis of these assumptions, a technique for the investigation of the discrete attributes in internal representations has been proposed. The technique makes use of a group of spatial transformations, smoothly parameterized by a single variable s, to generate a continuum of patterns. The visual discriminability of patterns perturbed in shape as a result of fixed increments $\pm \Delta s$ in s is measured as a function of s. Provided certain conditions are satisfied, the variations with s in the probabilities describing the assignment of values to a discrete attribute may be related simply to the characteristics of the discrimination performance. Thus, where assignment probabilities are maximum, discrimination performance should be minimum, and where assignment probabilities are changing most rapidly, discrimination performance should be maximum.

The experimental applications that were described concerned two putative discrete attributes, the one designating the collinearity or noncollinearity of points in a pattern, the other designating the acuteness or obtuseness of the angle between two lines. The characteristics of the discrimination performance obtained have been shown to be consistent with the predictions of the proposed technique.

APPENDIX

Let T_s be a family of spatial transformations, smoothly parameterized by a single variable s. Let the range of s be some interval I containing zero. The action of T_s on a pattern A is denoted by $T_s(A)$. The family T_s is said to be a *local 1-parameter group of smooth transformations* acting on A if the following conditions are satisfied.

1. The transformed pattern $T_s(A)$ depends smoothly on s and A.
2. For each s in I, the transformation T_s is smooth and has a smooth inverse.
3. If s_1, s_2, $s_1 + s_2$ are in I, then

$$T_{s_1}(T_{s_2}(A)) = T_{s_1 + s_2}(A).$$

4. When s is zero, $T_s(A) = A$.

A more formal definition is given in Foster (1978a, 1980b). For the present applications, the family of transformations T_s should satisfy the first three conditions; the fourth condition is not important, and in practice the range of s may be made all positive (or all negative).

REFERENCES

Aiken, L. S., & Brown, D. R. A feature utilization analysis of the perception of pattern class structure. *Perception and Psychophysics*, 1971, *9*, 279-283.

Andrews, D. P., Butcher, A. K., & Buckley, B. R. Acuities for spatial arrangement in line figures: Human and ideal observers compared. *Vision Research*, 1973, *13*, 599-620.

Attneave, F. Triangles as ambiguous figures. *American Journal of Psychology*, 1968, *81*, 447-453.

Barlow, H. B., Narasimhan, R., & Rosenfeld, A. Visual pattern analysis in machines and animals. *Science*, 1972, *177*, 567-575.

Beck, J. Similarity grouping and peripheral discriminability under uncertainty. *American Journal of Psychology*, 1972, *85*, 1-19.

Beck, J., & Ambler, B. Discriminability of differences in line slope and in line arrangement as a function of mask delay. *Perception and Psychophysics*, 1972, *12*, 33-38.

Beck, J., & Ambler, B. The effects of concentrated and distributed attention on peripheral acuity. *Perception and Psychophysics*, 1973, *14*, 225-230.

Beck, J., & Schwartz, T. Vernier acuity with dot test objects. *Vision Research*, 1979, *19*, 313-319.

Blesser, B., Shillman, R., Cox, C., Kuklinski, T., Ventura, J., & Eden, M. Character recognition based on phenomenological attributes. *Visible Language*, 1973, *7*, 209-223.

Bouma, H., & Andriessen, J. J. Perceived orientation of isolated line segments. *Vision Research*, 1968, *8*, 493-507.

Caelli, T. M., & Umansky, J. Interpolation in the visual system. *Vision Research*, 1976, *16*, 1055-1060.

Cutting, J. E., & Rosner, B. S. Categories and boundaries in speech and music. *Perception and Psychophysics*, 1974, *16*, 564-570.

Durlach, N. I., & Braida, L. D. Intensity perception. I. Preliminary theory of intensity resolution. *Journal of the Acoustical Society of America*, 1969, *46*, 372-383.

Foster, D. H. An approach to the analysis of the underlying structure of visual space using a generalized notion of visual pattern recognition. *Biological Cybernetics*, 1975, *17*, 77-79.

Foster, D. H. Visual apparent motion and the calculus of variations. In E.L.J. Leeuwenberg & H.F.J.M. Buffart (Eds.), *Formal theories of visual perception* Chichester: Wiley, 1978. (a)

Foster, D. H. Visual comparison of random-dot patterns: Evidence concerning a fixed visual association between features and feature-relations. *Quarterly Journal of Experimental Psychology*, 1978, *30*, 637-654. (b)

Foster, D. H. Discrete internal pattern representations and visual detection of small changes in pattern shape. *Perception and Psychophysics*, 1979, *26*, 459-468.

Foster, D. H. A description of discrete internal representation schemes for visual pattern discrimination. *Biological Cybernetics*, 1980, *38*, 151-157. (a)

Foster, D. H. A spatial perturbation technique for the investigation of discrete internal representations of visual patterns. *Biological Cybernetics*, 1980, *38*, 159-169. (b)

Foster, D. H., & Mason, R. J. Transformation and relational-structure schemes for visual pattern recognition: Two models tested experimentally with rotated random-dot patterns. *Biological Cybernetics*, 1979, *32*, 85-93.

Gibson, E. J. *Principles of perceptual learning and development*. New York: Appleton-Century-Crofts, 1969.

Goldmeier, E. Über Ähnlichkeit bei gesehenen Figuren. *Psychologische Forschung*, 1936, *21*, 146–208. Translation by E. Goldmeier. Similarity in visually perceived forms. *Psychological Issues*, 1972, *8*, Monograph 29, 1–135.

Green, D. M., & Swets, J. A. *Signal detection theory and psychophysics*. New York: Wiley, 1966.

Hakiel, S. R. *Variable and constant errors in perceived angle size*. Unpublished doctoral dissertation, University of Keele, Keele, Staffordshire, 1978.

Hoffman, W. C. Higher visual perception as prolongation of the basic Lie transformation group. *Mathematical Biosciences*, 1970, *6*, 437–471.

Kahn, J. I., & Foster, D. H. Visual comparison of rotated and reflected random-dot patterns as a function of their positional symmetry and separation in the field. *Quarterly Journal of Experimental Psychology*, 1981, *33A*, 155–166.

Liberman, A. M., Cooper, F. S., Shankweiler, D. P., & Studdert-Kennedy, M. Perception of the speech code. *Psychological Review*, 1967, *74*, 431–461.

Liberman, A. M., Harris, K. S., Hoffman, H. S., & Griffith, B. C. The discrimination of speech sounds within and across phoneme boundaries. *Journal of Experimental Psychology*, 1957, *54*, 358–368.

Liberman, A. M., Harris, K. S., Kinney, J. A., & Lane, H. The discrimination of relative onset-time of the components of certain speech and nonspeech patterns. *Journal of Experimental Psychology*, 1961, *61*, 379–388.

Ludvigh, E. Direction sense of the eye. *American Journal of Ophthalmology*, 1953, *36*, 139–143.

Macmillan, N. A., Kaplan, H. L., & Creelman, C. D. The psychophysics of categorical perception. *Psychological Review*, 1977, *84*, 452–471.

Marko, H. Space distortion and decomposition theory. A new approach to pattern recognition by vision. *Kybernetik*, 1973, *13*, 132–143.

Massaro, D. W. Auditory information processing. In W. K. Estes (Ed.), *Handbook of learning and cognitive processes IV*. Hillsdale, N. J.: Lawrence Erlbaum Associates, 1976.

Mavrides, C. M., & Brown, D. R. Discrimination and reproduction of patterns: Feature measures and constraint redundancy as predictors. *Perception and Psychophysics*, 1969, *6*, 276–280.

Naus, M. J., & Shillman, R. J. Why a Y is not a V: A new look at the distinctive features of letters. *Journal of Experimental Psychology: Human Perception and Performance*, 1976, *2*, 394–400.

Olson, R. K., & Attneave, F. What variables produce similarity grouping? *American Journal of Psychology*, 1970, *83*, 1–21.

Onley, J. W., & Volkmann, J. The visual perception of prependicularity. *American Journal of Psychology*, 1958, *71*, 504–516.

Pisoni, D. B., & Lazarus, J. H. Categorical and noncategorical modes of speech perception along the voicing continuum. *Journal of the Acoustical Society of America*, 1974, *55*, 328–333.

Pitts, W., & McCulloch, W. S. How we know universals. The perception of auditory and visual forms. *Bulletin of Mathematical Biophysics*, 1947, *9*, 127–147.

Prinzmetal, W., & Banks, W. P. Good continuation affects visual detection. *Perception and Psychophysics*, 1977, *21*, 389–395.

Prytulak, L. S. Good continuation revisited. *Journal of Experimental Psychology*, 1974, *102*, 773–777.

Reed, S. K. *Psychological processes in pattern recognition*. New York: Academic Press, 1973.

Rochlin, A. M. The effect of tilt on the visual perception of parallelness. *American Journal of Psychology*, 1955, *68*, 223–236.

Rock, I. *Orientation and form*. New York: Academic Press, 1973.

Rosenfeld, A. *Picture processing by computer*. New York: Academic Press, 1969.

Rumelhart, D. E. *A multicomponent theory of confusion among briefly exposed alphabetic characters*. (Technical Report 22.) San Diego: University of California, Center for Human Information Processing, 1971.

Shepard, R. N. Psychophysical complementarity. In M. Kubovy & J. R. Pomerantz (Eds.), *Perceptual organization*. Hillsdale, N.J.: Lawrence Erlbaum Associates, 1981.

Stevens, K. N., & House, A. S. Speech perception. In J. V. Tobias (Ed.), *Foundations of modern auditory theory II*. New York: Academic Press, 1972.

Sutherland, N. S. Outlines of a theory of visual pattern recognition in animals and man. *Proceedings of the Royal Society Series B.*, 1968, *171*, 297–317.

Sutherland, N. S. Object recognition. In E. C. Carterette & M. P. Friedman (Eds.), *Handbook of perception III*. New York: Academic Press, 1973.

Swets, J. A. The relative operating characteristic in psychology. *Science*, 1973, *182*, 990–1000.

Uttal, W. R. The effect of deviations from linearity on the detection of dotted line patterns. *Vision Research*, 1973, *13*, 2155–2163.

Weene, P., & Held, R. Changes in perceived size of angle as a function of orientation in the frontal plane. *Journal of Experimental Psychology*, 1966, *71*, 55–59.

Wertheimer, M. Untersuchungen zur Lehre von der Gestalt. II. *Psychologische Forschung*, 1923, *4*, 301–350.

Westheimer, G., & McKee, S. P. Spatial configurations for visual hyperacuity. *Vision Research*, 1977, *17*, 941–947.

17

The Two Modes of Processing Concept and Some Implications

Herschel W. Leibowitz
Robert B. Post*
Pennsylvania State University

INTRODUCTION

The first hundred years in the history of modern psychology have resulted in the development of a number of theories. In particular, the study of perception has been enriched by theoretical formulations, such as those of the Gestalt psychologists and of J. J. Gibson, which have played such an important role in the conference. More recently, we have been introduced to sophisticated information processing models and to the spatial frequency analysis of visual scenes.

There are many advantages to theoretical points of view. One advantage is to suggest new and different ways to look at phenomena. Even though the scope of a given theory may be limited, it suggests new "mental sets" and unique ways of approaching interesting observations.

The purpose of the present paper is to discuss a recent theoretical position that has stimulated novel analyses and interpretations of surprisingly diverse findings. The "two-visual systems" concept of concern here originated with Gerald Schneider's dissertation at M.I.T. in the early 1960s in which he discovered that object recognition and spatial orientation can be selectively impaired in the hamster by lesions of the cortex or the superior colliculus. In 1967 Schneider, along with Richard Held, Colwyn Trevarthen, and David Ingle, presented a symposium at the Eastern Psychological Association meeting where they described experiments, including studies on humans, which they interpreted in terms of the two systems concept (Held, 1968; Ingle, 1967; Schneider, 1967; Trevarthen, 1968). For anyone interested in the history and early development of this problem, these works represent a prime literature source.

---

*Now at the Department of Opthalmology, University of California, Davis.

Although the concept of two systems is derived from selective ablation studies and much of the literature has a strong anatomical flavor, the present treatment deliberately deemphasizes anatomy. This is of course not meant to minimize the ultimate importance of neurophysiology, however. Because the nervous system is much more complex in humans than in the hamster and our concern is primarily with perception and behavior in humans, it seems appropriate to follow Held's suggestion and to speak of "two modes of processing spatially distributed information" (Held, 1970).

The two modes of processing concept can best be described in functional terms. It posits two independent and dissociable modes of processing: (1) a "focal" mode that is in general concerned with the question of "what" and subserves object recognition and identification; (2) an "ambient" mode concerned with the question of "where" which mediates spatial orientation, locomotion, and posture.

In the original formulation of the two systems or modes of processing, reference was made to two *visual* systems, but this must be modified. Although visual information is adequate for the focal mode, the ambient mode involves the coordination of motor activity with the visual, vestibular, auditory and somatosensory systems, particularly, kinesthesis. In the discussion that follows, examples of the diverse basis of the ambient mode and the importance of interaction among its various components are described.

A number of distinctions can be made between these two modes of processing.

1. *Retinal Location.*   Focal vision involves primarily the central visual field. Although object recognition is possible in the periphery, this function is most efficient in the central field. Conversely, the visual contribution to the ambient system is mediated by the entire visual field. The discrimination of small spatial displacements which may be considered a localization function is superior in the central visual field, but others such as the sensation of self-motion or vection, which requires stimulation of large retinal areas, necessarily involve the periphery (Dichgans & Brandt, 1978).

2. *Awareness.*   Focal functions are typically well represented in consciousness whereas ambient functions often operate in the absence of awareness or with marginal conscious concomitants. This is not meant to imply that we cannot be aware of ambient functions, for example, by directing attention to their motoric consequences. Under everyday conditions, however, ambient functions are adequate without attentional effort.

3. *Luminance.*   Most classical visual functions such as acuity, intensity and stereoscopic depth discrimination, critical flicker frequency, and so on are very sensitive to luminance. Below about 1–10 cd/m² a systematic decrease in effi-

ciency is observed as luminance is lowered (Graham, 1965). In comparison, orientation functions such as localization of single points of light, vection, and nystagmus appear to follow an "all or none" principle (Grüttner, 1939; Leibowitz, Myers & Grant, 1955; Leibowitz, Shupert-Rodemer, & Dichgans, 1979). If stimuli are visible, orientation responses are adequately activated. A stimulus at scotopic threshold can be localized as well as one which is presented at high photopic luminance levels.

4. *Refractive Error.*   Focal vision is also extremely sensitive to the quality of the retinal image. Typically, focal functions such as reading are degraded noticeably by even a 0.25 diopter refractive error and an uncorrected error of 2.5-3.0 diopters corresponds to legal blindness in the United States (Borish, 1970). Conversely, ambient functions operate at maximum efficiency as long as a minimal pattern is visible. Uncorrected refractive errors as large as those which correspond to legal blindness have no effect on roll or circular vection (Leibowitz, Shupert-Rodemer, & Dichgans, 1979), radial localization of stimuli (Post & Leibowitz, 1980), or nystagmus (Post, Dichgans, Shupert, & Leibowitz, in preparation).

5. *Spatial Frequency.*   The differential effects of variables such as luminance, refractive error, and retinal location suggest that an underlying distinction between focal and ambient vision is in terms of the required spatial frequency content of the stimulus. Whereas blur (Regan, Silver, & Murray, 1977) and lowered luminance degrade the resolution of high frequencies, these same variables have little effect on the resolution of low frequency stimuli. It would appear therefore that whereas low frequencies are sufficient for ambient function, higher frequencies are necessary for focal discriminations. The contributions of different retinal areas to the two modes of processing are consistent with this analysis. The peripheral retina is incapable of mediating fine visual detail (i.e., is limited to processing low frequency information) and therefore contributes primarily to ambient rather than focal vision.

6. *Optical Rearrangement.*   Held (1970) has pointed out that while wearing prisms ambient functions such as eye-head coordination adapt readily but distortions of perceived shape persist.

DISSOCIATION

A simple demonstration of the dissociability of object recognition and orientation is illustrated by the ease with which one can walk while simultaneously reading. Although attention is concentrated on the reading material, locomotion and avoidance of large obstacles are readily accomplished. During simultaneous

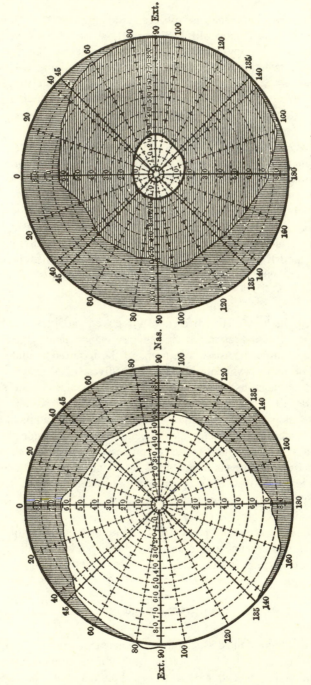

FIG. 17.1. Left: a normal visual field. Right: the constricted visual field of an hysterical patient (after Janet, 1907).

346

walking and reading, one is unaware of the role of vision in orientation, yet the process proceeds smoothly and with confidence.[1]

Experimental evidence for dissociation is also strongly suggested by a number of studies involving brain damage in humans. These tend to reflect the theme established in the work of Schneider and others that with severe damage to the geniculo-striate projections the ability to orient to stimuli is preserved.[2] In patients with cortical damage resulting in hemianopia or the inability to see in one-half of the visual field, several researchers have reported that a residual capacity for orienting is present (Perenin & Jeannerod, 1975, 1978; Pöppel, Held & Frost, 1973; Weiskrantz, Warrington, Sanders, & Marshall, 1974). This has been demonstrated by having subjects orient to where a stimulus (although unseen) might have been presented. The seemingly paradoxical nature of this ability has led Weiskrantz to refer to it as "blindsight." Additionally, lesions that result in massive deficits in form recognition have been found to leave the orientation reflexes and sensation of self-motion induced by large moving stimuli intact[3] (Leibowitz & Dichgans, 1977).

IMPLICATIONS FOR EVALUATION OF VISION

It follows from the two modes of processing concept and reports of dissociation in brain damage that evaluation of vision must be directed at *both* focal and ambient functions. The problem is that traditional clinical perimetry, which is invaluable for some purposes such as diagnosis of macular disease, does not assess orientation functions and therefore does not evaluate ambient vision.

Figure 17.1 presents an early report of narrowing of the visual field in an hysterical patient observed by Janet (1907). The left diagram presents a normal visual field and the right the patient's field during spontaneous narrowing. If one were to accept the implications of these results it would follow that this patient suffered from a serious visual deficit. Indeed, if such narrowing were caused by retinal disease, the behavior of the patient would be severely altered. In order to compensate for the loss of peripheral vision, patients with retinal pathology typically make additional eye and head movements and locomote in a characteristically slow and halting manner. As Janet has pointed out, however, the implications of classical perimetry in this case were misleading. This particular patient was able to "play very cleverly at ball" in the courtyard of the Salpêtrière

---

[1]The unconscious role of vision in walking is demonstrated by the lack of confidence when walking with the eyes closed.

[2]Sprague (1966) has demonstrated that localization after cortical ablation is also possible in cats but only after disconnecting the superior colliculi.

[3]The neural correlates of this phenomenon cannot be precisely specified at this time. In our experience, the majority of cortical scotoma patients do not demonstrate the ability to localize static stimuli.

Hospital. This behavior is typical of the observation that hysterical patients with narrowed visual fields do not seem to suffer orientation defects (Eszenyi, 1928). Janet concluded that normal visually guided behavior by hysterics with narrowed fields represents an example of "unconscious residual visual function." In the terms of the two modes of processing concept, Janet's "unconscious vision" may be attributed to ambient visual function to which classical clinical perimetry is not sensitive.

It is possible that other forms of visual narrowing which result from physiological causes may have a similar explanation, that is, that narrowing affects only the focal function in the periphery without influencing ambient abilities. This analysis would make biological sense as ambient functions would be preserved during times of stress when they are critically needed. This hypothesis is currently under examination in our laboratory with both psychological and physiological stressors. It is critical both in studies of perception during stress as well as in the clinic that evaluation of vision must include, in addition to a focal measure, some aspect of orientation behavior (Leibowitz, Post, Shupert-Rodemer, Wadlington, & Lundy, 1980; Leibowitz, Post, & Ginsburg, 1980).

PLASTICITY, LEARNING, AND DEVELOPMENT

In accordance with the developmental principle of ontogeny recapitulating phylogeny, Bronson (1974) has characterized the infant as having a relatively more developed ambient than focal system at birth. Although orienting responses are present in neonates, focal capacities such as high spatial frequency sensitivity are absent. The potential value of systematic investigation of ambient and focal functions in development is also suggested by animal studies which indicate differential effects, particularly with respect to recovery, of impoverished environments (Held & Hein, 1963; Mitchell, 1978).

In addition to the relatively late development of focal functions during maturation, these capabilities tend to be, once developed, more sensitive to disruption. Held (1970) has analyzed the effects of wearing distorting lenses in terms of the two modes of processing concept and concluded that orientation is rapidly modifiable through experience whereas form vision shows long lasting deficits under conditions of rearrangement. A striking example of the modifiability of an orientation process concerns the eye movements elicited by vestibular stimulation. The direction of the vestibulo-ocular reflex can be reversed by wearing an optical device which induces a left-right reversal of the visual field (Gonshor & Melvill-Jones, 1976). Similarly, prolonged exposure to optical reversal of the visual field also changes the direction of circular vection in humans (Oman, Bock, & Huang, 1980). Similar but less extreme adaptation of orientation responses may be observed if one's spectacle prescription is changed. Although visual stimuli may be mislocalized at first, there is rapid adaptation to the optical rearrangement introduced by the new prescription.

In contrast with the high degree of plasticity in orientation responses, form vision demonstrates less capacity for adaptation to optical rearrangement. Metamorphopsia resulting from "buckling" of the retina produces an irregular distortion of the retinal image which usually cannot be compensated optically (Duke-Elder, 1966). Because the distortion of perceived shapes shows little adaptation, it is very disruptive to the patient when in central vision. "Treatment" involves blurring the distorted image.

PERCEPTUAL CONSTANCIES

The value of a theory depends in part on the ability of its organizing concepts to summarize data and to suggest experiments. Relevant examples can be related with respect to the classical problems of perceptual constancy. There are many theoretical treatments of interesting and important constancy phenomena (Epstein, 1977), but these are not reviewed here. Rather, within the approach which attempts to identify the stimulus variables subserving different constancies, an analysis in terms of the two modes of processing concept has led to some testable predictions.

Size Constancy.   For unfamiliar objects located at distances beyond which the oculomotor adjustments can play a role, size constancy requires localization of stimuli relative to other detail in the visual field. The dramatic reduction in size constancy with a reduction screen which eliminates stimuli other than the test-object attests to the importance of orientation cues which provide a framework for the organization of visual space (Holway & Boring, 1941). We also know that low frequency stimuli capable of mediating spatial localization are unaltered by refractive error. These considerations led us to conduct a size constancy study in which specific amounts of blur were introduced and the effect on the function relating matched size to stimulus distance was determined (Leibowitz, Wilcox, & Post, 1978). Refractive errors were introduced by viewing through positive lenses, the strength of which was determined by means of a laser optometer to insure that the desired levels of blur were actually present.

The data are presented in Fig. 17.2 as matched size as a function of distance without blur and with 1.5 and 3.0 diopters of blur. It should be noted that the curves are superimposable—the size matching functions are identical for all conditions of the experiment. We interpret these data as evidence for the predominant role played by the relative localization of stimuli in size constancy.

Shape Constancy.   Shape constancy requires approximately 500 milliseconds exposure duration before reaching a maximum value (Leibowitz &

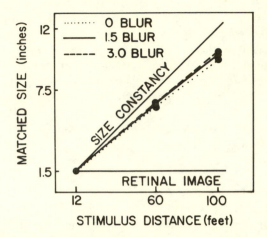

FIG. 17.2. Size matching as a function of distance at various levels of refractive error.

Bourne, 1956). This is particularly surprising because sensory functions which are related to duration of exposure are typically unaffected by presentations longer than the critical duration, that is, about 100 milliseconds (Graham, 1965). Clearly, the dependence of shape constancy on such long exposure durations reflects the operation of processes and mechanisms different from those involved in absolute threshold, localization, differential threshold, and so on. Whereas the impairment of these functions at short durations may be compensated by higher luminance, shape constancy for short exposure durations is not restored by increases in luminance. Because the resolution of high frequency texture gradations and binocular disparities require fine detail and are maximized with longer processing time, it seems reasonable that these processes are involved in shape constancy.

It has been established both psychophysically and by recording of evoked magnetic potentials that although responses to low spatial frequencies require only brief durations of exposure, more time is necessary for higher spatial frequencies (Breitmeyer, 1975; Kaufman & Williamson, 1979). If one views a shape test-object for a short duration, the first spatial frequencies to be processed are assumed to be those at the coarse or low end of the spectrum. These can accurately convey the retinal image shape of the stimulus but are not adequate for shape constancy. Whatever the actual shape of the stimulus, the retinal image shape would be accurately registered even for very brief durations of exposure. With increasing exposure duration, it is assumed that the progressively higher frequencies and disparities are processed which provide the appreciation of the slant of the stimulus object which is necessary for constancy.

The assumed role of high frequency mediated information and binocular disparities in shape constancy is also supported by evidence that two other procedures which eliminate high frequencies or stereopsis destroy shape constancy. Increasing viewing distance systematically reduces the tendency toward shape constancy (Meneghini & Leibowitz, 1967). Increasing distance would of course selectively and progressively eliminate high frequencies and reduce disparities. Similarly, for a stimulus at a constant distance, introduction of refractive error, which affects acuity and stereoacuity, also reduces shape constancy (Fig. 17.3) as does monocular viewing (Epstein & Hatfield, 1978; Meneghini & Leibowitz, 1967).

Thus, three different experimental procedures that share in common the reduction or elimination of high frequency information and stereopsis result in reduction of the tendency toward shape constancy. Other tests are feasible. We know that both acuity and stereoacuity fall off rapidly with increasing peripheral vision. If the assumed role of these factors in shape constancy is correct, off-axis viewing should also reduce the tendency toward shape constancy but not size constancy. Similarly, reduction of luminance should have a greater disruptive effect on shape than on size constancy.

The foregoing discussion was not meant to imply that shape constancy for static stimuli is mediated exclusively by high frequency information and stereopsis. Under appropriate conditions, not including those typical of laboratory studies, low frequency and monocular cues such as motion parallax may also be effective. It does seem heuristic, however, to consider the possibility that the striking dependence of shape constancy on exposure duration and the effects of refractive error and increasing distance all reduce shape constancy because of their effect on the elimination of high frequency components and stereopsis. This hypothesis could conceivably have been developed independent of the two modes of processing concept. It is clear, however, that consideration of perceptual constancies within this framework has some organizational value and has provided some interesting and testable hypotheses.

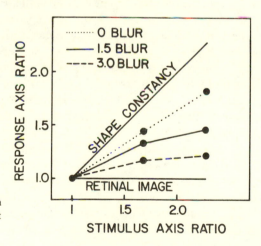

FIG. 17.3. Matched shape as a function of the stimulus-axis ratio at various levels of refractive error.

TRANSPORTATION SAFETY

It is always exciting when a possible solution to a longstanding problem is apparent. Perhaps the most rewarding aspect of the two modes of processing concept is its role in suggesting new ways of approaching phenomena which previously were not well understood. For example, it has been known for decades that automobile drivers do not reduce their driving speeds at night. One does not have to study visual psychophysics to appreciate the fact that visual capacities at night are simply not as good as during daylight. Despite the obvious degradation in visual function, most drivers (including many visual scientists) maintain the same vehicle velocities independent of the ambient illumination. This is even more difficult to understand in view of the fact that it is well known that a disproportionate number of accidents occur after sunset. Perhaps more surprising is that officials who have the responsibility to regulate highway speeds and are aware of the gruesome accident statistics have taken only marginal cognizance of this fact. In the United States very few states have ever posted different maximum velocities for day and night driving.

Simplistic explanations such as fatigue and alcohol consumption to account for night time driving accidents are apparent, but there is no question that visual factors are important especially in accidents involving pedestrians (Allen, 1970). Fortunately, the two modes of processing concept suggests a rational explanation for why drivers maintain fast speeds at night as well as a possible means for amelioration (Leibowitz & Owens, 1977).

The role of vision in automobile driving may be analyzed in terms of two separate subtasks that are mediated independently by ambient and by focal vision. Steering the automobile in order to keep it within the driving lane and following the changing contours of the road is essentially an ambient function. Analogous to the phenomenon of walking while reading, it can be demonstrated that steering a vehicle can be effectively and confidently carried out in the absence of high spatial frequencies. This can be demonstrated under appropriate conditions by putting the fists in front of the eyes which restricts vision to the peripheral visual fields. An ophthalmologist related to us that some of his patients with large central scotomas due to retinal pathology drive to his clinic which is located in a large city. Similarly, introduction of optical blur has no effect on steering ability as evaluated in a driving simulator (Merritt, Newton, Sanderson, & Seltzer, 1978).

The other task in driving, which involves focal vision, is the recognition of obstacles in the highway such as pedestrians, animals, potholes, and the reading or recognition of signs. These tasks are mediated primarily by the high frequency sensitivity of the central visual field.

Under daylight conditions, both the ambient-steering and the focal-recognition functions operate at their maximum capacities. As illumination is lowered, however, there is a *selective degradation* of visual functions. Focal vision, specifically resolution, stereoscopic depth perception and contrast sensitivity (Graham, 1965) as well as reaction time (Teichner & Krebs, 1972) are all extremely sensitive to reduced illumination. Below a level between 1 to 10 cd/m² the efficiency of these visual discriminations decreases systematically. Thus the detection of obstacles in the road and speed of reaction to such hazards are progressively degraded. Conversely it is a characteristic of ambient vision that its efficiency is *not* a function of illumination. As long as orientation stimuli are minimally visible, ambient vision functions normally. There are of course rare times when it is impossible to discern the borders of the road or the adjacent objects and under these conditions drivers are extremely cautious. Under typical night driving conditions, however, there is adequate illumination for orientation stimuli to activate ambient vision so that steering is as efficient as during the day. The net result is that the driver can steer accurately and confidently at night and is not aware of any compelling reason to reduce vehicle velocities.

The net result of this unjustified overconfidence is that night driving speeds often exceed the margin of safety of focal recognition vision. Hazards are not anticipated with adequate time to take evasive action and this contributes to the increase in night time driving accidents, particularly those involving objects on the motorway. Contributing to this overconfidence is the fact that steering is a continuous task and the driver is receiving unchallenged positive feedback confirming his or her ability to steer. Conversely, hazards appear infrequently and, in common with other low probability events, tend to be disregarded and therefore unanticipated (Starr & Whipple, 1980).

In effect, it is the selective degradation of the two modes of processing which accounts for excessive driving speeds at night and an increase in night time driving accidents. The confidence in the ability to steer the vehicle effectively "masks" the loss of focal capabilities and leads the driver into dangerously fast night time driving velocities.

To ameliorate this situation, drivers must be made aware of the implications of this unavoidable selective degradation of visual functions at night and traffic authorities should be encouraged to post different speed limits for day and night driving. Drivers should be made aware not only of selective degradation, but of the fact that the contribution of vision to orientation behavior, steering in particular, is primarily unconscious. Thus even the most prudent and well intentioned driver would most probably not be aware of these phenomena. The expression that it is not the "devil" you know that causes difficulty, but the "devil" you do not know, is relevant in this context.

ORIENTATION AND DISORIENTATION

The ability to orient in space reflects the coordination of multiple sensory modalities and motor information. Under most conditions the responses of the separate components are corresponding, that is, activity in one is usually accompanied by some specific level of activity in the others. One example of this correspondence is the afference from the visual and vestibular systems during head rotation. Under these conditions, both systems are simultaneously excited and provide corresponding information concerning the direction of head rotation. Under special conditions, however, a noncorrespondence or mismatch between the senses may be produced. When this occurs disorientation and, in severe cases, motion sickness may be experienced. Whether a pattern of activity in the different components is considered to be corresponding or not depends at least in part on the past history of the organism, that is, whether or not similar patterns have been experienced in the past (see Benson, 1978; Dichgans & Brandt, 1978; Reason & Brand, 1975).

The importance of the correspondence of visual and vestibular inputs has been elegantly demonstrated by Dichgans and Brandt (1978). Their subjects were rotated about the vertical axis at a constant velocity and requested to lower their heads to the shoulder thereby rotating the planes of the semicircular canals relative to the plane of whole-body rotation. This resulted in Coriolis (cross-coupled) stimulation which typically produces severe disorientation and frequently motion sickness. Dichgans and Brandt investigated the effect of systematic variation of the correspondence between information signaling direction of rotation from the vestibular and visual systems.

When the drum was rotated in the opposite direction from the subject so that the information from the visual and vestibular senses still agreed with respect to direction of rotation, rated discomfort remained the same even when drum speed was increased (Fig. 17.4, e-g). If, however, the drum rotated in the same direction and with the same speed as the subject so that information from the senses was in conflict, that is, vision indicated that the subject was at rest while the vestibular sense signaled rotation, estimation of discomfort doubled (b). The worst case is when visual and vestibular information indicate rotation in opposite directions, as illustrated in a, and this produced maximum discomfort. In this conflict situation, several subjects became motion sick and vomited after only one head movement.

These results conform nicely to the mismatch theory of disorientation and motion sickness. In effect, this study presented three levels of mismatch. Coriolis stimulation with a visual environment moving in the normal direction but at different speeds produced minimal rated discomfort. A visual environment which falsely signaled stationarity increased discomfort. The conflict resulting from sensory information indicating motion in opposite directions, however, produced severe disorientation and motion sickness.

These results recall the classical data of von Holst and Mittelstaedt (1950) in which they reversed the visual consequences of self-produced motion in the European dragonfly. This was accomplished by rotating the animal's head by 180 degrees so that the retinal image motion associated with movements of the

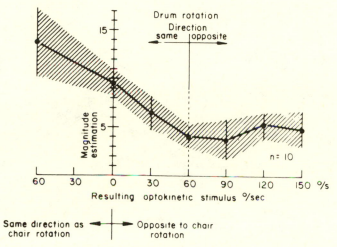

	a	b	c	d	e	f	g
Drum rotation °/s	120	60	30	–	30	60	90
Chair rotation °/s	60	60	60	60	60	60	60
Resulting optokinetic Stimulus °/s	60 R	–	30 L	60 L	90 L	120 L	150 L

FIG. 17.4. Magnitude estimation of Coriolis effects induced by head movements during constant velocity (60 degree/sec) chair rotation while direction and velocity of optokinetic stimulation provided by drum motion are varied (means and standard deviations). Stimuli are listed in the upper part of the figure. Weakest effects occur if the surround is stationary during chair rotation (d). Under these conditions the visual and vestibular signals correspond with respect to the direction and velocity of self motion. Similar effects occur with drum rotations which produce an optokinetic stimulus consistent with regard to the direction of chair rotation but corresponding to greater velocities (e-g). Coriolis effects increase with drum rotation consistent with direction of chair rotation but corresponding to lesser velocities (c). These effects are further increased if the drum and chair rotate at the same velocity, thereby eliminating visual information concerning self-rotation (b). Coriolis effects are markedly enhanced if the drum rotated in the same direction as the chair but at a greater velocity so that the visual and vestibular signals correspond to opposite directions of self-motion (a). Direction-specific interaction of the two stimuli is roughly linear within a range of ± 60 degrees of relative velocity (a-d) [modified after Dichgans & Brandt, 1978].

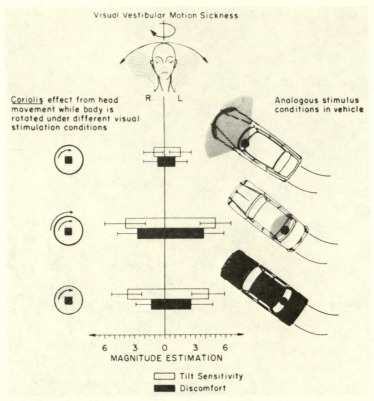

Visual Vestibular Motion Sickness

Coriolis effect from head
movement while body is
rotated under different visual
stimulation conditions

Analogous stimulus
conditions in vehicle

MAGNITUDE ESTIMATION

☐ Tilt Sensitivity

■ Discomfort

FIG. 17.5.   Magnitude estimation of tilt sensations and discomfort resulting from
sideward movement of the head (Coriolis stimulation) during stimultaneous chair
and visual surround rotation. The symbols on the left, from top to bottom, represent: chair rotation in the light, coupled chair and visual environment rotation, and
chair rotation in the dark. The right column represents comparable stimulus situations in a moving vehicle. Motion sickness is minimal in the front seat where body
accelerations and simultaneous visual stimulation are corresponding. Discomfort
is maximal when the vestibular accelerations are contradicted by visual information indicating no movement as occurs in the back seat with predominently stationary contours in the visual field (after Brandt, 1976).

animal were in the opposite direction to that normally experienced. For the
purpose of orientation, this procedure led to disastrous consequences. Any
movement of the animal resulted in initiation of the "following reflex" with the
result that the animal reflexively rotated its body until completely exhausted.

A recent study reported analogous results with human subjects. Moving the
visual field in a manner corresponding to the retinal image motion produced by
voluntary saccadic eye movements produced severe disorientation as measured
by postural stability (White, Post, & Leibowitz, 1980). In both the insect and

human studies, noncorresponding visual and motor information resulted in disorientation.

A less severe but more familiar example of a visual-vestibular mismatch occurs in automobiles (Brandt, 1976). The extent to which automobile motion results in discomfort depends, in terms of the mismatch theory of disorientation, on the extent to which "normal" simultaneous visual and vestibular inputs are available. As illustrated by Brandt in Fig. 17.5, the visual field of the driver permits a relatively large view of the stable outside environment so as to maximize the possibility for appropriately moving visual inputs during vehicle induced head motion. For a passenger in the back seat, however, because of the relatively smaller proportion of the visual field stimulated by the stable outside environment, appropriate visual input is reduced. This condition presumably accounts for the increased discomfort for rear seat as compared with front seat passengers. It is well known that reading in an automobile increases the incidence of discomfort. This should be expected since reading maximizes the proportion of the visual field which remains stationary during vehicle motion as compared to the normal pattern of *against* motion from the outside environment.

The mismatch theory of disorientation has been receiving increasing attention from the scientific and medical communities and appears to be heuristic in the interpretation of a variety of spatial orientation phenomena.

Disorientation In Aircraft. The suggestion that disorientation and motion sickness are associated with noncorresponding visual and vestibular inputs may help to explain disorientation in aircraft during instrument flight (Benson, 1978). Even experienced pilots report disorientation although the correct information is available from the flight instruments. When the ground is not visible, accelerations of the aircraft fail to result in appropriate simultaneous visual motion and the only reliable visual source of orientation information is the artificial horizon. Because spatial orientation is normally mediated by large portions of the visual field, the use of a relatively small (about five degrees of arc) artificial horizon in aircraft represents an unnatural situation. Human beings are extremely adaptable and can utilize cues which are abstract in nature and different from everyday experience. These "unnatural" abstract cues, however, are most vulnerable to interference by stress and/or unusual environmental conditions and the pilot may not be able to override the discrepant information provided by misleading orientation stimuli (Leibowitz & Dichgans, 1980). This hypothesis, although clearly speculative, may provide an explanation for disorientation during instrument flight rules. Fortunately, this possibility can and should be tested experimentally.[4]

---

[4]A wide artificial horizon, produced by optical projection, is reported to be more satisfactory in preliminary tests (Malcolm, Money & Anderson, 1975).

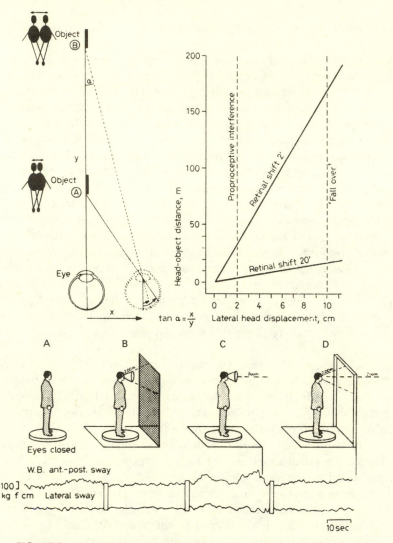

FIG. 17.6. Geometrical analysis showing that by increasing the distance between eyes and stationary surroundings body sway must also increase in order to be visually detected and stabilize posture. Minimum lateral head displacements are presented as a function of eye-object distance for assumed retinal displacement thresholds of either 20 or 2 min of arc. Fore, aft, and lateral body sway (original traces) are presented for conditions of eyes closed, eyes open in front of a wall, and eyes open on a high building with and without additional stationary contours in the peripheral visual field. Sway amplitudes, especially in the low frequency range, increase with height vertigo. The presence of simultaneous nearby stationary contours stabilize "height vertigo sway" (after Brandt, Bles, Arnold, & Kapteyn, 1979).

HEIGHT VERTIGO

The mismatch theory has been applied to the phenomenon of height vertigo (Bles, Kapteyn, Brandt, & Arnold, 1980; Brandt, Arnold, Bles, & Kapteyn, 1980). Figure 17.6 presents anterior-posterior and lateral plane body sway as measured by a force platform for a standing subject with (a) the eyes closed, (b) with the eyes open while viewing nearby contours. It will be noted that both anterior-posterior and lateral body sway are significantly reduced when contours are visible. In Fig. 17.6C the eyes are open but there are no nearby contours, resulting in a dramatic increase in sway. The authors suggest that this increase in body sway is associated with the feelings of subjective discomfort or height vertigo. The essence of the argument is that when the body sways normally we "expect" motion of visual contours. When these are located at a distance such that the corresponding retinal image motions are reduced, a mismatch results and discomfort increases. In Fig. 17.6D a frame is introduced into the visual field with the expected effect of stabilizing body posture.

The correlation between body sway and subjective estimates of height vertigo is illustrated in Fig. 17.7. Subjects assumed different postural positions while looking over the edge of a 20-meter high building. These positions were designed

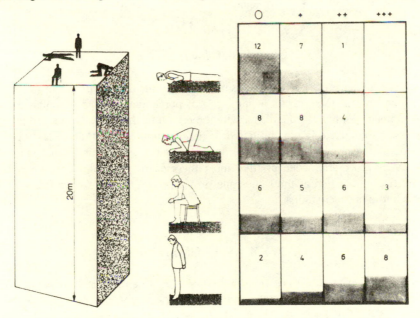

FIG. 17.7. Magnitude of subjective height vertigo as related to body position is maximal with upright stance (where maintaining postural balance is relatively most difficult). Scalings (0 = none: + = moderate: ++ = medium: +++ = severe height vertigo) for 20 volunteer subjects not particularly susceptible to height vertigo (after Brandt, Arnold, Bles, & Kapteyn, 1980).

to produce four levels of body stability from maximum in the prone position to minimum in the standing position. The figures on the right represent the subjective estimates of discomfort rated on a four point scale. Subjective symptoms increased as the body was progressively less stable. Although height vertigo can have a learned or phobic component, these data argue for the role of visual stimuli and their effect on body stability as a major contributing factor.

The mismatch theory of height vertigo suggests a possible interpretation for the visual cliff phenomenon. The fact that young animals, as soon as they are able to locomote, will avoid moving over glass when the underlying surface is far away as compared to one that is near has been demonstrated by a large number of experiments with many species (Walk & Gibson, 1961). The mechanism for this behavior is not as clear, however. Based on the body sway data described above, we have hypothesized that the basis for the avoidance of the cliff might be height vertigo which results from the reduced visual feedback during postural sway. A study was conducted which introduced contours over the glass on the deep side of the cliff to determine whether the simultaneous presence of visual contours would eliminate the response among newly hatched chicks. The avoidance behavior of the chicks was uninfluenced by the contours, however. We also attempted to eliminate motion sickness by giving the animals dramamine. The results of this study were also negative.

GENERAL COMMENTS

The general theme of this chapter has been to examine the two modes of processing concept in relation to a number of perceptual and perceptual-motor phenomena. We believe the reader will agree with us that there are indeed many interesting and exciting possibilities. It is perhaps appropriate that the last example led to negative empirical results. Such data serve as a reminder that the two modes of processing concept, like most theories in psychology, is an over-simplification, which at the same time provides suggestions for unifying concepts and empirical studies.

ACKNOWLEDGMENTS

Sponsored by grants MH08061 from the National Institute of Mental Health and EY 03276 from the National Eye Institute, and by a Senior Scientist Award from the Alexander von Humboldt Foundation (to H.W.L.) for study at the University of Freiburg, F.R.G. Many of the ideas presented in this chapter originated during invaluable discussions with Johannes Dichgans and with Thomas Brandt. The authors are grateful to Paul Cornwell, Jay Enoch, Fred Guedry, Richard Held, Eileen Leibowitz, Michael Leibowitz, Gordon Shulman, and Jane Raymond for a critical reading of the manuscript.

REFERENCES

Allen, M. J. *Vision and highway safety*. Philadelphia: Chilton, 1970.

Benson, A. J. Spatial disorientation; motion sickness. In G. Dhenin, G. R. Sharp, & J. Ernsting (Eds.), *Aviation medicine, physiology and human factors*. London: Tri-Med Books, 1978.

Bles, W., Kapteyn, T. S., Brandt, T., & Arnold, F. The mechanism of physiological height vertigo II. Posturography. *Acta Otolaryngologica*, 1980, *89*, 534–540.

Borish, I. M. *Clinical refraction*. Chicago: Professional Press, 1970.

Brandt, T. Optisch-vestibuläre Bewegungskrankheit, Höhenschwindel und klinische Schwindelformen. *Fortschritt der Medizin*, 1976, *94*, 1177–1182.

Brandt, T., Bles, W., Arnold, F., & Kapteyn, T. S. Height vertigo and human posture. *Advances in oto-rhino-otolaryngology*, 1979, *25*, 88–92.

Brandt, T., Arnold, F., Bles, W., & Kapteyn, T. S. The mechanism of physiological height vertigo I. Theoretical approach and psychophysics. *Acta Otolaryngologica*, 1980, *89*, 513–523.

Breitmeyer, B. Simple reaction time as a measure of the temporal response properties of transient and sustained channels. *Vision Research*, 1975, *15*, 1411–1412.

Bronson, G. The postnatal growth of visual capacity. *Child Development*, 1974, *45*, 873–890.

Dichgans, J., & Brandt, T. Visual-vestibular interaction: Effects on self-motion and postural control. In R. Held, H. W. Leibowitz, & H. L. Teuber (Eds.), *Handbook of sensory physiology, Vol. VIII*. Heidelberg: Springer, 1978.

Duke-Elder, S. *System of ophthalmology IX. Diseases of the uveal tract*. St. Louis: Mosby, 1966.

Epstein, W. (Ed.) *Stability and constancy in visual perception*. New York: Wiley, 1977.

Epstein, W., & Hatfield, G. Functional equivalence of mastering cue reduction in perception of shape at a slant. *Perception and Psychophysics*, 1978, *23*, 134–144.

Eszenyi, M. Zur differentialdiagnostischen Bedeutung der Gesichtsfeldveränderungen bei der Hysterie. *Monatschrift für Psychiatrie und Neurologie*, 1928, *70*, 147–160.

Gonshor, A., & Melvill-Jones, G. Short term changes in the human vestibulo-ocular reflex. *Journal of Physiology*, 1976, *256*, 361–379.

Graham, C. H. (Ed.) *Vision and visual perception*. New York: Wiley, 1965.

Grüttner, R. Experimentelle Untersuchungen über den optokinetischen Nystagmus. *Zeitschrift für Sinnesphysiologie*, 1939, *68*, 1–48.

Held, R. Dissociation of visual functions by deprivation and rearrangement. *Psychologische Forschung*, 1968, *31*, 338–348.

Held, R. Two modes of processing spatially distributed visual stimulation. In F. O. Schmitt (Ed.), *The neurosciences: Second study program*. New York: Rockefeller University Press, 1970.

Held, R., & Hein, A. Movement-produced stimulation in the development of visually guided behavior. *Journal of Comparative and Physiological Psychology*, 1963, *56*, 872–876.

Holst, E. von, & Mittelstaedt, H. Das Reafferenzprinzip, Wechselwirkungen zwischen Zentralnervensystem und Peripherie. *Naturwissenschaften*, 1950, *37*, 464–476.

Holway, A. H., & Boring, E. G. Determinants of apparent visual size with distance variant. *American Journal of Psychology*, 1941, *54*, 21–37.

Ingle, D. Two visual mechanisms underlying the behavior of fish. *Psychologische Forschung*, 1967, *31*, 44–51.

Janet, P. *The major symptom of hysteria*. London: Macmillan, 1907.

Kaufman, L., & Williamson, S. J. Biomagnetism and vision. *Investigative Ophthalmology and Visual Science*, 1979, *18*, 1101–1103.

Leibowitz, H., & Bourne, L. E., Jr. Time and intensity as determiners of perceived shape. *Journal of Experimental Psychology*, 1956, *45*, 277–281.

Leibowitz, H., & Dichgans, J. Zwei verschiedene Seh-Systeme. *Umschau in Wissenschaft und Technik*, 1977, *77*, 353–354.

Leibowitz, H., & Dichgans, J. The ambient visual system and spatial disorientation. *AGARD*

Conference on Spatial Disorientation in Flight: Current Problems. Conference No. 287, Bodø, Norway, 1980.

Leibowitz, H. W., Myers, N. A., & Grant, D. A. Radial localization of a single stimulus as a function of luminance and duration of exposure. *Journal of the Optical Society of America*, 1955, *45*, 76–78.

Leibowitz, H. W., & Owens, D. A. Nighttime accidents and selective visual degradation. *Science*, 1977, *197*, 422–423.

Leibowitz, H. W., Post, R. B., & Ginsburg, A. The role of fine detail in visually controlled behavior. *Investigative Ophthalmology and Visual Science*, 1980, *19*, 846–848.

Leibowitz, H. W., Post, R. B., Shupert-Rodemer, C., Wadlington, W. L., & Lundy, R. M. Roll vection analysis of suggestion induced visual field narrowing. *Perception and Psychophysics*, 1980, *28*, 173–176.

Leibowitz, H. W., Shupert-Rodemer, C., & Dichgans, J. The independence of dynamic spatial orientation from luminance and refractive error. *Perception and Psychophysics*, 1979, *25*, 75–79.

Leibowitz, H. W., Wilcox, S. B., & Post, R. B. The effect of refractive error on size constancy and shape constancy. *Perception*, 1978, *7*, 557–562.

Malcolm, R., Money, K. E., & Anderson, P. Peripheral vision artificial display. *AGARD Conference Proceedings No. 145 on Vibration and Combined Stress in Advanced Systems*, 1975.

Meneghini, K., & Leibowitz, H. The effect of stimulus distance and age on shape constancy. *Journal of Experimental Psychology*, 1967, 241–248.

Merritt, J. O., Newton, R. E., Sanderson, G. A., & Seltzer, M. L. *Driver visibility quality: An electro-optical meter for in-vehicle measurement of modulation transfer (MTF)*. Department of Transportation, 1978 (DOT HS 6-01426).

Mitchell, D. E. Effect of early experience on the development of certain perceptual abilities in animals and man. In R. D. Walk & H. L. Pick, Jr. (Eds.), *Perception and Experience*. New York: Plenum, 1978.

Oman, C. M., Bock, O. L. & Huang, J. K. Visually induced self-motion sensation adapts rapidly to left-right reversal, *Science*, 1980, *209*, 706–708.

Perenin, M. T., & Jeannerod, M. Residual vision in cortically blind hemifields. *Neuropsychologia*, 1975, *13*, 1–7.

Perenin, M. T., & Jeannerod, M. Visual function within the hemianopic field following early cerebral hemidecortication in man-I. Spatial localization. *Neuropsychologia*, 1978, *16*, 1–13.

Pöppel, E., Held, R., & Frost, D. Residual vision after brain wounds involving the central visual pathways in man. *Nature*, London, 1973, *243*, 295–296.

Post, R. B., & Leibowitz, H. W. The independence of radial localization from refractive error. *Journal of the Optical Society of America*, 1980, *70*(11), 1377–1379.

Post, R. B., Dichgans, J., Shupert, C. L., & Leibowitz, H. W. High contour-contrast is unnecessary for optimal optokinetic responses, in preparation.

Reason, J. R., & Brand, J. J. *Motion Sickness*. London/New York: Academic Press, 1975.

Regan, D., Silver, R., & Murray, T. J. Visual acuity and contrast sensitivity in multiple sclerosis-hidden visual loss. *Brain*, 1977, *100*, 563–579.

Schneider, G. E. Contrasting visuomotor functions of tectum and cortex in the golden hamster. *Psychologische Forschung*, 1967, *31*, 52–62.

Sprague, J. M. Interaction of cortex and superior colliculus in mediation of visually guided behavior in the cat. *Science*, 1966, *153*, 1544–1547.

Starr, C., & Whipple, C. Risks of risk decisions. *Science*, 1980, *208*, 1114–1119.

Teichner, W. H., & Krebs, M. Laws of the simple visual reaction time. *Psychological Review*, 1972, *79*, 344–358.

Trevarthen, C. Two mechanisms of vision in primates. *Psychologische Forschung*, 1968, *31*, 229–337.

Walk, R. D., & Gibson, E. J. A comparative and analytical study of visual depth perception. *Psychological Monographs*, 1961, *25*, Whole No. 519.

Weiskrantz, L., Warrington, E. K., Sanders, M. D., & Marshall, J. Visual capacity in the hemianopic field following a restricted occipital ablation. *Brain*, 1974, *97*, 709–728.

White, K. D., Post, R. B., & Leibowitz, H. W. Saccadic eye movements and body sway. *Science*, 1980, *208*, 621–623.

18 Illumination, Color, and Three-Dimensional Form

Sten Sture Bergström
Umeå University

In an earlier paper dedicated to Gunnar Johansson (Bergström, 1977a) I presented a vector analytic model for the perceptual analysis of a proximal stimulus into the perception of the illumination, color, and three-dimensional form of an object. The vector analytic model was initially developed by Johansson in a series of papers from 1950 to 1976 for motion perception (Johansson, 1950, 1976). In this chapter I try to develop the model in connection with the information about depth present in the reflected light.

THE VECTOR MODEL

The basic idea of the model is that there is a perceptual analysis of light reflected into the eye from illuminated objects into common and specific components. In the examples used in my earlier paper, the common component provides information about illumination. The extraction of that component from the reflected light (i.e., from the proximal stimulus) leaves specific components. The specific components provide information about the three-dimensional shape and the color of the object.

Figure 18.1 illustrates the analysis. There is in A a continuously decreasing luminance from left to right. It is not seen that way, however. Rather one sees a three-dimensional object like a white roofing tile illuminated from the left. The luminance gradient is analyzed into a common component (B in Fig. 18.1) that is a linear gradient corresponding to the illumination from the left, a specific component (C in Fig. 18.1)—the cyclic modulation—corresponding to the

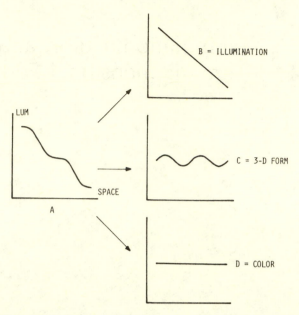

FIG. 18.1. The luminance gradient (A) analyzed into a common component (illumination, B), a specific component (three-dimensional form, C), and the resulting constant color (D).

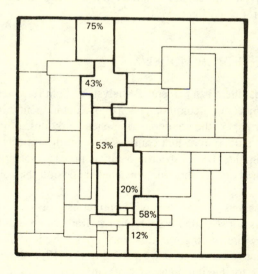

FIG. 18.2. A sketch of the achromatic "Mondrian" with the reflectance values along a track from the grey at its bottom to the white at its top. (From Land & McCann, 1971).

three-dimensional form of the perceived object, and, finally, a constant level (D in Fig. 18.1) corresponding to the constant color of the whole object.

A second illustration of the vector analytic model may be given by analyzing Land & McCann's (1971) achromatic "Mondrian" demonstrations. A Mondrian consisting of a lot of different achromatic color samples (Fig. 18.2) is illuminated from below in such a way, that a gray sample at the bottom of the picture receives the same mean luminance as a white sample at its top. Still the gray appears gray and the white appears white. My analysis of this color constancy demonstration is illustrated in Fig. 18.3.

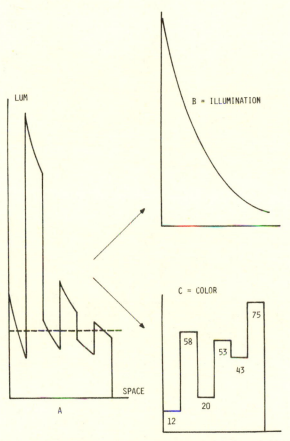

FIG. 18.3. The luminance distribution (A) along the track shown in Fig. 2 when the illumination from below gives the grey (12%) the same mean luminance as the white at the top (75%). The analysis gives a common Illumination (B), and specific lightness components (color, C). The figures denote reflectances of the different samples along the track.

The luminance profile along a path from the gray at the bottom to the white at the top is given in Fig. 18.3A. The illumination from below is adjusted to give the gray and the white the same mean luminance in spite of their different reflectances. The luminance profile is analyzed into a common component of illumination (B in Fig. 18.3) and a residual (specific) component corresponding to the reflectances of the samples (C in Fig. 18.3). This analysis is different from Land and McCann's explanation which assumes the visual system to be insensitive to the gradual variation of luminance.

The analysis assumes: (1) *luminance steps* correspond to perceived reflectance differences; and (2) *luminance gradients* correspond to perceived illumination and three-dimensional form of the object. The Craik-O'Brien and Cornsweet-O'Brien effects can be taken as evidence for the assumed functional

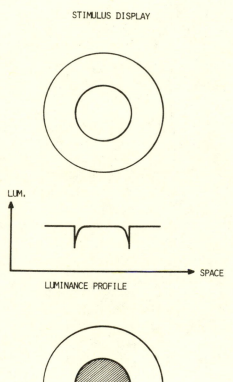

STIMULUS DISPLAY

LUM.

SPACE

LUMINANCE PROFILE

PERCEPT

FIG. 18.4.   The Craik-O'Brien effect. The center and surround have the same luminance. The center is demarcated by a contour, the profile of which is given in the diagram. The percept is a darker center field. The phenomenon is dependent on the very special type of contour.

difference between steps and gradients. Those effects mean, for example, that a center field and its surrounding look different in brightness though their luminances are the same. The fields are demarcated from each other by a very special type of contours consisting of a step and one or two gradients (Fig. 18.4 gives one example).

The gradual increase of luminance inside the luminance step can not compensate (perceptually) for the stepwise decrease. The result is a perceived darker center surrounded by a bright ring. (For more examples see, e.g., Cornsweet, 1970, pp. 270–276).

ILLUMINATION BORDERS AND
REFLECTANCE BORDERS

It is apparent that at least the first of the two assumptions made above must be qualified. There are, of course, in a three-dimensional world luminance steps due to color differences but there are also luminance steps due to illumination. Two walls forming a corner often constitute a luminance step without a color difference. We have to distinguish between luminance steps that are reflectance or color borders and those that are illumination borders. This means that the analysis of luminance or reflected light is essentially an analysis into color components and illumination components, the classical problem of color constancy.

Let us now reformulate the two assumptions above in the following way: (i) reflectance borders correspond to perceived color differences; and (ii) illumination borders like illumination gradients correspond to perceived three-dimensional form of objects and to their position in space relative to the source of light.

The distinction between the two types of borders has been discussed in a Scientific American article by Dr. Alan L. Gilchrist (1979). He assumes, however, that because the visual system recognizes the three-dimensional arrangement it also finds out that the two walls forming a corner are differently illuminated and not differently painted. In his discussion, color constancy is the result of depth perception and thus of more cognitive processes (unconscious inference?). I assume conversely that the visual system automatically performs an analysis of the light projected into the eye (i.e., the proximal stimulus) into common and specific components thus revealing the information about the illumination, color, and three-dimensional arrangement of the outer world.

According to my model the visual system distinguishes illumination from reflectance simply by the common component characteristic of the former. Thus the communality is the critical characteristic of illumination. This explains how the constancy can vanish as soon as the stimulus situation is reduced. The Gelb-effect and Katz's experiments with a reduction screen can be given as examples (see, e.g., Kling & Riggs, 1972, pp. 404, 409–420; Osgood, 1956, 272–273). Land and McCann (1971) consider the complexity of their chromatic Mondrian to be essential for the appearance of the marvellous color constancy they demonstrate. According to my own observations the constancy in these demonstrations remains as strong with a picture of only two fields or one field against a background (Bergström, 1977b). But when only a single field is presented color constancy does not occur. The reason is, of course, that there is no common component to extract and the color of the light can not be distinguished from the color of the object. The communality explanation can also be applied to the fact that painters by giving a common component to reflectances (i.e., colors) can paint a motif to look like being in a certain light. The old artist trick to look through a color filter to choose the right paint to "stimulate" a certain light illustrates the importance of the common component in this case.

Evidence for the type of analysis I propose can be found in the literature. Besides the classical experiments mentioned above (Gelb and Katz), the more recent findings by Arend, Buehler, and Lockhead (1971) on difference information in brightness perception, by Walraven (1976) on the discounting of the background in color induction, by Gilchrist (1979) on "classic and simulated contrast patterns," as well as the findings that a retinally stabilized infield takes on the color of the unstabilized surround (Krauskopf, 1963, and Yarbus, 1967) seem to fit my model very well because they all stress the importance of a common background or a common illumination. Gilchrist (1978) has explicitly analyzed his results in these terms.

From the assumptions made above some very specific predictions can be made about the effect of manipulating the illumination of an object.

PREDICTIONS AND TESTS

Illumination borders and gradients superimposed on flat surfaces will give the impression of depth, providing that the contradictory information is not too strong. Temporal variation of the illumination distribution superimposed on flat surfaces will give the impression of objects moving in depth, providing the contradictory information is not too strong. The automatic nature of the analysis means that the observers cognitive knowledge about the experimental conditions should have no negative effect on the predicted impressions, providing that he takes on a naive attitude.

Experimental tests of the predictions have been performed both as formal experimental sessions using phenomenological (i.e., impressionistic) descriptions of percepts and as informal demonstrations in front of an audience. As the demonstrations and the film shown at the Abano seminar can not be shown to the reader a few of the situations studied in experiments will be reported. Experiments 1 and 2 consider static situations and Experiment 3 dynamic situations.

EXPERIMENT 1

Procedure.   A picture resembling the "Mondrian" pictures used by Land was made from ten rectangular color samples (5 × 10 cm) from the Hesselgren Colour Atlas arranged to form a picture 20 × 25 cm. Nine of the samples were chromatic and one was white. The picture was illuminated by two projectors. One of them illuminated the left part of the picture (10 × 20 cm) and the other one illuminated the right part (15 × 20 cm). The two projectors had different intensities and the border between the two differently illuminated parts was either sharp or sharp on one side and blurred on the other (the *sharp* and *gradient* conditions, respectively). The *gradient* condition was made by having one of the projectors out of focus, the *sharp* condition by having both projectors well focused. The gradient had a width of 4 cm. The picture and the illumination conditions are sketched in Fig. 18.5, A and B.

Fifteen observers were presented each condition once with the instruction to describe verbally their immediate impression of the picture. The exposure time was about 10 seconds with a fifteen second pause between exposures. The viewing distance was 2.5 meters and the observers were allowed free binocular inspection.

Results.   All the observers under all conditions described the picture as having a three-dimensional shape.

The *sharp* condition was reported by all observers to look like a corner or a folded surface. Some of them reported the corner to be an outer corner, some reported an inner corner. A few reports of shifts between outer and inner corners were also given. But no one ever reported the picture to appear as a flat surface.

The *gradient* condition was always reported to look like a folded and curved surface. The fold was located at the sharp side of the border whereas the graded side was reported to be curved in depth.

Whether the left or the right projector was the more intense and whether the left or right was out of focus in the gradient condition seemed to play no role.

The shapes verbally described by the observers are outlined in Fig. 18.5, C and D.

The results of Experiment 1 show the effect of illumination on perceived shape. What we really did was to reverse the analysis described earlier. We added a common component of illumination to a flat textured and complex surface. And the illumination we added was modulated in space to simulate attached shadows and an illumination from quite another direction than from the projectors.

The picture was in no case reported to look flat, which stresses the importance of the information about three-dimensional form inherent in the light reflected from an object. All other information must have been about a flat surface.

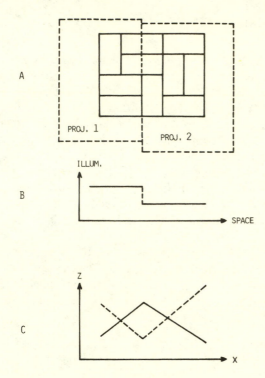

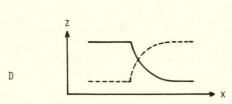

FIG. 18.5. A "Mondrian" picture illuminate by two projectors (*A*). The illumination profile is given in *B*. *C* and *D* illustrate the alternative percepts reported in the *sharp* and in the *gradient* conditions of Experiment 1, *z* representing the depth dimension.

The fact that the phenomenon reported appears in all the conditions for all our observers even though they were aware of the experimental arrangement confirm the assumed automatic nature of the perceptual analysis. The same phenomenon has been demonstrated quite a few times in front of an audience without concealing any part of the experimental arrangement and nobody has ever failed to see depth.

EXPERIMENT 2

Procedure.   In Experiment 2 the same picture was used as in Experiment 1. It was illuminated by two projectors but this time both projectors illuminated the whole picture. In one of the projectors a square wave grating was inserted as a slide, the other one just illuminated the picture evenly. Both projectors were connected to variable transformers to make it possible to adjust the intensities.

Two conditions were tested. In the *sharp grating* condition the square wave grating was superimposed on the illuminated Mondrian picture well-focused. The intensities of the projectors were adjusted to give a contrast value of 0.26, where contrast is defined as:

$$\frac{L_1 - L_2}{L_1 + L_2}$$

In the *blurred grating* condition the projector with the slide was defocused to give a smooth grating though not strictly a sinusoidal one. The illumination profiles of the two conditions are illustrated in Fig. 18.6, A and B.

The exposure time was approximately ten seconds with a minimum pause of fifteen seconds between exposures. Ten observers were presented with a single stimulus exposure.

Results.   The *sharp grating* was reported by eight out of ten subjects to appear three-dimensionally folded. Two of the subjects described the picture as flat. The eight observers were afterwards asked to draw the profile of the reported three-dimensional object. A typical drawing is illustrated in Fig. 18.6C. The blurred grating condition was reported by all the observers to look like a series of tubes. A typical drawing is shown in Fig. 18.6D. Figure 18.7 shows photos of a sharp and a blurred grating condition.

The conditions used in Experiment 2 have occasionally been demonstrated to audiences and three-dimensional percepts have always been reported in the gradient conditions.

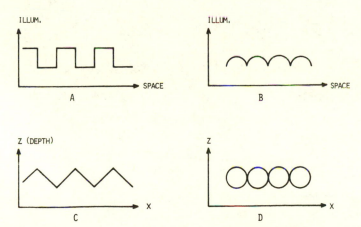

FIG. 18.6.   *A* and *B* are the illumination profiles for the *sharp grating* and *blurred grating* conditions of Experiment 2. *C* and *D* illustrate the corresponding percepts. *z* representing the depth dimension.

FIG. 18.7. Photos of a sharp and a blurred grating condition.

EXPERIMENT 3

Procedure.   The same arrangement was used as in Experiment 1 with two projectors illuminating one part each of the "Mondrian" picture (see Fig. 18.5). The sharp and the gradient conditions were as in Experiment 1. The intensities of the two projectors were modulated in time, however, according to an approximate sinusoidal variation. The two projectors were modulated in counterphase with a frequency of about 0.5 Hz (see Fig. 18.8).

Seven subjects (one at a time) were presented the sharp and the two gradient conditions (left and right) during the intensity modulations. The exposure time was fifteen seconds. They were instructed to describe their immediate impression of the stimulus.

Results.   In the *sharp* condition all the subjects reported movement in depth of the two surfaces of the picture. The reports were either of a corner folding out and in or of two surfaces moving to and fro in counterphase. In the *gradient* conditions the event was described as double doors opening and closing in counterphase or as double swing doors swinging in counterphase. No report of a two-dimensional picture in a varying illumination was made. These dynamic conditions have been shown to a few audiences on a 16 mm movie together with a number of various dynamic and static demonstrations of the same kind. The result has always been the same. Nobody has ever failed to see depth. The dynamic conditions used in this experiment give results analoguous to the static conditions: the spatial and spatio-temporal modulation of illumination gives very important information about the illumination, three-dimensional shape, position,

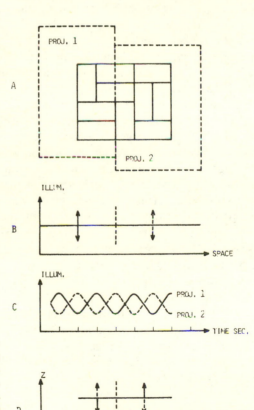

FIG. 18.8. The "Mondrian" picture illuminated by two projectors (*A*). The cyclic variation of the illumination from the two projectors is illustrated by diagrams *B* and *C*. *D*. illustrates the corresponding reported movement to and fro in depth.

and movement of an object in space. Compared to Johansson's (1964) experiment with the growing and shrinking square perceived as a constant "object" moving back and forth in space our results are still more compelling. He used outline squares with no other information present. In our experiment there is a lot of contradicting information from the geometrical contour projection of all the rectangles. We also use illuminated color samples compared to the CRT pictures used by Johansson. But the effect is the same. Rigid objects are perceived swinging in depth instead of the rigid flat picture in a complex and varying illumination.

DISCUSSION

The perceptual vector analysis of reflected light into common and specific components has been applied to color constancy phenomena. It can be concluded that the earlier assumption of illumination as a common component is strongly supported. The classical color constancy phenomena can be treated within a broader frame of reference including motion and depth perception. *Illumination is distinguished from reflectance by its character of being a common component, that is, by its communality.*

Any theory assuming independent information about depth to be a necessary base for distinguishing illumination borders from reflectance borders in three-dimensional layouts is rejected.

In Experiments 1 and 2, where spatially modulated illumintion is superimposed on a flat and complex picture, illumination borders simulating attached shadows give a very strong impression of depth. All other information about the picture is contradictory. Even though our observers were aware of the experimental arrangements the depth impression was compelling. This supports our assumption about the automatic character of the analysis.

In Experiment 3 a temporal modulation was introduced. It resulted in the perception of rigid objects moving in depth and with the illumination of the whole arrangement being invariant. This experiment is analoguous to Johansson's (1964) experiment with the growing and shrinking outline square, which was perceived as rigid and moving back and forth in depth rather than varying in size.

The experiments demonstrate very clearly that the information about depth in the spatial and spatiotemporal distribution of light is compelling and that color constancy is no more dependent on depth information than is depth information on the information about illumination. We seem to need a theory that handles both things at the same time rather than a two-step theory assuming one percept to be the base for decision about the other. An unorthodox stimulus description and an automatic analysis guided by some type of a minimum principle is preferred. In motion perception we begin to accept a vector analytic model mainly thanks to decades of ingenious work by Gunnar Johansson. We are less used to stimulus descriptions and analyses of reflected light in those terms, however, but so far the attempts to apply the same general model to the perception of illumination, color, and shape are very promising.

The proximal stimuli in our demonstrations and experiments are ambiguous and rules or "decoding principles" must be assumed according to which certain variations and certain constancies appear rather than others (cf. Restle's, 1979, analysis of some of Johansson's motion displays). So far such a hierarchy has not been systematically studied but our demonstrations indicate some interesting possibilities of testing certain organizing principles by bringing them into conflict. It is apparent from the experiments that motion in depth is preferred to change of form and also to shift of illumination, three-dimensional objects in one common illumination is preferred to a surface in two or more illuminations.

The phenomena studied in this chapter just touch upon the immense role for depth perception played by the projection into the eye of the spatial and spatiotemporal distribution of luminance. In my earlier paper the term "optical projection" was used to distinguish this aspect of the ambient optic array from another one, viz. the geometrical contour projection and its transformations traditionally described as a stimulus for depth perception. It was stressed that this 'optical projection'' has a very interesting characteristic which is missing in the geometrical contour projection, viz. its relation not only to the object and its observer but also to a point of reference out in space, that is, the source of light.

It is interesting to note that Johansson (1970, pp. 69–70) is astonished that Gibson has not explicitly treated this section of the ecology of light. Johansson even says that Gibson's declaration about the lack of adequate methods for stimulus analysis might be adequate here. According to my model, as presented here, Johansson was certainly nearer to those methods than he himself ever believed. Whether the ambient optic array containing both the "optical" and the "geometrical" projections at once carries unambiguous information about the outer world or not, the question of "decoding principles" is of interest. Because the information is not always unambiguous, the organism's way of handling ambiguous information is an important problem.

ACKNOWLEDGMENTS

This study is a modified version of the author's contribution to the Abano seminar June 25–29, 1979. The experiments briefly reported here are examples from a series of experiments to be published elsewhere. The author wants to express his gratitude to professor Gunnar Johansson for many valuable discussions of the topic of this chapter and to two of his collaborators, Mr. Karl-Arne Gustafsson and Mr. Jorma Putaansuu, both graduate students, who have taken active part in performing the demonstrations and experiments reported. This study was made possible by grants from the Swedish Council for Research in the Humanities and Social Sciences under contracts No. 588/78, and 61/79.

REFERENCES

Arend, L. E. Buehler, J. N., & Lockhead, G. R. Difference information in brightness perception. *Perception and Psychophysics*, 1971, *9*, 367-370.

Bergström, S. S. Common and relative components of reflected light as information about the illumination, colour, and three-dimensional form of objects. *Scandinavian Journal of Psychology*, 1977, *18*, 180-186. (a)

Bergström, S. S. *Colour*. Stockholm: Staff Training Department of Sveriges Radio, 1977. (b)

Cornsweet, T. N. *Visual perception*. New York: Academic Press, 1970.

Gilchrist, A. L. *Color perception without contrast (or why black rooms look black)*. Paper to the annual conference of Lake Ontario Visionary Establishment, February 24, 1978.

Gilchrist, A. L. The perception of surface blacks and whites. *Scientific American*, 1979, *240*, 112-124.

Johansson, G. *Configurations in event perception*. Uppsala: Almqvist & Wiksell, 1950.

Johansson, G. Perception of motion and changing form. *Scandinavian Journal of Psychology*, 1964, *5*, 181-208.

Johansson, G. On theories for visual space perception. A letter to Gibson. *Scandinavian Journal of Psychology*, 1970, *11*, 67-74.

Johansson, G. Spatio-temporal differentiation and integration in visual motion perception. *Psychological Research*, 1976, *38*, 379-393.

Kling, J. W., & Riggs, L. A. (Eds.) *Woodworth and Schlosberg's experimental psychology*. London: Methuen, 1972.

Krauskopf, J. Effects of retinal image stabilization on the appearance of heterochromatic targets. *Journal of the Optical Society of America*, 1963, *53*, 741-744.

Land, E. H., & McCann, J. J. Lightness and the Retinex theory. *Journal of the Optical Society of America*, 1971, *61*, 1-11.

Osgood, C. E. *Method and theory in experimental psychology*. New York: Oxford University Press, 1956.

Restle, F. Coding theory of the perception of motion configurations. *Psychological Review*, 1979, *86*, 1-24.

Walraven, J. Discounting the background—the missing link in the explanation of chromatic induction. *Vision Research*, 1976, *16*, 289-295.

Yarbus, A. *Eye movements and vision*. New York: Plenum Press, 1967.

Author Index

Subject Index